"Epstein masterfully lays out and puts together all the pieces of the Marvin puzzle without moralizing or salivating, the twin bad angels of movie biographers. All future writing about Lee Marvin will be measured against LEE MARVIN: POINT BLANK, which gives us the man in full. Like its subject, it will be a tough act to follow."—BILL KROHN, Author of *Hitchcock at Work*

"It being Valentine's Day, I can think of no more romantic way to waste the day (before I get to work) than by dipping in and out of a tender, caring, just-published biography of America's former sweetheart, Lee Marvin. In LEE MARVIN: POINT BLANK written by Dwayne Epstein, the action star who terrorized the West with a bullwhip in *The Man Who Shot Liberty Valance*, taught a squad of murderers and borderline psychos how to love again in *The Dirty Dozen*, and let Angie Dickinson use him as a punching bag for her furious little fists in the movie that gives this bio its subtitle weaves through the pages like the big rangy scary cat he was."— JAMES WALCOTT, *Vanity Fair* Online

"Epstein offers a great deal of insight regarding Marvin's approach to his work as an actor, and his process…
an entertaining and informative look at one of the most fascinating actors to appear on screen without once being exploitative. It is most highly recommended."
—THE EXAMINER.COM

"Considering what an icon Marvin has become it's really surprising that we haven't had more details on a man with over 100 credits to his name and countless memorable roles. Thankfully, author Dwayne Epstein has done cinephiles a solid, because his book LEE MARVIN: POINT BLANK is a well written and exhaustively researched book on the actor who was underrated as a performer and ignored when it came to biographies of our past stars… Biographies tend to drool over the subjects, creating an annoying air of idol worship. Others feel too academic and detached. Epstein spent a great deal of time researching the book and conducting interviews. He is clearly passionate about his subject but he never crosses the line into a sycophant. On the contrary, he treats Marvin almost as a curiosity; an enigma of rage and sadness who had a life peppered with tremendous success and equally significant personal setbacks. It's endlessly fascinating, exciting, and sometimes frightening. Lee Marvin lived fast, played hard, and punched harder, and Epstein created the definitive document on the actor who defined tough." —Daily Grindhouse

"Given Lee Marvin's legendary status in the film industry, it's rather surprising that his legacy has been so infrequently analyzed—especially since his real-life escapades dwarfed those in his reel life. Marvin was a genuine tough guy in an era in which there were no phony, wannabe tough guys. Like any actor, he had his share of cinematic misfires, but he made even those highly watchable. Author Epstein takes on the not-inconsiderable goal of fleshing out Marvin as a genuine person. His outstanding book presents meticulously researched facts about the man and his work, combined with insightful comments and interviews from those who knew him, including a short but poignant epilogue by his son Christopher." —Cinema Retro

"With his many iconic films, his record of combat action in the Pacific during WW2, his string of publicized woman problems, his off hours of drinking and brawling, Lee Marvin's life is so rich with biographical potential that LEE MARVIN: POINT BLANK, the new book by Dwayne Epstein, seems — at a little over 300 pages — almost like a summary, an outline, a breathless collection of life highlights and film critiques blurted out only at the few traffic lights its subject deigns to brake for. I mean that as a compliment; the author of many young adult biographies, a former newspaper editor, and respected writer on films, Epstein's unerring ear for conversational rhythm suits his restless, troubled subject and makes the book hard to put down." —BRIGHT LIGHTS FILM JOURNAL

"What makes this new biography so intriguing is that author Dwayne Epstein researched Marvin for several years, interviewing dozens of members of the acting profession in addition to his closest friends and family members. The result is a balanced book with even more depth than the previous full-length biography of Marvin, which was published before his death in 1987 at age 63. According to Mr. Epstein, more than 100 people were interviewed for this project. Two standouts include Lee's brother, Robert, and the actor's first wife, Betty. Others who offered insight include actors Angie Dickinson and Jack Palance, and directors John Frankenheimer and Stanley Kramer. A critic for *The New York Times* nicknamed Marvin "The Merchant of Menace" after seeing him shoot a scene in "The Big Heat." This film was notable for the scene where Marvin's character tosses a pot of scalding coffee into Gloria Grahame's face. It was only a supporting role, but the actor left his indelible mark on the final product. Ironically, it wasn't feature films that made

Marvin a household name, but a TV series, 'M Squad,' which debuted in 1957. LEE MARVIN: POINT BLANK is a rollicking narrative that comes about as close to the authentic Marvin as we are apt to get." —FT. MYERS, FLA. WEEKLY

"This is a great, fast paced book. Really enjoyed this! You get a great sense of Marvin's life before, during and after his filmic career. Through Mr. Epstein's book, you can really hear Lee Marvin's voice as he's quoted throughout the pages, and feel his struggles with being a WW2 veteran, a husband, an alcoholic and an artist."

—Documentary Filmmaker D.P. CARLSON

"Based on what I've always known about Lee Marvin, he seems to have been as interesting and multi-layered as any character he ever played onscreen. Up to now, though, I didn't know all that much. But thanks to Dwayne Epstein's first-rate biography I'll now watch even Marvin's minor films with renewed interest. Epstein is the ideal biographer for Marvin—well-versed in film history, dogged as a researcher and possessed of a writing style so engaging that LEE MARVIN: POINT BLANK reads like a novel. There's great background material on all of his important films and the great actors and directors with whom he worked. And I found Epstein's account of Marvin's early life to be thoroughly engrossing. There was never another actor quite like Lee Marvin and this biography does total justice to him. It's both deeply informative and completely enjoyable."

— Author & Historian FRANK THOMPSON

"This is the kind of biography Lee Marvin deserves."

—BOOKLIST ONLINE

Lee Marvin
Point Blank

DWAYNE EPSTEIN

schaffner
press

WWW.SCHAFFNERPRESS.COM

For permission to reprint, contact:
Schaffner Press, Inc., POB 41567, Tucson, AZ 85717

First Paperback Edition
ISBN: 978-1-936182-57-2

Library of Congress Cataloging-in-Publication Data

THE LIBRARY OF CONGRESS HAS CATALOGED THE HARDCOVER
EDITION AS FOLLOWS:

Epstein, Dwayne.
Lee Marvin : point blank / Dwayne Epstein ; afterword: Christopher Marvin.
   pages cm
ISBN 978-1-936182-40-4 (hardcover) -- ISBN 978-1-936182-41-1 (epub) --
ISBN 978-1-936182-42-8 (kindle) -- ISBN 978-1-936182-43-5 (adobe)
1. Marvin, Lee. 2. Actors--United States--Biography. I. Marvin, Christo-
pher, 1960- II. Title.
PN2287.M523E67 2013
791.4302'8092--dc23
[B]
                              2012048109

978-1-936182-57-2

To My Parents

Morris Epstein　　　　　　*Royce Epstein*
1927-2005　　　　　　　*1930-2008*

and

Claudia Leslie Marvin　　*Christopher Lamont Marvin*
1958-2012　　　　　　　*1952-2013*

In Loving Memory

"You plan the wars you masters of men
plan the wars and point the way
and we will point the gun."

from *Johnny Got His Gun*
by Dalton Trumbo

CONTENTS

Introduction: Marvin Matters   vii

PART I : BOOT CAMP

1: The Guilty Puritan   3
2: "Dogface" vs. St. Leo   16
3: "I Have Had My Fill of War"   31
4: "These Horrible, Animal Men"   48

PART II : IN THE TRENCHES

5: The Merchant of Menace   69
6: "You Look Like You Need a Hand"   84
7: Man in a Straitjacket   99
8: "Lady, I Just Don't Have the Time"   114

PART III : TAKING THE POINT

9: "Tension, Baby, Just Tension"   133
10: Everybody Gets Their "Vicaries"   149
11: "I Ain't Spittin' On My Whole Life"   167

PART IV : THE REAR ECHELON

12: The White Eye   189
13: May the Best Script Win   201
14: The Last of the Wintry Heroes   215

Epilogue: The Inglorious Bastard Sons Of Lee   233
Afterword by Christopher Marvin: My Father   238
Acknowledgments   240
Reader's Guide   243
    Author Q & A   244
    Topics and Questions for Discussion   257
Important Dates in Lee Marvin's Life   260
Unmade Films of Lee Marvin   264
Films Lee Marvin Could Have Made   266
End Notes   267
Bibliography/Author Interviews   282
Index   293
Photographic Credits   306
About the Author   308

Lee Marvin as he is best remembered, in the World War II classic,
The Dirty Dozen. *Of his own time in the war, he said, "I concluded it's every man for himself... The most useless word in the world is h-e-l-p."*

Marvin
Matters

APRIL 5, 1950, on a windy New York night, twenty-six-year-old Lee Marvin did the unthinkable. For young actors in the 1950s hoping to be the next Marlon Brando or Marilyn Monroe, their Mecca was the Actor's Studio in Manhattan, which taught the so-called Stanislavsky Method, pioneered by the renowned acting coach Lee Strasberg and the equally venerated director Elia Kazan. It was fated on that Thursday night that Lee Marvin, who was auditing the class, would do a scene to be critiqued by Strasberg. Marvin had prepared a monologue based on the Hemingway short story "The Snows of Kilimanjaro," in which a man dying of a gangrenous leg wound looks back on the disappointments in his life.

When Marvin had finished his piece, Strasberg led the students in deconstructing all that he decreed was wrong with Marvin's performance. He stated coldly that the scene failed since the actor never conveyed the pain of gangrene to the audience. But Lee Marvin, a former combat Marine, informed Strasberg that it was he, the teacher, who was mistaken. Marvin, having seen the effects of gangrene up close while fighting in the jungles of the Pacific, explained to Strasberg in the presence of his disciples that in the terminal stage of this condition there is no pain. The small theater fell into stony silence, which was suddenly shattered when Strasberg, furious at being corrected by a student, told the young actor to get out and never come back. Marvin had no problem with that, bellowing "fuck you!" as he turned on his heels, never to return.

Whereas young non-conforming actors were begging just to get into The Actor's Studio, Lee Marvin walked out. Although Marvin had shown Strasberg to be the emperor with no clothes, this school of modern acting still remained Strasberg's empire. Banished from the realm, and unwilling to conform to Strasberg's idea of a naturalistic—yet basically still European—method, Lee Marvin continued to toil in the Hollywood dream factories for over a decade before he was finally able to make his mark as a film star. He accomplished this by believing steadfastly that his time would come via a less refined but even more realistic concept based on this incontrovertible truth: Man is a violent animal, and the American male the most brutal of them all.

As noble as America had always tried to be in attempting to rise above this tendency, the fact is that this trait towards aggression had existed since the nation's inception. Benjamin Franklin had said as much in defending the colonies' right to exist autonomously. England's legal concept of a duty to retreat to the wall when confronted by violence was changed in America to standing one's ground in similar circumstances.

It is a peculiarly American point of view that has affected the nation's collective consciousness and culture. Author Richard Maxwell Brown stated succinctly in his book, *No Duty to Retreat: Violence and Values in American History,*[1] "...the metaphorical and symbolic impact of the transition from duty to retreat to standing one's ground is obvious and is crucial to the American identity. In the realms of both peace and war, it is not in the nature of America to approve retreat. Standing one's ground is an attitude that has deeply permeated our foreign relations and our military habits as well as the peaceful pursuits of daily life."

American films rarely reflected this violent nature as it truly existed, choosing instead to justify it with nobility and bravado. Lee Marvin, a veteran of some of the bloodiest battles of WWII, knew this better than most, stating some years later in a *Playboy* interview (January,1969), "In a typical John Wayne fight in a barroom... tables and bottles go along with mirrors and bartenders, and you end up with that little trickle of blood down your cheek and you're both pals and wasn't it a hell of a wonderful fight. That's fooling around with violence. It's phony; it's almost a character..."

The curtain had slipped from this facade following World War II, when war-weary audiences no longer accepted "the hero in the white hat" mythology. The true American character had peeked through on occasion in such action-oriented film genres as westerns, gangster films and war films, despite the puritanical restrictions set forth by production codes and societal standards of decency. While there was still an abundance of vacuous entertainment during the 1950s, a much darker tone was creeping like an uninvited guest into American popular culture, and staying long after the party was over.

A new breed of postwar male screen icons, beginning with Marlon Brando and rippling out to include the likes of exhibitionist Burt Lancaster, overly-sensitive Montgomery Clift, and apathetic Robert Mitchum, forced the stalwarts of the old guard to give their performances a previously unknown edge. Consider Tyrone Power in *Nightmare Alley* or James Stewart's later westerns and Hitchcock films. Even John Wayne, the champion of American virtue, portrayed such sadistic and psychotic characters as Tom Dunson in *Red River* and Ethan Edwards in *The Searchers*. Now, it seemed, movie villains of the era were required to be even more loathsome than ever.

Enter Lee Marvin. Middle-aged and not movie-star handsome, the most unlikely of film superstars, he would go on to forge a unique screen persona. He had his own "method" based purely on instinct and personal experience. Serving his apprenticeship by portraying countless villainous demons, he once told fellow grotesque character actor Strother Martin, "You know, as character actors we play all kinds of sex psychos, nuts, creeps, perverts and weirdoes. And we laugh it off saying what the hell it's just a character. But deep down inside, it's you, baby."[2]

By the mid-1960s, the studio fiefdoms had crumbled and the production code eventually morphed into a controversial rating system. By then, Lee Marvin had become an iconic figure with silver hair, granite features, and a voice to match, and his films were revered by audiences half his age. The year 1968 proved to be a turbulent time in the country and, by extension, the world. Assassinations, the Vietnam War, rioting in the streets and violence in general permeated the nation's consciousness.

Popular film, which had once been a haven from such ills, was suddenly being perceived as part of the problem. As a progenitor of this distressing phenomenon, Marvin, when asked by Richard Lewis in the aforementioned *Playboy* interview whether there was a connection between real and celluloid violence, responded, "Only in the sense that if the violence in a film is theatrically realistic, it's more of a deterrent to the audience committing violence themselves. Better on the screen than off. If you make it realistic enough, it becomes so revolting, that no viewer would want any part of it. But most violence on the screen looks so easy and so harmless that it's like an invitation to try it. I say make it so brutal that a man thinks twice before he does anything like that."

It was a philosophy derived from his own personal experience, resulting in brutality heretofore unseen in American films. His characters did not feel the need to be gentlemanly or apologetic concerning the extreme acts they perpetrated. This new concept of violence was Lee Marvin's pioneering contribution to American cinema. It had no name or title, but if it were given one, it would have to be as stark as the method and its creator himself: point blank.

Dwayne Epstein
November, 2012

[1]Brown, Richard Maxwell, *No Duty to Retreat: Violence & Values in American History*. NY: Oxford University Press, 1999, p.6.

[2] "You know, as character actors…": Shipman, David, *Movie Talk*. NY: St. Martin's Press, 1989 p.140.

Lee Marvin
Point Blank

PART ONE

BOOT CAMP

Six-year-old Lee (left) and older brother, Robert.
Lee is holding the family dog named, ironically enough, Whiskey.

CHAPTER I

The Guilty Puritan

I T WAS INEVITABLE that the name Lee Marvin would become inextricably linked with the theme of violence and its culture. During his belated ascent to stardom in 1967, Marvin was a popular media subject for interviews, in which this topic was always on the agenda. In fact, it was his predisposition to aggressive behavior that informed one of his earliest memories. In response to a question put to him by "Tonight Show" host Johnny Carson about his childhood, Marvin said: "I remember fighting with my brother. He'd hit me with a leash and I'd hit him with a stick, so we'd fight."

For Lee Marvin, this tendency towards violence would start early. He even recalled the first day of kindergarten as one filled with unchecked emotion and rage. "You've just been deposited here, right?" he would sarcastically state years later. "Boy, Mommy and Daddy are gone, and here's the big world, and it's working on you. And I remember I guess at one point I had to go to the john or something —it was probably down the hall—and when I came back some kid was sitting in my chair. And all I can remember is tremendous anger. I don't know whether I punched that kid, or if he punched me, or if I got into a fight. But I do remember my anger…"

The roots of physical aggression were genetically set in place long before his very existence. Its antecedents can also be traced among his ancestry, and the characteristic of the violence-prone male would go

3

on to wield a powerful influence over his life and work. The first of his paternal ancestors to come to America from England was Puritan civic leader Matthew Marvin, who went on to lead Connecticut's militia in the 1600s. But, when the farmers wanted to relax after a hard week in the fields, they would drift en masse to the local pub for some ale instead of going to church on Sunday morning. Brandishing his musket, in rode martinet Matthew Marvin and his militia to physically force the transgressors out of the pubs.

On his mother's side there was a distant relation to Revolutionary War general and first President of The United States, George Washington. His mother took such great pride in the lineage that when Lee was sweltering in the jungle islands of the Pacific during WWII, she attempted to rouse her son's spirit by writing, "Maybe blood is thicker than water, and maybe some of the qualities, both good and bad, do come down to us through the generations. In this case, I get a little more of George than you, being one generation closer."

In truth, he had strong feelings about his heritage, as his publicist Paul Wasserman once recalled, "I think he was a guilty puritan. Also, if memory serves, his ancestors were in the Revolutionary War. He was always saying, 'It's my country. We fought for it, we Marvins.' You know, shit like that." Yet, it wasn't so much those ancestors working menial jobs in the fields or factories whom the actor revered, but the valiant ones who fought and often died for glory in nearly every war and skirmish in American history.

The Marvin family first settled in New York after the Revolution when General Seth Marvin moved into the Hudson Valley. The following century, in the War Between the States, both the northern and southern sides of his ancestry suffered terrible losses, and as Marvin himself put it, "During the Civil War we were pretty well shot up and the family is very depleted." With such impressive names as Washington and even Robert E. Lee in his ancestry, Lee himself would often joke that he was "the charcoal gray not quite black sheep of the family."

The actor's maternal great, great grandfather William 'Uncle Billy' McCann became a local hero of sorts in the town of Elmira, New York and was the catalyst of an event that seems right out of a Lee Marvin movie. McCann, who lived well into his eighties, had been the County Under Sheriff in the Chemung County Seat of Elmira. According to *The New York Times,* "In 1863, while Sheriff McCann was in charge of the county bastille, a jail escape was planned by Leroy Channing Shearer, a soldier who was held for the killing of two comrades at the Elmira Prison Barracks. McCann, single-handed, fought a score of convicts. Shearer alone escaped after McCann had been left for dead [but survived]."

But, of his many illustrious and colorful ancestors, none proved to be more symbolic of Lee Marvin's legacy than his great uncle, Arctic explorer Ross Gilmore Marvin. Ross was born January 28, 1880, in Elmira, and was the youngest of Edward and Mary Marvin's six children. His father had been elected "Overseer of the Poor," but died when the boy was only six years old. His mother and older siblings raised Ross and, though small, he made a name for himself due to his determination to take part in school activities and sports.

Early on in his life, Marvin had exhibited a maverick spirit that seemed to foreshadow his great nephew's own outlook on life. Decades after his death, the *Elmira Star Gazette* wrote glowingly of Ross, "Marvin fought his way into everything. The places hardest to acquire were the places he sought. The things hardest to do, whether the road presented work or danger, were the things he wanted to do. He was that way from a boy."

That legendary perseverance would propel him through Cornell University where he graduated with a degree in civil engineering, as well as a stint on a training steamship for the New York Nautical School, conducting scientific experiments in oceans around the world. The same month of his graduation from Cornell in June 1905, in search of further adventure, Ross contacted Commander Robert Peary in the hope of joining the legendary explorer in his sixth attempt to reach the North Pole.

Peary wrote him back, stating, "I may say that your application is one of two or three which has impressed me very favorably, and though the time is limited, I trust that it may be practicable, in the event that, after personal interviews, my choice should fall on you, that you may be able to arrange your affairs so as to accompany the expedition. I assume that you are familiar with the program of the expedition and my plan of campaign in general." After hearing a short while later of his acceptance to the expedition, Ross Marvin quickly got his affairs in order and spent the next two years in the last unexplored territory on earth in the employ of Commander Peary.

In contrast, Ross's older brother Henry had a much less adventurous existence. He and his wife, Elizabeth, struggled to get by, but were plagued by bad luck. Their son Edward had died six days after being born on January 28, 1895, but a second child fared much better. Lee Marvin's father, Lamont Waltham Marvin was born December 19, 1896, also in Elmira, New York.

Monte, as he was known throughout his life, had a childhood marked by sadness. His father was rather sickly and, on a doctor's advice, moved his young family to Denver for his health where he obtained a job working for Wells Fargo. In spite of this, thirty-five year-old Henry Marvin's health continued to deteriorate at an alarming rate, and three years later, he was hospitalized. As Lee recalled his father telling him, eight year-old Monte, "Went out to Denver to see his father, who was dying in the hospital. It was Valentine's Day, and they wouldn't let him see him because he was already dead. My father slipped the card he had under the door. He never saw him again."

Monte and his now heartsick mother took the train back to New York where they stayed with relatives until they could figure out their circumstances. A single mother at the turn of the century had few options when it came to raising a child, and her own failing health was only making matters worse. Henry's siblings were willing to help out, including younger brother Ross, who, having just returned from Peary's unsuccessful attempt to reach the Pole in 1906, and upon hearing of his nephew's plight, petitioned the court to adopt Monte as his legal ward.

Monte idolized his uncle and with good reason. Uncle Ross had been described in both local and national newspapers as one of Peary's most trusted aides. His cool-headedness during the expedition's perilous retreat after a failed attempt to reach the Pole during an Arctic storm made headlines, and garnered him a teaching position of meteorology at his alma mater, Cornell. Ross relished his nephew's attention, in return filling the boy's head with amazing stories of the frozen North, and lavishing him with gifts of exotic animal pelts.

In 1908, Peary was ready to try for the Pole one more time, and so too was Ross Marvin. While Ross petitioned Cornell for a leave of absence, Monte was sent to Brooklyn in the care of his mother's sister and brother-in-law, Elizabeth and Thomas Wynn. When Ross met up with fifty-two year-old Commander Peary, he was informed that the crew and assistants had all been chosen. However, Peary decided to include Marvin in the 1908 expedition's bulging ranks, later writing, "Quiet in manner, wiry in build, clear of eye, with an atmosphere of earnestness about him, Ross G. Marvin had been an invaluable member of the expedition."

On July 6th Monte, accompanied by his aunt and uncle, bid farewell to Ross on Peary's specially built ship, the *Roosevelt*, as it prepared to leave New York harbor. Ross made Monte and his aunt and uncle promise that no matter the outcome of the voyage, his beloved nephew would go to school and finish college. Monte and his relatives said their good-byes and watched from the dock as the schooner sailed out of sight on its way to Greenland and into the history books.

The *Roosevelt* made several stops on its way, picking up supplies and crew until finally all the players were in place: Robert E. Peary (Commander); Robert A. Bartlett (Ship Master); John W. Goodsell (Medical Officer); Matthew Henson (Assistant); Ross G. Marvin (Secretary/Assistant); Donald B. MacMillan (Assistant); George Borup (Assistant), along with 15 ship crew members, 49 Eskimos (22 men, 17 women and 10 children), and 246 dogs. This would become one of the most debated and controversial expeditions in human exploration.

Much has been written over the years concerning the expedition and the individuals involved, especially the rivalry between Peary and former colleague Dr. Frederick Cook, Peary's questionable relationship with the indigenous people of the region, and African-American Matthew Henson's role in the race to the Pole. Largely forgotten amid these debates, however, is the vital part that Ross Marvin played on this expedition.

Never in question was Peary's unique method of travel across the frozen wasteland. He created a system of support teams that spread out on their dog-driven sleds, took readings, and doubled back to the ship as other teams advanced ahead of them. Peary and Henson would lead the first two support groups, with Marvin and then Bartlett behind them, each accompanied by two Eskimos. Marvin's Eskimos were two young male cousins named Kudluktoo and Inukitsoq, the latter nicknamed "Harrigan" by the crew for his ability to learn and repeat a popular song of the time.

After wintering on Ellesmere Island, the *Roosevelt* went up to Cape Columbia at the northern end of the island. Peary and Henson set out from there on the morning of March 1, 1909. They were accompanied by or met up with various advance teams along the way. By March 25th, Peary instructed Marvin and his team to work their way back to the ship. Six days later, Peary and other members of the expedition had arrived at the farthest point in the Arctic any man had reached, about 150 miles from the North Pole. What happened afterwards has been a point of contention for more than a century since Peary and Henson both claimed to have reached the Pole on April 6th. But, without having had the proper documentation as proof, and with possible miscalculations involved in their navigation, they were never able to confirm their exact location.

By the time Peary arrived at Cape Columbia on April 25 with the news, the celebration was short-lived. Captain Bartlett informed Peary that Kudluktoo and Harrigan had returned, but without Ross Marvin. When questioned, the two young men sadly recounted how, on April 10th, they had spread out as Marvin instructed but when he alone came to an area of thin ice, Marvin fell through, and the two Eskimos were too far away to reach him in time. By the time they got to the thin ice, they saw Ross Marvin sink face down and disappear into the current of the icy water. A makeshift marker was left near the site where twenty-nine year-old Ross was believed to have drowned. But, the body was never recovered.

Back in America, the many newspapers of the day wrote daily headlines of Peary's telegraphed progress as the world waited anxiously for any word they could get. Historically, the only thing comparable in recent memory would be the Space Race of the 1960s.

In Brooklyn, thirteen year-old Monte Marvin was more anxious than most; to compound matters, he was being interviewed several times by major dailies concerning his uncle. One journalist even accompanied him that morning on his regular routine to read the local paper. Along the way, several local kids taunted him that his uncle had died. He ran home without the paper and fell on his bed crying, while the reporter chronicled the tale of Monte sobbing to his Aunt Elizabeth about the tragic news he had just learned.

The news of Ross Marvin's untimely death,—the only fatality of the expedition—although reported, was quickly overshadowed by the controversy surrounding Peary's claim of victory. Dr. Cook made a similar claim, but stated he had reached the Pole earlier than Peary. The controversy continues to this day as to which, or for that matter, if indeed, either expedition had actually ever made it to the North Pole.

None of those facts mattered to the family and friends of Professor Ross Marvin, however. Young Monte was inconsolable and the family publicly acknowledged the difficulty in attempting to break the news to Ross Marvin's aged mother. Cornell honored their martyred alum with a memorial and additional plans of remembrance. Until his death in 1920, Peary continued to praise his fallen comrade by writing of Marvin in his memoir: "He who had never shrunk from loneliness in the performance of his duty had at last met death alone."

Monte's maternal aunt and uncle, Elizabeth and Thomas Wynn, made sure their nephew stayed in school as Ross had requested. According to Monte's first son, and Lee's older brother Robert, "Uncle was a big bookie with ties to Tammany Hall. They were Catholics so my father took the name Thomas. So his name was Thomas Lamont Waltham Marvin. He later dropped the Thomas." By the time Monte had turned seventeen, his mother had succumbed to cancer, leaving him a virtual orphan in the care of the Wynns. He was attending NYU as a business major when the United States entered World War I. Ross Marvin's wish that his nephew finish college was dashed when Monte volunteered for active service and left for the Front in May, 1917. He attended Officers Candidate School and went to Europe as a 1st Lieutenant in the Army Corps of Engineers.

His time in the war provided fodder for great storytelling years later.

"As a matter of fact, he said he was out in Leavenworth," recalled his son Robert. "They opened up Officer's Candidate School, and he was surprised they took him in. So, he was commanding officer of I think an all black infantry. They did this work, reinforce the trenches and stuff like that. They didn't do any real fighting. But still, it's military life and it was very strict."

Lee also recalled his father's experience retold to him about WWI: "My father was the classic puritan. Hold the emotions in check. Keep up appearances. Tight-assed. He had feelings but he'd never show them to you. I remember once he told me about a bunch of horses he saw in World War I. They were twisted and dead from mustard gas. He cried talking about them. He had feelings. It took something like that to bring them out."

Hoping to make the army a career after the war, Monte left active duty in 1919 but remained in the weekend reserves until 1925, working as a clerk at a midtown Manhattan branch of the Bank of Montreal during the week. Monte's request for a promotion in the reserves was denied as the Army stated it could not financially afford to approve his request. It was during this time, that, if family history is to be believed, Monte had a life-changing experience. "He said it was in a building in New York City," according to the story he told Robert's wife, Joan. "He was waiting for the elevator and this beautiful young woman walked off the elevator. He saw her and he fell in love with her but didn't know her name. It was love at first sight. "

He soon found out that the beautiful young woman was Courtenay Washington Davidge, the pride of northern Virginia. The oldest of William and Estelle Davidge's three children, Courtenay and her mother often called each other "sister" as was the southern custom. Her birth certificate states her father's occupation as lawyer, but according to Robert, he earned a living raising and selling horses to the military. Courtenay's siblings were close growing up but, as Robert points out, "William, Jr. ['Willie'] died in a car accident under mysterious circumstances. She never talked about it much." Courtenay's sister Anne, born Feb. 14, 1898, "…had a problem. Her father had to bail her out of a situation where she had been made the caretaker of a trust fund in which she had borrowed money to drink with. So he bailed her out. I think my mother had a, not a phobia, but a mild fear of booze. Her brother had been quite a drinker and maybe her father, too." It was a mild fear that, others noticed, diminished over the ensuing years.

As a young girl attending grade school in Washington, D.C., Courtenay entertained dreams of becoming a dancer. She graduated from Washington Business High School in 1915, and a few years later, sold war bonds during WWI. The closest she ever got to show business in her youth was designing the costumes for a musical version of the poem "Trees" in the early 1920s. She also loved the written word and continued to hone that craft through constant submissions to newspapers and magazines. Her masculine-sounding first name often got her work published, but when it came to getting into *The New York Times* training program, she was accepted, but only at half the pay a man would have received at that time.

It was while she was working at the *Times* to seek her fortune that she met Monte Marvin. "I didn't make my fortune," she would later say, "but I found my husband." After a brief courtship, Courtenay and Monte married September 3, 1921 in her parents' home in Washington, D.C. On their 20th anniversary she would later write Monte, " I see you again, quite as you were then, so young, so serious, and, I suppose, so frightened. I see you and me kneeling before Dr. Dudley who is no more. I see my father feeling for my elusive ring, and I hear plainly now words that were then just a sound. Now, I think of those words seriously. How serious was that act, how long reaching, how very indelible the effect on our lives. And from that came two more lives."

Such purple prose was typical of both her writing and personal style, which she utilized to the fullest in her correspondence to Monte. The young couple was truly in love during the heady early days of the jazz era. They lived simply in a sparsely decorated apartment, first in Washington after their marriage, and later New York. On a Father's Day in the early 1940s, she wrote Monte, "Since I can't send you a gift, let me send you a memory or two of you, as I shall always think of you, when I can push aside the dark, stifling curtains of the moment and look backwards. First, recorded for the duration of this life the sound of your footsteps coming down the long hall in Mrs. Beegle's apartment, where we first lived. Perhaps it was five thirty or so, and I would be there, because I was then looking for a job and would get home early. That hall had a kind of polished linoleum covering and the footsteps had a kind of pat and yours had a special swift rhythm. Later on in life, the footsteps transformed themselves to the sound of a key in a door, the click, the opening, you and your greeting. The nightly return of the loved one."

In the same letter, she wrote Monte a reminder of the event of July 18, 1922, when she gave birth to their first child, Robert Davidge Marvin, born in D.C. and named in part for her legendary Confederate ancestor, Robert E. Lee: "A very hot Saturday afternoon in Columbia Maternity Hospital. I knew you would come, but not just when. The door opened, and you stood there, still for an instant, and then it seemed you flew and were kneeling beside my bed. But it was the eyes I still see; your young face, taut and drawn, your eyes burning in anxiety and love and suffering, for Weensie had been born four or five days before. Though I could not turn or move, I can still remember that great desire to take you into the bed with me, only because you looked as if you had suffered. And then your face as you held Weensie with his little fattened head, and your deep, deep concern. Had everything been done for both of us?"

As flowery as they were, these letters were written as a way for Courtenay to get an emotional response from the usually reserved yet gentlemanly Monte. They were not necessarily physically affectionate with each other, but as Robert remembers, "Their gestures were different. Some of these guys are always pawing their wives, pulling them around. I didn't see much of that. My father could be a very warm and affectionate man, but he wasn't very demonstrative, the way you see some people are, guys who like to kiss all the wives and stuff." With a young family to support, the not quite thirty year-old Monte sought gainful employment wherever he could find it. Once his time in the army proved a dead end, he began looking for opportunities beyond his bank clerk job.

They were living in New York, and Monte was working in field sales for the Frank Seaman Agency when Courtenay next went into labor. As was the custom, the child was named for the same ancestor as Robert, Robert E. Lee, and on February 19, 1924, in New York's Booth Memorial Hospital, Lee Marvin was born. The actor would later joke that his memory was so strong he could actually recall his birth, stating proudly, "I once tried to figure out the first time I felt guilt, and it goes so far back that I might have been an inch long at the time."

It was while working in field surveys that Monte and the rest of the world discovered the truth surrounding his Uncle Ross Marvin's fate. *The New York Times* ran an exclusive article by then noted Arctic explorer George Palmer Putnam. Putnam would later gain fame as a publisher and as promoter of his wife Amelia Earhart's exploits, but in September, 1926, he was the english translator of a remarkable confession recorded the previous year: Danish missionary Knud Rasmussen had heard the testimony of Kudluktoo, the Inuit he had converted to Christianity which, told sixteen years after the fact, revealed that as one of two Inuit guides, he and his cousin nicknamed "Harrigan" were responsible for Ross Marvin's death.

The confession was thoroughly checked out before it was made public. Harrigan was questioned separately following Kudluktoo's statement, and the story stood up even in minute detail. When Ross and his guides were attempting their trek back to the ship over the frozen waters, Harrigan had stayed behind briefly to untangle the dog lines. Marvin and Kudluktoo diverged on foot approximately a half mile apart in an effort to chart the route back. Harrigan caught up with Kudluktoo's trail, and together they had waited until Marvin could catch up with their trail. "He lost his temper," Kudluktoo stated. "He threw Harrigan's things off the sled and said he could not stay with us." This sudden rage on the part of the normally restrained Marvin frightened the cousins. Harrigan knew he would surely die if left without food or water; he followed from a distance as Marvin continued to rail against the Inuits, and Kudluktoo wept in fear. When Marvin stopped the sled to check the trail ahead on foot, Kudluktoo waved over to the nearby Harrigan.

"He yelled at me that I should bring him his rifle," recalled the frightened Harrigan. "He had seen a seal in the open water. I brought him his rifle and went back again to the sled. I heard a shot a moment after and expected that Kudluktoo had shot the seal. But right away he came over to me and told me what happened, that there was no seal. He had shot Marvin in order to save my life... Marvin was shot just behind the ear and was killed instantly. We took the body out where the ice would cover him and wiped out all tracks." Four days later they reached the ship and told the concocted tale of Ross Marvin's drowning.

When *The New York Times* ran the confession on its front page, it was picked up around the world to instant repercussions. President Coolidge's Secretary of State Frank Kellogg ordered an official investigation into possible criminal charges, but none were filed. It proved to be not only a case of self-defense, but had occurred in an area of the world in which no jurisdiction existed. At the time of the incident, it was literally no-man's land until Denmark claimed the region a few years later.

Monte Marvin's legal guardian and beloved uncle died as a result of the ultimate act of violence on the last uncharted area on earth. The devastating effect this had on Monte was incalculable. For the rest of his days he kept his most vulnerable emotions in check as a result of this primal act. In contrast, his son, a recognized international film icon, would spend his adult life exploring the emotional impact of violence, and its effect on the human experience.

The surviving family decided the "official" explanation would be the only accepted one and never told Ross's then eighty-six year-old mother. In their minds, it would do no good to have her grieve again years after the tragedy in her weakened condition, nor did they believe the facts of the confession. It went against all that they held dear to think Ross had lost control of his faculties in the midst of his dilemma. Monte kept a meticulous scrapbook of the events as they unfolded but never mentioned it to his family. "If I didn't know about it, which I didn't" recalled Robert in 1995, "I can guarantee Lee didn't know."

Monte told his sons of his idolized Uncle's brave sacrifice but not the truth of his demise. By all accounts he never spoke of it to anyone. Any anger, resentment, or disillusionment he may have felt over the murder of his uncle was channeled instead through the puritan ethic of silence, hard work, and discipline. Ironically, the recipient of such discipline was his often rebellious youngest son.

Whether it could be called a response to discipline or abuse, Lee's reaction was swift and decisive: at the age of four he ran away from home. He had disappeared for two days before he was finally discovered hiding on a train bound for Baltimore. It proved to be the first of many such incidents perpetrated throughout his childhood, always ending with young Lee reluctantly returning to Manhattan and the brunt of his father's wrath. The actor later said of his constant conflict with Monte: "I wasn't having any too much discipline, even then. My father was tough. At least he thought so, and I guess I have a lot of his traits."

A year later he was confronting a fellow student in kindergarten over the territorial rights of that wooden chair. From Matthew Marvin's fiery pub raids, Ross Marvin's ill-fated Arctic adventures and his father's tightlipped discipline, Lee Marvin was on a collision course with confrontations that often led to pure physical violence. "I left kindergarten, and for the rest of my life I was never happy to go to school," he later said. "Because it was *my* chair wasn't it?"

CHAPTER 2

"Dogface" vs. St. Leo

THE STOCK MARKET CRASH in October 1929 that brought about the Great Depression of the 1930s had Lee Marvin's parents doing all they could to maintain a semblance of normalcy despite economic uncertainty. While other children were wondering where their next meal was coming from, Lee's 1929 letter to Santa told a different story. He dictated to his mother the following: "I am a good boy but sometimes I am bad. I am sorry that I am sometimes bad. I am 5 years old. I would like a soldier castle, a battleship, a cannon, a radio set, a war wagon, a soldier suit, a typewriter, a jack-in-the-box, a railroad station, a tricycle, a sand chute. Thank you for the toys."

Because Courtenay worked fairly frequently writing freelance articles for women's magazines, they were able to afford toys for the kids, and all the comforts of home. As Robert recalled, "She had a job in the Depression. She stayed home at night pounding the typewriter from time to time when my father didn't have a job. At least it was what you would call a middle-class life. See, the word middle-class now is spread so far it doesn't mean anything. Well, neither one of them had a college education so they weren't professional, in that sense. Otherwise, they were people who got creative jobs. We had a comfortable childhood. We went to both public and private schools. We didn't have what you might call a Depression-era life. Sometimes you get that impression of people's past but in our case it was pretty comfortable."

Robert recalled his father's work history somewhat differently: "He started off in the Bank of Montreal and I think a friend said, 'Why don't you try sales?' He had a very tough time for a while. Then he got a job with Eastman Kodak through the Frank Seaman Advertising Agency, one of the biggest in the world at the time. He made surveys about how to sell cameras and film. So, he went through all kinds of situations: coal mines, steel mills. He had a great deal of this sort of thing in his background. He wasn't a high-type executive in those years, where you sat in an office somewhere. He was a field guy… At the same time, my mother was working for magazines so she had an income. Between the two of them we were in pretty good shape."

The Marvin family was very keen on keeping up appearances no matter what the finances dictated. Lee's first wife, Betty, knew the family's inner workings and stated, "Well, there was money but there was no wealth. I think of wealth, I think of a lot of money. They lived okay. They lived quite frugally. Monte, you know what he did during the Depression? He went door-to-door selling 'Book of Knowledge' encyclopedias. People with financial means don't do that door-to-door."

The family's seesaw finances also meant moving a lot throughout the greater New York area, from Jackson Heights in Queens, to Brooklyn, to Manhattan's Upper West Side. Through it all, an African-American nanny named Erlene tended to Robert and Lee. Being from the South, such things were important to Courtenay, but as Betty points out, "Here's a little insight which I think was fascinating. It's like right out of Tennessee Williams or any Southern writer. When they were raised as children in New York City, Courtenay always had a Southern accent, with this little whisper. Monte, Robert and Lee always had such very fine English. Years later, Robert was in the army in a company from Brooklyn. That used to drive Courtenay crazy! His mother used to say, 'Oh Robert, how could you speak that way?' She'd go on and on and on about it. His mother was a complete snob. And those two guys, Robert and Lee, never had a chance with that mother."

Betty also recalled seeing for herself what Courtenay's relationship with Lee was like. "Lee had the most difficult time with his mother," who, she stated, "was a real Virginia Southern lady. Oh, tough as nails. I don't think there was a maternal bone in her body. Erlene, the maid whom they adored, raised both Robert and Lee. Their father was a real doormat to Courtenay. She never let anyone forget for a second about her heritage being of the George Washington strain. She came to New York from Virginia not as a fashion journalist but, well, she wanted to be a journalist. She was always exaggerating what she was. She was really more with Helena Rubenstein. She was more into cosmetics, not clothing. There was that interesting talk about matriarchy. I was the first woman that ever crossed that threshold. Robert never married until after his mother died. Lee, according to himself, really hated her. He would just go crazy when she was around. He would. He kept away from her."

Another reason for Lee's animosity towards his mother arose from the importance she would place on the facade of gracious living, while all around him he could see the effects of the struggling economy. "I always envied the street kids," he said years later. "Even though we went to public schools, we weren't allowed to have orange-crate skateboards or to wear the little stocking hats with the two buttons. We couldn't have them, and so the fights followed. I went to a lot of schools in New York City until I couldn't go anymore."

From Lee's point of view, school was a waste of his time, time he would rather have spent hunting or fishing. When the family first summered in Woodstock, five-year-old Lee discovered his love of fishing by walking off with his father's rod and reel, that is, until the state police found him and brought him back. He later went fishing on Sheepshead Bay but often ended up giving the fish away on the subway. "My parents just didn't know how to deal with fresh game," he explained.

He also loved going to the movies, Errol Flynn's being particular favorites. But the all-time favorite film of the often truant young film fan was the 1931 antiwar classic, *All Quiet On the Western Front*. He claimed it was the second film he ever saw and he never got over it, identifying closely with the tough but fair sergeant who oversaw his young charges.

School was an obvious letdown by comparison. "I didn't like school," he later reasoned. "Everyday it was a toss-up whether I'd go or skip." When he did go, the only things that held his interest were history and sports. When it came to grammar, spelling, math and other core curricula, his grades reflected his lack of interest. A teacher's note to his parents on his grade school report card read, "Please see that Lee gets to school on time."

Part of the problem went beyond his rebellious and non-conforming nature. Teachers at that time had no concept of either his Attention Deficit Disorder (ADD) or of his dyslexia. His first wife Betty witnessed it herself, and, when asked if her ex-husband was dyslexic, immediately replied: "Yes, and so is his son Christopher. Again, there was not the proper attention paid to Lee growing up, and I'm not blaming him because it was part of the times, but they were not sophisticated about dyslexia. I think Lee could have done anything if those problems had been worked out. He was a very slow reader. It's too bad because he had such a quest for knowledge. He used to say to me, 'Look at all the books around here.' It used to drive him crazy I was always reading."

Ironically, there were certain subjects and writers that held his interest, such as biographies of native-American warrior Osceola, the Civil War, and authors Bret Harte, Jack London, Herman Melville, and others. "Oh yes, and he would recite Robert Service by heart," recalled Betty. "When he read someone he really loved, he would do that. He loved literature." His ability to memorize passages while struggling with the written word itself aided him greatly with scripts when he became an actor, but frustrated his childhood teachers who were for the most part unaware of this coping device to compensate for his condition. Although dyslexia was recognized by astute and sympathetic educators, it would still be several decades before it would actually be treated in schools.

Most of the time however, school proved too frustrating to hold his interest, which resulted in another habit that carried over into adulthood: running away. His adventure to Baltimore at the age of four was just the beginning. To Betty, Lee's boyhood escapades became a regular part of their marriage. "It was a pattern," she recalled. "I believed that's how we really know people. Lee could say anything, but what he would do, from the time he was a little boy, he would run away. He would hide. While we were married, he wouldn't come home. He would call and say, 'I bet you don't know where I am.' That running away he did when he was at school. He was always truant and disappearing."

By his own admission, Lee stated, "I've never been able to accept any kind of discipline. My father was supposed to be pretty tough, and I rebelled against him by running away from home when I was four years-old. In school I couldn't see any sense to reading, writing, and arithmetic. Sure, they kicked me out, but for trifles like continual daydreaming and smoking that wouldn't be grounds for expulsion nowadays."

His transgressions were an ongoing concern to his family. "I once kicked [radio show host] Uncle Don in the shins at a performance in Jackson Heights," he once admitted sheepishly. Such actions required Monte to step in and, on more than one occasion, it got physical. "My father rarely punched my brother, rarely in any physical sense," rationalized Robert. "I can think of an incident or two when we were little children that he might have given him some verbal heat, which he could do in pretty good fashion. If your father can't do that to you, then what the hell is left?"

Upon further reflection, Robert recalled a particular time when Monte administered more than verbal heat to ten-year-old Lee: "My brother owed some kid some money, five or ten cents. Apparently, the kid came up and rang the apartment door. My father got wind of it. My father said, 'Okay, let's go out and straighten it out.' There was a gang of little kids, about eight to ten of them. My father said, 'Okay, you're going to take each one of them in a fight,' which Lee did. Of course, he was small. I remember I was awfully upset."

Such unorthodox—and in Robert's opinion, upsetting —discipline did not have the desired lasting effect on Lee. If he felt strongly about something, even at that age, he held his ground no matter the repercussions. The New York City Public School System relented and expelled him, first from P.S. 66 in Queens and then P.S. 69 in Manhattan. Following his expulsion, Lee's parents had no choice but to enroll him in a private school. The first was an experimental school in upstate New York known as Manumit. Robert remembered it as a "Very liberal private boarding school. The kids had their own garden. I think in those days it was probably considered Communist."

Priding itself on its reputation for nurturing a child's individual character, the school was progressive for its day, with group teachers, role-playing classes, and an emphasis on the arts and agriculture. Lee would recall it fondly, stating, "It was an outgrowth of the Little Red Schoolhouse-type of progressive education. When the Spanish Civil War broke out, the instructors defected to fight with the Loyalists. The school was run by Stella Ballantine, a protégé of the old anarchist, Emma Goldman. Stella's husband, E.J. [Ballantine] was a noted Shakespearean actor. They got me into acting and I was always very proud of that relationship." Letters he wrote home at the time told a different story. "I am writing this letter at the point of a gun," he would often start and then conclude with, "The other day I killed a mole and am treating its skin. Some of the girls are ordering moleskin coats."

Teachers were required to write regular summations of each student's progress and make it as positive as possible. The summary for Lee's brief tenure for the Fall/Winter term of 1937 was composed by group teacher William Mann Fincke, and included the following:

Lee is an exceedingly restless, extroverted, vital thirteen-year-old human male, but the Manumit environment appears to be big enough to take care of his restlessness. There are plenty of trees for him to get to the top of and he can build as many huts as he desires.

While Lee has arrived at the age at which he is well aware that girls exist, he has not yet, it seems arrived at the age where this awareness affects [sic] his washing and dressing habits.

From Lee's evidence of interest and stock of fairly accurate information, revealed in conversation about history, I am convinced that his difficulties with his history paper lay in his need for mastery of the simple tools of getting down the words.

...I have refrained from putting the screws on Lee in academic work pending getting completely next to him. This, I believe, I have gone a long way toward doing.

...In summarizing I should end on an optimistic note that Lee and we will be able, given time, to work out a solution of his problems and that his stay at Manumit will be on the whole a pleasant one. Occasionally I have had to speak sharply to him, chiefly to reassure him that there is present a friendly authority that does demand

from him certain standards. Lee's attitude either when advised or when sharply corrected is marked by a total absence of vindictiveness and seemingly by a bona fide desire to come through.

The school's friendly authority was sorely tested during Lee's short stay. He was caught smoking with several female students behind a shack and expelled. What upset him the most was the extra charges the self-proclaimed progressive principal heaped upon him. "We were smoking, that's all," Lee later stated. "But the principal was a dirty-minded man. He kicked me out of school and sent me home with a note for my father. It said I'd been having sexual intercourse with the girls. Hell, I didn't even have hair on my chest."

After the Manumit debacle, his parents tried a less progressive institution. The Oakwood Academy was a Quaker boarding school in Poughkeepsie, New York that Lee attended long enough to leave an indelible mark. In a letter to his brother he boasted, "Today we took four guys' pants down and put some Dr. Elles permanent wave set and mixed it with some scouring powder and poured it all over their wang. [One of them] practically bit my finger off!"

That particular incident remained undiscovered, but another one became one of the most legendary events of the actor's formative years. Waking up late one morning, Lee and his roommate scurried to organize their room in time for inspection. Lee put things away while the roommate swept. "He took the sweepings and dumped them out the window," the actor later recalled. "I said, 'That was a stupid goddamn thing to do. Now we'll have to go down there and clean 'em up again.' He called me a son-of-a-bitch, and I said, 'Call me that again and I'll throw you out the window.' He called me it again, and I threw him out the window. So, they kicked me out of school."

The roommate wasn't hurt, but over the years Lee proudly inflated the details of the incident with each retelling, such as the height of the window. Here is Marvin's own take on the repercussions: "They asked me to go home and commune with God and see the injustice of all this shit…"

Since progressive and Quaker did not work out too well, Monte then decided to enroll his son into a military school, the Admiral Farragut Naval Academy in Toms River, New Jersey. Lee was required to wear an expensive uniform and take flak from the retired sixty-one year-old naval officer, which did not sit well with the young rebel. His version was, "My uniform cost eight hundred dollars. I lasted a month. The guy in charge was a rear admiral. He kept pulling rank on us kids. I couldn't stand it. I called him a son-of-a-bitch." Lee was on the train back home in less than two weeks.

Over the years the actor boasted of having been thrown out of fifteen schools and of simply being misunderstood by his teachers and parents. Monte dispelled that legend by calling his son a "...wild, harmless, innocent but crazy kid. But there was never a period of misunderstanding. I wouldn't say that he understood me but I understood him. I used to take him fishing. He was thrown out of not fifteen schools, but let's say six schools. What a kid. I just had to put him someplace..." Lee understood what his parents were attempting, stating, "I'm not knocking what my parents were trying to do, but boy, did they waste their money."

Since Courtenay's freelance work was infrequent and Monte's job history remained sketchy, it was a waste of money they could ill afford. Then, a golden opportunity appeared for Monte in 1936 when he was offered a position with the newly formed Florida State Citrus Commission. On the face of it, financially speaking, it was an answer to the Marvins' prayers.

Unfortunately there were problems that went deeper than either finances or even Lee's incorrigibility. Monte was never one to show his emotions and Courtenay was never one to keep them in check. The family was spread across the country with Lee accompanying his father to Florida, Courtenay often in Hollywood or Manhattan on business, and Robert in Poughkeepsie at the Oakwood Academy after a brief stay in "The Sunshine State." The result left Courtenay feeling abandoned, as she pointed out in her letter-writing campaign to Monte, "The past few weeks seemed unbearable and I can't tell you exactly why," she wrote in 1938. "Perhaps I do jump to false conclusions but you must know I have little to live upon, mentally or spiritually here, so far as my family is concerned. Please do try to overlook this bad lapse and I will gird my loins once more. Oh Lord, would that I could in another sense. It has, darling, been kind of a concentration camp for years."

Monte, himself, was not having an easy time of it in Florida. He enrolled Lee into public school and battled daily with the growing politicization of the Commission. Because Monte was a sales manager and not a political appointee as were the rest of the Commission members, there were constant attempts to undermine his position by others in his office. The stress of this daily tug-of-war escalated his drinking and put an obvious strain on his long distance marriage. "For God's sake, don't let anything that can happen get to your morale," Courtenay wrote to her husband. "Don't let those crooks put anything over on you. Don't take the blame for the agency's refusal to give you good men to work with. Tell those damn fools to go to hell and get the hell out of that hole yourself. I tell you this, Monte, before it is too late."

Many of her letters ended with a plea so desperate she disregarded her facade of moneyed and privileged position: "As to money, oh hell, we got along when we didn't have it. At least we had family then. Dare I say it is a refuge here? The refuge you asked me to keep many years ago that will probably go on until I give out in a way. Florida is not the only place in the world. As to the boys thinking you are a failure ever, Monte, they would rather have a plain ordinary father than all the success in the world, and you know that. I, my dear, have learned, through you, the bitter price of success. I don't want it for myself or for anyone I love. The price is just too, too high and I beg you to remember this. Somehow I feel if we could both be together now, both of us cry, we might be better people."

As for Lee, he encountered his own problems in Florida. "My father had him in public high school," Robert recalled about his younger brother. "He did a lot of fighting. [Lee] said, 'I'm a Yankee.' You can imagine what those fucking redneck bastards thought. He came home one night, he had blood all over him. He said, 'I told some guy I'd meet him in the alley.' I said, 'What happened?' He said, 'I left him lying in the alley.'" Lee himself acknowledged his difficulty in Florida's Dade County public schools by once stating, "I had so many fists in my mouth that my folks pulled me out of there."

While Lee struggled in Florida, the relationship between his father and mother reached critical mass. Rather formally, Courtenay wrote to Monte, "Here on the afternoon of June 21, 1940, I write the letter of request that you once told me you would honor if put in writing. The request is for a divorce as promptly and painlessly as possible."

From that formal pronouncement, she then wrote for another several pages a litany of charges leveled against her husband. The most serious was, "I live in fear of you today, a fear that is built in chain fashion—first, because you stay out, and when you stay out you drink and when you drink you want to fight. I have grown afraid of those blows. Another bloody mouth, another black eye, and I can't fool the office or your friends that you expose me to, shamelessly, cruelly. You cannot be naive enough to believe that they think I walked into a door." Monte immediately returned to New York to talk Courtenay out of her request and upon his return to Florida began the long arduous task of extricating himself from the Florida Citrus Commission.

It is doubtful that Lee was fully aware of his parents' problems. If he had an inkling, he kept it to himself and followed his previous pattern. A Florida neighbor named Mrs. Walker recalled that… "{Lee} just appeared on the weekend or middle of the week and I never asked if he was supposed to be in school. He made our home his own though he never stayed overnight. He liked to help wipe the dishes while I washed. A companionable boy. He was exuberant." He showed his exuberance in often amusing ways. When Mrs. Walker served dinner for several RAF cadets, she recalled Lee suddenly jumped up and ran into the kitchen, returning later with a plate of homemade fudge. "He bubbled over, yet he was never any trouble and he was always very considerate."

He was considerate to neighbors, but exacerbated his parents' woes by knocking over trashcans, daydreaming in class, or fighting with neighborhood toughs. The young teenager knew his inability to walk the straight and narrow path of conformity would incur his father's wrath, but by the time he was of age for high school, that wrath was forced to diminish. When a friend once asked Lee when did his father stop beating him, he responded, "When I was fourteen. By that time, I was big enough physically that he became afraid to."

As in New York, the public school system of Florida had had its fill of Lee Marvin, and Monte was no longer of a mind to dominate his son physically. Lee was informed by his father that he had just one more chance to straighten up. After public, progressive, Quaker, and military attempts at an education failed, the young upstart knew Catholic school would be the end of a long line with no further options left to him.

The Catholic high school where Monte enrolled Lee had a well-de-served reputation for expecting and receiving excellence from its upper and middle-class student body. It was Lakeland Florida's St. Leo's School for Boys, with a faculty made up mostly of the Brothers of St. Benedictine. Despite the fact that Lee had been confirmed at St. Agnes Episcopal Trinity Parish of New York when he was twelve, having gone to Sunday school there, Monte was able to pull the proper strings to get Lee into St. Leo as a sophomore in September, 1940.

It would be natural to assume that Lee resented his father for his strict adherence to school and discipline, but such was not the case. "Lee just thought his father hung out the sun," recalled Monte's secretary, Cecil Gober, "He used to like to get his father to reminisce about his World War I experiences and the time he spent in France." His brother Robert saw it slightly different: "If you don't see a father as often as a guy who's home every night, you might tend to glorify him a little bit or compensate."

Lee's resentment was reserved for his mother Courtenay, who was spending most of her time writing for *Photoplay* in Hollywood. Lee loathed the way his mother put on false airs for friends and neighbors, and as a result, he harbored a lifelong disdain for phoniness and hypoc-risy. In 1966, another former neighbor was to recall how the teenaged Lee, tall and slim with a shock of dark hair, wore the resentment on his face: "He had very keen eyes and a cynical curl to his mouth. The same curl he has today."

Knowing he was out of second chances, Lee did make a concert-ed effort to succeed at St. Leo in spite of his undiagnosed dyslexia and ADD. His teacher, Fr. James Hoge, recalled, "He didn't care much for the academic part of it but he was great with his fellow students. He didn't fight with them or anything like that. He got along well." A classmate remembered, "We called him 'Dogface' because of his hangdog puss. He looked like one of Disney's pooches when you looked at him head on." Fr. Weigand, known for his gentle disposition, recalled, "I bopped him one time for doing something or other, and I rather surprised myself." As a six-foot, naturally athletic teenager, "Dogface" Marvin and St. Leo met their match in one another.

A saving grace for both the school and its most infamous student was its impressive athletic program. He wrote his parents at the time, "This evening I was 'told' to go out for track. I think that I will try the 440 and the low hurdles. I am glad that I have to go out because for the past month I have been just lying around and getting lazy. Maybe I will be a man yet." The maverick Marvin exhibited his prowess running the hurdles and throwing the javelin, as well as in competitive swimming. He set school records in most of the events he entered at St. Leo.

In spite of his athleticism, he still managed to get into some mischief even while under the watchful eye of the faculty. His dorm-mate Paul DeGuenther recalled his… "making a little wine out of the citrus fruit that we'd go out and pick and then squeeze. Let it ferment. It wasn't anything fancy. It was just something that had alcohol. It must have had some kick to it because we got a few [fellow students] a little tipsy. The guys after us had to report to the Abbot every week like a parole office because they got caught."

Being a healthy young man, Lee found time to explore another growing interest. Across nearby Lake Jovita and down the road from St. Leo was the Catholic girl's school and convent, Holy Name Academy. The St. Leo boys were often the guests at Holy Name dances. DeGuenther recalled once when he, Lee, and several others walked in just as the girls were about to have a contest to see who of the boys had the biggest mouth. The girls asked each of them to smile real wide, and they measured their mouths from side to side. He related warmly, "Well, Lee won and I came in second. I was always second to Lee Marvin." On occasion Lee, Paul, and several others ventured over to Holy Name uninvited. Sneaking down after hours to the lake's dock to borrow a rowboat and paddling over to the school, the transgressors were nonetheless gladly received.

Lee Marvin also experienced his first onstage triumph at St. Leo. The school production of "Brother Orchid"— based on the then popular Edward G. Robinson comedy film of a gangster who hides out in a monastery—proved to be an indicator of things to come. The amateur St. Leo's theater critic noted, "The auditorium was filled to capacity to see one of the greatest productions ever given at St. Leo… 'Solomon,' just one of the boys, slow thinking and willing to take a drink at the other man's expense, was a riot of comedy as played by Lee Marvin."

In the summer of 1941, Lee stayed in Florida instead of returning to New York until his father could finally extricate himself from the Citrus Commission. It was a complicated process and it was written in the local paper that for Lamont Marvin it was either resign or get fired. Whatever the case, Monte was clearly glad to be rid of it. The normally reserved Monte wrote his wife, "This is the last you will ever see an address from me in Lakeland. By the way, they got into more difficulty over a slogan for this fair city, selecting the second one, 'the roof garden of Florida,' which has been used for many years by a little dump called Lake Placid. Here is the slogan to end all slogans—*Lakeland, the asshole city of the asshole county of the asshole state of the nation.*"

Although the forty-four year-old business executive did not know what the future would hold, he managed to find work for the time-being promoting the vegetable industry in Washington, D.C.

While Monte was trying to figure out his future, back in Florida his son wrote of a valuable lesson learned during a football game: "I and four other boys took on the whole Dade City High School in a fight in the bleachers. We were sitting in the Dade City stands and making more noise for our team then they were for their team. So some lad stood up and told me to shut up. Consequently, I told him if he thought he could to come over and try it. Then about ten of his friends stood up. So did we. I looked around to tell one of the boys something and when I looked back there were a 150 of them standing. We said if they were fixing to start something then come ahead. About that time they started after us and by gum we were waiting. Then somebody hollered for them to sit down and they did. That just goes to show you that there is no use in throwing a bluff." In the same letter he made a revealing request: "Folks, there is one thing I would like to ask of you and that is that I may go to Oakwood next year. St. Leo is all right but it really is getting on my nerves. Now don't go and get worried about me flunking this year because I won't. But I really would like to go to Oakwood next year and play some football. It is a lot different than down here."

A few days later, on December 7th, 1941, Lee and a friend were leaving a movie theater. They had been making plans for a cross-country hike for the following summer when the news from Pearl Harbor came over the car radio. With America plunging into war, the seventeen year-old now found it even harder to focus on school. His brother Robert was the first to sign up, and joined the Army Air Corps. His father made plans to rejoin the Army and hoped to get a commission. As for himself, Lee grappled with his options, but finally wrote his parents in May of 1942, "I think that I have finally come to a decision about the service. I believe that I will join the Marines about the middle of summer. I was talking to one in Jacksonville last week and he was telling me all about it, good and bad. He was 22 or 23 and from Conn. He also said that it still is the best place for someone that wants to fight and raise hell."

CHAPTER 3

"I Have Had My Fill of War"

L EE MARVIN'S DECISION to join the Marines coincided with America's early setbacks in the war. In the eight months following Pearl Harbor, U.S. forces withstood staggering losses to the Japanese in The Philippines, The Aleutians, Indonesia, Singapore and Burma. This time of extreme patriotism had Lee's brother enlisting in the Army and going through training in New York to eventually serve overseas in the Army Air Corps ground crew. Monte was working in D.C. and was also itching to get into the fight despite the fact that he was in his forties.

The rebellious Lee Marvin was anxious to do his part through the auspices of the most rigorous branch of the service. What follows are excerpts of his letters home minus the usual salutations, the scuttlebutt, requests for spending money, and queries for family updates. What remains are his grammatically corrected firsthand accounts and revealing anecdotes of basic training, specialty training and warfare all within the confines of military censorship. The correspondence begins with "boot camp" on Parris Island, South Carolina and varies in tone depending on the recipient.

8/16/42, Dear Mother and Father:

Well we pulled in Thursday, noon. What a long trip. I certainly did not underestimate this one bit. We get up at 3:30 and hit the bed at 10:00. We work hard all day and I mean hard. There are 72 men in our platoon and I am the 1st squad leader. The platoon I am in has 72 men with 8 men to a squad. Though it's tough as hell, I really like it a lot.

The training is really tough and they work us all day. The one thing that they strive to do down here is to make you hate the Marines and, by gum, they do it.

8/23/42: We received our rifles and gear yesterday. In the morning we went on maneuvers in the swamps and had a very good time. Honestly, nobody could explain how tight this camp is. About once every three days you get five minutes to yourself. All it is is drill, sweat, drill, sweat.

They gave out the mail a few minutes ago and one guy got 15 letters from his girlfriend. Ain't it hell? We went swimming today and we had all looked forward to it for a long time. When it finally came, we did not feel like it. Oh well.

We also have to wash our clothes every night and everything you do you have to stand in line for. The food is very good, considering everything. One of the mess sergeants said it is all grade A, but then they cook it. A lot of the boys get heat prostration in the daytime because it is well over 100 degrees in the sun. Once in a while they give you 20 or 30 marches in a row and they get dizzy as hell and fall.

It is very pretty right now. The sun is setting and a few of us are sitting in the sand by our barracks in our bathing suits and shoes writing letters to our folks. There is nothing like an 18-hour solid workday and a good 6 hours sleep.

9/2/42: For the past three days we have been on the bayonet range and have learned the tricks of the trade. The range has all the plunges and lunges and it is a lot harder to do then you expect. Pop, you made a statement in your letter about training not being any tougher than I expected. Well, to be honest with you, the training was so hard on us that none of us could express it in writing. Pop, you were right, it was a bit tougher than expected.

A few days ago I applied for the Quartermaster School. That is they got our whole company together and asked all the men who *could do simple math and could type to fall out and I did. They told me that if I was not taken into any branch of the service for my former trade that I would probably go to the Quartermaster school and in three months I would be a Cpl. so I said O.K. Now all I have to do is to sit tight and wait.*

Having completed the normally thirteen-week Boot Camp in four weeks, Marvin was transferred to New River, North Carolina for his Marine Combat Training [MCT], which was also expedited for the war.

9/15/42: We arrived here at New River. After a filthy 12-hour trip, we got here. What a difference. At Parris Island we were treated like dogs by all the privates that were out of boot camp. Here, even the Master Gunnery Sergeants stand chow line with us.

We are camped in a tent area and they are cool as can be. I have my squad in the first tent and I have to take care of them and see that they don't shirk their duties. This afternoon we start "snoping in" which is learning the different stances for shooting. This is the most important part of our training, as a poor shot won't help win a battle.

As you know, this place is big, 200 sq. miles. It is a haven compared to Parris Island.

9/29/42: Well, here I am at the rifle range and I have had 3 days of firing. This is beyond a doubt the best part of the training. We fire 60 rounds in the morning every day and by noon my hip is about the size of a cow. The other day some man shot a foot behind the firing line and blew my ears off with the concussion. I wish you could hear 150 men firing rapid fire. It is terrific. I must go to chow now, as it is 6:30.

Today I shot 216, which is sharpshooter. It is a good improvement over yesterday. Today is record day and I did a little better but I should have made expert. I lacked just three points for the expert. On the Rapid Fire I did very bad but there is one thing I can say and that is that I shot the highest in my platoon of 72 men.

10/7/42: It took me a long time to get that phone call through to you but it was worth it. In the whole town there are only three phones that can get long distance and every night there are 10,000 Marines trying to use them. It is a pretty good set up around here with liberty every other night and every other weekend.

I am now in the Quartermaster School at Hadnot Point N.C. and it is a swell place with brick barracks and good chow. There is a big river just 100 yards from my barracks and I think I will do a little fishing soon.

I passed all my entrance tests. Classes won't start for about a week so all I do is 1 hour of police duty in the morning and for the rest of the day I loaf and fish. Really, there is very little I can tell you because there is nothing of interest and that which is, we are not allowed to tell.

10/13/42: I have started class and it is very interesting, about how to buy and distribute the things that you have. It is just like school here but not so much cutting up as in the classes at St. Leo.

10/28/42: About my schooling, it is coming along well at this time. My first test I got 85, which was good. In the last one I got 92 which is better. So far that gives me an 88.5 average. Yes, we go to school all day from 8:00 to 11:30. Then we start again at 13:00 and work until 16:00. We do a lot of typing and lecturing in the course. The job of the Quartermaster is to see that everybody has what they need and we have to learn the Marine manual, which is about 4 inches thick. We saw some pictures of the Marines in action in The Solomons and did they act mean. It really was very impressive.

10/29/42: It is so cold that in the morning the commanding officer issued an order that there would be no more blankets worn to roll call. Don't get me wrong, but this Marine Corps is so messed up I often wonder how it lasted this long. By that I mean that they never do the same thing the same way more than two times, and no one seems to know what is supposed to happen next or anything. All the boys get a big kick out of getting the officers all mixed up and telling them the wrong dope.

I wish that you could come down here for a few days and then you can understand why I send somebody in to [town to] get the things I want. I think that there are 72 million Marines in that small town of Wilson every night and what a mess it is. Everything costs three times as much as it does in other towns. I have not been out in the past three weeks and I am just as glad. The closest town that is of any size is Richmond, Va. which is too far away for a night's trip so all the boys stay home and gamble.

This QM is all right but the classes are very boring, as you can imagine. All this stuff about what the disbursing officer does in the case of a duplicate form going to Washington and what does he do when the field year is up, etc. After you get out it is a lot different they say and it is a good life.

Out of the seven shirts I have been issued I only have four left. The theft that goes on around here with clothes is terrific. When somebody takes yours you just find somebody that wears the same size as you and help yourself.

11/9/42: I received your phone call this morning. Sorry that I did not send you a wire telling you the situation but as you see, it was impossible for me to make it. A lot of the boys go AWOL but sooner or later they get caught, fined and kicked out of school, and I did not want that. Sometimes I wonder what I joined up for. A boy that sleeps above me left yesterday. Today they issue him books so he won't be here to receive them. They will check up on him and find that he has gone over the hill and then he will be in a fix.

I heard a program last night where a Major spoke about the situation on Guadalcanal. He stated when they landed there the Japs were sitting under the trees and then the commentator asked if they ran away. The Major quietly said, "No, they are still under the palm trees." He also said that the Japs are a little underestimated for they are good fighters and very tricky. They sneak behind our lines at night and then try to cause confusion by giving commands in English such as "Don't shoot, captain. I am bringing my platoon in." When the platoon does come in, it is a load of Japs. He also said that the American youth is not brought up to be a fighter but once he gains confidence in his weapons and is put in a situation, he can last better than the others.

11/15/42: Dear Mother,

Well, believe it or not, I got three letters today and two were from you and dated the 9th and the 12th. There is a good example of the mail system down here.

Mother, I have a funny feeling that Pop is lonesome from the way he writes and I have noticed it in all of his letters. That's why I will really make it to Washington on the weekend of the 29th. I will be able to get a 62-hour pass and that will be just right for the trip. Well I must quit and get to work or I will be shining brass for 583,986,000 days and don't think I am just kidding you.

12/7/42: Just a year ago today I remember clearly all that took place. In the afternoon I went to the show and when I came back somebody told me that the Japs had bombed Pearl Harbor. Of course I told him that he was slinging the bull but we went upstairs and listened to the radio and verified his statement. It seems impossible but it was a smart piece of strategy because we lost 25 ships there.

After spending the weekend with his parents, Lee wrote the following:

12/11/42: Well by some piece of luck or fate I just made it to roll call this morning. To be exact it was just 1 and 1/2 minutes past 6 when I crashed into the barracks as my name was being called off. If I can only stay awake in class today I will be all set. Pop, it was really swell to see you and Mother and you do know that I had a wonderful time while I was there. I feel that you went a little deep in your pocket for me but I will remember it. I will see that you get your Xmas present soon so that Santa Claus won't leave you empty handed.

I got 90 in my test Friday, which is about the average mark for me. We were just informed that we may have a two-week extension on our course but nothing is definite yet. Send those pictures along as soon as possible as my public is crying for them.

12/14/42: Good news! I have a 62-hour pass this weekend and I will be up in New York for an early afternoon. It will be good to see you all and I really mean it.

God, I really hope that Robert gets transferred to the East for a permanent post as I really worry about him. In my estimation there are very few brothers like us though we don't like the same things we get along swell together and I have a very deep love for him. Don't ever tell him this, it is a very personal feeling.

12/17/42: I am really sorry that I cannot make it this weekend but I did not wake up in time for roll call this morning. Subsequently, I went on report as absent and got restricted for the rest of my time here at New River. That will be about a week and a half.

On Christmas we are going to have a football game, the School Battalion against the Post troops. There are plenty of pro and college football players here so it ought to be a good dirty game. There will also be a track meet without the hurdles and javelin, which breaks my heart. There is a boy here who does the three-legged race with me and we really can move. We won it in the last meet. So the day will be pretty well filled in. Of course there will be little private parties and things like that. After that, there will be a dance with 56,000 Marines and 34 girls, so that ought to be something.

12/ 23/42: Well, we got the word today on the corporals. It did not sound very good. Of course I do not have the highest average in class but I do have 88. I guess that will only make me a P.F.C. at the most or just stay the way I am. It really makes no difference as I will get my stripes in the field. When I first got in this outfit I figured that stripes were everything but now I know different.

Completing his time with the Quartermaster, Marvin was transferred to San Diego's Camp Elliott for his Military Occupational Specialties [MOS] training.

1/5/43: Well at last we got here, after one full week of travel. The trip was really swell and it did not seem like 7 days. The country west of New Orleans started to get really flat until we got to New Mexico and then it got strange and quite hilly. Coming through Arizona was the best as we went through mountains.

I don't know yet what my duties are but it looks as though I will be here a long time. The boys call it Company B, as in B here when they go and B here when they come back. So you can see that I will be here for a hell of a long time.

2/ 8/43: I don't know how to tell you this but I will try, as it is only right that you know. It seems as if I have been working here for a month and I don't know what I did but I must have done something, as I had to see the first Sgt. Saturday morning. He handed me a sheet of paper and said, "I don't know whether you will like this or not, but it is yours, now you have to use it." It seems that it was a notification that I had been made a Corporal, which pleases me very much. Yes, Mother that is two stripes on my shirtsleeve. So in the next letter you will address it to Cpl. Lee Marvin.

2/23/43 Dear Robert;

Tell me one thing and that is how do you do with the women? As for me, I never go out with them much. When I was in New River I got my first ass, as you might put it. Let me tell you, that was a set up. She was a damn whore but it was damn good. She used to send me money to go up there and see her. Once she sent me 30 bucks and it only cost me about ten. She knew it but did not give a shit. It may not sound good to you but it was a hell of a lot of fun.

Well, how would you like to be back in college again or in civvies? One guy I was talking to said the biggest fight he is going to have in the Marine Corps is getting out and man, I believe that with all my heart.

3/8/43: Hello there, lad [addressed to his brother, Robert]

Damn Robert, don't ever get into any bad action and watch yourself because as you probably know I consider myself your big brother. I want to get back so you, Pop and me can have some more good times. I feel so damned sorry for Pop as he probably considers himself a flop in life. In reality, he is one of the best men. He is one of the few men that has two sons that look up to him with such esteem as you and myself. Believe me, every time I start to do something that will hurt him, I just think and then turn around and Don't. Yeah, he is the ace all right.

Do you ever think of the times we can have after this thing is over? Remember that time we went up to some park and coming home we had to take a piss so damn bad that we damn near drowned some couple over on the other side of the park? All of that was really good but you don't realize it until you get in some asshole outfit like the service. Now I know what Pop meant by saying that military life does you good. Yes sir, it makes you realize what a good time is. Hell, I can honestly say that I have not had a really good time since I have been in.

3/11/43: Pop, what did you do for enjoyment in the First World War? There is certainly nothing to do in this one and it costs a small fortune to get no place now. Oh well, it is a great life in the service as no one seems to know what you are supposed to do so actually you do nothing and get very tired of doing even that.

I will have to rush to get the 2200 show, as it is a good looking gal tonight and the boys really let out groans and sighs when she kisses one of the boys. O yes, it is only a movie but they have great imaginations.

3/20/43: I was transferred to the Base Depot here at Elliot and am now a correspondence clerk. I have to write all the letters that go out but they write them up in long hand so I don't have to trust my spelling. Boy, there can be no mistakes and it has to be perfect. I usually do each one for about 45 times before I get it right.

I just came back from the hills and you should have seen the things I saw. It was about 5:30 in the evening and the sun was just getting ready to go down. The sky was a limpid red with hills and valleys in different light. It was really magnificent. I did a lot of thinking while I was up there. That seems to be the only thing that I can do today and feel good. When I get annoyed at things in general and start to think about leaving, I just go out there and get good and disgusted at myself and then dream I have forgotten my troubles.

There is one thing that has me worried and this is that I have never found anything that I really want to do for a while. I guess you would call me fickle or something like it but it gets me worried once in a while.

Anxious to see action, Lee Marvin signed up for the 4th Marine Division attached to the Marines 24th Regiment. Known as the "Fighting Fourth," it was a new division and the first to be formed stateside to go directly into battle. Lee's training became even more intense in its short duration.

3/30/43: My stay at the Base Depot was very short (three days) and then I with another bunch of boys were transferred to this post. Last Friday they formed a new regiment called the 24th Marines and that is now where I am. It should take us at least 9 or 10 months to form. This outfit should see some real action when and where we land. Since Friday we have just sat around waiting for some more men as we have only 38. I and three corporals and a Mess Sgt. formed it, so no one can tell me they are "old salts" of the 20th.

Here at Camp Pendleton, it is really beautiful as there are mountains all around. Talk about a big camp, this is it. It covers 400 square miles and it used to be a big ranch. I went up to Hollywood this weekend and had a nice time. I saw Benny Goodman at the Palladium and had dinner there. All in all I had a nice clean time.

With both his sons in the military and having served in WWI, Monte sought their advice as to whether or not he should reenlist. Lee's letter helped him decide.

4/7/43: *Dear Pop;*

About your enlisting in the Army Engineers, well it is rather hard for me to tell your father what to do but I will give you all the dope I can on the different views. The first thing, you are not an old man. Please get this idea out of your head. If you did enlist you would undergo a hell of a social change, which you would get used to in time. The life and "chow" would really make you feel good and build up your body so that those little aches and pains you used to get would not bother you. So this is my decision, you would like it and also you would probably be a very good man in the outfit. If you did I would be the proudest son in this world. It is very seldom that you find a father doing so much for his sons and Robert and I both know that. Sure, Pop, go ahead and do it. That is what makes us Marvins.

5/3/43: *Dear Mother and Father;*

Things here have been going pretty rough. The Raiders attacked a company that was on maneuvers and they actually threw dynamite in their tents. They nearly lost some of the boys but that is the Marines for you. We have had a lot of problems this past week and they have really kept us going. I am still in charge of my platoon and I hope that I make the grade here. There is a lot of little things that get you balled up but slowly and surely I am getting them ironed out.

5/25/43: Things are starting to get straightened out in the company and now I really have to be on the ball. We have had a lot of classes in the tricks of fighting, the little things that save your life and make for perfection as a fighter. They are really very interesting and will continue to be.

I met a nice girl in L.A. last weekend and so I suppose that I will be going up there for a while now. Have to keep up my morale, you know.

6/23/43: Dear Mother and Father;

You would never guess what they put me into. Why I don't know but it is demolition, the art of blowing bridges, roads, etc. That is the safe part, as you are very seldom under heavy fire. But with that we are also snipers and have to dispose of booby traps and land mines. They now have booby traps that are so tricky that the best of them failed to dispose of them but we are figuring out ways to do it.

About this gal in L.A., well the old wolf in me led up to it. She is a damn nice girl. Good looking? Well I guess you know. I introduced one of my buddies to her and he stepped back, paused and his jaw dropped about 10 inches. We go out to the beach and movies and dance, etc. Just something to take up my spare time, yes, yes!

7/21/43: Dear Mother;

Well I seen Pop over the weekend and all in all I had the best time since I have been in the service. I got up to Camp Hood about 10 a.m. and I had to weigh in at the "M.P." station for 2 hours. I then decided to go up there to his barracks. I broke in on him just as he was getting dismissed from inspection. When we met I did not know whether to shake hands or hug him. Boy, he looked swell in his uniform and I think that he really likes the life. We went up to some town north of there and were lucky enough to find a room. We talked things over and had a swell time just talking to each other.

You asked for a description of Pop, well here goes. Mother, he looks young and as handsome as ever. His face is tanned and he is full of pep and is far more the father that I knew before. I now realize that I am afraid for him in the way that I can not express in words. You are and should be proud of our father, as he is unequaled. He expressed his great concerns for you and I think that things shall work out. Well I have to go so so long for a little while.

8/21/43: Dear Pop,

Remember when I told you the last time I saw you about the possibility of a transfer and demotion? Well lo and behold, it came. I am now doing the honorable job of chief messman in the chow house.

It is not the job that I like but as Private I do not request my job, etc. I hope to make back the rate quick but there is no line duty in this company.

I asked the Captain for a furlough the other day and he said as soon as I got out of the mess hall. So, there is a good possibility of 15 days to go see Mother. Personally, I do not care to go on furlough, as there is no place to go for seeing friends as I have none in New York. I know that Mother is lonely. She is my mother so I will go see her. I know it will do both of us good.

9/27/43: Dear Mother;

I am still in the mess hall and hope to get out the first but I can't be sure of anything around here. We are packing up all our equipment so I don't think it will be too long now until we shove off.

I'll bet that the weather is starting to get cool back there and in another month the whole Hudson Valley will be turning to the colors of fall. I do miss the east. The thing I most regret is the fact that I will no longer be able to be a boy in school with the simple non-thinking carefree mind. Well, I had better stop this talk before I get too deep.

By the end of 1943 the Marines had gone from defensive to offensive against the Japanese. The Japanese commanding officer of Coral Island had said, "It could not be taken by a million men in a hundred years." In spite of sustaining heavy losses at Coral, Midway and Tarawa, the Marines' aggressive island-hopping campaign took much less time than that. Fully trained and operational, The Fighting Fourth prepared to ship overseas and invade the Marshall Islands and their atolls in February of 1943.

Shortly before he shipped out for the Pacific, Lee Marvin received an unexpected surprise. Monte hitchhiked to Pendleton while on leave and took his son barhopping. "He gave me his .45 and said, 'Here kid. Don't lose it in a crap game.' I carried it with me everywhere with one in the chamber and seven in the back of the clip," the actor recalled. It was a story he often retold with pride, leaving out one important detail. According to Lee's first wife, "[It was] also then that Monte proceeded to seduce Lee's girlfriend at the time. Interesting isn't it?"

Once he shipped out, Marvin quickly discovered actual war was nothing like he had seen in the movies. "The war had an effect on me," he said years later. "I remember a native woman on one of the islands that was carrying a dead child in her arms—and she was nine months pregnant with the next one. She was walking around in shock. A Marine came up to her and said, 'Put that dead kid down.' She wouldn't do it. The Marine got sore. He told her to put it down. She refused. He took out a knife and sliced her belly open. He disemboweled her. The fetus dropped out. When he put his knife back in the scabbard, he was ready to fight a war. This insanity, this raving inhumanity—it was then I suddenly knew: This is what war does to a man, what war means."

With lessons learned from each of the Marines' previous skirmishes, they bombarded each island with artillery at dawn, having sent in trained Marine scout/snipers the night before for reconnaissance. The scout/snipers, of which Lee Marvin was one, administered silent death to any Japanese that were encountered. As much as he wanted to, these events could not be written about in family letters. Instead, he wrote the following:

> 2/14/44: *Dear Mother;*
> *Well here is the second letter, which will have to be fairly short. I guess the papers said that the Marshall Islands were taken. Our company was the first Marines that landed on them, in fact the first Marines to land on Jap held territory before Pearl Harbor. The job was done in good order and in good spirit. I am in fine health so don't worry. It is hard to think that it is winter back home, as it is pretty hot here, but to think of you and home is a blessing.*

Lee could not detail his experiences to his mother, such as staying on the island throughout the night until the bombardment began. He could not speak of the mosquitoes, leeches, dysentery, and the permeating wetness to be avoided or run the risk of jungle rot. Nor could he speak of the death encountered. "On Kwajalein there were six guys wearing white in a trench," he told LIFE Magazine in the 1960s. "I get up there waiting for them to move so I could pull the trigger. But none of them make a move. One of our guys comes along and says, 'What's the matter?' I said, 'I don't know. They look like merchant marine to me.' He looked at me and cursed and emptied his gun into the trench. Then he threw in a hand grenade."

Witnessing such behavior made it easier for Marvin to perpetrate it himself. A neighbor in California remembers the actor opening up to him about his war experiences: "He was assigned to go knock out a whole foxhole full of Japanese machine gunners. He went in there and I guess he laid out about 5-7 of them… Years pass and that's something you just don't kiss off easily… you could tell it was really hurting him." At the time, all he could do was write the following:

> 3/12/44: *Dear Pop;*
>
> *Lots has happened in the past few months but nothing that I can not speak of now, as the regulations are pretty strict on such things. I can tell you one thing and that is I have had my fill of war.*
>
> *Thanks again for the .45, as it is the best foxhole buddy a Marine can have. I hope that you won't mind the notch in the handle but you know how things like that are. I only fired it once but that was all that was necessary. It is in damn good condition and will remain that way. I am in good shape and feeling fine so don't let that worry you.*
>
> 4/11/44: *Dear Pop;*
>
> *I might not be writing so don't let it worry you. Our company got quite a good name for itself after those 17 islands and a night raid in rubber boats.*
>
> *They asked me to join another scout and sniper outfit but I don't think I will, as it is not until you sign on that you do realize its danger. I was lucky once and I don't want to tax it.*

He had good reason not to want to tax his luck. On the island of Eniwetok, he and five others rushed a machine gun nest that had kept the company pinned down. Crawling on their bellies on either side of the nest the six of them were able to get close enough to lob in grenades, killing half the men inside. When Marvin rushed in to kill the rest, his foot caught and sent him and his rifle sprawling. He rolled over to see his foot had caught on a sand-covered trapdoor that the other Japanese machine gunners were sneaking into. He made eye contact with one of them. "He popped out of that hole like a little animal," said Marvin. "For a second I just lay there on my ass surprised as hell while he blinked at me. Then he lunged. He tried to stick his bayonet in my eye. So I took it away from him. It wasn't hard to do because he was just a little bastard, maybe 5 feet 2 or so. I shoved that goddamned thing into his chest all the way to the gun barrel…"

While Europe was feeling the effects of D-Day on June 6, 1944, the invasion of Saipan in the Pacific the following week proved equally harrowing. Lee was there and later wrote his brother:

The first night on the island I had a damn close call. We were in a hell of a barrage and they were knocking the hell out of us. The hole I was in was about 4 feet deep and 12 across. There were four of us in it. You know you can hear [the mortars] coming so I would stick my head up and call the shots, that is if they were to come visiting 25 yards I'd better duck. If not we'd just let them go and hope for the best. Well I watched one of our batteries fire and heard them go off in the hills except it sounded like 3 times as many and sure enough they were Nip guns firing at us. I was looking for them and here comes one. I think it had all our names on it. Man, it sounded like it was in the hole with us. It hit about three feet from my head and blew off my pack, gas mask and canteen, killed one of the boys and wounded the next. But what I can't figure out is why it didn't blow my head off; that it didn't even scratch me yet it hit all the rest. Damn, I saw red for the next ten minutes and it sounded like Big Ben in my head.

It was also while on Saipan that Lee had taken a letter off a soldier he had killed and out of curiosity brought it in to be translated. It read, in part:

How is everyone and how is my home town? Please ease your worries since I am well as always. I'm doing my duties faithfully. I am determined to do nothing but my best for my country. I have no regret now. No matter where you are, the moon looks the same. Sorry that I'm always writing the same complaints.

This letter had a powerful effect on him as it transformed the idea of the Japanese soldier from that of a faceless enemy to a living and breathing fellow human being. To Marvin, it could have been written by a fellow American, or even one of the letters he had written home himself.

The battle of Saipan raged on until early July, but for Lee Marvin it ended on June 18th. Once he was evacuated from the island and safely ensconced on a hospital ship, he wrote his father:

7/3/44: Dear Pop;

I am writing you this letter mostly to tell you that I am really all right and that things are not as bad as they seem. I was on Saipan when I got hit. Not too bad but bad enough to hamper me if I stayed. I was hit in my left buttocks just below the belt line.

You may think it's funny to get hit in the can like that but at the time I was very lucky that that is all I got. I was pinned down and could not move an inch and then a sniper started on me. His first shot hit my foot and his second just about three inches in front of my nose. It was just a matter of time, as I knew I would get hit sooner or later. If I got up and ran I would not be writing this letter so I just kept down. I could see nothing to fire at so there I was.

Bang! It felt like someone hit me with a 2 x 4. The wound starts about 1/4" from my spine on a slight forward angle where it left the flesh. It was a sniper that hit me and he must have been using a flatnose slug, as it did not leave two little holes. It entered about 1/2" where it did and just laid it all open. Now there is more or less a gash 8" long by 3" wide and about 2" deep. It did not touch the muscle or spine at all. Geez, now you never seen creeping like I did but he kept on shooting. Finally, I got out of there and I am OK now. I am now on Guadalcanal and awaiting transfer south. They figure on letting the wound fill in so that will take about 4 or 5 months. They gave me the Purple Heart and all the trimmings but I still think that it was worth it.

Once he was on the hospital ship, he checked his belongings and saw the bullet hole in his wallet that left a gaping blood-soaked hole through a photo of his entire family. He also felt immense guilt over the loss of his father's .45 automatic. He had given it to one of the fellow Marines who had helped him get out after being wounded. The Marine's rifle had been shot up so Marvin lent him the .45, which saved his life after he too was wounded. Marvin had to later write his father:

My buddy was evacuated also but to a different place and he kept it until he got to a rear area that customs took it from him. The jerk didn't list it so the commander told us one of the officers noticed it and kept it for himself.

After twenty-one invasions in all for Private Marvin, such thoughts were foremost in his mind as he contemplated why he survived while the rest of his comrades continued to fight and die. Saipan was secured and on Lee's 21st birthday the 4th Marines invaded Iwo Jima. The battle was intense as the Fighting Fourth suffered devastating losses, 80% casualties in all and ultimately was disbanded. Marvin had hoped to get back into combat but for the next thirteen months he was transferred to different naval hospitals.

For Lee Marvin, the war ended when he was safely aboard the hospital ship after being evacuated from Saipan. Listening to the battle in the distance rage on into the night, nestled in clean sheets and being spoon-fed ice cream as Glenn Miller's "Moonlight Serenade" wafted through the sound system, twenty-year-old Lee Marvin broke down and cried.

CHAPTER 4

"These Horrible, Animal Men"

A S A CIVILIAN, mustered out from the Philadelphia Marine Barracks on July 24, 1945, Lee Marvin could not shake off the intense mixed feelings he was experiencing: anger, frustration and worst of all, survivor guilt as the war stubbornly wore on. On the bus ride back to his parents' Manhattan apartment an old woman angrily tapped his shoulder with a cane and asked why such a healthy-looking young man was not in the military fighting for God and country. Acting on reflex, Marvin turned and barked at her that he was physically unfit. Years later he told a reporter, "I won't repeat exactly what I said to her. Hell, I wanted to drop my trousers and show her exactly what I did for a legitimate 4-F classification!"

Lee's celebratory homecoming was short-lived, at least as far as his family was concerned. Courtenay was extremely glad her son was home safe and sound, but his war experiences made it extremely difficult to talk to him. She wrote in a letter to Robert, "Your brother is quite a man... I hear many strange and some horrible stories about his adventures, and at first it took a strong stomach to sit quietly and listen." As for Monte, Lee quickly discovered his father was finding the adjustment to civilian life even more difficult than he was. If Lee was damaged by the war, he said of Monte years later, "It ruined him. He came home from that half dead, totally broken. He was never the same."

During the war, First Sergeant Monte Marvin received a military citation from the British Government for his "Outstandingly meritorious service to the Allied Cause during the defense of the Port of Antwerp… Sergeant Marvin was called upon often to obtain a standard of continuous and excellent performance of duty by men under him… His own outstanding example, diligence and patience while under almost constant danger from long range rockets and flying bombs, were in large measure responsible for the efficiency which these men attained." However, as a civilian, he was unable to find gainful employment.

After another disheartening day of job hunting, he entered his 79th Street apartment building barely able to muster a businesslike smile for the doorman. He went in and ran hot water for a bath. The family maid found him. She immediately dressed his sloppily cut wrists and called the police. The police then contacted Bellevue, where he was transported in a siren-blaring ambulance for several days' observation. Unable to afford a private room, he was placed in a public ward where the rest that Monte desperately sought was impeded by the screams that went on through the night. He survived the suicide attempt and the family never spoke of it while he was alive.

Through an old friend Monte secured a sales job with the *Chicago Tribune* and the entire family moved to the "Windy City." At his father's urging, Lee enrolled in night school to get his high school diploma, but his heart was clearly not in it. He still had no plan for his future as the following excerpted letter to his brother illustrates:

> *I just got home from school to find your letter here at home and we were all glad to hear from you again. Boy just wait until you get out and see all the shit they hand you.*
>
> *Well, as you know I am now going to school and brother, that is a task, and I don't mean maybe. At the present I am taking English, Geometry, Physics and History. I just don't have any interest in the stuff but I am doing it for Pop. I don't have enough beer money so maybe that is the trouble with me. And then again I don't know anybody in this town but when I get settled, if I ever do, it might be different. So get the hell out of that lash up so we can get together soon.*
>
> *Funny thing, my feet are getting itching again and I want to be*

on the move. Where I don't know but just some place that I haven't been before, like the Yukon or some other desolate place. I just want to strike out and do something constructive with myself. In fact, I have often thought about going back into the Corps but I know that is just a way of trying to get back with the real friends I had. I mean real, because as you know when death is close at hand you don't do anything that you don't want to and the same with your friends. Boy, that was a real crowd and their only thought was to be happy while they could. So here I am still trying while the rest of them are dead. The main thing that I regret is that there is no longer any frontier to work on which is just my speed. Therefore I must conform to convention which I have a very deep-set distaste for. Officers, I hate their fucking guts but I will admit that there are a few good ones, but I have only seen a very damn few. Well now my problem is to see how much money I can get out of the folks for some brew. I will probably end up by getting fifty cents as usual which is a puny five glasses but it will have to do until that pension of mine comes through.

Lee struggled with his classes, but said years later, "It made no sense. After committing murder, it was hard to find sense in peace. How could a guy all mixed up in murder get an education? The two didn't make sense... I had to do something, though. They gave me a typing test and I couldn't spell half the words. I looked around and saw all those frivolous chicks and guys—what was I doing there? So, I quit." Forty years later 'The Sergeant,' his character in *The Big Red One,* would tell one of his charges, "We don't murder. We kill," a distinction that was not yet clear in young Lee's mind.

The day he quit class, he walked right into a Marine Recruitment Center. The officer in charge sympathetically responded, "Thank you for your offer and prior service, son, but due to your disability status..." Lee shook the officer's hand and proceeded to laugh it off at the nearest watering hole. As to his disability, a physical later that fall spoke the final word as only the military could: His sciatic wound disabled him exactly 20%. He received a check of $27.80, and would continue to do so each month for the rest of his life.

Monte's job in Chicago was short-lived, forcing the entire family to move back to New York. When the family returned to New York, the postwar housing shortage made it impossible to find worthy accommodations in the city. The Marvins decided on the Woodstock area since they had summered there often when Lee and Robert were boys. They purchased a home, and Monte eventually found work nearby with the New York and New England Apple Institute. He periodically attempted other employment and noted on his resume: "Natural hazards effecting [sic] apple crop greatly limit scope of accomplishment." Like an over-the-hill athlete dreaming his time would come again, he never saw the better employment materialize and stayed with the Institute until retiring in 1965. Through it all, Monte got by on the two things he could always rely on: his undiminished Puritan ethic and large quantities of alcohol.

Nestled in the foothills of the Catskill Mountains, the Woodstock community had long been a sanctuary for many of the colorful avant-garde artists and intellectuals of the day, decades before the eponymous historic rock concert that would take place in a nearby town. The small community even maintained three legitimate live theaters at the time: The Woodstock Playhouse, The Valetta Theater and the 1,000-seat Maverick Theater. On the surface, Courtenay seemed to enjoy the creative stimulation the area provided for her writing. The small social circle of Woodstock society made her feel like a big fish in a small pond, while Monte found the relative tranquility preferable to the hubbub of the city.

Lee took classes at Kingston High School to finally get his diploma around the time that Robert mustered out of the service. As he had done many times as a child, Lee frequently cut class to fish or hunt. When he did attend, his writing assignments gave a clear indication of what occupied his thoughts:

What I am trying to put over here is the unconscious will to live and enjoy also to keep with people their memories.

The Way of Life.
It was a late spring evening, full of the golden splendor of sunset. The clouds as if tinted by some past master were windswept and

exploding with the glory of nature, drifting on and on as they have done for centuries. The grass held the very fragrance and softness that they alone posses. At their bases were the sun-singed followers who too wanted life but had failed.

Sprawled in this magnitude of beauty was the once fine-formed body of a man. The passing rain had left the form dubbed with pellets of diamond like drops sparkling in the last rays of the disappearing sun. He too, as the blades of grass, wanted life but had lost in his all too sincere struggle.

This man, or rather lad, had at the age of eighteen met his maker. The clothes that he wore were of a rough cloth, originally green but now, after days of dirty living and dying, they were smeared with his very life, dried to the earthen ground from which it came.

To be buried? Perhaps, but that is of little importance to him now or ever. His clenched hands still but firm, grasping the dirt in his last attempt to keep from sliding into the unknown.

Monte had hoped Lee would get his diploma and use the G.I. Bill to become an engineer. Lee had contemplated several other careers, including forest ranger and car salesman, but when requirements like geometry became insurmountable, he again disappointed his father by dropping out of school altogether.

In Woodstock, Lee could often be found at a favorite hangout: The S.S. Seahorse. One longtime resident referred to it as "The greatest dive I've ever seen in my life. People used to line up in the summer just to get in to it." One attraction of the oddly shaped tavern was the architecture, which resembled a landlocked ship complete with appropriate decor and even portholes for windows. The local artisans and bohemians welcomed Lee as the most popular reveler in their midst.

The music and laughter offered only a fleeting refuge from the nightmares. According to Robert, "When Lee would come home, he was a little disturbed at night. He had a lot of nightmares. He wasn't exactly yelling but the poor guy would go through all kinds of convulsions." In rare moments of candor, Lee confessed to his brother he saw snipers in the trees just as he drifted off, or that he had relived the battle that decimated his outfit.

On occasion, he would drink at home with his family. The evening would start innocently enough, but would spiral out of control at the slightest provocation. Courtenay would sneak off to safer grounds when the dark clouds began forming. Inevitably, as the night and alcohol wore on, Monte would declare, "You Marines are a lot of bullshit!" or "My outfit in the artillery can do anything the goddamned Marines can do!" Sometimes Lee would be the provocateur, making the same pronouncements about the Army. Whoever started it, the end result was often physical.

Once, Robert brandished a hunk of firewood at his brother while Lee berated his father. When the intoxicated Robert missed his swing, the equally drunk Lee caught his brother with a fist that sent Robert sprawling face up on the front lawn. "I was wearing a good pair of pants and the next morning I saw a rip in it," Robert recalled smiling. "I said to him, 'Lee, would you mind putting up the money so I could get my pants fixed?' he said, 'Fuck you, too.' That was the end of that one."

Even though Monte and Lee were both dealing with the same issues, the men were too polarized to reconcile with each other. The guilt Lee suffered the morning after a family brawl often kept him away for days at a time. Sometimes he would inexplicably find himself in a bar somewhere in Brooklyn. Other times he'd wander down to Greenwich Village and hang out with the bums that drank through the night. They would string a rope across a building and hook their arms on to it so they could sleep standing up without getting arrested. The next morning, someone would untie the rope and send everyone sprawling. Marvin would then join the denizens in a concoction known as "smoke," a powerful mixture of illuminating gas blown into a jar of water that resulted in a high akin to LSD. Whatever he did, Lee could never travel far enough or drink enough to escape his war-induced or domestic trauma.

When he would return, dutifully apologetic, the cycle would start up again, often at Courtenay's subtle instigation. Her attempts at maintaining the facade of domestic bliss would result in Lee and the other Marvin men having to sit through meaningless social teas or Sunday afternoon art lectures. On one such occasion, the entire family made an appearance on local radio for a show based on "Thanksgiving in Strange Places." The

Marvin men discussed their war experiences while a Girl Scout Choir sang in the background. Unfortunately, no tape of the show exists, or of the drive home.

Monte had become fairly well known in the rural community, to the point he could get jobs for both of his sons. By early 1946, Robert was working for a printer and saving for college, while Lee became a plumber's apprentice under the tutelage of Adolph Heckeroth. A native of Diddledorf, Germany, Heckeroth had migrated to the U.S. in the 20's, and eventually settled in Woodstock, where he put his plumbing skills to good use.

To anyone willing to look, Bill Heckeroth—who now runs his father's business—will gladly point out a treasured memento carved in the wood of his father's wall-hung toolbox: "This is Adolph's. Help yourself." The engraver was, of course, Lee Marvin. Bill was just a child when Lee worked for his father, but he remembers with great affection the over-sized young man with the booming voice who'd put his feet up on his father's desk and tell fascinating stories to anyone within earshot.

Lee's work consisted of digging septic tanks and hand-threading pipes for $1.25 an hour. Hard as it was, this work proved therapeutic. "A guy digging ditches or a plumber wiping joints, it solves problems, you know?" Marvin later said. "You have to dig this hole so wide, so long, so deep. You dig it and that's it. You climb out and say, 'Boy, I don't know what it was, but I solved it today.' Good therapy for my back." Marvin found such comfort in this work that he maintained his union card even after his rise to cinematic stardom, and often worked on the plumbing in his Hollywood agent's house.

Adolph Heckeroth genuinely liked Lee, who impressed the veteran plumber with his natural prowess for the job. Once, when Heckeroth wanted Lee to help him measure the depth of a well, Lee told him not to bother with the old knotted string and weight device. Lee boasted he would merely drop a pebble and could tell by its acceleration the exact depth of the well. Heckeroth was astonished when Lee's measurement proved to be exactly what Heckeroth's string registered. He never knew Lee had measured the depth the night before.

Such pranks kept him in good graces when he would occasionally incur the old man's wrath. On a day off, Lee showed up with a deer he had shot out of season and nonchalantly asked his boss to keep it in his basement freezer for a short time. Bill Heckeroth recalls, "It wasn't long after, the state police arrived. Dad's in a tight spot with them now. They wanted to know if he knew anything about this deer and if he'd seen Lee. My father gave him hell after that."

In spite of these occasional trespasses, Lee and Heckeroth remained on good terms. Long after his success, Lee would sneak in the back door to visit Adolph and Bill Heckeroth whenever he was in Woodstock. His presence drew triple-takes from the current employees as the internationally famous film star would put his shoes up on the nearest desk, and with beer in hand announce, "My next film is going to be your life story, Adolph. It'll be called *Return to Diddledorf.*"

Lee's off-hour pursuits in Woodstock were often spent in the company of another local, David Ballantine. The diminutive Ballantine may have seemed an unlikely partner in Marvin's revelry, but the two shared many common interests. "We fished," recalls Ballantine. On one memorable occasion Ballantine—appropriately attired in hip waders—lost his footing and plunged into the roaring stream. Lee did eventually help his struggling comrade, after taking his time to cast his line first. "That was just Lee," adds his friend.

Ballantine had met Lee after his own discharge from the service in June of 1946. "I fought WWII in the Zone of the Interior, which is a euphemism for the United States. When I met Lee, I was in Woodstock on the 52/20 Club, the unemployment thing," he jokes today. "He was quite strong, too. He would do things I think sometimes to show everybody he was Lee Marvin and they were not, like carrying Heckeroth's big pipe-cutting tripod one-handed, or lifting up the front end of a car. When people ask me what was he like, I usually say, 'Try to imagine a non-effeminate Clint Eastwood!'"

Ballantine's interest in and knowledge of firearms, as well as his individualism made him a willing and able Tom Sawyer to Marvin's Huck Finn. Their mutual interest once took a near disastrous turn. To show their forays in gun handling were not all macho swagger, they took it upon themselves to demonstrate to a gathering of gawking youngsters the proper way in which to dispose of surplus gunpowder. Their good intentions resulted in a blinding flash. When the smoke cleared, the children laughed uproariously at a blackfaced Lee Marvin, sans eyebrows.

Studio biographies have said the Ballantines and the Marvins were good friends. "I knew Monte and Courtenay very, very slightly," corrects David. "Children now will invite friends in for dinner and such. In those days, there was a separation. I was Lee's friend, really. Not that they weren't friendly to me. Courtenay was pleasant enough and Monte had a dignity to him. Lee told me, if someone went in a bar to give everyone shit, they'd walk a wide circle around Monte. Monte was pretty tough."

David Ballantine did not often share his friend's penchant for what he called "the gargle." As he recalled, "A couple of times Lee was just snot-flying drunk. I remember many years later, when he came to visit, he was just causing shit in a bar. I took him aside and said, 'You know what's going to happen one of these days? You're going to walk around the corner and there's going to be a younger Lee Marvin and he's going to pound the shit out of you. Stop pushing your luck!' He understood. He wasn't stupid."

On a cool March night in 1946, Lee was sleeping off one such episode on a bench in the village green. At sunrise, children familiar with the sight of him in this condition as they passed him on the way to school, knew that even prodding the unconscious giant with a stick was a dare not worth taking. One local resident, either not aware or braver than most, disregarded the danger and proceeded to talk to the prone figure. When Lee's vision came into focus and the buzzing in his head had sufficiently dulled, he saw a very proper young woman beside him discussing the virtues of community services.

Scanning the area and realizing she must be talking to him, Lee smirked at the irony when she asked him to appear in an amateur Red Cross Benefit at Woodstock's Town Hall, titled "Ten Nights In a Barroom." He had been in school productions as far back as grade school and, as previously stated, had made a notable impression in St. Leo's production of "Brother Orchid." Figuring it might be a similar kick, he shrugged his shoulders and proceeded over the next several weeks to rehearse the farce with his young fellow amateurs.

"Lee's performance was the most hilarious I've ever seen," a proud Monte recalled in 1966. "The mustache kept falling off. Everybody in the cast forgot their lines and Lee's hands were very much in evidence pushing out scripts from the wings. Even then, he left them in the aisles."

Like the tales of Pecos Bill or Paul Bunyan, the story of Lee's professional acting debut has become the stuff of legend that begins with a kernel of truth and grows with time into larger-than-life proportions. Some versions claim Lee was being boisterous in a local bar, and instead of being bounced, was asked if he could be just as obnoxious onstage. There are even more creative tales, but the most consistent, started by Marvin himself, is that the door to acting was unlocked through his career in plumbing.

Marvin told several interviewers that it was while he had his head in the Maverick Theater commode that he heard his destiny beckon. As he recalled many times over the years, "The director needed a tall loud-mouth to play a Texan. The actor who played the part was sick. I was standing in the wings after fixing the head, eyeing this redheaded actress. Later, the director looked at me and figured I was made for the part. The other actor took longer to recuperate than expected. By that time, I was in the business and I loved it."

When told of this, Monte Marvin later commented, "Nothing could be further from the truth since the theater had no toilet, only a one-holer outside." David Ballantine also concurs on this point. However, the event that actually catapulted Lee Marvin into acting was just as good a story.

When David Ballantine turned twenty-one, his family held a celebratory birthday party in his honor. Lee always looked forward to any party but especially enjoyed the Ballantine family. David's brother Ian was publisher of Ballantine Books and his mother Stella was a founder of Lee's progressive school, Manumit. David's father, E. J. 'Teddy' Ballantine, had an illustrious theatrical history, which included membership in Eugene O'Neill's Provincetown Players and—most impressive to Lee— drinking bouts with the great John Barrymore. Teddy was also an integral part of the aptly named Maverick Theater. Among the guests at the informal soiree, Lee endeared himself with his usual array of outlandish and almost boorish antics. Also in attendance was Ian's wife, Betty. A petite woman known for wearing long flowing dresses, even in the muggy summer, she eventually became a confidante to the young Lee Marvin.

Lee himself recalled the events that transpired that night when his tale-spinning talent was still in its infancy: "I got swocked. I was dancing with a girl named Joy, which is what she was: 145 pounds and all of it pink and beautiful. At the party I found out the leading man of the local theater had run out on an upcoming production." It was just this fact E.J. Ballantine was discussing with the director when he noticed Lee jumping for Joy amid the other revelers.

"He was a very impressive character even then," recalled Betty Ballantine. "First of all, there was his voice. His voice was absolutely amazing. Then, he had a real gift for telling stories with a great sense of humor. He used body language, since Lee had an extraordinary control of his physical presence. He was the kind of a person who comes into a room and you damn well notice him. The play they were preparing was called 'Roadside.' They wanted a loudmouth Texan. Teddy said, 'We got a loudmouth right here. Hey, Lee! Come over here!' Of course, we were all feeling no pain. Lee with that wonderful voice he had, read for the play. He got the part and Saturday afternoon and all of Sunday, I sat with him. Teddy and I both walked him through it. Well, he never really learned the script. How could he? He only had a day and half."

When Lee heard his cue opening night, "It grabbed me just like that!" he would say with a snap of his fingers. "Suddenly I felt… Expression!" After years of rebellion, masked fear and uncertainty, Lee stepped out on to the stage that rainy summer night and made it his own. Lee's powerful voice rumbled through the Hudson Valley like a small earthquake to let one and all know that he had discovered his true calling.

On the last weekend in June of 1947, the *Ulster County News* proudly proclaimed, "Lee Marvin as the 6'3" 'Texas,' loomed even taller when silhouetted against the intense blue of the sky. It was very effective."

Lee found what he had been searching for during the short run of "Roadside." With absolutely no professional training, he came to acting fully endowed for what the work entailed. Although he never really learned all the dialogue for the opening show, "He had such presence onstage he could pick up and carry the story through and the other actors would pick up from him and keep the story going," recalled Betty Ballantine. "I went to the play I guess four or five times because he was so funny. He gave a different performance every night." He quit his job at Heckeroth's the very next day.

The summer of 1947 saw Lee devoting all of his considerable energy to the Maverick Theater's summer stock productions. He later reasoned, "It was the closet thing to the Marine Corps way of life I could find at the time —hard work and no crap." The camaraderie was key, but acting also did something else for the combat veteran: it gave him an outlet to express his inner demons that had been frustrating him since the war. "Acting is a search for communication," he later explained. "This is what I am doing—trying to communicate, get my message across. I can play these parts, these horrible, animal men. I do things on stage you shouldn't do and I make you see you shouldn't do them."

Although the Maverick did have an impressive roster of talent, only one other alumnus would achieve any level of celebrity. Canadian-born James Doohan, best known as 'Scotty' on the original "Star Trek" series, remembers the Lee Marvin of that summer and concurs: "Hard work and no crap, no doubt about it! We were a cooperative where everybody did everything to get the play going. Being Lee's first entrance into the theater, that was probably the thing he liked more about it than anything else. It was, 'Hey, I'm a partner here!'"

The short run of "Roadside" was not without other incidents— David Ballantine perpetrated a prank on his newly stagestruck friend. During a performance, Lee's intensity was tested when his gun exploded in his hand due to an abundance of gunpowder. He managed to stay in character, but privately fumed at the knowledge that only one person had the expertise to pull off such a stunt.

Following "Roadside," the Maverick staged ten other productions that summer, with Lee contributing to practically every one of them. Later he would recall, "When I put on the rags, I didn't feel it was make-believe. I felt it was real… Besides, a combat Marine doesn't get intimidated easily. The Corps teaches you when it's time to toe the mark, you toe the mark. I've applied much of what I learned in the Marine Corps to acting."

Doohan also appeared in every production that summer, honing a talent for accents and voices that would become a trademark. "We slept in cabins with three to four guys to a cabin. There were some terrific women there and I slept with a few. Hell, you needed it, you know? It was terribly romantic just by the setting alone."

Doohan was not alone in taking advantage of the Maverick's bucolic setting. According to Betty Ballantine, when it came to women, "Lee was a killer. Jesus, he had them trailing around him all over the place. At that time in his life, he had a very bad attitude about women. All he basically wanted to do was lay them… He had two or three affairs concurrently which I guess most of us knew about. He was only twenty-three then, but I wondered when he got married if he had changed at all."

Lee's attitude is apparent in the correspondence he maintained at the time. Letters from women he knew in Chicago, Texas and New York all profess undying love for him alone. "He also of course had an affair with the company's leading lady," recalled Betty Ballantine. "She was a very white-skinned, very big woman, which he liked, this kind of red-gold hair." A pretty young Woodstock resident named Pamela Feeley also fell under his spell. Their relationship was brief, and, according to her autobiography, resulted in an abortion.

Marvin followed his season at Woodstock by acting in road companies of popular plays. "Let me tell you, pal, touring was *fuckin'* tough," he later said of the experience. "Introducing the Great Drama to rural areas, see—holy shit, 33,000 miles of one-night stands, all in the wintertime and you got $75 a week and had to sustain all your own expenses with the exception of travel. We'd stay in places like the Pioneer Hotel in Pampa, Texas—two bucks a night, right? And about three in the morning the duck hunters would storm out on that frozen linoleum and—*aaaghh!*"

Since his father still hoped he would become an engineer, Lee had taken an aptitude test at the Rensselaer Polytechnic Institute (RPI) in nearby Troy. RPI also housed the Veterans Administration, which provided the paperwork needed to qualify for the G.I. Bill. He learned he could enroll at the American Theater Wing (ATW) and decided to tell his parents. "Lee told my father he wanted to be an actor," recalled Robert, "and my father almost went through the ceiling, naturally. My father told my brother, 'If you become an actor, don't expect any help from me. You're on your own.' He probably did help him. Besides, who cares? What's the good of having parents if they don't give you a hand every now and then?" A summary of Monte's ledger shows several loans made to Lee at the time, all of which his son paid back in short order.

He was accepted into the ATW's training program in April 1948, less than two years after it officially opened its doors. It was as if both the ATW and the G. I. Bill were created specifically with Lee Marvin in mind. The purpose of each was to help veterans get badly needed training. The G.I. Bill provided the money Lee needed with the ATW providing the hands-on training in the field he had chosen. The ATW did not have the lofty goals of the American Academy of Dramatic Arts or The Actors Studio, both of which sought to explore acting as art. Marvin took to the classes with all the enthusiasm and energy he had not mustered since first joining the Marines. "It was marvelous, like a halfway house," he said of the added bonus of the social interaction the classes incurred. "All the guys had been in the service, we knew one another's problems."

The actor also knew how to manipulate the instructors for maximum attention, a trait he would later use successfully on film directors. The foremost saber and foil expert, Giorgio Santelli, taught his fencing class. "Lee walked in and they showed him the saber," recalled David Ballantine. "Lee looked at the saber and said, 'A man my size should easily be able to beat the shit out of a little squirt like you.' Of course, the purpose of this taunting remark was so that none of the other people got any instruction at all. Lee got the shit beaten out of him. But he learned to do saber."

Practical advice in getting work was the ATW's main goal and proved to be the instruction that made the greatest impact on Marvin. As he made the usual rounds of agents, casting directors, and producers he often found work on live TV, radio, stage, and even military training films. However, what he desperately sought was a part in an original Broadway production. His datebook showed call-back auditions for the original runs of "Death Of A Salesman," "Mister Roberts," and other recognized classics. When he was turned down for the service comedy "At War with the Army" (later retooled into a vehicle for Martin & Lewis), he wrote in his runner, "I could turn that part inside out if they'd give me a chance which they won't."

Fellow New York actor Bert Remsen recalled the routine: "There used to be an agent in New York named Max Richards. He was one of the agents you would go see when you made the rounds looking for work. You would stick your head in the door and say, 'Anything for me, today?' I remember many years later, when Lee was a big star, he dropped by the Max Richards office, stuck his head in and asked, 'Anything for me, today?' The secretary said, 'Sorry, nothing today.' Everybody would see each other and talk about it. That's how you got work in those days. When Lee did *Paint Your Wagon,* he said to Josh Logan, 'You don't remember me, Mr. Logan. I tried out for "Mr. Roberts" but you said I was too skinny.' Life was different for actors in those days. We used to hang out at Nedick's or Horn and Hardart. They had the best coffee in the world. You make friends with actors and talk about work. I remember I used to see James Dean a lot in those days. See, kids starting out nowadays don't have that. There's no apprenticeship."

Audiences after the war were seeking more believable stories and characters, and plays and films moved towards more realistic productions to meet this demand for realism. There would always be a call for the handsome matinee idol, but villains and juicy character parts required the kind of performance that would keep Marvin working regularly once he got his foot in the door. "I think he might very well have ended up on the stage anyway," recalled Betty Ballantine. "He had a theatrical personality. You could see that right away. I don't think he had any second thoughts. You know, Lee was not a deep thinker. He went from moment to moment reacting, being himself, and doing what he wanted to do. I think he found a home in the theater. It acted as a release for some of his problems. Obviously, not all of them because otherwise he wouldn't have become a drunk. I think the theater or acting as a career is a form of release for a great many actors. I don't think Lee was confused about himself or who he was, but he needed to express a lot of feelings that are not acceptable in common society and he was able to do it through acting."

While the ultimate goal of any New York actor was to land a role on Broadway, Marvin honed his craft, establishing himself with critics who often singled him out for praise. The stage work was in revivals of "Murder in the Cathedral" as well as off-Broadway runs of plays like "The 19th Hole of Europe," "A Sound of Hunting," and tours of "A Streetcar Named Desire," "Home of the Brave," and "The Hasty Heart."

Fellow movie tough guy Leo Gordon would often run into Marvin at auditions, and recalled those days: "New York is a totally different scene than out here in L.A. is for an actor. Used to go to the Astor Drug Store and hang out. It was in the Astor Hotel, which is no longer there. There was the Green Room up at NBC. You know, you're fluid. You run into people continually, the same people. At any rate, I had some casual conversations with Marvin. One afternoon, I was walking down 6th Ave. Lee comes along and says, 'I'm looking for a place to move.' I told him I just moved in to a place on 46th St. He said, 'Yeah? How much?' I said $45.00 a month.' He said, 'Oh man, I could never cut that.' That was around 1949, I guess."

One of the few constants he was able to rely on was a hot meal every Tuesday night at Ian and Betty Ballantine's New York apartment. Many of their friends were struggling in the arts and with Ballantine's publishing company doing well, the couple was able to ensure them at least one home-cooked meal a week. Betty took note of the fact that, each week, Marvin sported a different injury somewhere on his person, but he brushed it off to simple clumsiness. Eventually she confronted him, and he told her the truth. "Look, I'm a trained killer," he told her in a moment of rare candor. "I'm very good at it. I can kill with my bare hands. I have a need for violence. I go into a bar and pick on some little guy. I make sure that there are at least four big guys that could take me because I don't want to hurt anybody. Okay, if I get a black eye or pick up a few bruises, nobody got seriously injured. Look, it's something that I gotta do."

The reason the actor felt as he did would remain unidentified throughout most of his life. According to historian Thomas Childers, author of 2010's *Soldier from the War Returning*: "Post-traumatic stress disorder (PTSD) went undiagnosed until 1980. Yet in the aftermath of WWII, depression, recurring nightmares, survivor guilt, outbursts of rage (often directed at family members) and anxiety reactions —all of which are recognized today as classic symptoms of PTSD—were as common as they were unnerving."

The diagnosis was based on the high level of problems noted in returning Vietnam-era veterans. Childers notes, "If veterans of WWII were mentioned at all, it was to draw a striking contrast. They had fought 'the good war' and returned home to a grateful nation, healthy, happy and well-adjusted, or so the story went... The reality was a great deal more unsettling. Although largely forgotten today, many of the profoundly disturbing social and personal problems arising from the wars in Korea, Vietnam, Iraq and Afghanistan were glaringly present in the aftermath of WWII."

Between bar room brawls, classes, auditions and short run work, lightning finally struck for the actor when Marvin answered a casting call put out by film director Henry Hathaway. Hathaway's call let it be known that, for his next film, he was interested in young New York actors who did not look like typical actors. Marvin remembers: "I hung around for three days. Then somebody came out and said, 'It's over.' I said, 'No, it ain't, pal. I've been waiting for three days.' So they let me in to see Hathaway, and he hired me as an extra. Charlie Bronson and I both got speaking parts later on." While filming in Norfolk's Naval Yard, Marvin also turned in a quick appearance as an extra in uniform for the film *Teresa*. Filming finished on the Hathaway film on the soundstages of 20th-Century Fox in Hollywood.

Neither film would be released for over a year, allowing Marvin to return to New York in hopes of finally making his Broadway debut. It finally happened in an almost insignificant role in a major production being mounted at the experimental American National Theater and Academy (ANTA) originally titled "Uniform of Flesh." Through workshops and lengthy tryouts it eventually became a lushly produced version of Herman Melville's "Billy Budd" on Broadway with Marvin on stage as a Marine in His Majesty's Service, 1798.

On opening night one of the play's authors, Bob Chapman, sent out traditional good luck notes to the cast. Lee Marvin's read, "Dear Lee, Good luck tonight, and if you feel the irresistible impulse to fire that flintlock, try [*New Yorker* theater critic Wolcott] Gibbs, in the sixth row on the aisle." On February 10, 1951, four years after debuting in "Roadside" he had finally made it to Broadway, with disillusionment following quickly. "There I was in a theater, and my entire part was seven sides of saying 'Yes sir, no sir.' There I was on this big stage thinking I really belonged in theater, and all that crap, and all I could see of the audience were those signs that said 'Exit.'"

David Ballantine recalled that "He stood at attention through three acts. He had, I think, one line in the whole thing. He didn't say, 'This part is below me,' or 'I won't take this part because it won't show what I can do.' He was a working actor. He went with what he could get and he did it well. I'm sure he stayed at attention. Somebody else who did it, who had never been a Marine, I'm sure would have melted somewhere along the line." The play opened at the Biltmore Theater, impressing critics but finding enthusiastic audiences hard to come by, forcing the production to close after a respectable 103 performances.

It was around this time that Marvin met up with James Doohan on a busy New York street corner. Marvin told Doohan that he finished work on the Hathaway film in Hollywood and had met an agent there who promised him more work if he came west. Marvin confided that he was not sure what to do since he finally made it to Broadway and had hoped it might lead to more work. "I said, 'Give Hollywood a try, for gosh sakes,' because I hadn't seen him in any plays or TV or anything else," recalled Doohan. Helping to seal the deal was the experience of finally being on Broadway. "It was a damned bore," admitted Marvin. "The New York stage is a hustle. The audience is half-boozed and you can't really wake them. I got my tail back to Hollywood."

PART TWO

IN THE TRENCHES

In costume as 'Chino'—rival of Marlon Brando in 1954's The Wild One—
Marvin cradles his infant son, Christopher Lamont Marvin.

CHAPTER 5

The Merchant of Menace

IN THE MIDDLE of what has often been called the American Century, Lee Marvin was at the crux of a serious decision concerning his fledgling career. Having to choose between making films in Hollywood or continuing to struggle in New York, he ultimately chose Hollywood.

The agent he had mentioned to James Doohan was Meyer Mishkin. The son of Russian immigrants who was raised on the Lower East Side of New York, the diminutive Mishkin had been a part of the movie business since the 1930s. As a casting director, he had convinced Hollywood executives that movie usher Gregory Peck was worthy of a screen test, and advised strangely ambling Tony Curtis to take the deck of cards out of his shoes when meeting producers. When director Henry Hathaway searched in vain to find the right actor to portray a demented killer in his film *Kiss Of Death*, Mishkin introduced Hathaway to a part-time schoolteacher named Richard Widmark, who landed the role and an Oscar nomination. His eye for talent convinced Mishkin to launch the Mishkin Talent Agency, which was established in Hollywood with his first major client, Ira Grosell, better known as Jeff Chandler.

Believing the fledgling talent agent should check out some of the novice cast, Hathaway had invited Mishkin to the set of *You're In The Navy Now*. An assistant was sent out to find the young extra Hathaway had hired out of New York to play one of the film's sailors opposite star Gary Cooper. Twenty minutes later, Lee Marvin showed up grumbling,

"Geez, can't I take a crap on my own time?" Marvin had actually been smoking a cigarette, but did not like being ordered around by the famously authoritative Hathaway, who was known for always getting his way. Mishkin, nonetheless, was impressed by the actor's brashness.

The dictatorial Hathaway then suggested that Mishkin take Marvin on as a client, to which the emboldened agent replied, "Let me see him work. I don't represent anybody unless I know they can act." Hathaway proceeded to give Marvin a few lines of dialogue and filmed the sequence. After it was shot, Mishkin asked Marvin if he needed an agent, to which Lee responded, "Before you showed up I didn't have a fucking thing to say. You arrive and I got lines in the picture. I'm with you."

The Cooper film was released in February 1951 as *U.S.S. Teakettle*, a WWII service comedy about an experimental steam-driven ship that, in spite of good reviews, sank quickly at the box-office. Re-released as *You're in the Navy Now*, the unsuccessful comedy still fared badly at the box-office, but the title has remained ever since. The mostly male cast included Eddie Albert, Jack Webb, and featured the debuts of Marvin, Jack Warden and Charles Bronson, in a showier role as an amateur boxer. "In my first picture I played seven sailors," Marvin later joked. "They even had me talking to myself over the intercom."

His even smaller role in *Teresa*, in which he appears briefly talking to someone against a ship's railing, hit theaters first. The film's story centered on the problems faced by returning veteran John Erickson in trying to get his Italian war bride Pier Angeli to adjust to America. Rod Steiger made his film debut as an understanding psychiatrist, but Marvin was merely an extra in the film directed by the legendary Fred Zinnemann (*From Here to Eternity, High Noon*, etc.). He probably had no contact with the Austrian director which is unfortunate since Zinnemann's first job in Hollywood was also as an extra in *All Quiet on the Western Front*, Lee Marvin's favorite film.

When both films were completed, Marvin told Mishkin he had to go back to New York for "Billy Budd." Mishkin assured him that if and when he returned to Hollywood, there would be work waiting for him. "I said to him, 'Before you go, I want you to do something…'" Mishkin remembers. "I had to give Christmas presents to the casting heads. I told

Lee, 'I want you to come and deliver them with me.' They were ceramic ashtrays that a friend of mine was selling. So, what we did was, we went to each one of the studios, and I introduced Lee to each one of the casting directors. He then took off for New York."

"I got a telephone call from Lee. He had been in a play. He was going to drive the star's car to California… I said, 'Okay, when will you be here?' he said, 'It'll take me five days. I'll be there.' So, I called Hathaway on the phone and I said, 'Henry, I want to tell you, Lee Marvin is coming back here. He's driving back. He'll be back in a week to ten days…' To me, when Lee says five days, he could have stopped off somewhere, who knows. So, I said, 'You know, there's a role in your new film that Lee could play.' I mentioned the part, and Henry said, 'Yeah, he's good for it. You're right.' So, by the time Lee arrived in town, he had a part in another Henry Hathaway picture. I guess it was *Diplomatic Courier* [as an M.P. encountering star Tyrone Power]. It ran for four weeks and he got $500 bucks a week, which in those days, was fairly good money… And so, when Lee arrived, I said to him, 'I got to tell you, you start working. You'll have to go to 20th-Century Fox. You get $500 bucks a week,' and he went crazy. I had called every one of the casting directors that he had met, and I said, 'By the way, I just wanted to tell you, Lee Marvin is coming to do another picture with Henry Hathaway.' See, that was important. I also told them he was going to live here. 'Oh, you mean the guy who gave us the ashtray.' So, I had accomplished my mission. Lee and I, from that time on, were together for thirty-seven years."

It wasn't until after the production of "Billy Budd" had run its course, that Lee Marvin took James Doohan's advice; he sold most of what he could of his possessions, took his life savings of $1,100, and migrated west. He had been in Hollywood before, when he was stationed in San Diego, and his mother had worked there in the 1930s. Courtenay had written about it to Monte at the time, stating, "Hollywood is the funniest place—all gossip and talk and dirt. Yet it is so funny. It would be grand to live here for a while and associate a little with the acting world. You have never known such morons. Lilyan Tashman, for example, has a huge appetite but she likes to keep svelte. So after gorging she goes upstairs and makes herself vomit. Did you ever?"

By the early 1950s, Meyer Mishkin knew Hollywood was changing. There were fissures in the old system that would eventually lead to the complete decimation of the feudal way in which the studios did business. With this in mind, Mishkin maintained a belief in putting his client's long-range career plans over immediate job placement. Asked if Marvin was ever under contract to any one studio, Mishkin said, "No, I didn't have that kind of deal. The thing is, when they were having contract players, there was no such thing as being able to use Lee in a series of films because of the things that I could get done. I had learned something from Spencer Tracy. 20th-Century Fox wanted him to play gangsters all the time. I did some thinking about this. [Lee] could have been an actor that very easily would have been sidetracked into a real typecasting situation. Oh sure, very easily."

By early 1952, the actor was able to write his brother, "Things are still going very well out here for me as I have run into some of the boys I knew in New York and they don't seem to be doing a damn thing. I was to start a western today at Universal International [*Duel At Silver Creek*] but the weather was cloudy so it will go tomorrow or Monday and has a guarantee of a week's work and $500. I have seen other things on the horizon but nothing definite. California is still a dull place for my money but what the hell, you can make money out here if you get the breaks, so I'll stick around a while."

The buzz started surprisingly early for Marvin when he was cast as a health food fanatic accused of homicide on a 1952 episode of "Dragnet." Jack Webb, the show's creator and star, was impressed with Marvin. He told an interviewer in 1969, "The episode Lee was on was a three-man piece, and we did a number of those in the beginning. In the conclusion of the story, Lee said he'd confess to everything if we bought him lunch. Well, the prop man needed something to substitute for food that could be photographed, so he got some plums. The prop man forgot to take the pits out and Lee was such a trouper, he never spit them out. Lee kept eating the plums during the scene until we forgot to tell him, we couldn't hear his dialogue. He stored them in his cheeks like a squirrel so the audience wouldn't know they were plums, and kept doing the scene."

Marvin's comical use of props and his ability to transcend the simplistic dialogue allowed Mishkin to say with pride, "Everything he did in the early days created interest. I was able to say to people, 'Look at it. See it.' What could they say negative about it? I can see any old movie with Lee today and he's so good."

Mishkin's instinct for spotting stars gave him insight into his new client's ability, whereas others might merely have seen a gangly, horse-faced heavy waiting to be bumped off by the leading man. He explained, "My offices used to be on Sunset Blvd. I knew Cary Grant. Cary Grant had a characteristic walk. I told somebody, 'When I look out the window and two blocks away there's a guy coming, I know it's Lee Marvin.' And he wasn't trying. It was Lee."

After the "Dragnet" appearance, Marvin was seen regularly on TV and film, appearing in a total of five movies released in 1952. The quality of the films and the length of his appearances may have varied, but the realism he brought to these mostly western and military roles did not. Betty Ballantine recalled the actor relating with pride his work in the forgettable Randolph Scott western *Hangman's Knot*. "I remember his telling me about a scene with this woman [Donna Reed], and he had her up against the wall. He takes maybe a scarf and he held it against her neck. You really could feel the tension in that. He told me that when he played that scene with her, she was absolutely terrified. She wouldn't let him come near her off the set."

When not frightening leading ladies, Marvin maintained an active social life. Being the owner of a Ford convertible and one Brooks Brothers sports coat gained him entry to industry parties within his own social strata. It was at one such party that he came out of the kitchen playing with a yo-yo, only to be confronted by a woman in need of a ride home. Since her friend had abandoned her, Marvin obliged the tall redhead he learned was named Betty Ebeling. Betty joked about their first meeting, "I was very attracted to his one Brooks Brothers jacket and his only possession, which was a Ford convertible." She was not enamored with him immediately as they were both seeing other people. The next day he called and she began warming up to him a little more. "Here's one of the dearest memories I have of Lee. We had met and I agreed to go out with him. I was really very busy and I was rehearsing with [arranger/pianist]

Roger Edens. Anyway, it was a Sunday. My free day to be working in Roger's home. Beautiful house. He was playing and I was singing. Then, there across the room, in the French window, is Lee. I'll never forget it. Just watching. He was just watching and all of a sudden, I hear him. Talk about being pursued… He made me laugh. Very few people really make me laugh but Lee could always make me laugh. He was very, very quick. Very bright. He had a wonderful sense of humor."

The two began seeing each other exclusively and as the relationship deepened, Marvin learned of Betty's background in Washington, her musical ambitions as a UCLA grad student, and her recent tenure as nanny to Joan Crawford's children. Together they shared an appreciation of fishing, movies, the writings of Jack London, and all the things Lee Marvin always assumed women did not care about.

"Lee was very shy, as a man with a woman, but he was a real romantic," recalled Betty. "I remember after we met, and we started seeing each other, he had an actor friend who was driving a cab. He'd come with Lee, and we'd get this guy to drive us everywhere so we could sit in the back. I remember this guy, Lenny was his name. Lee would say, 'Lenny, this is the only woman I have ever loved.' He would always say that. He'd take my hand and say, 'I could fall into your eyes.' He was very romantic. He'd buy me wonderful things. He really, in many ways, spoiled me. But he was also very tough. Although there were times I wanted him to baby me, he wouldn't do it. He'd say, "Listen, you got yourself into this, now get yourself out of it." I'd get mad and say, 'Oh, c'mon!' He'd say, 'No!' It was a great education for me. I don't know if I would have the courage to do what I'm doing in my life if I hadn't had that training from him."

Like most young couples, they went to the movies often, and Betty discovered an even more impressive aspect to her boyfriend: "Lee, from the beginning, knew every method used in acting. He knew what everybody was doing whether he attended those schools or not. He knew everybody that taught there. He knew what they taught. He approved of it or he didn't. He saw the performances. We used to talk shop all the time, he and I. 'Why did this work?' or 'Look what he did…' He was always right on. 'Look at this actor. He knows every line and he's got a broomstick up his ass.' He knew instinctively."

As the actor romanced his new love, Mishkin got Jack Webb to give him a copy of Marvin's appearance on "Dragnet." "I know that Webb made sure a lot of influential people saw that piece of film," recalled Webb's friend and frequent costar Martin Milner. "He was very instrumental in making sure that the film got on the circuit and went around town to different casting people. They were impressed with Lee's work. They wanted to help him. He [Webb] did the same kind of thing for me."

One such producer was Stanley Kramer who was about to launch a film he intended to call *The Dirty Dozen*. Based on the Broadway play "A Sound of Hunting," which had made a star out of Burt Lancaster, Kramer and director Edward Dmytryk decided to retitle the film version *Eight Iron Men*. The project allowed Lee Marvin to cap off 1952 with his fifth film appearance and first leading role. Marvin played Sgt. Joe Mooney, the leader of a small war-weary rifle squad unable to get to an abandoned comrade who is pinned down by a German machine gun.

During the film's production, the all-important German gun had jammed and studio prop men were stymied. It was Lee Marvin who got it working again. He also unobtrusively taught the other cast members the best way to realistically age their studio-issued uniforms. "For instance, when he put on his clothes, they were believable, the shoes that were half-laced, everything about him was," recalled Dmytryk. "We used him as a hint for how to dress the other actors who hadn't been in the war... Any director who would say, 'No, don't do that,' would be pretty silly unless [the actor] did something ridiculous, but Lee never did. He was very much with it. If he did it, believe me it was done by that kind of a character because he did his study. He studied his character and he knew his people."

Although Dmytryk had previously directed such gritty noir classics as *Murder, My Sweet* and *Crossfire*, Lee Marvin changed his perspective. "Oh, he was a wonder," Dmytryk recalled. "He did one thing that was very important. He showed me how people died at the front. He said, 'They didn't just all throw up their arms and land flat on their face or on their back. Sometimes you're up against a tree. Sometimes their legs are turned a certain way.' Obviously, [he was] a great observer... I should have known that people don't die the way they do in the movies, big dramatic pirouettes!"

Other than providing a greater sense of realism, Marvin began another career-long habit while making the film. As he had done in the Marines, to enhance the sense of camaraderie, he would buddy up with another cast member and go out drinking all night. In *Eight Iron Men* that buddy was Brooklyn-accented costar Bonar Colleano. When Dmytryk sternly admonished the two men against such binging, Marvin dutifully bowed his head, but smiled to himself knowing that sharing the punishment with another always helped to lessen the blow.

Although critics praised the effort, the film failed to find an audience when it was released. Marvin's performance, however, brought him to the attention of other Hollywood agents who tried to seduce him away from Mishkin. But, Marvin so believed in his agent's long-term commitment, he would simply say to them, "Sounds great, ask Meyer." Another client, for whom Mishkin got more work after he changed his named from Charles Buchinski to Charles Bronson, did not renew his contract. He told Mishkin, "I can't re-sign with you. Lee Marvin is getting all my parts."

On the set of *Eight Iron Men* Marvin had mentioned to costar Arthur Franz how much he was in love, but could not get his girlfriend to move in with him. When Franz suggested marriage, bachelor Marvin recoiled in horror. Franz offhandedly related the story to his neighbor who just happened to be Betty's best friend. Consequently, Betty was prepared when Lee broached the subject: "He went around and about. 'I don't think I could do better' was one of the lines. I said, 'Compared to what?' But the proposal is what was funny. We were in the Bantam Cock. He never actually said the words 'Will you marry me?' One thing he said, because it was wonderful was, 'I hope you can cook because I never want to eat out again.' I thought, 'Oh my God, what am I going to do for food?'"

A quick road trip to Las Vegas's Wee Kirk O' The Heather Chapel in February, 1952 (officiated by the clergyman of record, the Rev. Lovable) took care of the nuptials. "We had no witnesses, so the reverend woke up his wife," Lee recalled. "She wasn't dressed. She stood behind a curtain. The reverend said, 'See? There's her feet.' Her feet were our witnesses. Lovable said to me, 'Do you, Lee, take this woman to be your lawful wedded wife, to love, honor, and cherish?' and I said 'Yes.' Then he said—this is exactly what he said — 'And do you, Betty, and all that stuff?' He said, 'And all that stuff!'" On the road trip back to L.A. the newlyweds picked up a drunken hitchhiker, who coincidentally happened to be a Marine. For years, Marvin took great joy in telling people that his bride spent her wedding night with a drunken Marine.

When the couple later honeymooned in Mexico, Betty received an indication of the kind of man she married. He had several passions, such as fishing and an appreciation of the Blues. His love of the Blues grew out of his childhood habit of hopping trains from which he claimed to have once shared a boxcar with blues legend 'Blind Lemon' Jefferson. "On our honeymoon," recalls Betty, "I think it was meant as a challenge. He brought along 'Blind Lemon' Jefferson, 'Wee Willie' Williams, Lead-belly, Robert Johnson, all his fishing tackle and several rods to be wound. He said to me, as a challenge, 'If you don't understand any of this, you're undersexed.' Is that the best challenge ever?"

In November of 1952 Lee and Betty became the proud parents of nine and a half-pound Christopher Lamont Marvin. "He cried when I had a baby, when he'd see the baby," recalled Betty. "Someone asked me once in an interview, 'Is Lee really that tough?' I said, 'Tough? He's a bowl of mashed potatoes.' I remember, Dr. Mishell, the OB/GYN had by then become a family friend because he was so much in our lives. Lee was there talking, and Dan came in… Dan Mishell, the obstetrician. He was talking to Lee about fishing together and then started taking out my stitches, which is really nothing. Lee looked at this and went right into the bathroom and closed the door. I said, "What's the matter?" He said, "If I watch it, I'm gonna throw up. I can't watch that.'"

Fatherhood clearly had a maturing effect on the once rebellious student and war-hardened Marine. He wrote his brother about it after proudly sending out photos and cigars: "Did you see the pictures of Christopher? Everybody says he looks like me and he does. Actually he looks more like you, no kidding. His hair, what there is of it, is red too. He's a great little pooch and a great little boy. I like him. Already he is now a month old. Strange isn't it how short the present is. I'm reminded of a line from T.S. Eliot: 'Men grow old, grow old. They wear their pant legs rolled.'

Do write, Robert. I miss you."

Lee Marvin continued to find steady work despite the fact that audience attendance in the 1950s had dropped dramatically due to the novelty of television. As a well-cast bad guy in gangster, war and western films, Marvin gave able support to big name stars, claiming, "You don't make friends with the guys who are above you too much. Remember, I didn't make it until I was older... Up until then I was just a dog-assed heavy, one of the posse. My best friends were always stunt guys and extras. I've always seen myself as one of the masses. Besides, a lot of actors are just boring and pompous as hell."

Marvin carved a niche for himself within the confines of what was allotted to him. Fellow character actor and veteran movie bad guy, L.Q. Jones was also represented by Meyer Mishkin at the time and said that's what set Marvin apart: "He would have been with Raoul Walsh and Barrymore and that whole bunch. He realized the first thing you got to do, sports fans, is entertain the audience, then you can act. You got to entertain them first. Lee just instinctively understood that. So, he'll go too far in a lot of his stuff but it's not too far for the piece, and it worked... He was taking a chance and that's what acting is all about."

The chances he took were often wasted in such lackluster projects as *Seminole, Down Among the Sheltering Palms* and the 3-D Randolph Scott western, *The Stranger Wore A Gun,* in which Marvin was paired for the first time with fellow bad guy Ernest Borgnine. No matter the film, "That quality of violence in Lee showed up on screen, it really did," recalled Betty Ballantine. "I mean he was a menacing person when he was the bad guy and he was almost always the bad guy. He enjoyed it. He enjoyed physical contact and this was one way he could get it. He told me he loved to do fight scenes. For instance, that other handsome six-footer, Randolph Scott, he loved to do fight scenes with Scott because he must have also had this wonderful physical coordination. In the fight scenes they must have looked like they were murdering each other. They'd come away from it without a scratch. Beautiful timing, yes. That's another thing. Lee had a sense of timing that was inborn. That's why he was a good storyteller."

Marvin's reputation among the ranks grew largely from his own ability but also in part due to his agent. "Meyer had a whole bunch of people who were really busy," recalled L.Q. Jones. "I guess because at that point in time, if you were with Meyer, people knew you could perform just because you were with Meyer. He didn't take many people, comparably speaking. So, a lot of them were working and I was very fortunate to get in that group. We all just stayed busy all of the time."

Mishkin next got his client work in the Victor Mature vehicle, *The Glory Brigade*. Set during the Korean War, the film depicted the conflicts and growing respect between U.S forces and Greek-led UN forces. Most of his scenes in *Glory Brigade* were with fellow ex-Marine and Iwo Jima veteran Alvy Moore, later better known for his role as Mr. Kimball on TV's "Green Acres." "We met when he was coming up heading toward the bus this way and I was heading toward the bus this way," recalls Moore. "I said, 'Did you read the script?' He said, 'Yeah, did you?' And I said, 'Yeah.' Then we both started laughing. I didn't think we were going to stop. We got on the bus [to the location] and we were in hysterics. It was the worst piece of..."

Making matters worse was the location. The army base Fort Leonard Wood in Missouri doubled for Korea, but had been nicknamed "Fort Lost in the Woods of Misery." "It was a hellhole," recalled Moore. "The place was so bad they were volunteering to go to Korea to get out of there. It was not a good place, at all. There was nothing around the darn thing." In fact, a special effects man was also accidentally killed from a badly timed explosion during the film's location shoot.

Moore had a run-in with the film's director, but was amazed to see Lee avoid the same situation. "I think the biggest thing about Lee that stands out is his ability to overcome an adverse situation. He could appease somebody in a way that I've never seen anybody do. Using his short-hand speech, he had the ability for somebody to not fully understand what he meant when he was talking to them. Then [Lee would] go back and do it his own way. He's the only guy I've ever seen do that."

After having to endure the nightmarish conditions of the badly made and equally badly received *Glory Brigade*, Lee Marvin was rewarded with the plum role for his next film. Director Fritz Lang's ultra-violent *The Big Heat*, starred Glenn Ford as a tough cop out to break up the mob that corrupts the city's police force and kills his wife in a car bomb meant for him. Lee later remembered, "…I did ask [Lang] if there was anything that he wanted to tell me about the role before we started. He shook his head and said, 'Vot you are is vot I vant. I don't vorry about guys like you. You are great, huh.' Then he pointed across the stage and said, 'It's that over there I don't like.' He was looking at Glenn Ford, the star of the picture. So, I said to myself, 'He loves me. I'm accepted, right?'"

Marvin's career received a well-needed jolt in 1953 with a performance that became a classic of its genre. As fancy-dressed yet sadistic henchman Vince Stone, Marvin was well cast. First, he stubs his cigarette out in Carolyn Jones' hand. Later, when he thinks his moll Gloria Grahame has been talking to Ford, he angrily tosses a pot of scalding hot coffee in her face, creating one of the most horrific acts of brutality in movie history. It made James Cagney smashing a grapefruit in Mae Clark's face seem playful by comparison. *New York Times* film critic Vincent Canby appropriately dubbed Marvin, "The Merchant of Menace." A new era of filmmaking had clearly arrived, and Lee Marvin was poised to be at its vanguard.

During the making of the film, Marvin impressed the legendary Lang. "We're sitting around a coffee table between scenes, and Fritz Lang is reminiscing about the original *M* that he directed in Germany with Peter Lorre," recalls fellow henchman Chris Alcaide. "Sitting around the table was Adam Williams, who was also in the film as one of the henchmen, Alexander Scourby, and myself. As he's talking of it, Lee, who was smoking large cigars in the film, took the cigar out of his mouth and said, 'Tell me Mr. Lang, what other films have you done?' Fritz Lang got hysterical. Lang loved him for that line. Lang said, "You son-of-a-bitch, I love you."

His costar Gloria Grahame had a strange obsession of abnormally protruding her upper lip that effected her speech. Alcaide recalled, "Lee's girlfriend, Gloria Grahame, had a sequence where she was supposed to say, 'When he cracks the whip, you all jump. Hup Larry! Hup Vince!' Lang kept her going all morning on that. We were waiting outside the door, Lee, Alexander Scourby, and myself to make an entrance, all morning. We broke for lunch because in the middle of it, she kept saying

'Hump Larry! Hump Vince!' Fritz would say, 'Zere vill be no humping in ziz picture!'"

The graphic film noir resulted in Marvin getting more work, albeit still in support of bigger named but less talented stars. On the set of *Gun Fury*, another forgettable 3-D western, this time with Rock Hudson and Donna Reed, fellow bad guy Leo Gordon recalled, "In those days, the [3-D] cameras weren't quite as effective as they are now. The westerns in particular, it happened every damned time. The cameraman would say, 'Could you push your hat up, a little bit? I can't see your eyes.' That's why you'll notice in those pictures all the guys are running around with a forelock hanging out from their forehead. Lee said, 'To hell with that. All they gotta see is my mouth when I'm talking.' He'd pull it down to the bridge of his nose. They just accepted it. It worked."

In spite of the hard work, Marvin did manage to have fun, usually at another actor's expense. "He was a pretty muscular gun nut. So am I, or was," recalled Gordon. "We were on the set one day and I happened to have a Garand M-1. He showed me a little trick. He just brushed the trigger guard in a certain way and the whole assembly came out in one piece. So, I used to get a kick out of doing that with these actor types who wouldn't know a Garand from a plunger. I'd just take the whole assembly out and put it on the side. They'd go to pick up the gun and the rifle and the barrel and everything else would become detached. [They would shout] 'It broke! It broke!'"

Such pranks relieved the tedium of location shooting as the actor strove for better roles in better films. His wife recalled what his early goal in Hollywood was: "When he was a young actor, and we were just married, we were just kids. He would say, 'What I want more than anything is just to be a character actor. I only want to be a character actor.' That's what he loved."

Getting the chance to create a character role against one of the biggest stars in Hollywood was in the offing. He wrote his brother, "There are big things in the wind in a thing that Stanley Kramer, the producer of *Eight Iron Men* is going to do called *The Cyclist Raid*. It's a great idea for a script and they say they definitely want me for the second lead, a damned good part. The idea is it is a motorcycle club that has broken up into two clubs and you see what those crazy bastards are like. I will lead one group and the other group is led by a good quiet type, get this, Marlon Brando. If I get this part, which I think I will get, I think it would do the trick as far as a career is concerned. Keep your fingers crossed."

The wind was in his favor as both he and Brando were signed to the retitled seminal biker film, *The Wild One*. Remembered now mostly as a showcase for Brando, the film was actually based on a true story in which bikers wreaked havoc in the sleepy little town of Hollister, California shortly after WWII. As one of Brando's gang members, Alvy Moore watched as novice biker Lee Marvin wrestled with a Harley: "Lee passed me coming in over at the Columbia Ranch on a motorcycle. He asked me, 'So, you want a ride?' I said, 'Lee, I wouldn't get on that motorcycle with you for any amount of money.' He was in costume at the time. He took off, lost control, and ran it right into the women's john."

Marvin learned quick and, as Moore recalled: "When the director [Laslo Benedek] walked down the street one day and saw Brando and Marvin doing 'wheelies' he said, 'No! No! No more riding unless it's in the scene. When you see them doing that, take those motorcycles away from those guys.' That was the perfect picture for Lee. He loved that."

Producer Kramer remembered that in spite of the subject matter, the actors took their parts very seriously. "He [Marvin] and Marlon Brando… spent three days practicing getting on and off a cycle the way they would because it was a very special thing. It wasn't just a simple maneuver. It was a style, devil-may-care. He was very attentive to that kind of detail… Lee wasn't a fancy guy. He did a more difficult thing. He reduced to utter simplicity something that seemed terribly involved for most other actors."

Brando, the biggest star in Hollywood at the time and the one actor everyone wanted to emulate, met his match in Marvin—and vice-versa. "They got along but it was a tolerance," explained Kramer. "Two strong personalities that came on as actors, they were heads of rival gangs in that film, so it stood up. Marlon Brando was a star by then." Asked about any off-screen rivalry and Kramer responds, "Nah, neither one would have cared one way or the other."

In spite of the film's showcase of Brando, Betty Marvin recalled, "Lee was always, in the tense scenes, it was like a glass had been thrown against the wall and hadn't yet broken. When's it going to shatter?... You just saw that adrenaline pumping. Also, they were both young actors, but Lee had a maturity that Brando didn't have yet. Brando was kind of a kid next to Lee. Lee was like the adult in that gang. Remember, he was the older guy."

Over the years, legends have grown concerning the two actors' interaction, many of them fanned by Marvin himself. Off-camera, the two men were anything but rivals. "When they did *The Wild One*, he was our son's baby-sitter," recalled Betty. "We were together all the time. Brando taught me to play bongos on the peanut butter jars. We did things together. They were different in some ways in that Brando compared to Lee was very childlike. Brando was one who would make Lee laugh. He'd tell me that they would drive to the studio and he'd tell me later, 'Do you know Bud was trying to pick up a girl at the red light?' He was like a kid, flirting. I liked his honesty. I also think he's very bright."

Brando never cared for the film despite the fact that young girls swooned over him and young men tried to emulate him. Critics felt the film was exploitative, and singled out Marvin particularly as too old to play the rival biker. What the critics did not realize was that Marvin's look and over-the-top performance was actually more in line with the real bikers who had invaded Hollister. Future Hell's Angels founder Sonny Barger was so inspired by Marvin's character Chino, that he bought the iconic striped shirt that Marvin had worn in the film. After the movie was released, the real bikers it was based on camped out in front of the Marvin home. Betty made them meals, but in time they drifted off to greener pastures. When they were on the property, Lee avoided them, warning his wife, "Just don't make eye contact with them!"

Other than pioneering the genre of biker movies that flooded the theaters the following decade, *The Wild One* earned another footnote in cultural history. Though this theory is often disputed, the story goes that, when the film was released in Britain several years later after censorship battles, a young John Lennon was also inspired by Marvin's gang, especially its name, "The Beetles."

CHAPTER 6

"You Look Like
You Need a Hand."

WHILE AUDIENCES and critics enjoyed Marvin in some of their favorite films, industry insiders recognized his ability to do whatever was required of him. Lee Marvin clearly understood this role in the business, stating, "I was a troubleshooter. If they didn't know what to do with a role, they'd say, 'We'll give it to Lee Marvin. He'll do something without overpowering the stars.'" Stardom may have been out of reach, but his ability to do impressive work remained a constant.

He appeared in three films in 1954, securing himself a decent living of roughly $15,000 annually. The pay was well earned since not overpowering the stars was not always as easy as it sounded. Sometimes the star was a stuntman in a gorilla suit, as when the actor appeared in yet another 3-D opus, *Gorilla At Large*. The self-explanatory title takes place at a circus and starred such embarrassed actors as Cameron Mitchell, Lee J. Cobb, Raymond Burr and a very young Anne Bancroft. "I caught Lee's first screen triumph," Woodstock friend David Ballantine joked about his friend's minor role as a dimwitted cop. "I think his one line was, 'The ape has not been born yet that can outsmart Shaunessy'... Great writing."

Such lowbrow projects were the chaff he had to cut through to get to the wheat. In this case the harvest was a minor role in *The Caine Mutiny*. Based on the Pulitzer-Prize winning novel by Herman Wouk, the story concerned the breakdown of a mentally unstable captain of a minesweeper during WWII. Humphrey Bogart starred as Captain Queeg with

Van Johnson, Fred MacMurray and Robert Francis as the mutinous officers. The last half of the film included an impressive turn by Jose Ferrer
as their defense lawyer. Much further down the cast list was Lee Marvin
as 'Meatball,' who, along with Claude Akins as 'Horrible,' provided the
film's comic relief.

Producer Stanley Kramer liked what he saw in Marvin and hired him
for the third time for this production. *Eight Iron Men*'s Edward Dmytryk
again directed, and said of Marvin, "He was a goofball but he was a fun
goofball. The scene where he gives the watch to the retiring skipper was
a very nice scene." He also stated that none of Marvin and Akin's antics
in the film were scripted, allowing them to be wildly improvisational and
very funny within the confines of their scenes.

He also dispelled a popular myth that Marvin was an unofficial tech-
nical adviser on the film. This seems unlikely since a naval film would
certainly not go to a former Marine for advice, especially since several
members of the cast, such as Bogart and Jerry Paris, had served in the
Navy. The legend may have started due to an incident just prior to filming. Producer Kramer had a major headache trying to get the military's
cooperation for the film and, once negotiations were finalized, a celebratory cocktail party was held to smooth things over on the site of the
film's Pearl Harbor location.

"There they were, 'admiral' this and 'general' that, the high com-
mand," recalled Lee's brother. "They're all being introduced around. He
(Lee) comes to a fella, a Marine general. He's shaking hands and so, either
he or the general said, 'Don't I know you from somewhere?' My brother
says, 'Excuse me, were you Colonel Franklin Hart in the Second World
War?' All of a sudden, it turns out that Lee was in the colonel's battalion.
Then, the emphasis shifts a little. Now they're back in battle and so forth.
Hart is introducing my brother, according to him, to half of the people
there that they fought the battle of Saipan together. The whole show begins to shift. Now you have this somewhat obscure actor coming off as
one of those heroes. Kramer said to my brother, 'Never upstage me like
that again. I'm gonna blackball you.' It's a great story. Christ, how often
do you get this satisfaction in front of the crew?"

The fifty-four-day production also provided Marvin the only opportunity he would ever have to work closely with the legendary Humphrey Bogart in one of his last and best roles. Over the years, comparisons were often made between the two actors whenever Marvin was profiled in the media. Such comparisons were both obvious and inaccurate; obvious, since they did both work their way up the ranks playing small roles and villains until achieving major success later in life as unhandsome cinematic anti-heroes. This analogy would be acknowledged by Marvin, but only on a superficial level as he modestly thought he did not qualify to be mentioned in the same breath as Bogart.

The inaccurate comparison between the two actors can be seen in viewing any of Bogart's pre-stardom films. There is an undeniable quality of uneasiness that comes through in which the audience can discern Bogart's disinterest with his minor roles. Such was not the case with Lee Marvin at the same point in his career. Marvin's instincts and natural ability were infinitely more advanced in his early career, to the point the audience senses his mischievous wink of enjoyment while Bogart often seemed ill-at-ease or bored. Nonetheless, Marvin was humbled at being in the great man's presence.

His other film appearance of 1954 was in the Civil War era drama, *The Raid.* Based on the book *The Raid At St. Albans,* it told the true story of escaped Confederate P.O.W.'s who go undercover in a sleepy Vermont town only to betray the townsfolk's trust and burn it down. Van Heflin played the Confederate officer leading Peter Graves, James Best, and Lee on the raid. Lee never even makes it close to the titular event as film critic A.O. Scott wrote: "Lee Marvin plays his role more than effectively, still Mr. Heflin is forced to bump him off." A well-intentioned story was given the stereotypical Hollywood treatment while the lame plot concerning a secondary love triangle involving Heflin, Anne Bancroft, and Richard Boone helped undermine the proceedings.

Marvin's cowering death scene provided the film's highlight and, as he observed, "I was mainly hired as the dummy with the flat nose and the thick ear. I've got this sagging mouth, makes me look like an idiot— actually it's because I can't breathe through my nose. But I didn't mind it for a while. I figured it's the obligation of the bit player to make the star look better... I was earning fifteen thousand dollars a year and living well…"

The salary came in handy on the home front because, following the birth of Christopher, Betty became pregnant again. It was the mid-1950s and, despite having her own promising musical career, she abandoned it for domestic life. According to Betty, "We had babies one right after another. I was so determined on getting pregnant, I said, 'Well I'm pregnant now for nine months. Thank God, that's over.'" She adds with a laugh, "People would say to me by the fourth child, 'Betty, this is obscene.' But Lee loved it when I was pregnant."

The remaining Marvin babies were all girls: Courtenay Lee, born in 1954; Cynthia Louise in 1956; and Claudia Leslie in 1958. The names were Betty's idea, "The 'C' and 'L' names all came from family. Lee loved the idea. It was like we were naming orangutans or something," she stated whimsically.

This baby boom naturally required more room so the Marvins moved from their small West Los Angeles apartment to an actual house. "The first house we bought was up in Hollywood Knolls," recalled Betty. "We had two children when we moved there and had our third child there. It already was too small." Larger digs finally came in 1958 when the couple had their fourth and final child.

While *The Raid* was having its short run in movie theaters in 1954, one of its stars could be seen onstage in a musical performance at the San Francisco Opera House's premiere of Honneger's "Joan of Arc at the Stake." It was an oratorio with a full choir backing the speaking performances at the podium of Dorothy McGuire as Joan and Lee Marvin dramatically reading as Father Dominic. The two-week run would have made the Brothers of St. Leo proud.

Marvin did not sing for the oratorio; that dubious distinction would come later in his career. However, he did audition for the role of Jud in the film *Oklahoma!* that same year. "Lee had never sung," remembers Betty. "I had all this voice training. I was mezzo-soprano. I said, 'C'mon, I'll take you to Irv, my voice teacher.' He was the head of voice at UCLA and I worked with him for years. Irv works with him a couple of hours and says, 'Oh God, you could be the greatest singer in the world.' He had Lee singing full voice and just fabulous! So that's a natural gift."

In 1955 any fans Lee Marvin may have had at the time would have been overjoyed with the presence of the actor in eight different films that year. The first was *Bad Day at Black Rock*, one of the best ensemble films of its day, and, arguably, one of the most influential of all time. It starred Spencer Tracy as a one-armed man on a mission coming to a desolate desert town lorded over by vicious Robert Ryan and his even more vicious henchmen headed up by Marvin and Ernest Borgnine. Millard Kaufman's Oscar-nominated story unfolds expertly under the underrated direction of John Sturges who ratcheted up the tension like the slowly tuned strings of a guitar nearing the breaking point. "Like Lee, he was another guy who did things that were so good they went unnoticed, except subcutaneously. You felt them," remarked Kaufman.

Kaufman and Marvin, both former combat Marines, became friends and mutual admirers while filming. "I also knew the first time I met him that he was unusually bright," recalled the writer. "He was a very smart and articulate man. I think, but I'm not sure from the way we talked, but it might have been part of his excessively masculine macho romanticism that he was kind of a black sheep."

One of the stand-out details the actor created for his character concerned his shirt tails. "I didn't have anything in the script about that," recalled Kaufman. "Lee was the greatest actor in the history of show business for trying to get the tail of his shirt in his pants and never succeeding... Also, he had quite a bit to do with a kind of character outfit: the hat he wore, the boots he wore, the soiled jeans, that kind of thing. He was a bright guy... Also, the way he carried himself. Other things he did, he did brilliantly. For example, when he's playing around as Spence is trying to get out of town. He takes out a pistol and he twirls it in his hand. He did that better than any cowboy actor I've ever seen."

Friend and neighbor Alvy Moore remembers seeing Marvin in the film, and had a slightly different take: "See, Lee was the kind of guy that hated gimmicks. He would point out a gimmick on a guy and he was one of the biggest gimmick actors there was. In *Bad Day At Black Rock* he had that shirt tail hanging out. He always had some gimmick and I used to laugh at that because he was always one of the first to point out somebody else using some kind of thing, which is all right. If it all fit with the character, that's fine."

Holding his own within the powerhouse cast that also included Walter Brennan, Anne Francis, and John Ericson, Lee Marvin had several other moments that stood out. One of Marvin's first lines in the film remains one of his best. When he and the others watch one-armed Tracy lug his suitcase into the hotel, Marvin sneers, "You look like you need a hand." He was of course speaking in character, but he could just as easily have been speaking sarcastically of his career in support of other actors. When it came to such support, Marvin was experienced enough to state his personal favorite. "I'll grant you one basically fine actor is Spencer Tracy," he said in 1961. "When he turns it on, he's really a rough guy."

The tedium of the film's Lone Pine, California location often led to Marvin playing poker with the cast. The card game was a popular pastime in Hollywood and the actor played regularly at home with his other friends. "One night there was this poker game in his home," recalled Alvy Moore. "There was Neville Brand, James Garner, L.Q. Jones, and a stuntman I can't remember. I didn't gamble. Number one, I was afraid of my money and the little bit that I had, so I served drinks and just sort of watched the game. Jim Garner hadn't done anything at that time. He was gone in fifteen minutes. They whacked him clean. He was gone. Neville Brand got really drunk and they took him to the cleaners. He didn't show up for work at Paramount the next day. They couldn't find him the whole next day or the next."

When Marvin won or was working steadily as in 1955, he was an effusive gift giver to his wife. Betty recalls, "Like on my birthday he would give me a bicycle with a basket, the old fashioned kind and it would wind up being in the room. Then, in the basket, there'd be a little box with a beautiful diamond. He gave me the most beautiful gifts of any man I've ever known... He always was a class act. I'm telling you, he was classy. That's what most people don't know about him. He had amazing taste. Did not give me one gauche piece of jewelry. Nothing gaudy. Beautiful sterling silver bangles and beautiful turquoise belts."

Next for Marvin was *Violent Saturday*, a hybrid of two different genres, noir and soap opera. He played one of three hoods who come to a small town to rob its bank in the midst of the strange and perverse habits of its citizens. The film costarred Richard Egan as a drunken philanderer, Sylvia Sydney as an embezzling librarian, Tommy Noonan as a peeping tom, Ernest Borgnine as a conflicted Amish farmer and Stephen McNally, J. Carroll Naish, and Marvin as the bank robbers.

The headliner was Victor Mature, a popular hunky star of the 1950s who never took himself too seriously. While filming one of the many "Sword and Sandal" epics he made in his career, he once walked into a local bar in full Trojan dress as the patrons stared in shock. He smiled and asked, "What's the matter, don't you serve servicemen here?"

Directing *Violent Saturday*'s cross between *The Asphalt Jungle* and *Peyton Place* was the prolific and underrated Richard Fleischer, the son of animation pioneer Max Fleischer. He remembered Lee Marvin fondly, stating, "All you had to do was meet Lee. You knew he would fall right into a slot. When you see somebody like Lee, you know just where he's going to fit into your cast. If there's a part for him, it's his the minute he walks in... Well, I probably interviewed the usual suspects. With him, when you meet him, you know what he's going to play. I think that comes across in one of my favorite scenes of any picture I've done; the night before the robbery. It's a unique scene and it's Lee's scene, of course. It's a hilarious moment in a serious situation. I don't think anybody else could've pulled it off."

Years later, film critic Judith Crist marveled at the same scene in 1965, writing: "If you just ignored Victor Mature, the nominal star... you could concentrate on Marvin as a Benzedrine-sniffing hood, catch every nuance, watch his perfect pace, revel in a superb monologue on the skinny broad he married whose perpetual contagious colds gave him the Benzedrine habit. And you realize, watching his performance, that Marvin stood distinct and apart from the maudlin melodrama swirling around him. A pity we had to waste 10 years watching any number of 'stars' do ineptly what he had clearly mastered long ago."

He continued to etch interesting portraits of humanity's dark side by playing a cynical med student in *Not As A Stranger*. The film was Stanley Kramer's directorial debut, and he cast Marvin in the small role because of Marvin's ability to give the part, as he described it: "Sincerity and giving the role a character beyond what was written. In other words, he sought out an identification, and once he found it, he played it that way." Marvin came away largely unscathed, but Kramer's lengthy homage to the medical profession flopped in spite of the presence of Robert Mitchum, Olivia DeHavilland, Frank Sinatra, Broderick Crawford, Charles Bickford, and Gloria Grahame.

Lee's next film gave him much more screen time as well as a trip to Mexico City. The quickly made low-budget *A Life in the Balance* cast Marvin as a deranged killer who kidnaps the young boy who witnessed his crime. In a classic noir twist, the police blame the boy's luckless widowed father, played by Ricardo Montalban for Marvin's deeds. Anne Bancroft also appeared in the film as Montalban's love interest. In playing such unsavory characters, Marvin rationalized, "I got to do things on film that, if you did on the street, they'd send you away... I think we're all potentially violent. But most don't get the chance to act it out. And those that don't, sometimes do it. All those mass-murderers that their neighbors remember as such peaceful guys..."

He was next seen playing an aging musician during the gangster wars of Prohibition in Jack Webb's *Pete Kelly's Blues*, released the same month as *A Life in the Balance* but with much more fanfare. Webb produced, directed, and starred in his tribute to the roots of jazz, and lined up an offbeat cast that included Janet Leigh, Martin Milner, Edmond O'Brien, Andy Devine, Ella Fitzgerald, Jayne Mansfield, and Oscar-nominated Peggy Lee. "I think everybody was certainly in awe of Ella and Ella was so self-deprecating," recalled costar Milner. "She would say, 'Oh, is that okay?' or 'Did I do that right?' Of course, she was wonderful. And everybody was very impressed with the acting job that Peggy Lee did because nobody expected it."

Marvin next tirelessly lent a hand in the proceedings of *I Died a Thousand Times*, a full-color, almost scene-for-scene remake of Humphrey Bogart's *High Sierra* with Jack Palance taking over the lead. Marvin was back in henchman status in support of Palance and costars Shelley Winters, Earl Holliman, and Lon Chaney, Jr. However, unlike other less than matinee-idol-handsome contemporaries, such as Palance or Ernest Borgnine, stardom and name recognition continued to elude Lee Marvin.

His eighth and final film of 1955 was one of the strangest of his career while being one of the most rewarding for him on a personal level. It was *Shack Out on 101*, in which he played the aptly named 'Slob,' a cook in Keenan Wynn's roadside beanery with Terry Moore as the waitress everyone drools over, although she is in love with nuclear scientist Frank Lovejoy. Cold War paranoia infuses the film, as one of the many characters may be a Communist spy. The bizarre unintentional comedy was filmed in just ten days and includes an uproarious scene of Marvin and Wynn working out with weights that Moore states was totally ad-libbed. "Lee was an amazing actor," said Moore. "He had split-second timing. In the scene where he hits me, he did it so real by coming so close, but he never touched me. I really passed out at the end of the scene."

Moore, the former Mrs. Howard Hughes, also claims that both Marvin and Wynn imparted their wisdom of the sexes upon her. "They even gave me advice on how to treat men," she said. "Lee and Keenan both told me, 'Whatever you do, don't go beyond normal sex. Pretty soon, other things won't turn you on. Pretty soon, you become a voyeur who won't enjoy anything.' I always remembered that."

During the filming Marvin and Wynn bonded in friendship that deepened quickly and lasted throughout their lives. According to Wynn's son, Ned, "They were the best of pals and always got along. Dad adored Lee. I think it was because Lee was a no-nonsense kind of guy. He just was who he was. My dad admired that because he was like that. My dad thought Lee was a tremendous actor and thought he would be a big star. He always told him so."

One of the ways in which they bonded was through their love of motorcycles, which they occasionally roared through the showroom of the Beverly Hills Mercedes-Benz dealership. Bud Ekins, stuntman and motorcycle store owner, remembers the days when the likes of Marvin, Steve McQueen, and especially Keenan Wynn, would frequent his store: "Yeah, I guess there was a time or two they'd be in the shop or with a group of about a half a dozen. They [Marvin & McQueen] hardly knew each other, really. They'd see each other maybe two or three times, but it was always in a crowd. Keenan knew Steve better. Keenan knew everybody. Keenan knew you even before he met you."

The work kept coming, and Marvin's first offering of 1956 was one of his all-time best. Cult film director Budd Boetticher's *Seven Men From Now* was produced by John Wayne's company and starred Randolph Scott as a former sheriff seeking the men who killed his wife and robbed his town's bank. It was the first of a series of now cult westerns made by Boetticher and Scott in which vengeance and redemption are intertwined.

A few days into the production of *Seven Men From Now,* Scott was so impressed by Marvin's performance as his nemesis, he mentioned to Boetticher, "This kid's good. You should give him more lyrics." The director agreed, and he and screenwriter Burt Kennedy expanded the role. Enlarging the role of the villain set a precedent for such succeeding films in the series as *The Tall T, Ride Lonesome,* and *Comanche Station.* Marvin indirectly helped the careers of Richard Boone, James Coburn, Stuart Whitman, and Pernell Roberts.

It was on the set of *Seven Men from Now* that Marvin first met the iconic Wayne. "Lee comes out and he's got this coat on," remembers Kennedy. "He went up to Duke who introduced himself and Lee said, 'This coat had your name in it at wardrobe but it's a little tight for me.' That's what he said every time he saw him, and Duke loved it."

"Lee was great," proclaimed Boetticher. "When he came on set for me to approve his costume—you know, 'How does this look? Is this all right?' He had a hooker's bright, red garter on his left arm. It was just magnificent. He wore it through the whole picture, keeping the audience guessing when he was going to explain and he never did. That's the kind of thing Lee Marvin would bring to a part. That's what you want from an actor."

The director was so impressed with Marvin it resulted in the creation of an inventive twist to the standard western showdown. "He was one of the few actors who really knew how to handle a gun," Boetticher said of Marvin. "It made me want to try something I had never seen in a western before. I've never seen in a western a gunfighter practicing his draw. So, what I did was every chance I could, I had Lee draw and practice. His death was so dramatic when Randy shot him because of that. He just stood there for a minute and stared at his hands in disbelief. The audience loved it. The reaction, when we previewed it at the Pantages, was some-thing I had never seen before. They stopped the film and reran the scene." Years later, even when Marvin could no longer remember the name of the film, he always claimed it was his favorite death scene. Unfortunately, the film remained largely forgotten until the advent of home video.

In each of almost every decade of his career, Marvin successfully col-laborated on films with renowned director Robert Aldrich, the first of these being 1956's *Attack!* Based on the play "Fragile Fox," which was the film's working title, it was also the first time the actor would play a com-manding officer. The gritty World War II era film had Eddie Albert as an opportunistic captain whose cowardice under pressure causes the death of so many of his men that one of his lieutenants, played by Jack Palance vows, "If I lose another man on account of you, I'll shove this grenade down your throat and pull the pin!" The all-male cast of Robert Strauss, Richard Jaeckel, Buddy Ebsen, William Smithers, and Marvin as Albert's wily commanding officer, interacts around this conflict.

Aldrich put his cast through their paces by rehearsing them in full uniform for nine days and then filming some of the dangerous battle scenes in the early hours between 4:30 and 7:30 am. A record 657 pounds of gunpowder were set off for these scenes, resulting in the kind of stark and realistic war film that Marvin would make a staple of his career. Aldrich's cinematographer Joe Biroc recalled, "Well, we made that local and it didn't cost much... Marvin was a damned good actor. He was well-respected. Hey, that's why Aldrich hired you."

As the politically ambitious Colonel Bartlett, Marvin convincingly drawled in a southern accent, intimidated and cajoled the weaker Albert, and just generally lent his powerful presence to the moody action film's non-battle scenes. "He was totally in charge," recalled costar and deco-rated veteran Eddie Albert. "He was always in charge. He had done his work." Having worked with him on live television, Albert recalled, "Ev-ery time I saw him he had grown tremendously in charge of the peculiar-ities of acting. He had a wonderful voice." Most of the cast and crew had also seen action during WWII, helping to create one of the best films of its kind. Unfortunately, it too failed to find an interested audience when it was released.

Lee Marvin had hoped the role would lead to other impressive projects but the follow-up was more of a step backwards. *Pillars of the Sky*, an over-ripe western of Cavalry and Indians starring Meyer Mishkin's bigger-named client Jeff Chandler, was a serious letdown compared to *Attack!* Fifth-billed, and doing a badly Irish-accented cavalry sergeant, Marvin seemed to base his performance on mimicking costar Ward Bond. "Lee, in those days, was very much like he was after he became a star," recalled his *Pillar* costar Martin Milner. "He was proud of his military background and he made a big deal out of that. You hand him a rifle to do something in a scene and right away he'd be playing with it. But, he was very opinionated, even to the point of being real cocky, beyond what somebody of his particular niche in the industry was at that point."

That cockiness brought about a confrontation on the film's set with movie veteran and political conservative Ward Bond. Marvin very rarely let his personal politics enter the workplace, but when Bond railed against the Communist threat and expressed his opinion that the U.S. should attack Russia, Marvin could not contain himself. He silenced Bond by stating, "Ward, what war did you ever fight in? I was in the Marine Corps. Infantryman. I know what it's about. You fought your best wars right here on the backlot of Universal."

Marvin was next seen, but just barely, in the Paul Newman Korean War era film *The Rack,* based on Rod Serling's TV drama about the abundance of traitorous American soldiers who were complicit with the enemy. In June of the same year, he gave what would be his last stage performance in the La Jolla Playhouse production of "Bus Stop." He had appeared at La Jolla in a production of "The Rainmaker" with James Whitmore the year before. In "Bus Stop" he essayed the lead role of Bo Decker, the big, lovable cowboy just off his Montana ranch to find a mate in the big city of Phoenix.

Frank Cady, later best known as Sam Drucker on "Green Acres," who played Marvin's partner, recalled how Marvin inadvertently skipped over the dialogue that lead to Cady's one big scene. Such occurrences are common in live theater but it bothered Cady since his wife had gone to great pains to drive down to see the play that night. "After the play," recalled Cady, "the actors would all meet at the bar at the La Jolla Inn. I introduced my wife to Lee while we were there and he said, 'I'm sorry you had to travel all that way and miss Frank's big scene.' He then jumped up and the two of us acted out the whole scene for her right there in front of everybody in the bar. So, my impression of him changed dramatically from that moment on. I thought he was a prince of a guy."

Marvin had planned on doing more live theater but, as he later stated, a successful film career kept him from ever trodding the boards again. His wife Betty remarked, "I feel very strongly that the longer you stay away from the stage the more frightening it is. You always hear actors saying, 'I gotta get my chops. I gotta go back.' They get frightened. Live theater is a bigger responsibility too, let's face it. You get to do another take on film. But on stage, there you are, totally naked without retakes."

The limited run of the play was done through the graces of MGM which granted Marvin time off from shooting *Raintree County*. The massive production was the studio's unsuccessful attempt to capture the magic of *Gone With the Wind*, but from the point of view of the North. Montgomery Clift starred as an idealistic young Hoosier in search of the legendary Raintree. Along the way he forsakes his true love, Eva Marie Saint, for beautiful but unbalanced Southern belle Elizabeth Taylor as he gets swept up in the events of the Civil War.

Marvin is a standout as Orville 'Flash' Perkins, a brash rival of Clift's who transforms from a local braggart to a war hardened soldier during the lengthy film. It is a wonderfully nuanced performance, but lost in the gargantuan production. Marvin was able to show off his high school athletic prowess during an early scene in which his character challenges Clift to a foot race and then believably appears to have lost to his less coordinated rival. "There's a scene in the bar in which he goes kind of wild," recalls the film's writer Millard Kaufman. "He attacks a post in the building and swings completely around on it. We had a stuntman in for that. The stunt guy couldn't do it. So, Lee did it himself."

Early in the production Clift survived a horrific, near fatal car accident. His painful recovery hampered the remainder of the filming during which he immersed himself in massive quantities of pills and alcohol that resulted in very erratic behavior. Costar Rod Taylor recalled Marvin's feelings towards Clift: "I think he felt like I did and felt sorry for him. Lee didn't socialize much with him. I did that and I was the one who had dinner with him and got mashed potatoes thrown in my hair."

Off camera, Marvin got along with Rod Taylor who said, "Lee and I went with photographer Bob Willoughby and actor Nigel Patrick on this picnic. Now I'm from Australia and have some knowledge about waters and what not. Bob accidentally dropped this very expensive camera into the water. Everyone looked at the fucking swimming champ. I jumped into this murky water to look for the camera. I looked and looked. Nothing. Lee put down his tall, frosty, mint julep, cut through the water like a knife and brought up the camera as if guided by the hand of God, while I sputtered and choked on the swamp water."

The film proved to be an expensive failure upon its release, but the role did earn the actor enough money to finally purchase a larger house. The former home of Johnny Weismuller was nestled in a region of Santa Monica known as the "Uplifter's Ranch." Betty had discovered it by accident while Lee was filming *Raintree*. "Lee was on location so I called our business manager Ed Silver," recalled Betty. "I said, 'Ed, I found this great house for us. It's the most wonderful house for us to raise our family.' He said, 'I'd love to see it.' So he came out, looked around and all he saw was this mess. Then Ed called Lee. He said, 'Lee, you don't want this house. This house is a big mistake. It's a mess. It's going to take so much work.' Lee said, 'Uh-huh, uh-huh. Does Betty like it?' Ed said, 'Well, yes.' Lee said, 'Then get it.' He never saw it. He just said, 'If she wants it, if she likes it, she's gonna have it.' That's what I mean about him being a feminist. Not: 'What does she know?' He'd never admit it, but he was a real feminist."

Marvin finished out the decade with *The Missouri Traveler*, a folksy turn-of-the century family film starring Brandon DeWilde as a young runaway who finds comfort in a small town of quirky characters but is mistreated by Marvin's wealthy and unscrupulous character, Tobias Brown. All works out in the end with Marvin getting his proper comeuppance and for the first time ever, actually getting the girl.

His leading lady was Mary Hosford, making her sole film appearance before marrying wealthy Cornelius Vanderbilt Whitney. The scion of two of the richest families in America and a financial backer on the film,

Whitney made the mistake of acting unnecessarily snide towards Betty at a dinner party during the making of the film. Lee Marvin witnessed all this and held his tongue. The next day on the set he approached Whitney when no one else was around and said, "If you ever talk to my wife again, I'll tear your head off. Now, let's roll. Let's shoot this movie."

After nearly a decade of great performances, major stardom still eluded Marvin. Audiences might have been able to remember his face or possibly his name, but in order to put them both together required working in a medium he despised. Television would help audiences remember exactly who he was on a weekly basis. After much cajoling from his agent, who pressed this argument on his recalcitrant client, Marvin finally gave in to Meyer Mishkin's pleadings and agreed to do a TV series. The decision to move the actor to TV proved Mishkin correct, but the effort nearly ruined their partnership, Marvin's marriage, and any future he may have had in film.

CHAPTER 7

Man in a Straitjacket

LEE MARVIN HATED television. Despite several previous offers, Marvin had avoided being tied down to a TV series. The emphasis on commercials over content, the rushed schedule, and the mediocre output, all conspired to make the actor feel, in his words, like a man in "a straitjacket." Having appeared on the small screen since the very beginning of his career, he knew of what he spoke.

Despite his initial aim to become a successful character actor, after nearly a decade of doing just that in feature films, his goal had morphed into something else entirely. As such contemporaries as Ernest Borgnine, Rod Steiger, and Jack Palance ascended to stardom throughout the 1950s, Marvin was understandably anxious to attain the same status. Meyer Mishkin finally convinced Marvin that the best chance he had to break through was by starring in a weekly television series. It would take some time for Mishkin to win over his client, because Marvin's relationship with television—as recounted in the following pages—was a tempestuous one.

Marvin often claimed he appeared in more than 200 live TV shows. While that number may be questionable, the abundance and variety of his work within the infant medium—concurrent with his movies—did give him the opportunity to prove his talent much more than films did during that time. Ironically, some of the most impressive and realistic acting he would ever do would be on the network soundstages.

Starting out mostly playing henchmen and heavies in westerns and crime shows, Marvin quickly discovered that television provided him the opportunity to display his amazing versatility in every genre imaginable. In both early anthology and later episodic shows, he played complex individuals in genres running the gamut from science fiction/fantasy, biography, medical shows, and he even made appearances on variety and game shows. His various roles included everything from an astronaut to an immigrant grape picker, and he also once played a believable Lenny Bruce-styled comedian.

Chronologically, Marvin's first foray in television occurred while he was still working in New York, in such early shows as "T-Men In Action," "Escape," "Suspense," "The Big Story," and other holdovers from the radio era. Many were aired live, resulting in infamous gaffes that have become the stuff of legend. When *TIME* magazine profiled Marvin years later, he recounted a story of working in live TV with Rip Torn, who was supposed to shoot Marvin in an old-fashioned western showdown. According to Marvin, he drew a bead and shouted, "Now!" so convincingly, Torn dropped his gun. "No matter how fast they are, when you've got a white eye for a guy, it really gets them," Marvin told Richard Schickel. In response, Torn wrote a letter to the magazine, stating: "Lee is a mythomaniac. Enclosed is the moldy kinescope of that show… It shows I hold on to the pistol even when dead. As my father once remarked, 'That boy's dropped a lot of things in his life, but I doubt he would drop a pistol.'"

Marvin's own questionable myth-making aside, there were other incidents that costars recalled more fondly with the passage of time. Eddie Albert remembered working with Marvin on "Outlaw's Reckoning," a western episode of an anthology show that was broadcast live on November 3, 1953. The actors had rehearsed diligently for more than a week on the climactic fight scene at a nearby gym on 57th Street. In spite of their preparation, when the show aired, things went slightly awry: "The fight was supposed to last about four minutes, but went for seven minutes on screen, which is a long time for such a physical workout," recalled Albert. "After a round, or two minutes, you get pretty winded. That's why we worked so hard on it. Lee was a pretty impressive physical athlete, and knew how to do a fight on stage.

"What happened, we had some furniture in that room. It was real furniture, heavy furniture. Since we weren't supposed to hit each other with it, the furniture was not break-away. I think we did about four minutes, and were still fighting when he picked up this big table. Well, it happened because he took it easy with me to give me a chance to duck, but it hit the floor and fell the wrong way. He threw this thing, and he hit me, and down I went. It caught my leg underneath, and I couldn't get up to fight anymore. Remember, this went out live, and I was supposed to win the fight! He jumped on me with his back to the camera and wriggled me so I could get out, and we went for four minutes on that thing. We were so tired, we'd hit each other and then pick each other up. It was a wonderful battle. I have nothing but the highest respect for him as an actor because of that."

In spite of such unplanned gaffes, Marvin still managed to have fun within the confines of the small screen. Veteran actress Beverly Garland remembers appearing with the actor on the 1955 pilot of the popular Richard Boone series, "Medic." It was a somber tale of newlyweds, in which the pregnant wife was dying of leukemia. Filmed at a real hospital, Garland wore a very believable prosthetic to make her look eight months' pregnant. "We would walk down the hall to go to the cafeteria, all these people are coming in and out," recalled Garland. "Lee would go, 'Pow!' He'd hit me in the stomach and I'd go, 'Arrgh!' People would say, 'My God, did you see what that man did to his wife?' I'd say, 'Lee, you've got to stop doing this.' He thought it was the best thing that ever happened. I thought somebody was going to lynch the man."

Generally, Marvin got along with his fellow actors, save for one possible exception. According to Meyer Mishkin, "In the early days, he was doing a show with Reagan. I asked him, 'What do you think of Ronald Reagan?' He said, 'He's a jerk.' I don't remember him ever blasting any other actors or putting them down." Marvin did not elaborate further, but would go on to work again with the future president in Reagan's last acting role, and would not find reason to change his opinion.

Working in the medium also allowed Marvin to forge relationships with directors who would later prove beneficial to his film career. "I did 'Bailout At 43,000' on 'Climax!' in 1956, I guess it was," recalled John Frankenheimer. He later directed Marvin in 1973's *The Iceman Cometh*, but recalled,

"He didn't drink at all when we were doing 'Bailout.' No drinking problem whatsoever. He and Richard Boone used to race their sports cars up and down Sunset Blvd., but there was no drinking."

The prolific TV and film director Buzz Kulik directed Marvin several times, and remembered, "He was a terrific personality. A real ballsy kind of guy. Had a great humor about him. He was a Marine, through and through. He wasn't one of those kinds of guys who were into method acting. He didn't dig deep into his inner soul. He was very instinctive. He wouldn't ask what his motivation was. It was all instinct with him. He had very good instincts… He had a wonderful presence that came from the energy he generated. Some actors go through all kinds of machinations for a role. Lee would have none of it. He just worked through his incredible energy. I think that's why he drank, [to] work off some of that energy."

The heyday of the live anthology show ("General Electric Theater," "Pepsi-Cola Playhouse 90," "Studio One," etc.) did not last long as the more creative entities found it frustrating to establish plot and character development within the medium's time constraints. According to veteran TV director Leslie Martinson, "You must understand that anthology TV is a very difficult form. The canvas is very small in which to develop… Audiences had to latch on in Scene One, Act One with the character. That's why anthology never worked. The successful shows were rare ones…"

Martinson directed Lee Marvin in one of the actor's most offbeat TV anthologies. "How Charlie Faust Won a Pennant for the Giants" was a 30-minute episode of "TV Reader's Digest" that aired April 1955, and, according to Martinson, "The truth is it was Lee Marvin's show. He was just tailor-made for the part of Charlie Faust." It told the 1911 baseball legend of a not-too-bright big league pitcher who never played the game, but was considered by manager John McGraw a good luck charm just by being in the dugout. "He was simply great," Martinson said of Marvin's performance. "In comedy, he had a built-in thermostat to his humor. Some comedians don't, and would go over the top, but Lee instinctively knew what his limit was. When you encounter a performer who doesn't [have a built-in thermostat], that's when you need a strong director."

Marvin's film appearances had yet to take advantage of his comic timing, but television certainly did. On a 1961 episode of "General Electric Theatre" titled "The Joke's On Me," the actor played a cynical nightclub comic opposite comedy legend Bud Abbott as his long-suffering agent. Marvin's delivery of his standup material in the beginning and end of the show's otherwise pedestrian plot is executed with razor sharp timing and gestures that lead one to wonder why he was not allowed to do more comedy in his career.

One of the best and least known of Lee Marvin's TV performances was in an episode of "Studio One" that aired in 1955. "Shakedown Cruise" was directed by future Oscar-winner Franklin Schaffner (*Patton*), and costarred Richard Kiley, Don Gordon, and a very young Walter Matthau. Marvin played Lt. Mark Peele, the executive officer of a submarine who desperately wants his own command, and says as much to Captain Kiley who is about to transfer. During a routine assignment, the torpedo room floods, and the lives of fifty men are now at risk. Peele shows his true colors during the crisis and becomes unhinged, shouting, "I've sunk in one of these things before!" The live show was a remarkable example of the dramatic capabilities of television: the creation of a premise in which tension can be built through plot and characters in a claustrophobic setting.

"In those days I did a lot of "Studio One," recalled Don Gordon. "It kept me alive. Don't get me wrong. It didn't pay that well. Only about $200, but it kept you going. I did one or two a month in those days, and it was hard work. You would rehearse for about ten to twelve days, and then go out there live. The next day, you'd be walking around New York and all the cab drivers would say, 'Hey, I saw you last night in that show, and you were great.' So the reaction was immediate. Cab drivers are the best that way. They wouldn't have any problem saying, 'Hey I saw you last night, and you stink!' I love New York cab drivers."

By the late 1950s, when Lee Marvin's film career had reached a plateau of portraying brutal bad guys and interesting second leads, the actor reconsidered the idea of a series. "Everybody knew me, but nobody knew my name," he later said. "Every young actor should do a TV series to establish himself. That's the only way you can stand out from the crowd."

Now that he had acquiesced to do a series in an effort to improve his film career, he ironically had no time available to make any films during the entire run of the show.

The program he chose was "M Squad" and, as was the custom, it first aired as a pilot during an anthology series, in this case, "Schlitz Playhouse." What sold the American Tobacco Company sponsor on Marvin was the way in which the actor handled his four-pack-a-day cigarette habit. "That kid really smokes," noted one admiring executive.

"M Squad" premiered in September 1957 on NBC with Marvin as Lt. Frank Ballinger, detective of a special detail of the Chicago Police Department called in to handle difficult cases. Episodes with titles such as "Grenade for A Summer Evening," "Lover's Lane Killing," and "Ten Minutes to Doomsday" were played out in gritty black and white in which the crime is committed at the outset, and the remainder of the screen time belongs to Marvin as he solves the case. The only other regular cast member was Paul Newlan as Ballinger's boss, Captain Grey. Marvin described Ballinger's bristle-haired, .38-wielding detective as "No broads, no mother, no sleep, no eat, just a dumb fair cop." The show was done in the popular procedural style of "Dragnet," with Marvin providing voice-over narration as he hunted down his prey in each week's 30-minute episode.

"M Squad" did fairly well in the ratings, and Marvin smoothly made the transition from movie heavy to TV hero. He also made money with his Latimer Productions co-producing, but the grind was anathema to the actor. "Making movies rather than a television series is like the difference between playing for the New York Yankees and the Peoria Tigers," he later claimed. "You're in the big leagues with one team and you're struggling in the minors with the other."

A month after the show had premiered, Marvin did promotion, but audaciously remarked, "Cops and robbers series sell. You don't make TV shows for fun—you make them for money." Interiors were filmed mostly in Los Angeles, but once or twice a month Marvin filmed in Chicago for background exteriors. He said of the Chicago police department, "They arrested our cameraman twice. They don't like the idea a bit. They go on the theory that there is no crime in Chicago." When asked if the show had a message or a purpose, he said, "The purpose is to enable me to get rich so I can quit the show in three years knowing my wife has a paid-up insurance policy of $100,000 and my kids are taken care of. Then I'll go to Tahiti, take it real easy, and do the Gauguin bit with the paints. As for the message, I have only one—watch the show!"

While journalists loved the actor's candor, the network and sponsor executives were less amused. Marvin got heat for such comments, and made sure to cover his flank with such statements as: "I'm never ashamed of anything I do. If you accept a part it's because you think you can do something with it. I'll play the worst scene in the worst script and you can judge me by it. If I'm out in front of an audience, I'll answer for it. There's no such thing as a lousy script—there's only lousy actors."

Keeping the show fresh, even after just a few episodes, proved a challenge to Marvin. One aspect that set the show apart was the popular, swinging Count Basie theme that Marvin himself commissioned for the second season, and also wrote the liner notes to the bestselling soundtrack album. Frequent costar and fellow movie bad guy John Dennis noted the way in which Marvin kept the proceedings from becoming mundane. "You never quite knew what he was going to do," recalled Dennis. "Lee was a very challenging actor to work with because he really made you watch the little things that were happening. You'd watch that twinkle in his eyes when there should be no twinkle."

Specifically, Dennis noted how Marvin changed from rehearsal to performance: "He was, all of a sudden, in rehearsal like this with the booming voice. In the filmed take, he'd be down here like this [speaking softly] and you're up here anticipating what you rehearsed. But, he didn't do it that way. 'Son-of-a-bitch! Where the hell is he going?' Well, we were doing it in rehearsals. So, when he dropped, I dropped. But now I knew that when I got low, Lee couldn't get any lower because you couldn't understand him. He was on top of it. He had an intensity, it was just great."

As was common for the time, several future stars appeared on the show, such as frequent film costar Charles Bronson, as well as a young Burt Reynolds, Tom Laughlin (*Billy Jack*), James Coburn, and Leonard Nimoy. Marlon Brando's sister Jocelyn appeared in an episode as well as a fairly unknown actor named Duncan McLeod. At the time, he happened to be the second husband of Pamela Feeley, whom Lee had dated back in Woodstock, and with whom he remained in periodic contact through the years.

Angie Dickinson, another actor to make an early appearance on the show, was to recall, "That is one of my good early jobs, when I probably had five or six lines. I don't remember anything about that except that I got the job and I did it. I was very nervous at those times, especially working with people like Lee, or any kind of good job. I was still very new. I was literally three years in the business. It was just something… I was probably too involved with my own personal life—which was rather in turmoil at the time—and trying to do a good job."

On the domestic front, at least on the surface, the Marvins were doing well. Betty and Lee made a good team when it came to providing a home and maintaining a social existence. "We had themes and what not," recalled Betty of the Marvin family get-togethers. "We never went out much but I could entertain for a hundred people and not think about it, seriously. I'm not exaggerating. Lee would call and say, 'Listen honey, what's going on? Everybody's on location, and I'm tired of eating out…' I'd say, 'How many?' 'Oh, about thirty.' 'See you then.' It was great, because I was good at what I did and he was good at what he did. It was okay."

Lee invited his brother to stay for the summer while Robert awaited word from the New York Board of Education concerning his teaching position. Robert would go on to become an art teacher in the Fort Apache district of the Bronx, but in the summer of 1958, the heated topic of conversation for the Marvin brothers was baseball, which led to a revelation. "We got on the subject of the Brooklyn Dodgers, who had moved out to California," recalled Robert. "With Lee were one or two guys, and I know one man was a lawyer. I had said, 'What the hell kind of baseball team leaves its fans…?' You know, the usual beef. The lawyer said, in effect, they went where the money is. Of course, I immediately hated the lawyer. Then I asked Lee, 'What do you expect to make?' I was making about four thousand. I was just starting out as a teacher. My brother mentioned $250,000, and I said, 'Christ!' Then I got mad at him… I had no idea what was going on. That's how dumb I was."

The effect the financial success and growing fame of "M Squad" had on Lee Marvin's family became apparent to Betty. "When Lee became somewhat successful, Robert at times became quite vicious," she recalled. "I don't want to say jealous, but very resentful. His life wasn't working. As Lee became more and more successful, the family's behavior towards him changed. I don't know, maybe it's just human nature. Someone said to me once, 'You know, Betty, you never let Lee get away with a thing.' I said, 'Why should I? I loved him.' It used to upset me so much that in the business, that there was so much ass kissing."

For all of his instinctual good sense, Lee Marvin was not entirely immune to the industry's seamier underbelly. Former cop and actor Bob Phillips became a close friend of the actor and related this example: "Lee told me a story during the time of "M Squad." He had a little notoriety. So, this independent producer contacts him. He wanted to do a picture about the Marine Corps, and a lot of it was going to be shot down in Camp Pendleton. So, Lee's all enthused. It was going to be kind of a low-budget picture, but what the hell, he was going to have his name above the title. The guy makes the arrangement for them to go down Friday night and tour a Marine base. They went out to dinner and drink, drink, drink. They come back to the motel and the guy says, 'Oh, I forgot to tell you, all I could get was one room, just one bed. I'll sleep on the floor.' Lee said something like, 'Fuck it. I don't care. As long as you don't snore.' Something like that.

"So, they go to bed and Lee's sound asleep. All of a sudden, an arm comes over. A fucking leg comes over. Then he's moving in and all that kind of stuff. Lee said, 'What the fuck are you doing?' The guy says, 'What? What? Oh! I was asleep.' Lee jumped out of bed, got himself a fucking blanket, got a little chair and curled up. The morning comes and he told the guy, 'Let's get the fuck out of here.' The guy never said a word. Drove all the way back to L.A. Lee said he never seen him since. He was a total phony. Lee Marvin got taken in."

By the middle of the second season of the series, Marvin was clearly fed up and frustrated. He told *TV Guide*, "I would get out of this series if I could. It's a straitjacket. Anything that's that much work, I'd try to get out of. Trouble is, I don't know how to do it legitimately. Can't pull the morals clause. And anyway, darn it, I agreed to do it, so I have to live up to my word." After explaining that he could speak so bluntly because he owned fifty percent of the series, he added, "I can't slough it, because I've never walked through anything in my life, and I don't want to have to apologize for anything I do. That makes the strain doubly great."

Not surprisingly, the series began to take a toll on his marriage. "We were really tight it seems to me until 'M Squad,'" recalled Betty. "He was working those long hours, and he was not happy with the series. He had this outrageous sports car, and he was drunk and driving like a maniac. I was trying to think of everything I could do to keep him alive. To keep him there… I leased an apartment for him right across the street from the studio. I furnished it. I put in the best of everything. I said, 'Now, sweetheart, you just crawl over there every night. Don't drive. Don't go anywhere.' Great setup, right?"

The series also had a detrimental effect on his relationship with Meyer Mishkin. The studio system had lost a number of debilitating, high-profile lawsuits that diminished its control of the industry. With the studios' autonomy wavering, the Music Corporation of America (MCA), under the auspices of Lew Wasserman, decided to take advantage of their weakened condition. Branching out beyond artist representation, MCA pioneered the concept of packaging deals between actors, writers, directors and producers to create projects in which all concerned received a percentage of the profits. It was during this innovative period in the industry that Lee Marvin, frustratingly trapped in a TV series, found himself vulnerable to a new offer from the interested third party.

Although MCA successfully wooed him away from Mishkin during the end of the show, when he tried to get out of 'M Squad,' he was put on suspension. "Well, Lee was wined and dined by MCA, Jennings Lang, and that whole group," recalled veteran agent and family friend Bob Walker. "Then he left Meyer, but it didn't take him long to figure out that this wasn't the answer. Lee Marvin said to me, 'Every time that there's a part for me, Charlton Heston is up for it.' They were looking for big bucks. Of course, Lee was the big bucks, and they just weren't aware of it. He didn't stick with MCA very long. He went back to Meyer about a month later."

At the time of his suspension, Betty was in the midst of setting up the first French Haute Couture salon in Beverly Hills. She remembered, "'Well,' he said, 'I don't want to do 'M Squad' anymore.' MCA was not like Meyer. They said, 'Swell, we'll put you on suspension.' He didn't want anything like that. Of course, every now and again they'd offer him jobs, and he can't do it, so he got suspended again… And I was in Paris, and he got real depressed. He said, 'You got to come home.' That's when they had him on suspension at MCA. It was so horrible. He sat it out and then went back to Meyer. I don't remember the details of how he got out of the contract with MCA, but he got out of the series. He was so desperate, he flew back east to the sponsors, Pall Mall, and said to them, 'Get me out of here!'"

The last episode of "M Squad" aired June 28, 1960, and no one was happier to see the series draw to a close than its star. Marvin was extremely anxious to get back into feature films now that he had established his name and face with audiences. Moreover, the grind of doing the show made him feel the closest he would ever come to actually dreading his chosen profession. "Creatively, an actor is limited in TV," he said after he left the show. "The medium is geared for pushing goods. Sell the product, that's the goal… But, I'm not interested in pushing the products; I'm interested in Lee Marvin, and where he's going as an actor. There's the rub. Lee Marvin was going nowhere creatively in the series. Now that I'm back in feature films, I can feel the excitement all around me."

Marvin may have been excited to get back into films in the early 60s, but his contentious relationship with TV continued throughout a good part of his career. When film roles were scarce, he turned in excellent performances in several episodes of such shows as "The Untouchables." Series regular Paul Picerni remembered an episode titled "Fist of Five" in which Marvin gave a revealing glimpse into his acting persona: "Ida Lupino was directing that one. Lee and I were sitting on the set, and it was the last scene of the picture. He's trapped in a tunnel or something, and he's caught. It's a very powerful scene. We shot one take, the master, and he came out. He sat next to me, and I said to him, 'Lee, you know, wouldn't it be interesting if you broke down and cried in that scene?' He looked at me strangely and said, 'You might cry, but I wouldn't.'"

By the time "M Squad" left the air, live TV and anthology shows had faded, replaced by quickly filmed, character-driven series. When the film work was hard to come by, Marvin still found suitable work guest-starring in episodes of "Wagon Train," "Dr. Kildare," "Bonanza," "Combat!," "The Virginian," (directed by Sam Fuller) and other popular series. A "Twilight Zone" episode (the last and most enduring of all the anthology shows), penned by cult writer Richard Matheson, titled "Steel" would be proclaimed as the writer's favorite of all his episodes, and later became the basis for the 2011 Hugh Jackman feature, *Real Steel*.

Not all of Lee Marvin's TV work was episodic or formulaic. In early 1960, he gave one of his most poignant performances in the dramatic special "The American," directed by John Frankenheimer. He portrayed Native-American Ira Hayes who, as a Marine, helped raise the flag on Iwo Jima, but, as a civilian, died an alcoholic. Unlike his film roles up to that time, Marvin was able to convey with amazing restraint the postwar guilt and trauma he was still grappling with himself. The performance remains one of the most realistic and heart-wrenching he would give. Marvin said at the time, "He [Frankenheimer] called me, outlined the story, and asked if I'd like to play the role. I said, 'Yeh,' because I sympathize so much with Hayes. You know he never could escape being a hero. He was buried at Arlington."

The following year, the actor again played a psychologically tortured soldier in a special titled "People Need People." Based on the true story of Dr. Harry Willner, who introduced the idea of group therapy to traumatized veterans, Marvin played an emotionally unreachable and violent Marine as therapist Willner—played by Arthur Kennedy—forces him to confront his demons. The harrowing performance earned the actor his only Emmy nomination, and costarred James Gregory, Keir Dullea, Marion Ross, Jocelyn Brando, and Bert Remsen. Marvin made friends with the real Willner during the show, and even helped him stage the story for inmates at San Quentin the next year. "The prisoners and I hit it off without any trouble. One of them came up to me and said he didn't think of me as an actor, but as one of them. It was a great compliment—I think," joked Marvin.

Marvin also hosted and narrated another short-lived series titled "Lawbreakers," which is largely forgotten now. "I regard the series as a public service rather than a dramatic effort," he said at the time. "Many people in a TV audience think of a cop as some s.o.b. who gives out parking tickets for kicks. With this in mind, we thought it would be beneficial to give a complete picture of police work in a realistic way. To achieve the broadest possible spectrum, we'll utilize the police files of major cities from all over the country." The ill-fated syndicated show went off the air in April 1964 after only twenty-six episodes.

While "Lawbreakers" was still airing, Marvin lent his name to an interesting promo for the show. A movie magazine used his name for an article, "There's Not Enough Violence on TV!," written by the show's publicist, Peter Levinson, but credited to the actor. Cop shows, westerns and documentary style shows like "Lawbreakers" were coming under fire for their violence, and ironically, the soon-to-be pioneer of film violence found himself defending the concept in the context of television. An abbreviated excerpt of the piece proves the words were Levinson's but the sentiment was pure Marvin:

"Violence on the screen is totally different from violence in real life... [it] seems to me pretty ridiculous because the fights are so exaggerated, it's obvious to the viewer that they've been carefully "staged."

"[...]If the situation isn't "real," the question isn't: Is there too much violence? The question really is: Is the violence plausible — is it understandable or constructive in relation to the story being told?

"[...] I play these violent roles to the hilt, but the reason I handle these parts so graphically is pretty simple: I figure out what action or words might be injurious or painful to me, and I project that on the other character. What offends me will pretty generally offend the other character — which, in effect, offends the viewer.

"If I can demonstrate the horror that violence entails I feel I have made a contribution against violence to society. If violence isn't effectively portrayed so it captures the viewer as a participant in a show, then it becomes violence for violence's sake and I'm against that!

"... In my own life, I've seen a lot of guys hurt and killed in a number of different violent ways. That's why it seems to me when a war or fight scene isn't made vicious and horrifying — the way it really is — it loses its impact. War should be shown in all its horror. Otherwise, it becomes an

attractive "adventure" to the audience.

"[...] I admit I sometimes underplay violence in vicious fight scenes. If I played such scenes with realism, it would really horrify you—and myself! But I am still as close to realism as my own censorship will allow.

"You see, I have my own code of ethics on acting.

"I think to myself, 'Does it have a theatrical value to the audience instead of being realistic?' Sometimes I go past realism for theatrical value— yet the effect is even more realistic than it would otherwise be.

"[...] Regardless of how I play a violent scene, you'll always see me making it as violent (theatrical or otherwise) as I know how. If I can show how horrible it is to kill a guy slowly, I know the audience will see it, too."

Karma had its say, however, during the filming of an episode of the popular travelogue show "Route 66." Frustrated with his career, at odds with director Sam Peckinpah, and hating the dreary Pittsburgh location, the actor drank too much during work hours, and paid the price. "What I remember most was his eyes," recalled costar Bert Remsen. "He'd come in from the night before with his eyes all red with that strange walk he had, and say with that voice, 'Hiya baby! You going out drinking with me tonight?' I'd say, 'No way! I gotta work the next day.' He could do it though. He'd come in all disheveled and go throw up in the corner. Sam would say, 'Wash his face. He's fine.' He'd do the scene and never miss a line. He was a total professional."

But, in a climactic fight scene with costar Martin Milner, either Marvin stepped incorrectly or Milner did; the end result was that his costar accidentally broke Lee Marvin's nose wide open. "I'm not quite sure how it happened during that fight scene; it could be either one's fault," recalled Milner. "Lee said on that occasion that the only reason he didn't punch me back is because we were such good friends. What was funny was when we took him to the emergency room, the intern looked at Lee's bloody face and my bloody hand, and asked, 'Okay, what happened?'

"By the time we got back from the hospital all stitched up, Lee started to get these big black eyes. For the rest of the show we really had to be careful how we photographed him. It either had to be from the side or in a darkened room, not up close or anything. It was almost impossible to cover with make-up."

Marvin was given the choice between medications that would either help him deal with the pain or contend with the repulsive swelling and discoloration. Knowing his familiar face was his fortune, he chose to live with the excruciating pain, and silently drank himself into a stupor on the plane back to Los Angeles.

Before drifting off, he was struck by the ironic fact that television, the medium he despised, had quite possibly ruined any chance he might have had for film stardom. Getting slowly drunk on the flight back, he tried to shrug off the realization that timing and events were working against him. The film industry was in flux but, now, poised to star in film projects in which he could take advantage of both his recognized talent and TV-spawned popularity, as well as his by-now familiar craggy features, he found himself instead with his nose plastered all over his face. He loathed to admit it, but, at this point in his life, after all his hard work, he wondered if he might have any film career at all.

CHAPTER 8

"Lady, I Just Don't Have the Time"

BY 1960, THERE was no denying the fact that Lee Marvin's career had hit an impenetrable ceiling. Charlton Heston, Marlon Brando, and Sidney Poitier were all the same age as Marvin, and had been popular leading men from the onset of their careers. Even younger stars such as Tony Curtis, Jack Lemmon, Paul Newman, Rock Hudson, and Steve McQueen had all surpassed Marvin in their ascendance to fame. "M Squad" publicist Peter Levinson summed up Marvin's frustration: "He's been around this town ten years, he got a lot of work, but he never went anywhere. Then, come the 60s, he got into TV, 'M Squad,' and so forth. It's very rare that it takes a guy that long and the guy makes it. If they don't make it in three to six years, it rarely happens."

Lee Marvin was well aware of this on the plane back to L.A. from Pittsburgh. His thoughts were on John Ford, the one director the actor wanted to work with more than any other. Although he would again play a secondary character, he had been looking forward to his role as the ultimate western villain, and was even more excited to work with the director who had practically invented the American western. He knew if he stood any chance at all of breaking out of the pack, it would be with the kind of role he could sink his teeth into with the aid of a master filmmaker. Just before touching down at LAX, he drunkenly confided to actor Bert Remsen that he thought Ford would take one look at his swollen and disfigured nose, and recast the part.

After "M Squad," it was to be a full year before he would appear in front of film audiences again, this time in the 1961 John Wayne horse opera, *The Comancheros*. Wayne played a Texas Ranger trying to discover the bad guys of the title who are selling rifles to the Comanches. In a ten-minute, scene-stealing turn as larger-than-life, half-scalped villain 'Tully Crowe,' Marvin's sequence with John Wayne breathed the only life into the run-of-the-mill production.

The film also holds a footnote in cinema history as being the last work of the prolific Michael Curtiz, director of all of the greatest films to come from Warner Brothers during the studio's heyday. Wayne sat in for the ailing veteran during several days of production, but Curtiz eventually succumbed to cancer a few months after the film's release. Another footnote of the changing times was the fact that the often-used 1936 backlot known as Tombstone Street was razed to the ground during the filming. At the time, 20th-Century Fox proudly proclaimed, "It will be the site of a huge new housing development known as Century City."

Lee Marvin's brief scene-stealing performance did result in his being recommended to Ford for Wayne's and Ford's next film. When Marvin arrived to start work on *The Man Who Shot Liberty Valance*, the swelling of his nose had yet to recede, further enforcing his fears that he had confided earlier to Bert Remsen. Luckily, it was a black and white film, which would hide the discoloration, and the shooting schedule was rearranged so Marvin's first scene would be accomplished with a bandana covering most of his face. His fears allayed, Marvin proceeded to give one of the most memorable performances of his entire career.

The schedule was rearranged for the simple reason that the cantankerous Ford took an instant liking to Marvin. Western bad guy L.Q. Jones was visiting the set one day when he witnessed the unique way the legendary director showed his appreciation: "Ford gave Lee a piece of direction I don't think the old man ever told anybody before or after. He told him, 'Lee, take the stage!' And he did! From a non-actor's point of view it won't mean much, but to me, to ever hear Ford say, 'Take the stage' was phenomenal! That's what he did with Lee, just turned him loose. That in itself is one of the great kudos."

At the time the film was in production, Marvin told a reporter, "I think he's one of the most intelligent directors I've ever worked with. Duke Wayne's the star of the piece even if I have the name part. I worked with him in *Comancheros* too and both of my roles are corkers." Over a decade later, his respect for Ford would not waver, as he would tell *Rolling Stone*: "It was a kick in the head workin' with Ford on *The Man Who Shot Liberty Valance*. I mean, shit, man, he's the guy who made *The Iron Horse*—and the old bastard'll never let you forget it, either. Of course, I caught Ford pretty late in the game. He was still just as alert as ever, if not more so, but I guess he was more physically incapacitated than I was. But he was a bright motherfucker to screw around with, and I used to have fun teasin' him."

When Marvin took the stage as Ford directed, the actor obliterated any previous image of a villain in a John Ford opus. In just a handful of riveting scenes he conveyed the anger, maliciousness, and sadism of a man who symbolized all the lawlessness of the old west, and who refused to step gently aside to encroaching civilization.

Marvin enjoyed playing the larger-than-life 'Liberty Valance,' which he did to the hilt, opposite iconic costars John Wayne and Jimmy Stewart. When he became frustrated with his costars' leisurely pace, he did what he often did in that situation. Woody Strode remembers such an occasion on the day he first met Marvin: "Here's how we meet… I come to the set and John Ford told me, 'Woody, Lee came in drunk. He's raising hell. Will you get Lee Marvin off the set, please?' I walked over to Lee and said, 'Now, Lee, you know Papa Ford told me to put you off the set— will you please leave?' Lee said, 'To hell with those bastards. Those sons-of-bitches think they can act. I'm out-acting everybody.' He was pissed off."

Strode acquiesced when Marvin wanted to go out drinking, even though Marvin knew Betty was planning a dinner party that evening. Marvin and Strode finally arrived around 11:30, drunkenly acting out scenes from *Liberty Valance* until 2:00 am. Marvin eventually passed out, Strode was driven to John Ford's house, and the entire fiasco was remembered by Strode as "That's how I met Lee Marvin."

It was also further proof that the fissures in the Marvin marriage were deepening. It was not the first time Lee Marvin had ruined a dinner party Betty had planned, and as one of the attendees that night, Alvy

Moore recalled, "We were just sitting there bored with the whole thing; 'Who needs this?' Lee is doing all this stuff, and that's when Woody said he wanted to be driven to John Ford's house. We drove Woody there. Basically, it was the beginning of the end for Lee and Betty, and he told me so later on."

When the now recognized classic was released, it was lambasted by some critics who claimed that Ford had lost his touch. Many felt the film appeared artificial and that Wayne and Stewart were too old for their roles. Audiences did not agree, and understood that Ford was actually summing up the mythology of the West he himself had created, with Wayne and Stewart playing dual archetypes of the myth: the grizzled veteran cowboy and the idealistic, young, city-slicker lawyer.

Marvin again stole every scene in which he is featured away from his famous costars. He later explained one of the methods he used to accomplish this: "I move faster on screen. Creates a sense of danger and ahh… I mean, if you're in there, then do it and get the hell out." As to the fear-inducing Ford, he stated the following epigram, "I can work with tough directors. I always say if you're gonna be a bear, be a grizzly."

The character of 'Liberty Valance,' as vicious as he was, still had his defenders. "We had a dog named Liberty, too," recalled Christopher Marvin. The actor's son genuinely feels *Liberty Valance* captured much of his father's soul, stating comically, "After dad did the movie, Duke came over to the house once and I wouldn't shake his hand… I was being really rude. Duke got off on that. He loved it. That was one of my favorite films. I've got only one on video and it's that one."

Although even those critics who did not care for the film lauded his performance in *Liberty Valance*, Lee Marvin's frustration with the roles he was subsequently offered continued unabated. And, while he did take great pride in being able to add to his resume that he'd performed in a John Ford film, it unfortunately did not result in more work for him except on television, which he despised. Consequently, he was spending more time at home trying to be a good father and husband, but with often mixed results. "I remember once, when I was about twenty-two or twenty-three, seeing him working on a bike for Christopher," recalled Keenan Wynn's son, Ned. "I had gone over to his house because I needed him for a reference for a job, or something. He was in the garage working on the bike, and was on his best behavior. He was supposed to be doing chores around the house while everybody was gone. We wound up getting drunk. It was largely my fault. He never set out to get drunk and really tried to do the right thing. We went inside, and he offered me a drink and said he wasn't drinking. Watching me drink, he said, 'Well, one drink won't hurt.' He had this way of monitoring drinking that was pretty strange. He'd tip the bottle, and when the vacuum was there so he couldn't get any more liquor out, he'd go, 'There! That's my drink.' It was pretty funny. He'd just go 'glug! glug!' and 'bam!'

"Within the hour, we were throwing darts at the wall and the ceiling. When Betty came home, she was livid. She had a right to be. She yelled at him and she yelled at me. He just looked at me kind of sheepishly and said, 'I think you better leave.' He was on probation with her. But like I said, he never set out to get drunk, and he tried to do the right thing. In fact, he said he would sign the reference form, but only after he finished the bike. He really tried to be a good dad."

Hanging around the house more than usual did not always bring out the best in Marvin, but did result in some sitcom-like scenarios. To blow off steam, he would often be found showing off his Bristol Ace, a British sports car. "Absolutely fantastic," remembers neighbor George Rappaport. "It was a green one. Yeah, but they're racing cars. A little English car and it also had little bumps all over it, like little dents. It cost him an arm and a leg. That was a pretty hot car, then. We're all sitting in the garage looking at it and my friend Don says, 'Gee, Lee, that looks just like a Volkswagen with acne.' I thought Lee was going to deck him."

Another domestic anecdote involved his beloved Bristol and fellow movie tough guy Neville Brand. According to Alvy Moore, "I remember one time, he and Neville Brand were in his car, the Bristol. One thing Lee would have to do when you first rode in it was he'd go around the corner at about 70 mph. He'd choose the corner, and I knew I'd have to live through that. Once he did that, it was okay.

"Apparently, Lee collected records by Leadbelly, Jelly Roll Morton, and all that. He said to Neville, 'You gotta hear some of these records I got.' So, they drove up in front of the house and he got out. They had been talking about how Lee runs his house: 'I'm the boss. Whatever I say, goes.' They get to the house and he goes to the closet. Betty said, 'What are you doing?' He said, 'I'm getting my records that I want Neville to hear.' She said, 'Look, I'm cleaning this house. I want both of you to get out of here until I get this place clean. I don't want to see hide nor hair of you.' Then Lee said, 'Oh, okay.' They left, and on the way Neville said, 'Yeah, you run the place.'"

According to his son Christopher, there were times when he and his father bonded through their mutual love of classic Blues. "A couple of times he used to wake me up when he'd come up with a raging… not a raging heater, but feeling good. He'd come home, wake me up and we'd be out in the living room. I just remember dancing behind him to his Blues records. I'd be about five or six years-old and he'd be just going in circles and I'd be right behind him. Then mom would come out and say, 'What the…?' Then I'd say, 'Okay, okay…' That I remember well."

Not all of Lee's domestic time was as comical. "I remember when he didn't drink, it wasn't fun to be around him," recalled Betty. "I always knew when he was going to drink. I knew that man so well, I knew by his energy when he was going to have a drink. I knew by his voice when he had one drink. I knew. It started to change. He would come in after not drinking for several days and say, 'Hi, honey.' I'd say to myself, 'He's gonna drink.' It was an awful life, in that way. I was like the barometer. Red flags would go up. 'Oh boy, he's going to be drunk in the morning. I gotta get bourbon.' I just knew."

Even when Betty did know, sometimes she could not predict the results. After Lee had appeared on TV's "Wagon Train," he made friends with its star Robert Horton, who also happened to have dated Betty before Lee. Horton and his wife Marilyn became good friends of the Marvins and invited them to one of their parties. "There might have been about a hundred people there," recalled Horton. "People like Lew Wasserman came to the party. Somebody said, 'When Lew Wasserman comes to the wrong side of the hill, you know you're an important client.' Anyway, Lee arrived with Betty. Lee was dressed very properly for the time. He had on a tweed suit with a vest, big gold chain, and a watch and a fob with a big flower in his lapel. He really looked, if I can use the word cute, he looked cute.

"There was one of those moments when it got quiet for no particular reason. At that moment, Lee Marvin was across the room with a woman who had been a former Miss America. At the time, she was married to one of the executives at NBC. She was a beautiful woman. In this quiet moment, all of a sudden you hear Lee say, 'I'd like to fuck you!' This lady handled him beautifully. She in essence said, 'That's a very interesting proposition. Why don't we go over here and talk about it.' She's not in any way offended by it. I went over to Lee, and I said, 'Lee, maybe you've had enough to drink now.' He looked at me, and he looked at me, and finally said, 'I'm gonna tear your fucking head off.' I said, 'Maybe that's true. The main thing is, though, you've had enough to drink.' 'I'll tear your fucking head off!' I had no aggressive response to it. Eventually, I lead him over to a window seat where he sat down with Betty, and then became very quiet. In a little while, they left and went on home. He colored the afternoon party."

Betty also remembered that knowing when he was going to drink was often not nearly as bad as when he did not drink at all: "I also knew when he wasn't drinking. It was so painful—for all of us. When an alcoholic is not drinking, it is just 'God forbid, let's just not make noise.' It was craziness. I remember one day, he hadn't been drinking for several days. We went down to where we used to go a lot to have a hamburger. I remember we were driving back, and Lee stopped the car and took my hand. He said, 'Betty, it's been two days, eight hours, twenty-four minutes, and five seconds since I've had a drink, and I don't think I can stand it.' That's the way it could be. This is no fooling around here. We tried everything. We tried AA. We tried detox. We tried doctors. I'm telling you, it was endless."

To show the lengths he was willing to go, Marvin began seeing a therapist: "His drinking was getting pretty bad," recalled Betty. "He said to me, 'I really need help.' It wasn't just that he had said, 'Okay.' He had tried a number of things. I was in analysis and he said, 'Ask your doctor if he could find someone to help me.' I said I would. My doctor recommended an analyst at UCLA. I really had very mixed feelings about it because I had enough treatment then to know it's very hard to treat alcoholics with analysis. You cannot have drugs and treatment. You have to be pretty much there and deal with the pain. Lee would think nothing of having a couple martinis on his way. Then he would laugh. I know he wanted the help but it really wasn't working for him, I don't think. Lee came in one day after a session and he started laughing. He had already had a few drinks. His doctor's first name was Charles, and Lee said to me, 'Can you believe this Doctor so-and-so? I turned around and said, 'Fuck you, Charlie!' Can you imagine? That's so in character."

In an interview a few years later, Marvin told his own version: "The guy never said anything. It really began to bug me, and one day I said to him, 'What would you say if I came over there and really took a swing at you?' That moved him! 'Let's discuss that,' he said. I spent some time setting him up for it, and then I told him I couldn't pay him for a while. For six months, I didn't give him a nickel, 'til I owed about $6,000. Then I told him I decided to quit… I let him sweat for it. Then one day I thought, 'what-the-hell,' and wrote out the check. Sent it off without a letter."

As with many actors, often, when things were at their worst domestically, work would prove to be the saving grace. "There's a thing that happens with actors," stated Meyer Mishkin. "They sometimes are governed not only about what they would like to do, but what a director is going to do. Well, Lee liked working with Ford." In fact, one of the actor's proudest moments was when Betty reported that, while visiting the set during the shooting of *The Man Who Shot Liberty Valance,* as she was watching her husband work, Ford leaned over and said to her, "He's quite a kid, isn't he?"

Marvin got his chance to work again with Ford, but his involvement required some convincing. It was again a John Ford/John Wayne project, but this time the curmudgeonly Ford wanted to make an old-fashioned, rowdy comedy with serious overtones, titled *Donovan's Reef.* Marvin was hesitant at first to once again take second billing, but Ford worked on him, explaining the location filming would take place in Hawaii, where the entire Marvin family could partake of the tropical paradise. Ford asked Marvin, "Don't you want you and your family to all get brown as berries?"

There was another factor that weighed on Marvin in making his decision. He was still not happy with where he was in his career, and did not want to constantly repeat himself. "Have I ever had a part where I didn't get killed?" he asked rhetorically in 1962. "I die beautifully. The trouble is, how do you live? It's not nice to look at a character and see him die. After all, every character to a degree is yourself. But there's a great necessity for dying in this business. Why do I play these roles? You know, if you live by the gun, you die by the gun. And I hate guys who do that. They deserve to die. But maybe someday I'll mature enough to where the audience will let me put the gun down." Although the script was not yet complete, at least the rollicking comedy meant no guns, and that his character would survive to the final reel. Mature or not, he signed on to work again with John Wayne and John Ford.

Ford himself had ulterior motives for making the film. For tax reasons he had to sell his beloved yacht, *The Araner*, so he decided to use it in the movie before selling it off, and figured he could have a good time drinking on board during the film. But, for health reasons the 68-year-old was not allowed to drink during the production and had to referee as Wayne and Marvin imbibed. Betty Marvin recalled those moments fondly, and observed an interesting contrast between her husband and John Wayne: "Duke would talk slow. The more he drank, the slower he talked. He was a big kissy bear. Lee was fast. Lee was like a leopard. So, you have these two animals, you could imagine. I'll say one thing, Duke was very honest about himself: 'Look, I'm not an actor. I just stand and move.' He was not pretentious. Not at all. But Lee was a totally different breed. I don't remember that Lee and Duke ever discussed filmmaking. They were instinctual. Lee Marvin's presence was very different than what John Wayne's was."

The production started out to be the fun romp Ford had intended, with cast and crew taking full advantage of the tropical setting. Betty had fond memories of teaching her husband and John Wayne the hula, which was in keeping with the film's theme of rowdy yet harmless shenanigans in the South Seas. Wayne played Michael 'Guns' Donovan, proprietor of the saloon, "Donovan's Reef." He and his former WWII cohorts, Thomas Aloysius 'Boats' Gilhooley (Marvin) and Doc Dedham (Jack Warden), remained after the war, and made a life for themselves away from the structured, and in their view, hypocritical lifestyle back in stuffy Massachusetts. Enter Warden's grown daughter Amelia, played by Elizabeth Allen. She has come to judge her father's lifestyle, but inadvertently falls for Wayne, whom she is led to believe is the father of Warden's native children.

By film's end, Ford has managed to throw in a good many barroom brawls, the best of which is the comical opening between Marvin and Wayne. There were a number of exasperated nuns and priests, a statement about racial intolerance, an older Dorothy Lamour for Lee Marvin, and a dated yet appropriate happy ending, all of which proved to be the swan song of Ford and Wayne's many years together.

According to Marvin, whenever the script became dull, Ford staged a brawl, and, in spite of his experience with his broken nose, Marvin did most of his own stunts. "I won't jump out a third story window, but I'm willing to do anything short of that," he said. "I have an identifiable way of moving, which most men can't duplicate, and scenes usually ring true if I do them myself. Besides, I'm a pretty physical guy, and since I don't go in for pushups or gym work, this is my only outlet... With a face like mine, one more scar or less doesn't really matter anyway."

The tropical bliss soured, however, when Lee continued to drink too much, far beyond the capacity of the rest of the cast and crew. Back in Los Angeles, neighbor George Rappaport and his wife were sound asleep when they heard someone at their door. "This is like six in the morning," recalled Rappaport. "My wife Page says, 'I think I hear the doorbell.' I go downstairs, open the door, and there's Lee. I said, 'What the hell are you doing here?' He said, 'I got to borrow a razor.' He was in skivvies, had a T-shirt, canvas loafers. I said, 'How did you get here?' He said, 'I just got on a plane.' How he got on that plane, I really don't know, because he didn't have any money. Somehow, I guess they knew who he was. I didn't know what to do. I ran to my wife, 'It's Lee Marvin.' She said, 'It can't be Lee Marvin. He's in Hawaii.' I said, "No, Lee's here.' So she said, 'Why?' I said, 'I don't know.' I asked Lee, 'What do you mean you want to borrow a razor?' He said, 'Well, I got some things I gotta do.' I said, 'You gotta be crazy!' He said, 'Just give me a razor.' I said, 'Come in and I could make you some coffee.' 'Nope.' So, I gave him a razor, some shaving cream and he took off. I got on the phone to Mishkin and he said, 'Where the hell did he go?' I said, 'I don't know where the hell he's going.' I guess Meyer knew, all along, the haunts he would go to."

The recalcitrant Marvin was willing again to take the pledge, but this strange occurrence would be a sign of darker things to come. As he waited for the right role and tried to stay sober, there was still the occasional ray of hope. One in particular proved to be amazingly prophetic. "I was talking to what's-his-name, Eddie G. Robinson," recalled Marvin years later. "I was stuck at some fucking party. One of those lawn-type things, right?… And I'm not drinking. But I'm sitting at a table with all the Jack Lemmons, all the quick one-liners, you know? And Johnny Carson. Snappy conversations, zing, zing, zing. And you know, I don't worry about it 'cause they ain't in my league anyway. Or I'm not in theirs—let me put it that way.

"And Eddie G. walked by with a cigar. The first time I ever met him, right? 'Hello, Lee, how are you?' And I said, 'I wanna tell you that I never got over *Tiger Shark*.' He said, 'You ought to play that role.' And I said, 'I couldn't.' He said, 'Yeah, you could.' And all the guys have stopped, right? The smarties. He said, 'Lee, I give you the torch.' And he walked away. And they all looked at me…"

After a few months of frightening sobriety, news came from Woodstock that on March 23, 1963, Lee's mother Courtenay had died suddenly of a massive stroke. Mother and son had never truly reconciled, and becoming an actor, husband, and father did little to rectify his feelings towards her. The Marvin clan attended the funeral with Lee on his best behavior, until the return trip to Los Angeles. Betty recalled, "On the plane is when he said to me, 'Well, I don't have to go back anymore for treatment.' He had a drink and said, 'Here's to analysis.' My heart sunk because I thought maybe this would work. I said, 'Why have you decided now, all of a sudden?' He said, 'Because Mother's dead. I can deal with it.' I know that torment was so deep. I think it was very indicative. When Lee would be drunk, he would always call me 'Mommy.' 'Mommy' this and 'Mommy' that. I used to say, 'Your mother is in New York.' See, I would get irritated, but I think that's a longing for a mother he never felt he had. I really feel that very strongly."

Neither Lee nor Betty would be fully aware of a contributing rea-son why he started drinking again following his mother's death. According to a report cited by the Veteran's of Foreign Wars (VFW) in 2009, WWII veterans were showing up in VA hospitals as late as the 1990s with renewed symptoms of PTSD, despite their having made a relative adjustment throughout most of their civilian life. "Yet they still suffered from recurring nightmares, problems with close relationships or anger," stated the study. "Big life changes, retirement, a death in the family, di-vorce, could trigger symptoms of PTSD, reviving long repressed traumatic experiences."

At the time of Courtenay's death, Marvin's career remained stagnant, and he found himself still playing second lead roles of villainy in film and occasional interesting leads on television. Years later, he explained his desire for leading roles in film: "As you progress from bit to feature player, they naturally look at you as a type. Don't forget —when it came to dramatic roles with good dialogue, they went to the leading men and ladies for that. Because there was no such thing as a sympathetic heavy in those days."

There was no way he would know, but that would soon change due in part to his physical appearance. Gone was the gangly posture of his youth, and as he neared the age of forty, his hair had gone prematurely gray, and had even begun to show signs of a silvery steel hue. His face had filled out more with age, making him appear more world-weary, bordering on ruggedly handsome. He may have thought these physical changes would again hamper his chances of success, but in reality, they would actually enhance those chances.

The personal and professional events in the actor's life came to a symbolic crescendo later in 1963. The decade had begun with the same optimism and high hopes of the 1950s, as an energetic young Demo-crat was sworn in as president. Lee Marvin had actively campaigned for Kennedy and appeared onstage with Frank Sinatra and oth-er celebrities for the inaugural ball. When it came to Marvin's political philosophy, neighbor George Rappaport remembers, "When he was re-ally lucid, and off the stuff and feeling good, you could not find a better guy to talk with. We had some really nice conversations about everything… You would figure the macho guys were always like the rednecks and all. But that's not true. That's why I say on the inside, he was as soft as a pillow. He really cared about people and he cared about issues."

After the news from Dallas on November 22nd, 1963 stunned the nation, Marvin would never again publicly endorse a candidate. The assassination occurred on Christopher Marvin's 11th birthday, for which Betty had planned a party. "I called the parents of the kids I invited and canceled," she recalled. "School was dismissed and Christopher came home. I said, 'I canceled the party' and (according to her), he said, 'Oh good, mom.' He said, 'I have to tell you something. Well, you know dad gave me a gun. I knew I could never shoot it. So, I took it down to the garden and I buried it.' He said, 'Don't tell dad. I would never know what to do with it.' Here we are, a gun had assassinated our president. Even before that happened, our son got up and buried a gun in the garden."

The project Lee started just one day prior to Kennedy's assassination was a remake of Ernest Hemingway's short story, "The Killers." It was to be the first movie made directly for television and, for the first time in his career, Lee Marvin was top-billed as an aging hitman, costarring with Clu Gulager as his protégé. As the title characters searching for the reason why their target, John Cassavetes, gives up without a fight, they encounter a tangled history involving femme fatale Angie Dickinson, and in his last acting performance before switching to politics, mobster Ronald Reagan.

"Movies went to TV from the theaters until *The Killers*," stated Dickinson. "It was Lew Wasserman who said, 'Hey guys, how about making movies that go right to television?' That was the genius of Lew Wasserman, and they made three. The other two I don't remember… It was a low-budget movie that looks like a B-movie because it is a B-movie. But it was made as a TV-movie for people who don't realize the production qualities are vastly different than they are for a good movie. That's why it has that look of it, of cheap. And yet, it's very good."

The project was directed by the versatile Don Siegel (*Invasion of the Body Snatchers, Dirty Harry*, etc.) who, during a lunch meeting, attempted to convince Marvin to play the older hitman. Marvin suggested a preference for the role of the younger hitman. Exasperated, Siegel claims in his autobiography that he asked Marvin, "Are you going to play the older killer?" The actor replied, "Always was from day one." With an impressive supporting cast that included Claude Akins, Norman Fell, Bob Phillips, and Virginia Christine, the production shut down for a day of mourning before resuming what would be one of the seminal films in Lee Marvin's career.

Clu Gulager appeared in practically every scene with Marvin, and states emphatically, "He was, in my view, one of the foremost actors of his time. You never know about actors in their formative stages. Lee formed fairly early on and became a great actor, fairly early. Whereas an actor like Paul Newman, for example, became a great actor in his older age. I think Marty Landau did also. You never know. But Marvin was… by way of contrast, we all have our time."

The making of the film became an interesting drama unto itself as Gulager did little bits of scene-stealing business during his and Marvin's dialogue. Marvin let the younger actor have his way, but created an interesting competition no one but Gulager was aware of. "He started putting down and condemning every other actor on the set," recalled Gulager. "Well, every actor except me. Then again, he may have done it with another actor about me too, who knows. I don't think so, though. He said, 'You know, these actors are just shit.' And one by one he would do things to them, but before he did it, he would say 'watch.' He did this while we were making the movie, before rehearsal, before scenes… I'm going to name the names because it's fascinating to me. Each time, 'I'm going to get them all.' That's what he said. Say, for instance, Norman Fell was a great actor. He had his sweatbox scene. So Lee had told me he was going to get every actor: 'You watch me.' He got up behind him during rehearsal, right behind his head. He held up two fingers; 'This is the second actor I got.' He did some things to Norman that were not too good."

On this, Norman Fell concurred, "I used to look at his body language. His hands and arms were totally relaxed, which I can't say for all actors. He was just there… that was a joy to see. I didn't see any tension. I didn't see any acting. That's the ultimate. That's the key. Basically, that's what it's all about." When it came time to shoot the scene in which Marvin terrorizes Fell, who's locked in a steam box, Fell recalled, "Well, being who he is, he scared the crap out of me. I was in there with my head sticking out and this guy comes in. I knew that he could kill me within half a minute. Just absolutely rip me to pieces. So, he gave me a chance to give that to the scene. The fear you saw was real. But then again, afterwards, I knew he was a pussycat. But he helped me by really scaring the crap out of me."

Such results turned an otherwise mediocre project into a full-fledged watershed production in which Lee Marvin was the catalyst. Angie Dickinson took note of his performance and said, "He was a gifted actor who could rehearse and perform. Don't give me these guys that say, 'I had to pull your hair because I'm a method actor...' 'Well, fuck you!' Don't give me method actors out of control. Give me method actors in control and that's what Lee was. Lee was a method actor in control, and that's the brilliance of him... Everything was unexpected, mostly in his acting. He was just brilliant in his realism, and yet to be so interesting and exciting, you might have to create a lot of schtick. He was just a fascinating man. Fascinating. Brilliant, brilliant movie actor..."

When it came to Ronald Reagan, Marvin still did not care for the man, but kept his distance for the sake of the project. In the handful of scenes they had together, Marvin quite simply acted circles around the former SAG President, changing the moments to suit his whim while Reagan stubbornly played every scene the same. Marvin then told Gulager, "This guy couldn't act worth shit. He couldn't act his way out of a fucking paper bag."

The film's climax remains one of the best of its kind. Following a wonderful moment of dialogue, the mortally wounded Marvin stumbles out of a suburban home, only to topple in a heap just as the police arrive. A memorable piece of business adds a perfect Marvin touch that Gulager proclaimed, "That's the greatest death scene I believe I've ever seen. I don't know if you noticed it or not, but he was drunk. Many times, a drunken body doesn't feel what we feel. Did you see him come down the stairs from the porch, fall right on the cobblestones? He fell hard. He didn't put on knee-pads. He didn't put on elbow pads. No one knew he was going to fall. He just went down and hit hard. I thought he was never going to be able to continue. He got up and went on with the scene, which amazed me. Then, when he fell at the end, he's a big, huge hulk of a guy. When he falls, you can break all kinds of bones, collar bones, everything. He just hit the deck. When he did those two falls, without any rehearsals, any pads, no one knew what was going to happen. It was marvelous."

Ironically, following the President's death, NBC executives deemed *The Killers* too violent for television, and instead released it in theaters in 1964 where it became a financial gold mine. When it played in England, Marvin won the British Academy Award for Best Foreign Film Actor, for a film that was made for television. According to Clu Gulager, "Schools like NYU, UCLA, and USC, and all kinds of film schools around the United States, somehow took that film on as a cause celeb. They made it theirs, and all of the film students for years thought that was one of the greatest films ever made."

Marvin's last line in the film, "Lady, I just don't have the time," was uttered just before he murders his cowering victim. It became a classic moment of macabre humor, later emulated by every action film star from Clint Eastwood to Arnold Schwarzenegger. Just as Eastwood's "Go ahead, make my day" came to mean more than just its literal meaning, Marvin's line symbolized something deeper as well. As the 1960s progressed, the decade exploded violently with the Civil Rights movement, race riots, the assassinations of Martin Luther King and Robert F. Kennedy, and most polarizing of all, the Vietnam War. America underwent a belated midlife crisis, and no longer had the time to be polite about it. As a silver-haired, granite-faced, middle-aged man of violence, Lee Marvin came to represent the anxiousness of the times, and, as far as his career's impenetrable ceiling was concerned, he too, just didn't have the time.

PART THREE

TAKING THE POINT

Lee Marvin in the aptly titled The Professionals *(1966). In describing his character's opponent he solidified his own screen persona with such economic dialogue as, "Men tempered like steel. Tough men. Men who learn to endure." The audience knew he could have been describing himself.*

CHAPTER 9

"Tension, Baby, Just Tension"

I F THE MEDIA HYPE from the time was to be believed, 1965 was hailed as "The Year of Lee Marvin." It was almost impossible to pick up a periodical or turn on a TV talk show without seeing his by-now familiar visage. Paradoxically, his personal life spiraled into freefall, just as two films released the same year established forty-year-old Lee Marvin as a major film star beyond anyone's expectations.

It was not accomplished overnight of course, but Hollywood was taking note of his ascension. No less an authority than veteran columnist Louella Parsons wrote, "Lee is in kind of a special category in Hollywood. He's not really a star but sort of a secondary actor in status. But he's never made it as a hero. He doesn't look like a hero... Yet he is attractive in an offbeat way with his prematurely gray hair and his considerable sex magnetism. In this era of the so-called 'anti-hero,' who knows what Lee's future might hold?"

What the immediate future held would indeed be encouraging, but in the meantime, the ongoing frustration proved practically overwhelming. When he got lost driving home from a gin mill one night, he bought a map to movie star homes, only to discover he was not listed on it. "It was at that moment that I realized my career hadn't reached the peak it should have," he wryly commented years later.

The frustration was partially as a result of his trying to decide on the right project. Helping with this process was his agent Meyer Mishkin, as well as his wife Betty, whom Marvin often introduced as his best friend and toughest critic. He was mulling over several possible projects and said at the time, "Whatever picture I do next had better be the right one!… I kinda like to wait until the last minute 'cause then you know whether it's raining outside or not. I like to know all the elements and what the chemistry will be…"

Ultimately he chose a project he had initially resisted. "There's a thing that happens with actors," stated Meyer Mishkin. "They sometimes are governed not only about what they would like to do, but what a director is going to do…"

In this case, the director was Stanley Kramer. Kramer liked Marvin from their previous efforts (*Eight Iron Men, The Wild One, The Caine Mutiny, Not As a Stranger*) and, through Mishkin, approached him with his next project. At first Marvin balked at the idea of costarring in a film version of Katherine Anne Porter's bestselling novel, *Ship of Fools*. "Hell no. A book by a seventy-two-year-old broad? Not me," he said. Later he added, "I didn't like the book, *Ship of Fools*, but when Stanley Kramer told me the setup and who was going to be in it, I got interested and excited."

Kramer and scenarist Abby Mann had managed to condense Porter's five hundred-page tome into a workable screenplay of multiple, disparate characters onboard a luxury liner from Mexico to Germany at the dawn of Nazism. Joining Marvin in the international cast were Austria's Oskar Werner as the ship's doctor, Puerto Rico's Jose Ferrer as a strident Nazi, France's Simone Signoret as an exiled patrician, Spain's Jose Greco as a sleazy flamenco dancer, Slovakia's Charles Korvin as the captain, Germany's Heinz Ruhmann as a kindly Jewish businessman, and in her final screen appearance, England's Vivien Leigh as a fading Southern belle. Fellow Americans Elizabeth Ashley, George Segal, Barbara Luna, and Michael Dunn rounded out the massive ensemble.

The character Marvin would play was a conglomeration of several from the book, and, as the actor recalled, "In essence, it's the 'Ugly American.' Stanley Kramer sent me the first forty-seven pages of the script, knowing it would interest me. I thought I understood that character. He's an ex-ballplayer, a has-been, a washout, a drunk who's spent his life pursuing Mexican whores—there's a load of them aboard ship. He's a childlike adult, a little afraid, trying to work out values in his own way... a little like me."

Marvin's own description of the character was remarkably accurate, especially in reference to himself. The failed ballplayer drowning his troubles in alcohol and childlike behavior was an individual his wife was quite familiar with. "I think he drank sometimes to stop the pain," theorized Betty. "He would withdraw so much. Once, I couldn't find him. He was late for some kind of an appointment. I forget if it was an interview or something. The cars were in the garage, so he hadn't driven anywhere. I called the neighbors. He wasn't anywhere, and I'm looking all over. I finally find him. He was sitting in the bottom of the pool with his scuba gear on. Just sitting there. Is that a shock? I yelled at him, 'You gotta come up now!' It was amazing."

At the time *Ship of Fools* went into production, Lee and Betty were in the midst of a trial separation. There was not one particular incident that led to the separation, but enough had occurred to erode the marriage. Although Lee was older at this point, much of what he had experienced in his younger days still raged within and boiled to the surface on occasion. "Yes, he could be irrationally enraged," recalled Betty. "He was always very gentle with me, except once when he thought I was his mother, then he tried to choke me, but that was very brief. He stopped it very quickly. But he could be very outrageous."

The most outrageous behavior meant something more dangerous. "Yeah, he got the guns out after a certain point," remembers Ned Wynn. "It usually would happen if he started talking about his Marine days, and stuff like that. You got to understand that after a certain point, he'd just stop talking and he would gesticulate. He'd drink so much he couldn't form words, and his mannerisms and gestures were supposed to convey all these different thoughts. He'd just say, 'Got that baby?' He'd wave his finger in the air like a gun and go, 'Boom!' He'd just go into the whole Marine-military-gun thing."

Real guns would be used on very rare occasions, such as when, after getting drunk, he would try to shoot the gong that was over the bar in their Santa Monica home. Another time, he was looking to shoot some squirrels that were perched outside on his tree. When Betty asked him what he was doing out there, he said, "If he just showed his head just an inch, that's all I need." In frustration once, he shot at the house. Where others would consider it crazy, Betty saw that as the perfect symbolic gesture. "He'd rather have been on Pluto than be tied down with a wife and kids," she reasoned. "Those were the three times he ever fired a gun in the house. Otherwise, the guns were always, repeat always, locked up, and the kids never saw the guns."

Firearms were not the only weapons in his arsenal of anger and frustration. Betty recalls a bright and sunny afternoon at a restaurant that, after a few drinks, quickly turned dark and ugly: "We were at the intersection of Wilshire and Westwood Blvd. Traffic is crazy. Of course Lee had insisted on driving. Beverly and Paul Fix are in the back [with us] in this big convertible and we had the top down. Of course, he runs right into the car in front of us. He gets out of the car. Here's this woman sitting in her seat, she'd just been hit and Lee says to her, 'Start your car and drive away from here, or I'll kill you!' She is just beside herself. She drives on, you know the cops are coming. We drive away. He said to me, 'I don't want to talk about it. That's it.' The phone rings the next morning. Of course, he has hit the executive secretary to the head of the studio at MGM, I think it was. That's who he hits. He's ready to sue Lee, right? They had to quickly settle that. I must say, Meyer had his work cut out for him."

Such was the state of the Marvin marriage at the time Lee began work on *Ship of Fools*. He had moved out of the house and taken up residence in his dressing room on the studio lot. He and Betty kept in contact with each other, but for the most part, he lived a life similar to the one he was playing on film. He generally got along with the cast, one of whom noticed his similarities to the character he portrayed. "He would look at you from under his eyebrows," recalled costar Barbara Luna. "He'd give you a look of, 'Kid yourself, but don't kid me.' He was an honest guy, he really was." Taking note of his drinking and the way in which it affected him, she added, "Any time there's alcohol, comes anger. I think people like Lee drink that amount of alcohol, it's really because they don't like the way they feel. I really believe that. I really think we have to anesthetize ourselves, because there's something always there that we don't want to deal with."

It was at this point that the actor's work and his personal life came to a head-on collision of sorts. "He literally would black out, and he could find himself in many, many compromising situations," stated Betty. "It was very sad to have him say to me after we separated... He was so frustrated at the end of our relationship he said, 'I wish you would go out and have affairs. So that we could have equal footing.' Doesn't this sound like a man in pain? I said, 'I wouldn't give you the pleasure.' I believe very strongly, not just talking about me, necessarily, I know in that kind of behavior, there's a great need to sabotage happiness. I'm not going to analyze Lee, per se. I know we had so many good things going for us. He even said to me, 'I'm so ashamed. I don't think there's anything I haven't done to destroy us.' Sabotaging his own happiness. It's sad."

On the set of the film was a young brunette singer who had been hired as a stand-in at the behest of Barbara Luna. "I was in Robinson's Dept. Store, and I heard this little voice behind me," recalled Luna. "Now I'm pretty little, but there was an even littler person standing behind me. She was in tears. She said, 'I'm at my wit's end. I have nowhere to live. I have no job.' She just about asked if she could move in with me. I was living in a four-bedroom house in Beverly Hills... I didn't know her that well, but I knew her enough where it was really okay. You know, what always starts out as, 'I'll only be here for a week or two,' of course with anybody, it turns out to be a little longer. So, I took her in. I went to [producer] Mike Frankovich and said, 'She needs a job, and I need to come to you and see if I can get her a job as a stand-in.' So, I took her in and got her a job. Of course, she was never around the camera whenever they needed her. She was busy chasing Lee. That was the start of their relationship."

The petite, wayward brunette was Michele Triola, and besides working as Luna's stand-in, she can also be seen on screen as an extra in the film's dining room scenes. Triola was recently divorced from actor Skip Ward, and struggling to make it as a nightclub singer, when she got the job on *Ship of Fools*. Lee was separated from his wife, binge drinking, and attempting to portray a character on film that was of a similar mindset.

The stories of their meeting have varied sources. Triola often told an amusing tale of falling asleep in a deck chair wearing dark glasses while Marvin spoke to her at length. When he found out she was not listening but sleeping, he laughed and set out to talk to her all over again.

Marvin crony Ralph O'Hara recalled a different version, involving Marvin's stand-in Ty Cabeen. "Lee got drunk and he [Cabeen] put him in the [motel] room. Then, got Michele and he put her in there... He woke up the next morning with Michele. He had fucked and sucked or whatever. The next day, it was 'Why don't we go here or go there... During the trial in '79, [Marvin's lawyer] David Kagon's investigation found out that Lee was number five of people she was already blackmailing... Dave wouldn't tell me who the others were."

Years later, Barbara Luna discovered that she proved to be an unaware player in the scenario. "I didn't even know that they were coming to my house when she was still staying with me during the making of the film," Luna said of the revelation. Triola told Luna about it a few years before Triola succumbed to cancer in 2009. "Apparently, she was bringing him to the house, unbeknownst to me, when I was maybe locked in my bedroom. I don't know that they were doing any hanky panky. I don't know even when they started their hanky panky. It could be that they were just getting to know each other. I don't know. When she told me [years later] I was just, 'Oh! I see.' I didn't hear anything."

Although producer/director Stanley Kramer had his hands full with the gargantuan logistics of the film and cast, one of the easiest tasks for him was dealing with Lee Marvin. Asked what impressed him the most about Marvin, he stated, "The first thing was his personality because he was full of defense mechanisms. Defense mechanisms, so you couldn't get to his real character which was very soft and generous and kind. He created an image of the protective mechanism to cover that. If you penetrated it, he felt somehow that you pierced his or ego something. But in a relationship, once you became personally involved with him, you realized how sensitive he really was; which was unusual for a man who had such a facade... God, what time he spent on the facade. I said to him one day, 'Jesus, you waste a lot of time pretending that you don't care.' It's true. He said, 'You know I care, brother.' Just like that."

When *Ship of Fools* was released in July 1965, critics lauded most of the cast, but found the film's overall impact to be both preachy and somewhat melodramatic. The praise for Marvin was unanimous, especially for two key scenes. In one, near the film's climax, he withstands a vicious beating from the heel of Vivien Leigh's shoe when his character mistakes her for a prostitute. Marvin himself was so enamored with Leigh he kept the shoe as a prized memento.

In an even more dramatic moment—one of the film's best—Marvin's ruined ex-ballplayer breaks down and confides to diminutive Michael Dunn about his failed career. Utilizing pathos, mime, and just raw human emotion, Marvin does the miraculous task of turning an unsympathetic character into a tragic member of the film's title. "Among those that stand out in the best sense," wrote Archer Winsten of the *New York Post*, "foremost is Lee Marvin, the ex-baseball player who could not hit a curveball, low and outside…" Stanley Kramer concurred: "I think he was a hell of an actor, much better maybe than he would admit. I think he thought so, down deep, in the pit of his stomach. But he didn't look like a star. See, he was cast as more of a character lead. So, that limited role, to a certain extent, in a romantic situation, affected him. But still, that's what made him effective in his relationship with Vivien Leigh in the picture."

Even before the release of *Ship of Fools,* Marvin was earning even greater praise for a film he made right after, but which was released just a bit earlier. The novel *The Ballad of Cat Ballou* by Roy Chanslor had been floating around Hollywood since its publication in 1956, before the film version finally saw the light of day. Several well-known leading men had been considered for it long before Lee Marvin was chosen. "He was the seventh guy after six of them turned it down: Kirk Douglas, Burt Lancaster, a whole list," recalled Don Gurler, who worked in Meyer Mishkin's office. "He worked it for $30,000, something like that." Jack Palance lobbied hard for the part, but did not even make the list. By the time Lee Marvin had been approached, the film had evolved from a straight western to a comedy-parody.

The executive producer, Harold Hecht, had just come off several recent high profile flops, including *Taras Bulba* with Yul Brynner. Several decisive changes to *Cat Ballou* were in the works, including the selection of who would ultimately direct the movie. According to veteran Western film director Burt Kennedy, "We had lunch in Bel-Air at Harold's house. We made a deal for me to write *Cat Ballou.* When I came back, the phone was ringing and it was Harold, and he fired me!… Then they made it a comedy, and Harold gave me the script. I said, 'I don't know how to do this.' I hadn't done *Support Your Local Sheriff* or any of those others, yet. Of course, they didn't have Lee and Jane Fonda at this time. If they had, I would have probably done it. At this point, it was early on, right after they had done a first script. Then I said [to Hecht], 'I don't know how to poke fun at the thing…'"

Veteran TV director Elliot Silverstein was eventually assigned to direct, and remembered, "The first script was rather a female adventure story. It was [associate producer Mitch] Linderman, I think, that first came up with the idea of mocking it, doing a satire. [Co-screenwriter] Frank [Pierson] and I, each in our areas, took it one step further. What he did was really, I think, probably the key of the movie." It was Pierson, who would go on to write such classics as *Cool Hand Luke* and *Dog Day Afternoon,* who offered Silverstein this sage advice. "You must be careful. You're dealing with an American mythological hero: the cowboy, the gunslinger." Having worked in television, Silverstein was used to pressure, but had never before encountered someone as nervous as Harold Hecht, who wanted to increase the film's chances of success by using a big name star.

Silverstein was bedeviled by the casting choices he was given until *The Wild One* happened to be on television one night. Watching Lee Marvin fall off his motorcycle, Silverstein knew he would make a better choice than Hecht's pick of either Kirk Douglas or Jose Ferrer. Silverstein recalled, "I was concerned that Kirk Douglas, as a major star, would not feel comfortable doing some of the crazy things I was going to ask the actor playing 'Kid Shelleen' to do. In fact, I had not the leverage that I would have liked." When asked, Silverstein boldly stated, "I would like you try to get Lee. You got to try to persuade him."

Betty Marvin had read the script and passed it on to her husband during their reconciliation. "I told him, 'It'll get you out of playing the heavies. It'll get you out of that whole genre. Do it. It's like heaven-sent.'

Reading scripts, to me, is torture. It's like a bad play. It's hard work. But I laughed out loud. I thought, 'Hmm, I'm laughing at a script?' That, to me, was worth a lot right there." Lee still valued his wife's input, and when he agreed to read the script, he so loved the concept of playing both a broken-down drunken, gunslinger and his evil twin brother, he would often quote the dialogue at parties.

Following his wife and agent's recommendations, he read the script, and recalled, "I started laughing when I read the first line. I didn't know how good it was, though. Nobody did. I thought it would just be another little flick. But the part of 'Kid Shelleen' hit pretty close to home for me. It became a reprimand of my drinking habits. I got a look at myself." He signed on along with young stars Michael Callan, Dwayne Hickman, and Tom Nardini, as well as veterans J.C. Flippen, John Marley, Reginald Denny, Stubby Kaye, Nat 'King' Cole, and a youthful Jane Fonda in the title role. Several actresses had been considered, and when Ann-Margret later learned her agent had passed on it without telling her, she fired him.

The finalized version of the story revolved around Catherine Ballou, a young school teacher returning home to Wolf City, Wyoming in 1894, only to discover her rancher father harassed to death by an unscrupulous railroad magnate and his henchman with an artificial nose (also played by Marvin). She and her newly formed outlaw gang—headed up by the once infamous, but now broken-down, drunken gunslinger, 'Kid Shelleen'—wreak havoc on those who "done her wrong" while two strolling minstrels, Nat King Cole and comedian Stubby Kaye, sing to the camera of the gang's exploits.

During the early rehearsals of the film, Hecht became even more nervous watching Marvin not really doing anything as the cast ran lines. Silverstein suggested to Marvin that he have some spasms or something just to appease the anxious-ridden producer. Marvin chuckled, "Sure, kid," but three days later Hecht called Silverstein into a meeting just before the company was about to leave for location shooting in Colorado. Hecht wanted Marvin fired and replaced. After much discussion, Silverstein boldly told his boss, 'There's too much chaos here and it's too much uncertainty to begin with. So, I'm telling you, now. We're going to Colorado in forty-eight hours. We're going with Lee Marvin, or you're going with a different director." Later in the production, when Hecht considered firing Silverstein, Marvin returned Silverstein's favor by making the same pronouncement.

Such pressure was not the best environment in which to make a comedy, but it did not seem to faze Marvin, at least on the surface. "He was a wild man," remembers costar Dwayne Hickman. "The police used to stop him all the time on PCH and cuff him. It didn't take much to set him off. I remember one day, we were shooting at the old Columbia Ranch on Hollywood Way. We shot most of the interiors at the studio on Sunset & Gower. He used to go to the Blarney Castle for lunch. Naturally, he wouldn't go to a restaurant unless it served cocktails. He came back from lunch and rear-ended the producer's car. He got out and yelled, 'I am here!' He went to his dressing room and slammed the door. That's the kind of thing he would do."

As he had in the past, Marvin would bond with one or two other costars, in this instance his younger cohorts, Callan, Hickman, and Nardini. "As filming went on, we socialized in California at my house a couple of times, and I got to know him pretty well," recalled Callan. "When we were filming in Colorado, we hung out on the set a lot, or in the hotel room. We were both going through some tough times in our personal life, so we talked about that. I talked to him about my ex-wife and he talked about Michele, I guess it was at the time."

One of the cast members Marvin did not bond with was his young leading lady. While the passage of time has allowed Jane Fonda to write warmly about working with Marvin, observers during production saw it differently. "What bothered Lee about Jane was that she was kind of pretentious," observed Hickman. "Jane was a product of Henry, and finishing schools in Europe, and was a proponent of 'The Method.' She was very serious about acting. Lee was serious in his own way, but also a bit outrageous, so she was his target. Of course, she was very good, too, but approached her role in a different way. He was crude and bawdy, and kind of offended her sensibilities."

When the production moved to Canyon City, Colorado, the cast stayed at a hotel an hour's drive from the location. "I remember early on, Lee had the driver stop and get a bottle of vodka," Hickman recalled. "I thought to myself, 'Geez, it's 7:00 am.' I must say, to his credit, his first scene was a tough one. It was the scene where he starts drinking and explains how sad a gunfighter's life is when he grows old and is forgotten. He was brilliant. In all fairness, it was the first day of location shooting and it's usually pretty easy in the beginning, because everyone is just familiarizing themselves and getting to know one another. But he had a hard day's work ahead of him. He would take little nips from the vodka throughout the day. When I asked if he was okay, he just said, 'Tension, baby, just tension.' He was a lot of fun, but I enjoyed him from a distance."

The brilliance did not come forth right away, as the actor who rarely required more than two takes per scene was racking up several for his difficult, yet all-important opening monologue. In front of the entire cast and crew, producer Hecht would call Silverstein over to the side after each take, wanting to know why they were not moving on to the next set-up. The director of many episodes of television's 'Have Gun, Will Travel' and 'Naked City' had something in mind that he was not quite getting from his actor.

Silverstein approached Marvin after the seventh take, and as he recalled, "He had seen Harold call me over each time... I said to Lee, 'We got seven in the can that are pretty good. I'd like to try one more that's completely different.' He said, 'Yeah, yeah. What do you want me to do?' I said, 'Try to play this like a 'Naked City' bum. Don't make me laugh. Make me cry. Let me see the sadness of this guy because in the sadness, I think there may be some fun.' He thought about it, and answered in that mumbling way of his, 'Naked City' bum, yeah. What the hell, let's give it a whirl.' I stepped back, and we rolled it. Then, he broke me up. I printed that take and looked at Harold, breathing a sigh of relief. That was take eight. That set his character... I later bought a boat and called it *Take Eight*."

The rest of the filming in Colorado was fairly uneventful. The flipside of Marvin's professionalism concerned his escapades away from the camera. "Well, I remember one day," recalled Michael Callan whimsically, "We were shooting a scene, and the light was going down. Lee was kind of depressed, because it meant he was not going to be able to get his close-up. I told him, 'I'll take you out drinking tonight, and I'll match you drink for drink…' Well, you probably know how the story ends. I was drunk under the table, and he was fine. The next day, I was totally hung over, and he just had a little headache."

The day the company left Colorado to return to California, life seemed to imitate art. According to Callan, "Another funny incident was on the last day. He was in his hotel room when we were getting ready to leave. It was a pretty funny sight when we came to get him. He had a hairnet on, had both his legs in one leg of his shorts. I mean he was a mess. He had to be poured into the car, and then the plane. Somehow he had gotten a hold of a .45, and started shooting things on the road as we drove. If you think about it, it was just like his character in the movie. After we got back, he found out he had to shoot a scene."

The scene Marvin was called in to shoot, on what was supposed to be his day off, was a relatively simple one. Wearing his full gunslinger regalia, he was to walk slowly down the corridor of a whorehouse, and check each room quickly for the presence of his nemesis. The scene required a specific rhythm to his movements, but Marvin's inebriated state made it difficult. Director Silverstein tried everything he could think of, including handclaps and, at one point, a metronome to time the actor's steps. After five takes, the director managed to get what he wanted. "If you watch that scene closely," adds Silverstein, "you'll see he lumbers a bit." According to Silverstein, there was actually very little difficulty in working with Marvin. Whatever he suggested, the actor was willing to try. "Lee was a kind of 'do-it' guy," recalled the director. "He wasn't for talking much. He just did it. If there was something different I wanted, we would talk about that. I never had any problems with him as an actor." When Silverstein thought it would be funnier if Marvin sang "Happy Birthday" to a corpse in a voice like Mortimer Snerd, Marvin was up for it.

The company's return to California also meant a return to Lee Marvin's domestic problems, as well. When he told Betty when he would be home, she went to buy herself a new dress for the homecoming. "I was in a changing room in I. Magnin's trying on something. Lee was due to come back that evening. He had called me from location, I don't remember where. He had his problems and I know Michele existed... I was actually trying on something in a dressing room. Who should come into the dressing room next to me but Michele and a friend. We're trying on clothes, and they're talking about Lee coming home. Isn't that eerie?"

Lee's wife found out about Triola's existence when Triola called their home, bluntly asking for Lee: "This woman calls and I answer, 'Hello.' She says, 'Betty?' and I say 'Yes.' She says, 'Michele.' I said, 'I'm sorry?' She says, 'You know, Michele. You know who I am.' I said, 'I'm very sorry. I don't know you.' She said, 'I'm Lee's mistress, you know.' I was so shocked.

"Meyer called shortly thereafter, something for Lee. I said, 'Meyer, who's Michele? She just called here.' Poor Meyer started with the 'Oh-my-God!' Poor Meyer never knew what hit him. So there was Lee, stuck between a rock and hard place and I was just devastated... I couldn't believe this woman. Then of course, everybody started calling me and started telling me, 'Oh well, she's a hooker from Vegas, she's a call girl, etc.' This one guy said, 'I don't know of any actor in town who hasn't had her.'"

These painful episodes required that Lee move into the Malibu beach house the couple had purchased. At one point Betty told her husband, "I wish you well but it's so hard for me to understand that you choose a woman so different from me." He responded, "Why wouldn't you understand that? I don't have to be with her. I don't have to talk to her. I don't care about her." Years later, Betty considered her husband's words and said, "I thought that was so fascinating. He was always honest about us. I feel, to the best of his ability, he did the best he could. I know that in my heart. He was always totally honest with me. When he deceived me, when he disappeared and he was very bad. He didn't bring that home. It was the dark side of him."

At the same time, Marvin was finishing his work on *Cat Ballou*, which included one of the most famous sight gags in movie history. When 'Kid Shelleen' is found, having fallen off the wagon, both he and his horse appear to be drunk and leaning against the wall in a parody of the iconic James Earle Fraser statue, "The End of the Trail." It also proved to be one of the film's most difficult sequences to shoot. Before the days of high-tech wizardry, filmmakers had to rely solely on their ingenuity to achieve the impossible, which is precisely what Silverstein did to make the horse appear drunk and leaning against the wall.

The problem arose due to the simple fact that horses do not lean, and when Silverstein thought the illusion could be created if the horse were to cross his legs, the wrangler explained to him that horses do not naturally cross their legs. Silverstein told the wrangler, "When I first came to town, I was told a director could have anything he wanted, and I want the horse to cross his legs. How long will it take?" When the wrangler said, "Oh, about two days," the director told him, "You got an hour and a half." Marvin went to his dressing room to study his lines, another shot was set up, and the wrangler coaxed the horse named Smoky to cross his legs briefly with the help of a sugar cube and a strand of piano wire.

Silverstein recalled, "The horse uncrossed his legs, and the wrangler rapped the horse's shin with his hand or a stick, or something. He repeated that over and over again until the horse got the idea that crossing his legs would get him sugar. All I needed was to hold it for ten seconds. We got it. We then brought Lee back out, and he got up on the horse. He said, 'What's happening? What's this?' I said, 'Nothing, Lee. I just made a little change in the way the horse behaves.' He got up there and leaned against the wall. We got a little piano wire tied to the horse's bridle, and pulled it around to the corner of the building. So, we kept the horse's head down with the piano wire.

"The wrangler placed the horse's legs in a crossed position. He let the horse see the sugar, and then backed slowly out of the scene. We insulated, which means we didn't use the clapper to begin the scene, so we wouldn't spook the horse. We just rolled, silently. Then, with a visual nod, the piano wire pulled the horse's head over to the left. They let loose the piano wire, and the horse turned away. So, I had my ten seconds. The producer, as it turns out, had walked by on that take. I said, 'Harold, Harold! Look at that.' He said, 'Yeah, yeah, yeah.' He was very concerned, because I think we were a half a day behind or something like that, which is nothing. He was very nervous."

The difficult situation, solved with old-fashioned ingenuity, provided one of the most talked about comedic moments of the year. In fact, the film was a major success. "The film was a lucky strike," declared Silverstein. "It just happened that everything came together. Out of all the chaos came something I don't think anybody expected, including me. I had a conversation with Frank Pierson during all these troubles I was having with Harold. I said, 'Frank, if we could just hang in there and get through this, we will open the golden door to doing other features. We'll have a nice little film. It'll be different.' I remember saying that. I had no idea. I knew what we were doing was something unusual, but I had no idea that it… I'm not one of those people who knows what's commercial and what's not commercial."

The moderately budgeted, twenty-eight-day scheduled shoot took everyone by surprise when it was previewed. Receiving the lion's share of the credit was Lee Marvin, in spite of the good work done by all concerned. "I've been doing good things for years, but no one had ever seen it before. But *Cat Ballou* was something else," explained the actor. "Know what I was thinking when we were making *Cat Ballou*? I was thinking that this would be my last picture. I was going to quit the business. It was that difficult for me. Nobody has to work that hard for a million dollars—constantly reaching beyond himself. Or at least I thought so. I'm not over it yet. If anything, it's getting worse. I have a feeling this reaction is going to set in after every piece of work I do from now on. Now that I think I know what I'm doing, I'm scared. Before this, I just didn't know any better."

Just prior to the general release of both *Ship of Fools* and *Cat Ballou* there was a positive buzz in Hollywood. Mishkin had talked Marvin into hiring a publicist a few years earlier, and it proved a wise investment for 1965. The interview requests were almost overwhelming, and, at the time, Marvin was able to proclaim, "The slow growth for me into the big time was actually planned ahead. It was the idea of my agent, Meyer Mishkin. He believes in selectivity, and his taste is impeccable. I wouldn't have had it any other way because I've had the opportunity to develop my craft. If I'd come in slam, bang! I would probably have remained a frustrated one-part type actor."

The interview requests via the buzz in Hollywood were growing loud and incessant. Publicist Paul Wasserman recalls, "I went to a [prerelease] screening of *Cat Ballou.* I called him [Marvin] up on the phone after-wards, and said, 'I'd like to sit down with you and talk to you about the Oscar campaign.' He said, 'What Oscar campaign?' I said, 'I think you are going to win the Oscar…'"

CHAPTER 10

Everybody Gets Their "Vicaries"

T HE MID TO LATE 1960S was a period of immense change in both America and the film industry that reflected it. The studio system had become a memory only to be joined soon by the old production code, which would eventually be replaced by a controversial rating system. With such massive changes taking place, it was inevitable that the concept of the American leading man would also undergo a metamorphosis. New actors were being touted and each would fall into a pattern for audiences to admire. Jack Lemmon may have been funnier, Steve McQueen cooler, Paul Newman sexier, even the aging John Wayne more reliable, but when it came to channeling the angst and violence of the turbulent era, only one actor did so with every performance.

Lee Marvin was so much in demand during the 1960s, that whenever he granted an interview, reporters found him to be immensely entertaining and eminently quotable. Meyer Mishkin believed his client did his best acting for the press, and, rising to the occasion, Marvin would often do his best to challenge his interviewers with unsettling mindgames, by playing with a knife during the session for instance, or making frightening pronouncements accompanied by strange gesticulations. Just a small sampling of some of Marvin's quotes bears this out:

— "Let's just you and me face it, buddy. War isn't like it is in the movies, and death is not the worst of war—after all, everyone's gotta die.

No, what's left is the worst."

—"If someone's going for my life—and it's a question of him or me—well, it ain't gonna be me. The Marquis of Queensbury went out of style with wing collars."

—"Most people only wise up when they are down on the floor with the blood everywhere."

—"The only thing in life that's really interesting is the contest. We are all contestants—whether we admit it or not. If you read a good book—the author has won. If I read 20 pages of a book and they're no good, I put it down. Maybe it's good after 100 pages, but I can't wait. The author lost."

—"The whole thing of success is just a big accident. I don't think a man even has a 'stride' till he's about 40. I'm not talking about the brain-work you can do at the age of 22, as a construction worker or a plane engineer, say. But around 38-45 is the time when a man develops whatever his 'smell' may be…"

—"I like a martini. I like rum. I love tequila straight. It is the perfect drink. You keep right on drinking until you finally take one more and you know you've reached your limit. A very polite drink. It tells you when to quit."

—"When I do a scene I make it as rough as I can. Knock a man down with one round, then walk up on him and put three or four more in his face. Roll him over and put one in his back. Make it ugly… I say make it so brutal that a man thinks twice before he does something like that."

— "People get a vicarious thrill out of what I do; I know that. But I don't reckon my films have a bad influence on anyone; they won't send people out into the street with axes, or anything. The Shirley Temple movies are more likely to do that; after listening to 'The Good Ship Lollipop' you just gotta go out and beat up somebody. Stands to reason."

Depending on his mood, which largely had to do with his alcohol intake that day, or the opinion he held of the interviewer, he often peppered such comments with his own vocabulary, which included Marine barracks jargon, sound effects for punctuation, and made up words, such as "vicaries" (pronounced 'vy-care-rees') for "vicarious." Sometimes, what transpired could not translate to the printed word. "He had a body language that was altogether different than most people," recalled Alvy Moore. "It was almost laughable at times because he had that light, easy way of explaining something. When he explained something, you assumed you understood what he just said, but it was amusing watching him say it. He was always emphasizing his words with 'Crack! Bang! Phfft!' He did manage to say something in all those gyrations and motions he went through. He would have some gyrations that were really something else."

Generated by the rave reviews and word-of-mouth attention in the wake of his performances in *Ship of Fools* and *Cat Ballou*, these non-stop interviews were to become a necessary evil to Marvin; for along with the widespread publicity came better film offers, such as his next project. Based on the novel *A Mule For Marquesa* by Frank O'Rourke, and adapted by writer/director Richard Brooks, *The Professionals* was a rousing adventure story about four mercenaries in 1917 (Marvin, Burt Lancaster, Robert Ryan and Woody Strode) who are hired by a rich man (Ralph Bellamy) to retrieve his wife (Claudia Cardinale) from the clutches of a Mexican revolutionary (Jack Palance). Brooks managed to include salty yet quotable dialogue, graphic violence, a twist ending, and, for the first time ever in the sacred genre of mythic westerns, a glimpse of frontal female nudity.

Given that the veteran cast was one of the first in which seasoned actors, all in their forties, played all the leads, the film was aptly titled. "They were some group," recalled production assistant Phil Parslow. "Lee came to the set in a big, white Caddy limo. So would Burt. Claudia came in a Lincoln, and Palance had a Mercury. It pissed him off, because he was supporting guys that used to be supporting him, and now it's the other way around. But, he got the last laugh because he practically stole the picture. I remember Robert Ryan would put his hand on my shoulder and say, 'You and I are the only sane ones in the group.' I got to be pretty tight with Ryan and found out he had his own problems."

Ryan was apparently not alone in that department. Like Lee Marvin's, Burt Lancaster's decades-long marriage was crumbling, he was having an ongoing liaison with his hairdresser, and, worst of all, his underage son had eloped with Ernie Kovacs' underage daughter. Marvin and Lancaster could have commiserated over some of their troubles, but Marvin sized up the situation of the entire cast differently when he noted, "Shooting was postponed one day because of rain. I turned to Burt Lancaster and joked about rain never bothering a Marine. Lancaster nodded and said he'd been a Pfc. in the Army. I told him that didn't count. Brooks, Ryan, and I also held the rank of Pfc. —in the Marine Corps. Then the irony of the situation dawned on me—all those millions riding on the backs of Pfcs made me wonder what the colonels were doing on that day."

Despite their wonderful chemistry on film, Marvin and Lancaster did not warm up to each other off camera. Instead, Marvin found one of the perks of the film was in being reunited with his old companion, Woody Strode. Although they had not worked together since *Liberty Valance* three years earlier, the two men had held a genuine affection for each other ever since. "From then on [after *Valance*], we were cool," said Strode. "We were together all the time. We didn't go into nothing crazy... I would go to his Malibu home. He was going with this little girl, Michele. I would sit around there with him, and we'd just be looking at that ocean, having drinks and cooking steaks. If I got too drunk to drive home, I'd stay overnight... From 1960 on, anytime that I had to go, that's the only time I'd go to Malibu. I wouldn't go out there because it was all white places. But for Lee Marvin, I would go... Those were good years."

Strode and Marvin were good enough friends that Marvin was able to pass on some confidential information to him. Each character had an opening vignette before the credits, and the well-chiseled muscles of Strode were on full display as he was shown riding into town wearing little more than jeans and a leather vest, but only in the opening. "See how I was cut out in that vest?," reminded Strode. "Lee Marvin said to me, 'Burt couldn't take that.' That's why they put clothes on me. I could have run through the whole picture naked, but Lancaster was jealous, yeah. Didn't want me looking that way, and he's the star. Lee Marvin told me. That's how good Lee was. Lee didn't give a shit… If an elephant was there, he was going to out-act it. Hear me? That's what a great actor he was… He told me why they took it [the costume] off me. He was sitting with the muscle when it went down."

Tony Epper, the six-foot-four, solidly-built member of a movie stunt family dynasty, began his long professional association with Lancaster on *The Professionals*, although the acrobatically-trained fifty-two-year-old Lancaster did scale the side of a steep cliff on his own for the film. As for Epper, "He had no fear," said Phil Parslow of the legendary stuntman. "Some guy picked a fight with him in a bar once, and Tony hit him and killed him. He was charged with involuntary manslaughter, I think. It was self-defense, and he didn't do any time. There was nothing phony about him. He was the real thing."

Nevada's blistering Valley of Fire desert region became the location for the film, during which Epper formed a bond with Marvin. Since both men were familiar with the weaponry used in the movie, they took it upon themselves to clean and maintain all the guns. Epper was also an aspiring actor and had a small role in the film. He recalled a moment when Marvin shared his wisdom garnered from years of playing supporting roles to the stars: "Lee Marvin told me one thing that set in my mind my entire career. He said, 'Look, this is Burt Lancaster's picture. We are supporting actors. Let's do our very best to find our niche and make him look as good as we can.' That right there is Lee Marvin… You ever watch him handle a gun? Those were well thought out moves. I don't know if anybody is aware of that."

Epper was also impressed by Marvin's ability to do difficult and dangerous stunts if called upon. "Yeah, he'd do a lot of fight scenes. He fell down some stairs one night," recalled Epper. Asked if the fall was in a film, Epper wryly responded, "No, from coming out of a bar with me. It would have killed anybody else. He'd brush himself off with that look he gets about him, you know? You'd say 'Buddy, what happened?' He'd say 'Nope, nope, didn't hurt me.' Sat down, glug, glug, glug. 'Ahh!' That was Lee."

Richard Brooks was an old-fashioned, screaming director who drove his cast and crew to exhaustion, causing them in turn to blow off steam at night when they got back to their hotel in Las Vegas. Marvin, Epper, and Strode created legendary debauches in the casinos, but still managed to perform the next day. Not included in the masculine reverie was Jack Palance, of whom Epper claimed: "He's crazy. He pulled a thing, once, geez! We were sitting with some hookers… God, Palance had a weird sense of humor. I remember, he went and bought condoms. Must have spent twenty bucks on them… He dumped them all on the bed and shouted, 'Now we can all fuck! Ha, ha!' You can hear him all over. I don't know what he thought was funny about it. I still, to this day, don't understand it."

No matter what they had been up to the night before, Marvin was a total professional by the time they got to the set the next day. According to Strode, "I saw it when we'd drive to the set. He'd study the dialogue, and by the time we got to the set, he got it all in his head. He'd say, 'Now, watch me make Burt blow all his lines.' Burt's been up all night studying and going through the regular routine actors would go through. Lee didn't have to do that. Guy was gifted!"

Some of their nightly escapades even outdid the antics of the legendary "Rat Pack." They dangled nude showgirls out of their hotel-room window, and shot out the famous "Vegas Vic" sign with armor-piercing arrows. The trio almost landed in jail, but Marvin's newly acquired stardom kept them at peace with the local constabulary.

Phil Parslow was the person responsible for making sure Marvin and the others got to the set. As far as he was concerned, "The sober people on that film gave me more problems than the drunks. As long as Lee made it to the Caddy, I knew he was going to be okay. When he got to work, he was professional. The trouble was sweating out whether he was going to make it or not. I remember he'd get in the limo, and you'd throw in a six-pack with him to keep him happy and he'd be fine. He would shout out for Woody, 'Where's my nigger?'—and Woody would show up with a six-pack. Lee would be the only one who could get away with saying stuff like that. Woody loved him dearly."

The company mercifully left Nevada after more than a hundred days and finished filming in the California desert town of Indio. Just as Parslow may have thought being away from Vegas would end his troubles, he encountered another. Marvin's stand-in was his friend Boyd "Ty" Cabeen, a dubious figure in the film industry, who often bragged about stepping in to take punches for Marvin and Robert Mitchum. According to Parslow, "Cabeen was an asshole. He was a parasite, but Lee liked him. Michele hated him. They were eating in a restaurant we were staying at in Indio. We stayed in small motels. It was one of those typical little road-house motels with the pool and stuff. We heard a racket going on in the restaurant. Tyrone and Michele were fighting about something, and he threw his drink in her face. The only thing is he forgot to keep the glass. He wound up breaking her nose."

The film did very well with preview audiences in 1966, and, while most critics praised it, they rarely commented on the advanced age of all the leads playing action heroes, or that an African-American had second billing in the cast. "Oh, if it weren't for Lee Marvin, I wouldn't get billing," stated Woody Strode. Due to his immense popularity, the studio gave Marvin the choice of selecting which actor's opening vignette, after his own, would be seen by the audience; Marvin picked Strode to appear before Lancaster. That one magnanimous gesture helped establish Strode in the world market, and got him steady work in Spaghetti Westerns. "He got me some kind of half-assed billing for *The Professionals*. He was a nice, decent Marine. Pure in heart."

For Marvin, his solid performance as Henry "Rico" Fardan, a leading role in this wildly successful film, built on his growing screen persona. The muscular, well-written production allowed him to demonstrate his unequaled prowess with firearms, substitute gestures for dialogue, and give a rugged new look to the cinematic anti-hero. It also firmly set in place a trend in his work that began with 1964's *The Killers*, which was to continue for more than a decade, during which he would make a string of now classic action films that redefined their various genres. Some were wildly popular upon release, others took time to find an audience, but all of them helped to create the first modern action hero. Void of either sentiment or family, his characters were loners with a past who allowed film audiences to get their "vicaries" watching them pursue a mission or goal with singular purpose. The scenarios found Marvin thrust into violent situations, leaving a trail of blood in his wake, often mingled with his own, by film's end.

Other film stars had dabbled in similar projects and characters of course, and the popular foreign films of the likes of Akira Kurosawa and Sergio Leone had also helped transform film violence. However, only Lee Marvin maintained this persona in his canon of work, thereby cementing the most purposeful and consistent portrayal of man's violent and primal inner demons in the history of modern American cinema.

It was also the beginning of award season in Hollywood for the previous year's films, which added yet more gasoline to the considerable fire of his success. When Marvin was named Best Actor in a Comedy for *Cat Ballou* in February of 1966 at the Golden Globes, he graciously accepted his award and quipped, "Oh—I didn't think it was all THAT funny." Other awards followed, and the goodwill media attention he gained through columnists' write-ups proved Paul Wasserman's prediction: Marvin was nominated for an Academy Award for Best Actor.

Marvin knew that comedy performances rarely, if ever, won Oscars, and his fellow nominees were some of the best actors in the industry. His competition consisted of: Laurence Olivier for *Othello*; Richard Burton for *The Spy Who Came in from the Cold*; Rod Steiger for *The Pawnbroker;* and Marvin's *Ship of Fools* costar, Oskar Werner. Handicapping such competition, Marvin at first said, "Two will get you twenty that I'll win no Oscar. The competition is too stiff, but I'll be there." He then predicted the winner would be Werner, graciously proclaiming, "I want to be in competition with the best. I'm in tremendous company… I think I have a fifty-fifty chance." Four days before the awards show, he said, "The men with whom I'm competing for the Academy Award can all act circles around me, but this is the land of milk and honey. If you have the right gimmick, you're in. I never got out of high school, and here I am making many more times the money the president of the United States makes. It's pretty ridiculous really, but that's how it is."

The night of the Oscars, Marvin had flown in from the London location of *The Dirty Dozen* to fulfill his promise of taking his wife to the awards ceremony, even though by that time they had already separated. However, just a few hours before the show, Lee informed Betty that Michele told him she would commit suicide if he didn't take her instead. Betty recalled with a laugh, "I just said, 'Oh Lee, I think you should reconsider it.' I took the dress, folded it up, and put it away. I put on my sweats or something. It wasn't a big deal to me that I didn't go to the Academy Awards. It was just the whole thing he did was so tacky. A friend called, and I said to him, 'I think I'm going to dress the kids up in something shabby and I'll go in some rags. We'll go down to the Academy Awards, and I'm going to sit inside and have the kids say, 'Hi Daddy!' My friend said, 'You wouldn't do that.' I said, 'Oh, I don't know. I probably could…'"

Betty graciously changed her mind, and Lee sat nervously chain-smoking, and hiding the cigarette under Triola's dress during the ceremony. To ease his tension, he leaned over to fellow nominee Rod Steiger, and whispered that, if Steiger won, he would trip him on the way to the stage. When Julie Andrews announced the nominees for Best Actor, Meyer Mishkin recalled, "Lee was on the aisle. I was next to him, and then Michele, and then my wife. So, he's sitting on the aisle, they announce the winner is Lee Marvin. He gets up and buttons his jacket. He always had an attitude with it. He buttons his jacket, and says to me, 'I love you, you cocksucker.' I said to him, 'Go get it!'"

He came to the stage to the largest applause of the evening. Tears welled up in his eyes, and when the applause had died down, he composed himself and famously said, "Thank you, thank you all, very much. I don't want to take up too much of your time. There are too many people to correctly thank for my career. I think, though, half of this belongs to a horse, someplace out in the Valley. Thank you." After his acceptance, he left the stage, got to a phone, and immediately called Betty to thank her for all that she had done for his career. He tried calling his father, but Robert answered and told him that, though Monte had watched the acceptance on TV, he refused to come to the phone when he saw that it was Michele and not Betty in the audience.

Backstage, Marvin fielded the usual harangue of questions from the Hollywood press corps as cameras flashed and fellow Oscar winners congratulated each other.

"He certainly didn't act like that tough, hard-drinking character of *Cat Ballou*, because he cried more backstage than Shelley Winters," wrote columnist Sheila Graham. "I asked him if he thought the award would change his life, and he said, 'Hell, yes, I'm not Superman.'" In the limo on the way to the after-party, Meyer was able to get Monte on the phone, who told his son how proud he was of him. At a red light Marvin then saw Rod Steiger in the car next to him, hunched over in the backseat and apparently crying. Marvin tapped the glass, and when Steiger made eye contact, he held up his Oscar and beamed a smile.

The next morning, a slightly hung-over Marvin was photographed at LAX on his way back to London receiving the impromptu surprise of a bridal bouquet of flowers from his best friend Keenan Wynn.

By the time Marvin had landed at Heathrow, he'd missed a good deal of the hubbub over his acceptance speech. Asked if he was bothered by the speech, director Elliot Silverstein said, "Yes and no. Yes, because everybody likes some acknowledgment. Frank Pierson was very upset by Lee's statement. He said, 'The only half of the horse not represented that night was the head.'

"No, because Lee did what he had to do. We worked professionally, and he was not a person for love, hugs, and kisses. I guess I wasn't either. There's a whole lot of that that goes on in the filmmaking world: 'Oh, I couldn't have done it without you...' The fact is, he may have been able to do it without me. I may have been able to do it without him. I don't know. The only thing I contributed, I think, was standing up for him when the chips were down. Not because I loved him, but because I thought he was right for the part and would deliver it."

Over the years, talk would arise about a possible sequel to *Cat Ballou*. There were two 1971 TV-movie pilots, one with Jack Elam and the other with Forrest Tucker. Silverstein remembers meeting Marvin at a party and mentioning a sequel: "I was willing to try it, and Lee mumbled something that's still not clear to me. He said something like, 'Ahh, mumble, mumble, CAREER!' I think he was trying to say he wanted to broaden his career and not simply repeat. I think that's what it was."

Back at work on the early stages of production on *The Dirty Dozen*, Lee Marvin received hearty congratulations from the all-star cast and director Robert Aldrich. The World War II film featured Marvin as maverick Major John Reisman, chosen to train a group of violent and condemned military prisoners for a suicide mission behind enemy lines the night before the D-Day invasion. The almost all-male cast consisted of actors who either had starred, or would soon star in their own films. Charles Bronson, Ernest Borgnine, John Cassavetes, Robert Ryan, Telly Savalas, George Kennedy, Jim Brown, Robert Webber, Richard Jaeckel, Ralph Meeker, Donald Sutherland, Clint Walker, and Trini Lopez, all played in support of Lee Marvin's leading performance.

Marvin had worked with many of the actors previously, and got along well with both the cast and director. Aldrich however, was not always in the best of moods during the shoot since he was not allowed to use his regular crew. "Well, the English government wouldn't allow American crews to work in England," stated Joe Biroc, Aldrich's veteran cinematographer who was replaced by England's Edward Scaife. "Aldrich hated it. They were very, very slow. Bob didn't work that way. He was used to doing a lot of shots in a day when they only did two or three. He was glad to get out of there."

It being England, the weather did not always cooperate for Aldrich either, and Marvin could be found at the nearest pub on more than one rained-out occasion. His partner in crime this time was former Chicago detective Bob Phillips, who had a small role in the film as Corporal Morgan. The two ex-Marines frequented many of the local watering holes, and Phillips recalled one particular night in which disaster was barely averted. They had been drinking and winning at darts all night, angering the locals, but earning the affection of the bartender, a sixty-year-old, six-foot tall, brunette beehive-wig wearing Lee Marvin fan whom Phillips had dubbed "Black Helen."

When a patron started removing the darts from the board while Marvin was still playing, one landed in the man's coat between his shoulder blades. A voice then immediately rang out, "The Yank stabbed me mate!" The owner of the voice was taller than Marvin and huskier than Phillips, and proceeded to advance on the duo. "Lee swings with a John Wayne roundhouse right. Lee missed him by three feet. Not that the guy ducked or anything. Lee sailed over right behind him. I went in and I hit that son-of-a-bitch right, and he went down and out. Lee stands up, and he looks down at the guy. 'Anybody else? Who's next?' Honest to god, in his best passionate style. Well, here comes about five or six of them. Boy, out of nowhere, with her beehive, is 'Black Helen.' Nobody's going to punch out Lee. She saved our ass. I grabbed Lee and I said, 'Let's get out of here.' He said, 'What about our drinks?' He's worried about the drinks!" Thanks to Helen, they were able to beat a hasty retreat, and make it back to their hotel unscathed.

Marvin and Phillips appeared on the set each day ready to work despite such adventures the night before. Phillips also bonded with Marvin through their mutual war experiences and their schoolboy antics. "Bob Aldrich used to always say 'Zabba, zabba, zabba,' about a scene," recalled Phillips. "Then he'd shoot it and say, 'That's a thing of beauty. Print it. Next shot.' We'd imitate him when he wasn't on the set. Lee and I would talk, 'Zabba, zabba.' One of those kids playing one of the *Dozen* would walk up, and we'd say, 'We're running lines.' We'd always catch somebody with that."

They also took to playfully calling Charles Bronson "Charlie Sunshine," due to his often dour disposition. Years later, Marvin recalled about his frequent costar, "He wants to intimidate you, but there's a little gleam way back behind the eyes, if you can see it. We were sitting in London once in a very posh club, wearing black suits, talking to a girl. Charlie says, 'Yeah, sweetheart, it's tough lying on your side in a coal mine.' I said, 'Jesus, Charlie. You ain't been in a coal mine in thirty years. You drive around in a Rolls Royce...'"

Lisa Ryan, daughter of actor Robert Ryan, remembers her father would often laugh to himself and mutter, "What a character," whenever Marvin's name was mentioned. She discovered what he meant when visiting the London set one morning: "I was just standing around, and then Lee Marvin just sort of walked over to me and was sort of leaning over me. He seemed drunk, and I knew who he was. I was just sort of like, 'Ooo, Lee Marvin!' He was like, 'Oh, what are you doing here?' I mainly remember that he was kind of listing toward me. I wasn't upset or anything. I thought it was really cool that I was standing there, talking to Lee Marvin. The next thing I remember is my dad came marching over and said, 'Lee! That's my daughter!' I remember, he literally jumped backwards. I mean it really was like he got zapped with a cattle prod or something. He just jumped backwards and kind of stumbled away. That was the end of it. I don't recall anything unpleasant. I think it was funny. I think maybe my dad thought it was funny, too."

Costar Clint Walker remembers the experience of working with Marvin as a pleasant one, stating: "Lee's a pro. Sometimes there's a problem that'll pop up that you simply don't anticipate. Maybe the gate on the compound fence swings the wrong way, so you got to change a scene a little bit, or something. Other than that, like I say, Lee always knew his lines. I think there were a few times he may have suggested something to Bob Aldrich. I think for the most part, Bob went along with it. Don't forget, Lee had a military background. He was right at home with what he was doing... I think everybody had a great deal of respect for Lee. Usually what he did or said made sense. I can't even remember any problems or friction or any real difference of opinion... I think everybody got along quite well."

Walker's major scene in the film had Marvin's character taunting him to lose his temper and stab Reisman with a knife. Walker recalls: "I had cut my finger the night before fixing a chicken for my supper. I had to go to the hospital. I think it took about five stitches in my right thumb." As Aldrich explained to Walker how the scene would work, "He grabbed my thumb instead of my hand. He started leading me around by it and Lee starts tapping Bob on the shoulder and saying, 'Um, Bob...' Bob kept on going and he said, [louder] 'Bob!' He said it a third time, and Bob stopped and said, 'What do you want, Lee?' Lee says, 'Let go of Clint's thumb.' Bob looked and said, 'Why?' Lee said, 'Because he cut it last night and he had five stitches taken in it.' Bob said, 'Oh!,' let go, and then started laughing. That was the beginning of the scene. So as you can see, Lee certainly had a consideration for his fellow man."

Production finally drew to an end, but not before Marvin was approached on set by an enthusiastic young British filmmaker by the name of John Boorman, interested in making a film with his favorite American actor. Boorman discussed his idea for the film *Point Blank* with Marvin and found a receptive audience. They maintained contact with each other after Marvin returned home to southern California and worked out the details.

Marvin, in the meantime, hosted and narrated a TV documentary that utilized rare color footage of the Marines in WWII, titled "Our Time in Hell." After it aired, Democratic California Representative James C. Cameron paid tribute to Marvin as part of the Congressional record, "As a patriotic American who is donating his entire fee for this narration to the Marine Corps Civic Action Fund, which is currently being used to rehabilitate civilian victims of Vietcong attacks."

By 1967, Lee Marvin was soaring high in the rarified air of film stardom. Since he never had done things in the usual way in his career, being in the driver's seat proved no different. According to Boorman, Marvin dispensed with the usual protocol and set up a meeting himself with him, that also included several producers, the head of MGM, and Meyer Mishkin to work out the details of *Point Blank*. The way Boorman recalled the meeting was that, "Marvin asked: 'I have script approval?' They agreed. 'I have cast approval?' 'Yes.' 'Approval of technicians?' 'Yes.' For the first time in his career, he had assumed the heady powers of superstar. Rising to leave, he lobbed the grenade in their midst. 'I defer all these approvals to John.'" Marvin's characteristic gesture allowed Boorman to state, "Making my first picture in Hollywood, I was fortunate enough to have the gift of freedom. And he backed me all the way with a belief and loyalty that was inspiring."

Based on the 1962 novel *The Hunter* by Donald E. Westlake (writing under the pen name Richard Stark), *Point Blank* is a modern noir thriller in which Marvin's character, Walker, is double-crossed by his wife and best friend, and then left for dead before the opening credits. What follows is a highly stylized tale of Walker's systematic attempts to get back the money that is owed him as he battles his way through the hierarchy of the Los Angeles crime syndicate. The only help he gets is from his ex-wife's sister, played by Angie Dickinson, and Keenan Wynn as a mysterious stranger known only as Yost.

Dickinson noted a distinct contrast from her previous outings with Marvin. "*The Killers* had a different situation already," she stated. "It was not a friendly atmosphere because of all of our grief [over JFK] so you can't really judge anything accurately... It [*Point Blank*] was concentrated. They were constantly working on the script, he and Boorman. I don't want to say it was strained, but it was constantly challenging. So, between Boorman's great ideas and of course the genius of Lee Marvin, I wasn't privy to what they were struggling about."

The challenge was to create a unique vision of noir, a sort of art-house action film. According to Boorman, Marvin rose to the challenge: "He was endlessly inventive, constantly devising ways to externalize what we wanted to express. He taught me how actors must relate to other actors, objects, settings, compositions, movements. He has a dynamic relationship with the camera, a knowledge of its capacity to penetrate scenes and find their truth."

The axiom of art imitating life was certainly borne out during the filming of *Point Blank*. Several of the scenes in the film seemed drawn from Marvin's personal experiences such as Walker's wife's suicide, which mirrored Michele Triola's attempt to take her own life. The film's opening scene, when John Vernon's character of Mal desperately entreats the drunken Walker to help him out of a financial jam, also parallels a similar real-life experience for Marvin. At the Malibu bar known as The Raft, bartender Ralph O'Hara struck up a friendship with the actor and witnessed the event himself. "Lee was having one of these anxiety attacks from being in the Marines, and he got to drinking and…he got juiced. This guy, [a friend from San Francisco] puts him there in the bar. Lee was laying there on the ground, and this guy was saying, 'You got to loan me the money!' So, Lee give[s] him a check for $9,000 and he [the guy] never paid him back."

O'Hara observed something else during the making of the film in the chemistry between Marvin and Dickinson. "He felt the world of her. He really liked her, and I'm sure she did the same. On *Point Blank*, when we were down at The Raft, she couldn't take her eyes off him. There's something about people that you could see, that no matter how you're trying to hit on that woman yourself, or someone else's, they're not even listening to what you have to say…"

Asked about this, Dickinson acknowledged, "Well, I'm very flattered by that. On *Point Blank* we did have an eye thing… Oh, it was wonderful! But as I say, Lee never made any kind of move of any kind; emotional, physical, or anything towards me that would make me think he was ever interested in me… I would say if you asked me, 'Do you think Lee digs you?' I would probably have said at the time, 'No, I don't think so.' If he did, I wasn't aware… My guess would be that from him, a look would be comparable to a pass from somebody else. Again, so hard to read Lee." Had he been less shy in her presence, who can say where it may have gone.

Another bizarre moment when events in the film and his own life seemed to intersect, and which further resonated for the character he was portraying, occurred when Carroll O'Connor came to shoot his scene. Unbeknownst to Marvin, O'Connor and his wife Nancy had become good friends with Lee's estranged wife. "So, Carroll said to Lee during the film, that he was looking for a house to buy," recalled Betty. "Lee said, 'I think my house is for sale. You should see it. It's a wonderful house.' Carroll said, 'I know your house very well.' Lee said, 'You do?' And he said, 'Betty and I are good friends.' He said, 'You are?' Carroll said, 'Absolutely.' That seemed to be the end of their communication." Just as Walker's life had seemingly gone on without him, so too had Lee Marvin's.

A few years before his death, Marvin ruminated on these parallels between art and reality: "I saw *Point Blank* at a film festival a year or so ago and I was absolutely shocked. I'd forgotten. It was a rough film. The prototype. You've seen it a thousand times since in other forms. That was a troubled time for me, too, in my own personal relationship, so I used an awful lot of that while making the picture, even the suicide of my wife."

As he had succeeded in doing with 1965's dual release of *Ship Of Fools* and *Cat Ballou*, film audiences of 1967 also got a double shot of Lee Marvin with the releases of *The Dirty Dozen* and *Point Blank* coming just two months apart. The box-office returns for *The Dirty Dozen* surpassed even the most generous estimates. It became the highest grossing film of the year, the sixth highest in MGM's history, and made Marvin the number one male film star in America. The violent WWII-era action film remains one of the most popular of its kind, spawning a cottage industry of both sequels and thinly veiled rip-offs. Even though the demographic of film audiences of the day was considerably younger than

Marvin, the film struck a chord with the youth market in its depiction of social outcasts. Marvin's character, Reisman, brashly conflicting with the authoritative establishment, reflected the younger generation's growing disenchantment with the U.S. military.

It is worth noting that John Wayne understandably had turned down the film when he was offered Marvin's role. Neither Wayne, nor his loyal fans could possibly imagine seeing The Duke do some of the things Reisman and his men perpetrate by the climax of the film. Wayne could be violent, but not to the extent as Lee Marvin, who sought to give his fans their "vicaries" by incinerating countless Nazis locked in a bomb shelter. Aldrich reportedly fought the studio to keep the scene in the film, which may have cost the director a possible Oscar nomination. But, regardless, the film did finally receive four nominations, including one for John Cassavetes as Best Supporting Actor.

The movie *Bonnie & Clyde*, released later the same year, proved to be even more violent, and resulted in the early retirement of *New York Times* film critic Bosley Crowther, who had refused to write a retraction of his review condemning the graphic gangster film. Producer and star Warren Beatty loved the free publicity, which would not have been possible without *The Dirty Dozen* having paved the way first. Crowther usually liked Marvin's films, often comparing him to Bogart, but, though he condemned *Dozen*'s ultra-violence, his critique had little effect on its box office appeal. When *Bonnie & Clyde* followed the next month, the stage was set for Crowther's ire to peak, which precipitated the end of his career with *The Times*.

The release of *Point Blank* took another path to success. Largely overlooked at first, it has since become one of the most influential cult films ever made. This is due in part to the enigmatic, surreal style that was just slightly ahead of its time, as well as Marvin's haunting portrayal of the emotionally hollow, psychopathic Walker whose single-mindedness of purpose and almost robotic, killing-machine persona, set against the alienating landscape of modern Los Angeles, has inspired many revenge-themed films ever since. The movie itself has also been remade several times, most recently with Mel Gibson in 1999's *Payback*. That film's ad line was "Get ready to cheer for the bad guy!" Lee Marvin fans had clearly learned to do that a long time before.

A remake was surely something the actor had in mind when he called Betty into the bedroom during one of their several reconciliations. After countless drunken mishaps, car accidents (Marvin's license had been revoked for a good part of the year), infidelities, and screaming matches, Betty recalled, "We sit down in the master bedroom. He's there and I'm here. I said, 'What is it, Lee?' He said, 'Well Betty, this is nothing personal, but I don't want to be married anymore.' Is that a great line? *Nothing personal.* I said, 'I wish you would have told me this four children ago.'"

CHAPTER 11

"I Ain't Spittin' on My Whole Life"

A MERICAN FILMS of the late 60s and early 70s emphasized themes of sexuality, violence and realism more intensely than ever before. Young filmmakers and stars of this new Hollywood were clearly rebelling against the way films had been made previously, and it became a struggle for some postwar male stars to find projects worthy of their talent. The middle-aged Lee Marvin was luckier than many of his contemporaries, making some of his best films during this period. At the time they were cast aside by "The New Hollywood" and youth-oriented audience, but in recent years technology has allowed these films to be rediscovered by a whole new generation of filmgoers.

Following his divorce from Betty in January of 1967, the actor's attempt to simplify his personal life with bachelorhood was complicated by the presence of Michele Triola. He often vacillated between entreaties to his ex-wife, truces with Triola, and occasionally taking advantage of his newfound celebrity in ways his previous status as a feature player never could. While filming *The Dirty Dozen* in 1966, for example, he invited both his soon-to-be-ex-wife and his live-in girlfriend to London, but spent most of his time hanging out with his costars.

Actor and costar Bob Phillips recalled another aspect of Marvin's use of his celebrity power: "A female reporter from New York came to the London set to interview Marvin. She was over six feet tall, and asked embarrassing questions about his marriage. Marvin told me, 'Watch me get her.' Later that night, I come to meet Marvin in his limo. When I opened the door, the reporter was on her knees blowing Marvin who just had an 'I-told-you-so' smile on his face."

When he was home in southern California, he and Michele cohabited on his Malibu beach property not too far from where Betty lived. "He didn't have a place to live so, what I did, I had his power of attorney, and I bought him a house in Malibu on the sand," recalled business manager Ed Silver. "What I paid for it was seventy-two thousand, five hundred, and it was furnished! He lived there until he moved to Tucson. It was on Pacific Coast Highway. His neighbors were Lloyd Bridges and Ryan O'Neal. It was a damned good house. Burgess Meredith lived a couple of houses down. It went from the highway to the sand…"

Another means by which Marvin was able to leverage his celebrity status lay in his ability to nurture promising movie projects, a case in point being *The Wild Bunch*. In this instance, over the course of several months, he had been helping a friend named Roy Sickner write the screenplay, and had then passed the finished treatment on to friend and Malibu neighbor, Sam Peckinpah. Revisions on the gritty western continued for some time, however, forcing Marvin to look elsewhere.

Although offers were plentiful, the actor's expectations were set extremely high when it came to evaluating scripts; he would only read those that he felt were worthy of his time, and that he believed would result in projects in which he would not be repeating himself artistically. Publicist Paul Wasserman recalled, "I don't know if I remember it correctly… but [Lee] would always look for the thing in the character that reminded him of himself. That he was aware of the feelings or experience that he shared."

He turned down more films than he accepted, and without regret, even after they were bona fide hits, such as was the case with *Patton*. Marvin had his own unorthodox method of choosing projects. "He's one of the very few stars that would bring a bunch of scripts that was sent to him, to his agent to read," stated Mishkin associate Don Gurler. "Usually, the agent gets it and calls up to say, 'Lee, I'll messenger this stuff over to you.' He didn't read anything until Meyer got it all. He'd come into the office with a bunch of scripts. Stars didn't do that."

Although his last film, *Point Blank*, did not find a responsive audience until somewhat later, the experience of working with John Boorman had been so rewarding for Marvin, he was willing to listen to the director's idea for a new film. The subject intrigued Marvin, but another aspect proved even more enticing. Marvin admired only a handful of other actors, and the one that towered above all was Japan's Toshiro Mifune.

When Marvin was first married, "Lee and I always, from the beginning, would see Japanese films," recalled Betty. "He loved Toshiro Mifune so much. He used to call him on the phone. Couldn't understand a word of Japanese. Mifune spoke no English. It was just a joke. They'd have these long conversations, about what? He just adored him." Marvin himself expressed his admiration for Mifune by glowing, "This guy hypnotizes you with his genius. Those eyes! The battered samurai warrior standing alone, not wanting outside help."

Boorman's project was *Hell in the Pacific*, an allegory in which Marvin is cast as an unnamed American pilot and Mifune as a similarly anonymous Japanese soldier, stranded together on an island during WWII. Marvin was sold on the concept in spite of the unfinished script. Mishkin negotiated the actor's fee at three quarters of a million against ten percent of the gross, setting the stage for the on-location project to begin with an international crew.

The promising concept proved to be extremely difficult to film with its problematic location shooting in Micronesia and a multinational crew further hampered by language and cultural conflicts. According to Marvin, the problems within the film mirrored the problems of the filming: "It all paralleled beautifully. The more tense things became between us all, the more tense the plot was supposed to be getting. Let me tell you, the plot got pretty rough."

As the tension increased, so too did the problems of language, culture, living accommodations, and more. Marvin lost almost twenty pounds during the film and it showed in the final product. Although communication was strained, the one constant throughout remained Marvin's admiration for his costar. "Mifune is beyond professionalism, he's even better than that. What he did off the set was his own business and I won't discuss that. I admire his talent and abilities tremendously… Let's just say Mifune was displeased, and that we were all fed up with living on a ship… Oh yes, and Mifune had his troubles with the director, too. I kept out of that, even tried to make the peace a couple of times."

Mifune had his own concept of how the film should play out, having deep-rooted feelings about the war. Like his costar, Mifune had been in the war, but as a petty officer for seven years, the last few spent giving ritualistic sake to Kamikaze pilots. At one point during the film, Marvin and Mifune both visited the battleground of nearby Peleliu, laying wreaths in memory of the dead. Later, Mifune solemnly told a visiting reporter, "Those who died, if they were still alive, they would be the same age as Lee here and myself. Their deaths were useless. It is hard for me to explain how I feel about the bones in the caves, in the jungle, along Orange Beach. How wasted…"

According to Meyer Mishkin, the film opened successfully in Tokyo. He remembered the night of the premiere as one of the last times he had ever got truly drunk. Mifune had invited him and Marvin to his home for dinner and kept the sake flowing all night. "We had a limo that we had come in from the hotel," recalled the smiling Mishkin. "When we got back to the hotel, Lee Marvin stepped out of the limo and disappeared. We did not see him until the following night. We don't know where he went. He was not at the hotel. When we did see him again, he was surrounded by Japanese fans saying to him, 'Oh, wonderful male! Great actor!' and so forth."

Mishkin proudly framed a letter from the trip that he had translated, and hung on his living room wall. It read: "Mr. Meyer Mishkin; Seeing your truly happy, smiling face has blown away all the hardship and unhappy moments we had in our work. I sincerely appreciated your calling Lee Marvin, the drunken Santa Claus, for the great reception party. I sincerely hope I can do the next work in Japan with you two. Toshiro Mifune."

The film was less favorably received in Marvin's native land, however. The allegorical style and ambiguous ending left American audiences scratching their heads. Friend L.Q. Jones recalled, "They released it during the Christmas weekend in Westwood. For some reason, I was over there and talking to the manager and some of the ticket takers. I asked him how it was, and he said, 'You can't believe this disaster. You can not believe it. We don't get sixteen people a day.' It was the wrong timing for the picture. It's a strange picture anyway. During the holiday season, who's going to go see *Hell in the Pacific*?"

The box office failure and mixed reviews greatly disappointed Marvin, who felt the film expressed much of his own sentiments concerning war. He later claimed that he would never work that hard again, despite how much he personally liked the finished product. When a friend told Marvin that his fans were disappointed by the film's lack of violence, the actor snarled, "Screw'em. Let'em do their own killing!"

What Marvin planned to do next looked to be his most impressive endeavor yet. Old friend and sometimes-drinking rival Sam Peckinpah was preparing *The Wild Bunch*, and Marvin definitely wanted in. A series of memos from producers Phil Feldman to producer Ken Hyman illustrate how desperately they too wanted Marvin to play the lead.

August 30, 1967: "A friend of Lee Marvin's called Roy Sickner wrote a story some time ago which Lee Marvin wants to do. Sam subsequently collaborated on a screenplay based on the property and in his recent conversations with Lee it was brought up again. Sam tells me he spent several hours with Lee just the other day on it... Meyer is aware of *The Wild Bunch* and is not in favor of Lee doing another 'violent' picture... Meyer would like to get him in a romantic lead at this time... My own feelings on *The Wild Bunch*, now having read it is that's it's a 'gasser.' It needs changes that Sam and I have discussed and I think if you have time to look at it, it will prove to be the kind of picture with Lee Marvin that you would be most sympathetic with."

September, 12, 1967: "Marvin suggests that you and I and Sam meet with Mishkin, who, as I advised you is not in favor of *The Wild Bunch*, explains the facts of Marvin's desire to do it and make a deal. Marvin does not want to be present but will advise Mishkin that he wants to deal... Sam is of course pre-approved by Lee as director and writer..."

December 5, 1967: "I have been advised among other things by Meyer Mishkin that Lee Marvin has accepted the *Paint Your Wagon* book... that makes him totally unavailable in the year 1968..."

In signing instead to do *Paint Your Wagon,* based on the 1951 stage musical, Marvin had earned his first million-dollar payday. Paramount had hoped it would repeat the success of *The Sound of Music.* This might have been the case had not Alan Jay Lerner tinkered with the script by Paddy Chayefsky that Marvin read and loved, or had not the manic-depressive director, Joshua Logan, skewered the production. In a misguided effort to seem relevant, the musical numbers were wrapped around a new plot of 19th century California gold miners involved in a menage-a-trois of Marvin and costars Clint Eastwood and Jean Seberg, who were both paid considerably less than he.

Filmed in rustic Baker, Oregon, the overblown production became a standard-bearer for out-of-control Hollywood. The chaos began to escalate when Chayefsky butted heads with Lerner over the script. Chayefsky quit, had his credit changed to adaptation, and later fumed, "I don't think there were six pages of mine left in the whole picture. A couple of ideas of mine are left, but barely recognizable."

When filming began in Oregon during the summer of 1968, things became progressively worse. The fifteen million-dollar budget quickly went to nineteen million as Lerner tried to wrangle control from Logan for ruining his picture, and Logan accused Lerner of pretty much the same thing. A cast of more than two hundred, as well as animals of every shape and size, converged along with transient hippies, bikers, groupies, and lumberjacks on the location that had turned into an unmanageable three-ring circus. Unsavory characters, such as Dr. Max "Feelgood" Jacobson, were seen lurking about, and daily stories persisted in the trades that Richard Brooks was on standby to take over the reins from Logan. Through it all, when the production was at its maddest, Lee Marvin simply found the nearest establishment that served any available libation.

"I saw what happened there," stated Tony Epper. Epper, officially hired as a stunt man, worked unofficially with Marvin to rehearse his singing and watch over him when he traversed the watering holes. "I saw them shut the company down for a week, waiting for some ponies to come from France. They also built realistic sets they wound up not even photographing… Over it all was the fear of Josh Logan. They never knew which way he was going to go. As I think back on it now, he was totally unprepared in a lot of ways."

When *Paint Your Wagon* finally wrapped, post-production kept the film from general release until October 1969. In April, Marvin accepted an invitation to receive an honorary Doctor of Fine Arts Degree from St. Leo, along with several other luminaries. Accompanied by both Michele Triola and his ailing father, he met and reminisced with old schoolmates, and was introduced by his former teacher, Fr. James Hoge, who recalled, "He and I were standing there by the microphone. I mentioned that, 'I taught Lee in his high school classes and I have to say that he was not the best I ever had, nor was he the worst. He was the damnedest student I ever had!' It got a roar of applause from the people. When I said that, Lee sort of ducked as if I was going to attack him or something. You know, as a student would do if the teacher were wielding a rod. He was a great actor."

Back in California, the biggest buzz in Hollywood concerned *The Wild Bunch*. Peckinpah biographer David Weddle recalled, "They had a screening at Warners and Marvin was invited. He showed up totally bombed. During the film he's shouting out stuff: 'More blood!'; 'Aw, c'mon, kill'em some more, Sam!' One person even said he was crawling down the aisles saying things. Someone finally said, 'Shut up, Lee!'

"They went to dinner afterward, and Sam's sister Fern Lea was there with her husband, Walter Peters. She said she took one look in Marvin's eyes and she was petrified. He sat down opposite her with Walter Peters sitting right there and he looked at Walter Peters and said, 'So, is this your cunt?' She got up and went over to sit next to Sam. She said, 'Sam, you know…' He said, 'I know, I know. Just leave him alone.' They ignored Marvin and he finally left. About a week or two later, they went to some other gathering and Marvin showed up sober this time, totally different guy. He had iced tea or something. He's standing next to Fern Lea and he said, 'I'm drinking iced tea tonight because people don't seem to like me when I'm drunk.' Fern Lea said, 'That's right, and I'm one of them.' He didn't say anything."

Marvin never publicly claimed disappointment in not starring in the film that remains one of the greatest American films ever made. Instead, he said, "[Sam] approached me about doin' *The Wild Bunch*. Shit, I'd helped write the original goddamn script, which Sam eventually bought and rewrote. Well, I mean I didn't do any of the actual writing, but I talked it out with these guys who were writin' it, Walon Green and Roy Sickner. Sam said, 'Well geez, aren't you even interested?' I told him I'd already done *The Professionals*, and what did I need *The Wild Bunch* for? And when the picture came out, I don't think it really succeeded. It didn't have the—I mean, it had all the action and all the blood and all that shit, but it didn't have the ultimate kavoom, you know? It didn't have the one-eye-slowly-opening aspect it should've had."

Paint Your Wagon premiered in October to scathing reviews. In time it turned a small profit and, other than Lee's lack of singing ability, the remarks aimed at Marvin were not that bad. In fact, he managed to give a perceptive and enjoyable performance when Chayefsky's surviving dialogue allowed Marvin's character to pontificate on the state of the world and his place in it. Marvin received a Golden Globe nomination for his performance and when his song "Wanderin' Star" was released as a single in the U.K., it knocked The Beatles out of first place in the charts. The critic David Denby may have summed it up best when he wrote, "Lee Marvin is a superb physical actor and a much more interesting one than Clint Eastwood. That long face with its great, heavy warlord's brow, sardonic eyes, and huge snout, is a movie all in itself, both funny and threatening. The voice is a rich actor's bass, gravelly and black, yet with a surprising lilt that makes the simplest line vibrate with insinuation."

Marvin was already in the midst of his next project when *Paint Your Wagon* was playing in theaters. It was another change of pace for the actor who specialized in films of graphic violence. *Monte Walsh* was based on a lesser known novel by *Shane* author Jack Schaefer, an elegiac tale with Marvin as the title character, who along with his cohort Chet Rollins—played by Jack Palance in a rare sympathetic performance—must confront the stark reality that their cowboy days have come to an end. As Rollins poignantly tells Walsh, "Nobody gets to be a cowboy forever,

Monte."

Officially credited as an actor, Marvin was more involved in the production than on any other film of his career. He met with producers, suggested actors, and even convinced William Fraker to make his directorial debut. Fraker, a multi Oscar-nominated cinematographer, had also worked on *The Professionals* and *Paint Your Wagon*. It would also be the first time in which Marvin would have a true romantic interest in a film, something he had wanted as far back as 1962, stating, "I would love to do love scenes. In fact, I don't have a friend who doesn't love them. Maybe I'm not fascinated by death any more. I think life is much more interesting and love is one of the most beauteous forms of life. I play what I hate. Now I'd like to play what I love." Producers Bobby Roberts and Hal Landers suggested Deborah Kerr to play Marvin's romantic interest. Instead, Fraker and Marvin flew to Paris and convinced French film icon Jeanne Moreau to help Marvin play what he loved. The rest of the cast was made up of such veteran western regulars as Jim Davis, G.D. Spradlin, John 'Bear' Hudkins, Ray Guth, Matt Clark, Billy Green Bush, and Bo Hopkins.

For the pivotal role of 'Shorty Austin,' a character who starts out as a protagonist but inadvertently becomes an antagonist, the producers and director approached Mitch Ryan, having been impressed by his stage performance in O'Neill's "A Moon For the Misbegotten." Ryan had first appeared in Robert Mitchum's 1959 cult film *Thunder Road* but had not been in a film since. Marvin not only approved of the choice, he stood by Ryan when the producers raised concerns over Ryan's admitted drinking problem.

Ryan first met Marvin and Palance in a meeting prior to production, which he recalled with a laugh, "It was really very strange. The first thing Lee said after I came in was, 'What's the story with this Eugene O'Neill? I mean what's his problem?' And Jack said, 'What the fuck kind of talk is that? Jesus Christ! Welcome, Mitch, come in.' Then Lee said, 'Oh shit, tell us about *Shane*, Jack. That was your last big hit, wasn't it?' So, it was like that. They were great and then Michele came in with Fraker. She angrily said, to Lee, 'I thought you weren't going to drink today.' He was drinking a beer. He said, 'Mitch, this is Bill Fraker, the director, and this is Michele, the cunt.' This is my initiation to Lee. Then after that, everybody left except Lee, and he and I had a nice chat about acting."

Once Ryan got past Marvin's verbose veneer, the two became fast friends. "One of the other things he did was when we first got there," recalled Ryan, "we all went to the wardrobe, and he very meticulously picked out a hat, that great hat he wore. He must have gone through ten hats until he found the one he really liked. Then the kerchief that he wore, and the chaps, he went over those." Ryan also took note of Marvin's attention to detail: "Well, he knew really who the guy was. I mean he really knew. He'd say, 'The way I needle Jack, is exactly the way these two characters in *Monte Walsh* should behave with each other.' So he would bring all that on, but he never let on anything like it was acting. Jack was really funny because he sort of took it rather well, but he also didn't like it a lot. He wasn't about to show that it was getting to him."

Western film historian Neil Summers worked on the film, and was also impressed. "Lee Marvin was not a tough guy acting like a tough guy. Lee Marvin *was* a tough guy. He didn't take any garbage off of directors, fellow players, big guys like Jack Palance, or anything. He was well respected and people trod easy around him. He was a hell of a guy." Summers also noted Fraker's ingenuity on the Tucson location. "Lee's drinking was legendary, but it didn't necessarily inhibit his work. There was one shot they had been trying to get for weeks. The director wanted to get a sunset shot, but because of Lee's work habits, keeping him around that late to get a sunset shot usually didn't work… So, they gave him a 3:00 a.m. call to get him out there for a sunrise shot, which would be used as a sunset shot. I remember that vividly because we all had to get up at 3:00 in the morning."

Jack Palance, Marvin's frequent costar, recalled, "I remember one time we were in some restaurant and waiting at the bar for a table. A producer walked in with his family and saw me. Lee was on the other side and wasn't able to be seen right away. The producer fellow wanted to talk to me and walked up to greet me. When I leaned out of the way to introduce Lee, the producer had a look of horror on his face. He turned to his wife and said, 'It's Lee Marvin! Get the children out of here!'"

The cast and crew were very aware that the project they were

Monte Marvin (above) in his W.W.I uniform. (Below) Lee (left), mother Courtenay (center), and brother Robert (right) enjoying a late summer day in Woodstock, New York.

Ross Marvin (above), Lee Marvin's great uncle, in full Arctic regalia prior to his ill-fated polar expedition with Adm. Peary. Baby Lee (below) wagging his tongue as he would later in many villainous roles.

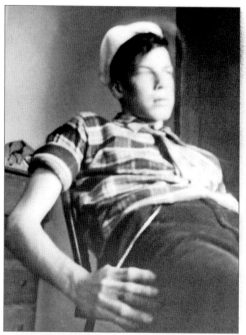

(Top left) Young Lee attending upstate New York's experimental Manumit School in 1937, the sense of abandonment writ large on his face.

(Above right) Lee, on the far right, treks through the swamps of Florida with several fellow adventurers.

(Left) A gangly, teen-aged Lee, nicknamed "Dogface" by his peers, under a palm tree on campus at St. Leo's School for Boys in Lakeland, Florida in 1940.

U. S. MARINE CORPS
Identification Card

MARVIN, LEE (n)
Name

Signature

Color Hair BROWN Eyes GRAY
Weight 180 Birth 19 FEB 24
Void after INDEFINITE

T.R. HISE Capt Phm (jg) USN
Validating Officer

(Above) Monte and Courtenay visit
with their son, Pfc. Marvin, following
his completion of both basic and Marine
combat training which were expedited for
the war. Note the sharpshooter pin on his
breast pocket.

(Left) Marvin sporting a mustache for his
USMC identification card, on the back
of which he had penciled in a girl's phone
number.

(Above) Lee shares a bottle with several friends while stationed at California's Camp Pendleton in May, 1943. On the back he simply wrote, "Tucker, myself, Millinich, Hodges, Maffesoli. A few of the boys in my platoon."

(Left) The logo of the 4th Marine Division attached to the 24th Marines and activated Stateside specifically for action in the Pacific. The Division suffered a total of 17,722 battle casualties during the four assault landings on Roi-Namur, Saipan, Tinian, and Iwo Jima.

(Below) Lee and fellow Marine Wade Rayborn pose with some of the Japanese armaments captured in battle.

Memorial Day . . 1946
Ulster Detachment, Marine Corps League

(Top) The telegram sent to Lee's parents after he was wounded on Saipan.

(Above) Probably the last time he wore his dress uniform, Lee is shown marching (at front) in the traditional Memorial Day Parade in Woodstock, New York.

(Right) At Woodstock's Maverick Theater, Lee made his professional stage debut as "Texas" in the 1947 production of Lynn Riggs' "Roadside". He quit his job as a plumber's assistant the next day, but kept his union card his whole life.

Visit Our Nautical
Restaurant
and Bar

(Top) Finally on Broadway as Hallam, a bit player in the 1951 adaptation of the Herman Melville classic, "Billy Budd."

(Left) Logo for one of Marvin's favorite hangouts during his summer stock days.

(Right) In Shakespearean garb while studying at the ATW.

(Below) 1952's "Dragnet" with Jack Webb (center) and Barney Phillips.

(Above) In the Korean War action film *The Glory Brigade* (left in glasses) aside longtime colleague and friend Alvy Moore. (1953) and (Below) as Lt. Frank Ballinger on TV's "M Squad (1957-60).

(Above) Looking down on frequent costar Ernest Borgnine in 1955's *Bad Day At Black Rock*. (Below) John Ford's *The Man Who Shot Liberty Valance* (1962).

(Top) In Hawaii for Donovan's Reef, with daughters Courtenay, Cynthia, partially hidden Claudia, wife Betty, and son Christopher.

(Above) From 1965, taking a beating from Vivien Leigh in Stanley Kramer's Ship of Fools and (below) on top of old Smokey in Cat Ballou.

(Above) Monte, Lee and Christopher Marvin. (Below) Keenan Wynn presents Marvin with a wedding bouquet at LAX after his Oscar win for Cat Ballou.

With Burt Lancaster, Robert Ryan and Woody Strode in The Professionals *(1966). By the time the film was released, Marvin was an Oscar winner. Lancaster wired, "Welcome to the club." In 1972, when Lancaster was arrested for drunk driving, Marvin reportedly said, "Where's a Western Union office? I have to wire him, 'Welcome to the club.'" (Below) In John Boorman's 1967 'arthouse' action film,* Point Blank, *avenging angel Lee Marvin looks down on nervous bagman Michael Strong.*

(Above) The only known photo of the entire cast of The Dirty Dozen *at the initial script reading in England. Clockwise from the bottom left are Charles Bronson (Joseph Wladislaw), Richard Jaeckel (Sgt. Bowren), George Kennedy (Maj. Armbruster), Trini Lopez (Jimenez), Al Mancini (Bravos), Bob Phillips (Cpl. Morgan), Jim Brown (R.T. Jefferson), Donald Sutherland (Vernon Pinkley), John Cassavetes (Victor Franko), Ralph Meeker (Capt. Kinder), Robert Webber (Gen. Denton), director Robert Aldrich, Lee Marvin (Maj. John Reisman), Ernest Borgnine (Gen. Worden), Telly Savalas (Archer Maggot), Robert Ryan (Col. Breed), Clint Walker (Samson Posey), Colin Maitland (Sawyer), Ben Carruthers (Gilpin), Stuart Cooper (Lever), unidentified, and Tom Busby (Vladek).*

(Below) Marvin jokes with career-long agent Meyer Mishkin (center) and drinking buddy/fellow marine Bob Phillips (left) one typically overcast day on the English location of 1967's The Dirty Dozen.

(Above) Working with his favorite actor, Toshiro Mifune (right), in one of Marvin's favorite projects, John Boorman's 1968 WWII allegory, Hell in the Pacific. (Left) Monte (far left) visits his son on the set of Paint Your Wagon. (Below) Marvin dries his boots while waiting for a decision to be rendered during Paint Your Wagon (1969).

(Clockwise from top) As the title character in the elegiac Monte Walsh (1970), another of the actor's favorite films in spite of the unfortunate editing.

(Right) As Hickey, nervously meeting the great Fredric March during production of John Frankenheimer's adaptation of Eugene O'Neill's The Iceman Cometh (1973).

(Bottom right) With wife Pam at JFK Airport reacting happily to the verdict in the palimony suit rendered in Los Angeles Superior Court.

(Below) A return to classic villainy playing 'Jack Osborne' in Michael Apted's Gorky Park.

(Above) While filming part of The Big Red One *in 1978, Lee and writer/director Sam Fuller (center) met up with Marvin's former director John Boorman (left) in Ireland. (Below) Discussing the D-Day Invasion scene on* The Big Red One's *Israel location with Fuller. The heavily edited film was was not released until a year after Marvin's 1979 palimony suit, and was later restored in 2004 by critic/historian Richard Schickel.*

Wearing a gown she designed, Cynthia delights in the presence of her father at her 1982 nuptials.

(Above) Son Christopher (left) visits with his father in Tucson to discuss the ways and ills of the world.

(Left) Having put a sizable dent in the environs of Malibu, Marvin chose to live out his days in the more tranquil desert of Tucson, AZ.

The Many Faces of Lee Marvin

(Above) As the aptly named 'Slob' in the so-bad-it's-good Cold War quickie, Shack Out on 101 (1955), Marvin clashes with Len Lesser in the backroom of the eponymous roadside joint.

(Above) As Orville 'Flash' Perkins in Raintree County (1957), MGM's failed attempt to recapture the glow of Gone With the Wind.

(Above) Returning to the screen after "M Squad" as the half-scalped, strangely-attired, scene-stealing 'Tully Crow' in 1961's The Comancheros opposite the equally oddly-garbed John Wayne (center) and nervous Phil Arnold (right). This was to the first of three films in which Marvin would co-star with 'The Duke.'

(Above) As Charlie Strom, the mortally wounded Marvin gives 'the white eye' in Don Seigel's The Killers (1964).

(Left) Marvin as Walker visits wife Sharon Acker in Point Blank.

(Below) Riding the rails with Paul Newman in the buddy movie, Pocket Money (1972). As he had done as a supporting actor, Marvin created an interesting portrait by reaching into his bag of tricks of mugging, pantomime, and a solid sense of humor to steal the film from producer/star Newman.

working on was special in more ways than one. They joked and jibed each other in their bonding but, as Ryan recalled, "One thing that Lee and some of the stuntmen said was that this was the end of an era of big money, studio westerns. Everybody said to me, 'You're lucky, kid. This is probably the last one of these that's gonna be done. You got out here just in time.' That kind of thing was said a lot."

Much of the camaraderie continued throughout the filming, but changed in the presence of Jeanne Moreau. "Then came Jeanne Moreau," recalled Ryan with a chuckle. "How could I forget Jeanne Moreau? She was great. He was a little… I don't know exactly, but I got the feeling he [Marvin] was a little nervous about Jeanne Moreau." Asked about the couple's chemistry, Ryan stated, "Oh yes, and it was very quiet. It wasn't obvious. It was obvious on the screen, but it was… I mean the whole thing was weird. Well, he told me once later, 'Hey, she wants me to live in Paris. How can I go live in Paris?' I don't know how much bullshit that was or whatever. Obviously, there was something going on and they were quite fond of each other. There were a lot of things going on. I didn't see any of it, and they were very discreet." Neither one would comment publicly on their relationship, but Moreau did say, "He says more in less words, sometimes in no words at all, than any other American actor I've ever met."

Unsure of its appeal, nervous producers had trimmed the film by almost fifteen minutes when *Monte Walsh* premiered in late 1970. *The Hollywood Reporter*'s Larry Cohen took note of the editing and wrote, "The decision to cut the film is unfortunate, for the picture I saw was one of the best American films of the year; a strong contender for numerous end-of-the-year awards in virtually every category, a candidate for critical praise, and a major box-office possibility… In its longer running time, *Monte Walsh* is a classic which stands up with the best of recent American films; it would be a shame to have to accept less." The film fared better in Europe than in the youth-oriented American film market, which was greatly disappointing to Marvin.

It is indeed unfortunate, because the middle-aged Marvin was touching and poignant in his scenes with Moreau, and he showed a level of intimacy audiences had never witnessed before from the macho actor. His performance is wonderfully nuanced throughout, such as in the scene when a huckster offers the unemployed Walsh a job in a wild west show, to which he nobly responds, "I ain't spittin' on my whole life." It was a philosophy that resonated with historical novelist James Michener, who mentions the film in his novel *Centennial* as being a modern classic that only true believers in the old west could genuinely appreciate.

Marvin's on-set romance with his costar may have been what prompted the strange phone call to Paul Wasserman when the actor called to tell him he was flying to Las Vegas to get married. The stunned publicist asked if it was Michele Triola or Jeanne Moreau. "Neither," said Marvin. "It's Pam Feeley, from Woodstock." Apparently, according to the official press release, after a promotional tour of *Walsh* in New York with Moreau, Marvin had driven to Woodstock to visit his ailing father where he then met with his former girlfriend from his summer stock days. Their reunion prompted the call to Wasserman a week later with his news. What is often left out is that, prior to this event, the forty-six-year-old actor had attempted another reconciliation with Betty Marvin, who had rebuffed him. Marvin and his new bride moved into his Malibu home and proceeded to make every effort at a new life.

Following his marriage to Pam, Marvin made the lackluster *Pocket Money* with Paul Newman, in which the two actors played bumbling modern day cattle brokers. Marvin was enamored with the script fashioned by Terence Malick, saying at the time the film was in production, "It's kind of a comedy of a couple of con men who really think they know how to operate and they just end up on their feet walking back… It's dumb, dumb stuff but thought-out dumb." Marvin did give an engaging performance as a man not nearly as smart as he thinks he is, but when the film flopped, he publicly blamed the failure on Newman, whose company helped make the badly received comedy.

The author of the autobiographical novel *Jim Kane* on which it was based did not care for the film either, but for a different reason. "They didn't get it," writer JPS Brown said of the filmmakers. "They made every Mexican in *Pocket Money* a low-down person. In fact, they wanted to do it in Mexico so they had to show the Mexican censors the script. They went to Mexico City to meet with the censors and showed them the script. The censors refused them permission to do it in Mexico [after reading the script]. With that, I had cattle and property in Mexico. I had a bunch of cattle ready to come out and they took away my visa. The Mexican consulate was in Nogales then. She called me up and told me she had to take away my visa. I couldn't go back to Mexico until I straightened it up. She told me she would help and send five copies of my book *Jim Kane* to the censors so they could see I hadn't made Mexicans look bad, that I was friendly and respectful of the Mexican cattle people that I worked with. Well, I couldn't get my cattle out for six months... So, when the censors read the book, they let me have my visa back." Neither Marvin, Newman, nor anyone else connected with the movie was ever aware of the author's film-induced travails.

The failure of *Pocket Money* was hardly at the forefront of Marvin's thoughts in early April of 1971. Over the years, he had kept intermittent contact with his father who had retired in 1965. A few years after the death of Courtenay, Monte had literally married the widow next door. He had also taken up genealogy, attempting to piece together the Marvin family tree, at his son Robert's urging. The effort also included extensive clippings covering his son's acting career. Mostly, he simply drank, and at age seventy-four, he lapsed into a coma while visiting friends in Florida.

In a tragic echo of Monte's own childhood, Lee rushed to see his father when it was already too late. Years later the actor recounted, "When the Chief died... I went down to Florida... He was in a coma... I came over and kissed him on the head and said, 'That's it, Chief. I'll see you down the line?' And then I got on a plane and guess what was playing?—*I Never Sang for My Father*. People hated it, man, but I loved it. It got it all out there... Gene Hackman and Melvyn Douglas... Melvyn Douglas is amazing. What a great actor. One of the greatest of all time. I remember that after the movie, people were saying how depressing it was, and I started an argument with them. I was holding forth, man, to the whole plane. It was great. I got it out. Like that... I felt, you know, cleansed of it... I think I understand my father more everyday. On some days I can almost..."

Marvin went back to work filming *Prime Cut* in Canada, which he had agreed to make during *Pocket Money*. The project was a bizarre action film with Marvin as a Chicago mob enforcer grappling with Kansas meat packer and white slaver Gene Hackman, who was fresh off his success from *The French Connection.* The film also starred Hackman's real-life *French Connection* counterpart Eddie Egan, as well as Gregory Walcott, Angel Tompkins, William Morey, and, making her film debut, a young Texan actress named Sissy Spacek.

Walcott recalled a telling incident early on during the film: "Lee invited Gene and me to drive out with him on location about forty miles out of the city. Lee was in a very talkative mood that morning and kept up a continual commentary all the way to the location. Gene mainly listened. He seemed a little amazed at Lee's uncanny ability to chatter using his 'shorthand' method of speaking. Gene had just received rave reviews of his performance in the film *I Never Sang For My Father.* Lee said, 'I haven't had a chance to see that film with you and Melvyn Douglas. What's it called? *I Never Sucked My Father's Cock?'*

"Then the topic segued to his own father. He told how they had a bitter relationship and it had been years since he had seen him. Then he went on to add that on his [Lee's] birthday a couple of years prior, he got word that his father had died. 'Wouldn't you know that the bastard had to die on my birthday, and spoil it for me.' I looked at Gene, and by now he was wondering if he should take his costar serious. His shock approach seemed to be one of his favorite ways of dealing with people. As the weeks progressed on the film, I began to wonder if the shock method was not a way to cover his insecurities. With all of his two-fisted bravado, I could not help but sense some insecurity in Lee Marvin."

Lee Marvin feuded with director Michael Ritchie during production, balking at the romance between his character and Spacek. "Actually, I thought Lee was protective of her in that thing," stated Walcott. "I know in the original script, he was supposed to make love to the girl, the child. Lee didn't go for that. Lee nixed the idea… I think it was Lee that had that changed. Once again, I want to stress, that as wild as he could be, maybe deep inside there was a moral streak in him that came out." Marvin himself commented, "I've made some mistakes I wish I hadn't. One of them was workin' with Michael Ritchie on *Prime Cut.* Oh, I hate that sonofabitch. He likes to use amateurs, because he can totally dominate them." The offbeat film has its supporters and does indeed have some wonderful moments in it, such as the juxtaposition of the agrarian splendor of the prairie landscape against Marvin's high-powered weaponry, but the overall effect was far from successful.

His surprise marriage to Pam, the death of his father, and his uncharacteristic feud with Ritchie, all pointed to an apparent mid-life crisis. Marvin dealt with his demons best when creatively challenged, and the challenge came in his next two films. As he had managed to do in previous years, 1973's *Emperor of the North* and *The Iceman Cometh* gave film audiences two distinctly different performances in a single year in which to revel in Lee Marvin's versatility.

The genesis of *Emperor* began with veteran screenwriter Christopher Knopf's research into the late 19th and early 20th century legend of Leon R. Livingston. Knopf became fascinated with this man who called himself 'A No.1,' who claimed to have tramped the countryside from the age of eleven, and had self-published several books recounting his hobo adventures. Livingston had learned the ropes from Jack London, who had the hobo name "Sailor Jack" and later, "Cigaret." London also wrote about these adventures in his book *The Road*, with an emphasis on the social injustices perpetrated on the country's downtrodden, and the attempt to organize "Kelly's Army of 1894" to revolt against the status quo.

Knopf chose to update London's tale to the more familiar 1930s' Depression and make the social injustice more symbolic than polemic. These changes still allowed Knopf's screenplay to include London's graphic depiction of a tramp's mistreatment at the hands of the railroad employees. The project went through several directors, including Martin Ritt and Sam Peckinpah, before Robert Aldrich was locked in. The folksy image of the beloved hobo was obliterated in director Robert Aldrich's violent fable of the individual battling the establishment. Aldrich assembled his *Dirty Dozen* cast and crew, which included Ernest Borgnine as the sadistic conductor "Shack" who symbolized the unyielding establishment; newcomer Keith Carradine as "Cigaret," the fickle, and unreliable youth tramp; and as the symbol of rugged individualism, Lee Marvin as 'A No.1,' Knopf fashioned a story in which Marvin bets he can ride Borgnine's train with Carradine alternately allying himself throughout with whomever seemed to be winning at the time.

Given that Marvin had always claimed to have ridden the rails as a child in the Depression, casting him in the lead proved a stroke of genius. "I met Lee Marvin in Bob [Aldrich's] office on the Fox lot before filming began on location," recalled Knopf. "There was that squint in his eyes and the so familiar baritone voice as he held court, dissecting his role. 'The guy's a philosopher, a disciple of Kant's metaphysics and ethics, right?' 'Right,' I nodded. 'Bullshit.' The man was already in character."

As he had done in 1955's *Kiss Me Deadly* and 1967's *The Dirty Dozen*, Aldrich pushed the limits of screen violence more than ever before, and he had a very willing partner in Lee Marvin. Marvin held Aldrich in rare esteem. "Bob has a knack of gettin' a kind of cast together that does the show beyond the script, even though the script may be strong in itself. That's happening on this one, I think," he stated. "In the whole show, Ernie Borgnine and I have about two lines to each other. It's plus attracts minus, and that's that."

A climactic fight scene aboard a moving freight train between the two titans remains one of the most intense of its kind. "We were on the damned thing for a week," recalled cinematographer Joe Biroc. "That was hell. We stayed on the train, and it was tough. We shot part of it from the boxcar. Some of the scenes were shot with the train not moving and a couple of our guys wiggled the cars. See, I never had a challenge in my life. I just called it a day's work... Anything is hard if you don't know what you're doing. We always found the easy way to do the hard thing."

The colloquialism-laden dialogue, the 'king-of-the-hill' storyline, veteran cast, impressive photography of Oregon's Cascade Mountains, and the use of vintage trains, all conspired to make a film that was again overlooked in its time, only to find an appreciative audience decades later. At the time, Lee Marvin simply felt, "I get a special kick playing rebels over establishment types. I've always been a bum, so I'm being paid to act out my fantasies."

He was not only able to act out his fantasies; as a major film star he would have the opportunity to challenge his acting ability as never before with his next role. In director John Frankenheimer's film version of Eugene O'Neill's classic *The Iceman Cometh*, Marvin played 'Hickey,' an early 20th century salesman who forces the denizens of a skid row bar to confront their pipe dreams. The film version of O'Neill's marathon-length play was the most anticipated offering of the experimental American Film Theater [AFT]. The belief was that audiences who could not get to Broadway or other theatrical venues, whether geographically or financially, might still be willing to see great plays on a limited subscription basis. Frankenheimer had his pick of any actor to play 'Hickey,' and narrowed it down to Marvin, Marlon Brando, or Gene Hackman. Of Marvin he said, "He has that wonderful face. That tortured face, and he looked like a salesman. He told stories so well, in life and he was such a good actor. I loved working with him. Of all, of the three, I think, secretly, I really hoped to be able to do it with Lee... It was a really wonderful experience. For me, he was perfect for it."

Publicist Paul Wasserman remembers encountering Marvin: "I saw him someplace, and he gave me the shooting script of *The Iceman Cometh*, and said he'd probably be doing it. I remember it like Tolstoy: long, long, long. I said to him, 'Are you up for O'Neill?' He said, 'I was doing O'Neill when I was in my diapers.' Meaning his Woodstock days." There were certainly thematic connections Marvin could draw to Hickey, such as his father's salesman background, his own drinking problem, and the fact that the character of Hickey's relationship with his wife resonated with his own history with women. Marvin knew Hickey well, but the intimidating words of a master playwright in conjunction with the stellar cast of Robert Ryan, Fredric March, Moses Gunn, Bradford Dillman— all of whom were much more familiar with the material than he—would be daunting to say the least.

Also in the cast was a young Jeff Bridges, who had at first been reluctant to sign on. As he recently confided, "Yeah, it was at a stage in my career where I wasn't sure I wanted to be an actor. I mean I had made a few films and all, but I still wasn't completely sold on the idea. In fact, when I was offered *Iceman* I didn't want to do it. The last film I had made was *The Last American Hero*. That film's director Lamont Johnson told me I had better do it, and he was right."

Once he did sign on, "I found it wouldn't be done like other films.

On most other films you're lucky if you get a few weeks' rehearsal and then you shoot for, like, eight weeks. On this film, we rehearsed for eight weeks and then shot it straight through in two weeks. It was done more like a play. It was an incredible experience. It was some time ago, so my memory is not that great, but I'll always remember how it was working with these seasoned professionals. These guys, all of them, March, Ryan, Marvin, they all still got a little nervous before they worked, and they were all so committed."

Bridges also recalled learning a valuable lesson from Marvin during the film: "In acting there are certain unspoken rules. One of them is that when the camera moves in for a close-up, you have to be subtle in your performance because your face is going to be forty feet high on the screen. Marvin said, 'That's when I play it big.' and he did! See, I learned from him that you have to learn the rules, but once you do, you can do what you want to them to make them work for your performance."

Fredric March had come out of retirement to play 'Harry Hope,' the owner of Harry Hope's Last Chance Saloon, and was in frail health. Robert Ryan's wife had passed away not long before the film began, and Ryan himself was battling cancer. The presence of such veteran and legendary actors in their element and at the end of their lives deeply affected Marvin.

Robert Ryan's son Cheyney was present during the lengthy rehearsals, and remembers one early incident: "Marvin came in literally carrying an entire case of beer under his arm. We're talking about probably seven or eight in the morning. He proceeded to start to drink it. One thing that happened, and Frankenheimer got very, very upset… They were rehearsing it, but the whole time, Lee Marvin was just drinking. He was getting very, very drunk, and I was actually the only person there for him to talk to… he got into a thing about what a big star he was. It was really unpleasant… He said, 'Your father's not a big star, anymore. I'm a big star. He used to be a big star and now I'm the big star.' This went on and on and on. I thought the guy was kind of un-centered, to tell you the truth. My father didn't talk like that. I think it was important for him to be successful, but he would never talk about who was a big star and who was not."

Frankenheimer also recalled the incident, and felt, "Lee just couldn't handle it, because he had been working with a stand-in for Fredric March up until that time. Suddenly, to have the real Fredric March there, Lee just said to me afterwards, 'I just couldn't deal with it in front of him. I just couldn't.' So, he got drunk… The next day, I went in, and I really had it out with him. I said, 'Lee, if you do it again, I'm just going to walk off this picture, and I'm going to pull everybody off with me because there's no way you're going to take us down with you. No way.' He said, 'I won't. I won't touch anything while we do this movie.'" After the initial embarrassment, Frankenheimer stated, "Lee Marvin was sometimes not called for a week and a half, but he was there every day. He was almost an assistant director, trying to quiet people down while I worked with other actors on a scene."

When it came time to film 'Hickey's' lengthy final monologue in which he unveils all the events of his life leading up to a shocking confession, Marvin gave all concerned a reason to pause. "We went over the points we wanted to make, the beats," recalled Frankenheimer. "I kind of did it in about six different takes. Six different setups so that he'd have, 'Go to here, cut,' then, 'go to here…' you know? So, it really worked out very well… I don't know what he did to prepare… I just know he knew his lines. We talked it over. I don't get into the preparation an actor does, especially if he's a trained, wonderful actor like Lee Marvin. That's what he's going to do… I merely created an atmosphere there where we were ready for him. Cameras were ready. Everything was ready. We worked it out and, boom—he nailed it."

Veterans Fredric March and Robert Ryan received the lion's share of deserved praise for their swan song performances, but Marvin more than held his own as the affable yet ultimately tragic 'Hickey.' After *Iceman*'s short subscription run, legal problems with AFT's eventual bankruptcy kept the film from being viewed for decades. Frankenheimer and others helped the film eventually get a new lease on life and, like *Emperor of the North*, it has since found new audiences with the recent DVD release.

While other postwar actors at the same time had careers that devolved into self-parody—such as Charlton Heston's disaster epics, or Marlon Brando's excessive paychecks—Lee Marvin continued to challenge himself and his audience's expectations. It was important to him to maintain a high quality of excellence in his projects despite their initial financial disappointment. Like Monte Walsh, Lee Marvin had no intention of spitting on his own life.

PART FOUR

THE REAR ECHELON

Costarring in Delta Force *(1986) with Chuck Norris, Marvin played Col. Nick Alexander, head of an elite antiterrorist group in his swan song film appearance.*

CHAPTER 12

The White Eye

W HEN LEE MARVIN's personal life was in turmoil in the 1960s, he made some of his best films. Inversely, in the mid to late '70s, whereas his personal life had become fairly stable, his career appeared to take a nose dive. Part of the problem might have been due to the fact that his ex-wife had ceased to be involved as much in his life, which removed her from the decision making process. Another reason was that Lee Marvin never sought to become a hyphen, as in "actor-director" or "actor-producer." He looked over the scripts that were offered to him strictly as an actor for hire, which in itself required having to wear several hats. "It's getting very difficult to be an actor because you have to be an attorney, an agent, and a judge of scripts all at the same time," he said.

In choosing his projects, that certain quality he looked for was, as he put it, "the white eye," his term for that intangible yet resolute sense of the inescapability of imminent danger, or death. He had been the first actor to bring that feeling to American films on a consistent basis, resulting in his involvement in both popular and cult films. However, the unprecedented success of 1975's *Jaws* created the new phenomenon of the blockbuster, which proved to be the beginning of the end for the experimentation in America's cinema of the early 70s, thus closing the door on the kind of films Marvin preferred.

The first in a series of well-intentioned misfires for Marvin was *Spikes' Gang*. It was a western saga in which career outlaw 'Harry Spikes'

(Marvin) "recruits" three young drifters (Gary Grimes, Charlie Martin Smith and future Oscar-winning director Ron Howard) into the world of bank robbery. Director Richard Fleischer, having worked with Marvin years before in *Violent Saturday,* found the key to talking Marvin into playing the role: "I could see his eyes widen a bit when I explained why I thought it was an allegory… that he was really the devil. He and these boys' stories were about the loss of innocence. There was a mystical quality about him because he shows up in all the right places at the right time. His job was to lead the innocent astray. He was Satan, and Lee ate it up… If you look for it in the picture, you see that there is a mysterious quality; why he shows up, and leads the boys astray, and introduces them to a life of crime."

For the role, Marvin grew his hair out, put on a few extra pounds for the first time in his career, and sported an elongated mustache that gave him a walrus-like appearance. While in production, he described 'Harry Spikes' as a likable devil. "'Spikes' is not only a bank robber but also something of a philosopher, always ready with some little pearl of wisdom when he has an attentive audience such as his young trio of followers… You can't tell if 'Spikes' is a good bad man or a bad good man, and you are inclined to place him somewhere in between, always ahead of the game, when he is not one step ahead of the law."

Unfortunately, the end result looked like a TV-movie and came and went just as quickly. "As they say, it never opened," recalled Fleischer. "It didn't get any kind of reception. I really don't know what Lee thought, because by the time the screening was over, he was gone. He was dodging people. I never did talk to him about the picture. I never saw him again. He became very much like the mysterious stranger, 'Harry Spikes.'"

While it is axiomatic that no filmmaker sets out to make a bad film, Marvin's follow-up to *Spike's Gang* remains arguably the worst film the actor would ever be involved in. *The Klansman* was based on a novel by noted author William Bradford Huie, to be directed by the legendary maverick Sam Fuller, who also drafted the script. This pedigree resulted in a cast of Marvin, Richard Burton, Lola Falana, Linda Evans, Cameron Mitchell, and, making his film debut, Buffalo Bills running back O.J. Simpson.

The film had potential in its tale of Marvin as a sheriff in a southern town rife with bigotry and racial tension, that was ready to explode. "It's dangerous, for the same reasons antiwar pictures are dangerous," Marvin said as to why he had agreed to make the film. "It's a dangerous financial thing to go into, because they're usually money losers. It's anti-bigotry, and to show that aspect, you have to present the ultimate in bigotry. I was afraid that nobody else would make the film. I was afraid that it would it end up being a third-class product, and I thought the subject important enough so people should look at it squarely."

Unfortunately, the Northern California location of Oroville became a paparazzi feeding frenzy concerning Marvin's and Burton's marathon drinking bouts. Marvin proudly stated later, "I'll either drink the town dry or I won't touch a drop. When I'm in the mood, I'll take hold of any kind of bottle and drain it. Just as long as it's got a hole in it. But I can go for days with none at all." Those days of "none at all" were rare on *The Klansman*, but nothing compared to Burton, who was surly to the locals, drunk more often than Marvin, and caused the swift appearance of Elizabeth Taylor when she heard her husband had bought a local waitress an expensive bauble. She also was present during Burton's alcohol-induced hospitalization. The internationally famous couple divorced not long after the film wrapped.

The film also briefly reunited Marvin with his good friend Millard Kaufman, who had been nominated for an Oscar two decades earlier for his screenplay of *Bad Day at Black Rock*. Marvin's drinking almost ended the reunion shortly after it started, when he invited Kaufman to his hotel for an early morning drink, but Kaufman got word that his son was sick. "I said to Lee, 'I have to go back, I'm sorry.' He asked what was the matter, and I told him. He said, 'Don't be a goddamned Jewish mother.' I said, 'Fuck you.' I started at him, and he came at me. Now this guy, who's as big as a horse, his driver, came between us and that was it. Of course, the next time I saw him we both ignored it."

Future film historian John Gloske was working as an extra on the set, and remembered seeing Burton and Marvin regularly consume tumblers filled with straight vodka and ice. Intended moments of levity were also tainted by the mood of the proceedings, as Gloske recalled: "There was a film Lee Marvin and Cameron Mitchell did called *Gorilla At Large* and Cameron Mitchell's name I guess was second or third billed. Marvin's name on the poster was really small. In the *Klansman* scene in a train station, Burton rips down a poster. Well, a friend of mine, with Lee Marvin's permission and everybody—except for Cameron Mitchell— put a poster of *Gorilla At Large* behind that. He ripped it down and there's *Gorilla At Large*. Cameron Mitchell thought *The Klansman* was going to give him a big break. He thought it was going to put him back where he was. He got a little upset. Everybody was laughing at him. He wasn't laughing at it."

The elements of tabloid fodder certainly contributed to the film's failure, but problems began long before filming had commenced. According to Sam Fuller, "I was going to direct it. Business is business and [James Bond director] Terence Young, who told me he didn't care about America's social problems, was assigned to it, changed my script and the movie! It was nothing like what I had written or would have directed. The results made me sick to my stomach."

Millard Kaufman, credited alongside Sam Fuller, was co-writing the script. His opinion of Marvin had not wavered, however, and he felt the problem lay elsewhere: "Yeah, Lee was very good. As a matter of fact, everybody in the picture outside of Lee was terrible. They were awful. The curious thing in this was [producer] Bill Schiffrin, who didn't know what the hell he was doing. Later, when the picture fell on its ass, [Schiffrin] wrote a piece in a local paper where it's quoted as saying that it was all my fault. He said he really wanted Sammy Fuller in this piece, completely lying about the fact that he had Sammy Fuller, and fired him."

Marvin himself quickly soured on the whole disaster, calling the film "The Clownsman" and stating, "It's a load of bull. They didn't pay me for my last week, so I don't see why I should try to boost it." The well-intentioned film was justifiably jeered and laughed at during previews, in spite of Marvin's impressive performance as a sheriff trying to keep the peace. He told a friend jokingly after an embarrassing preview of the film, "Can you tell I did that one for the money?"

Released in 1974, *The Klansman* would be the last time audiences would see Lee Marvin on screen for two years. For the first time in his career, he took a lengthy vacation from film work. The lack of good scripts made it easy for him to take time off, or as he said at the time, "The thing I look for now is how I really feel, beyond other people's opinions. I've never done something for money, not just the money. And, sure, that makes me sound a total phony."

Marvin's long-time business manager, Ed Silver, had wisely advised the actor on his investments in order that he could afford to move anywhere he wished. "I was always proud of what I did with Lee," stated Silver. "The first thing I did for him, when I started taking over his affairs, I had a little investment money and I bought a little apartment house in Las Vegas. When I sold it, a few years later, I made a profit of $12,000. That may not seem like a lot but it seemed like a lot then…"

"I had very close relations with Lee and I watched his funds very closely," Silver continued. "There were several cases of big money people really being taken advantage of by the business manager… The business management business was very unique at that time. There were just maybe five or six major firms of guys that were the go-to people… One of my principles in my own operation, when I used to go to work, this is the truth, I used to go to work and say, 'Well, what can I do for Lee, today?' He was my mainstream client. In my mind, I went through that."

On occasion, the actor would whimsically indulge in such investments as speculative oil drilling in the Dakotas, or a working gold mine in Nevada. Strangers would approach him in a bar, offering stock tips, whereupon Marvin would pass the information on to Silver, who made sure the actor could afford to lose the investment if necessary. His film work allowed Marvin to indulge in the occasional financial wildcatting and prospecting forays, and as added security, Silver's shrewd purchase of a southern California apartment complex kept his client solvent.

At the end of the day, if Lee and Pam Marvin had wanted to pack up and purchase a twenty-acre property in Tucson, they were in the rare financial position to do so; and they did just that. At first the San Fernando Valley was considered, but ultimately, he and Pam decided on a clean break from California's smog and Malibu's dampness for health reasons. The Tucson property was large enough to accommodate the four children from Pam's three previous marriages and the occasional visits from Lee's four children, most of whom were old enough to be on their own.

At fifty years old, he and Pam chose to leave his wild Malibu lifestyle in hopes of putting his past behind him. Friends had noticed a difference in Marvin since marrying Pam, and the slower paced lifestyle of Tucson helped accommodate that change. "Well, to tell you the truth, Lee changed," said Keenan's Wynn's son, Tracy. " When he met his wife Pam, she put him on the straight and narrow. People like Keenan got phased out of his life. See, when they [Lee & Keenan] were together, they were just like little kids. They really were. When Lee would drink, he'd get very tough. He was a very mean drunk. Keenan was the opposite. He'd get very melancholy. Lee went the other way. He could get obnoxious and cantankerous but he was able to back it up. Keenan used to say about Lee, 'Don't let the gray hair fool you.' Yeah, Lee was a very tough character."

Marvin cut down on his drinking but, according to longtime buddy Ralph O'Hara, who lived with the couple periodically, his personal security was still a priority ingrained from the military. "It's a thing you continually do. It's from not being deprogrammed from the military. You still have to secure the perimeter," claimed O'Hara. "Lee had a machete he carried underneath the seat of his pickup truck. He went around Tucson in shorts, a shirt, and a big floppy hat, same as I. At times, he didn't strap the 9 mm gun. He'd put it into that little ditty bag, and I had it in my holster on my hip. Not just me. There's an awful lot of people who walk around Tucson with a gun on their hip. It's legal."

On occasion, old friends would visit, and celebrations were required. Keenan Wynn's son Tracy had become a successful writer and was present when he and his father were in Tucson to shoot a TV-movie, and met up with Marvin for the last time: "We were at the Holiday Inn or something like that. Lee had fallen off the wagon and we were eating dinner in some restaurant. Lee was getting kind of loud, and some older guy started to complain. Lee responded, but Keenan put his hand on his shoulder. I'm paraphrasing, but I remember asking my dad why did he buy that guy a bottle of wine. He said something like, 'That's just something you do for those kind of guys.' I later learned that he [the complaining customer] was a retired Mafia Don."

Lee's children were less welcome at the new house, however, according to Lee's ex-wife Betty. "I'm going to be very candid about this: Lee's widow, Pam, did not invite or want the children in the house... I certainly can not describe their relationship. I only hear from my kids, so maybe there's a prejudice there. They used to have to call and she would say, 'You can stay for one day.' He was in Tucson, Arizona. The kids were really hurt by that."

America's bicentennial year of 1976 also saw the return of Lee Marvin in two films. American International Pictures (AIP) wanted to establish itself beyond the low-budget teenage drive-in fodder it was known for, and signed Lee Marvin for two comparatively high budget pictures. *The Great Scout and Cathouse Thursday* was a return to the farcical comedy style of *Cat Ballou*, but with a much raunchier attitude, and not nearly as many true laughs. Marvin is the ridiculously named frontiersman 'Sam Longwood' who, along with his partners, half-breed 'Joe Knox' (Oliver Reed) and 'Billy' (Strother Martin), travels to Colorado to get back the money swindled out of them by their former partner and now respectable businessman, 'Jack Colby' (Robert Culp). Along the way, Knox kidnaps a wagonload of prostitutes in his own plan of vengeance on the white man by personally infecting the race with VD. The smallest of the prostitutes (Kay Lenz), having developed a crush on the legendary scout Sam Longwood, stays on with the trio, even after her coworkers have been freed. Such was the level of humor in the bawdy, slapstick comedy set against the backdrop of the 1908 presidential election of William Howard Taft.

Filmed in the uncomfortable climes of Durango, Mexico for nine weeks and directed by former actor Don Taylor, the disparate cast got along surprisingly well. According to costar Kay Lenz, who was only twenty-two at the time, "You couldn't have gotten seven people who were more different. I was there for about three weeks before either Sylvia [Miles] or Elizabeth [Ashley] came, so it was me and all the guys. Most of my stuff was with all the guys. I became close with Strother, because he and I drove out to work every day together. He was just an incredibly wonderful man! Multifaceted. He collected opera. I think he was an Olympic diver, at one point. He was fascinating."

Working with Marvin was an especially memorable experience for Lenz. "He's not a man of many words," she chuckled. "I rode double on a horse with him for I think ten days of filming. I knew he always had an eye on me in terms of wanting to make sure I was okay, because there were a lot of stunts. My stunt girl broke her leg. The stunts were… there were a lot of little bumps and bruises… I just knew he was always making sure that I was going to be okay… It's not that he said, 'I'm looking out for you.' It's not that he made overt gestures. I just knew that he was. He was just always very aware of making sure that I was safe, and okay with all the stuff that we had to do."

Marvin's drinking bouts with costar Oliver Reed proved to be more interesting to the press than the film. When not being asked about the marathon sessions, Marvin would bristle at the obvious comparisons to *Cat Ballou*: "Any time you do something like that—revert back to the hit of your life—they say, 'Oh, he's pulling that stuff again.' It's called pigeon-holing, and I don't have a lot of patience with it." Promoting the film during its June, 1976 release, Marvin described it as: "A fun picture, a summer romp, if you're out of school and have nothing to do… I can't say this is my greatest film or my worst… I did my message films and they've all bombed. I wanted a lets-have-another-beer-type film and I liked the script." Audiences and critics did not agree.

His next film for AIP, *Shout at the Devil,* was based on a popular novel by Wilbur Smith, which in turn was based on the same true story that was the basis for the climax of the classic Bogart/Hepburn film, *The African Queen*. Marvin's character of 'Flynn O'Flynn' and costar Roger Moore as 'Sebastian Oldsmith' played ivory poachers in WWI-era Africa who plot to sabotage a German gunship. Moore also romances Marvin's daughter, played by Barbara Parkins, resulting in an old-fashioned brawl between the two men, a scene that seemed straight out of a rowdy John Ford comedy. Actor Reinhard Kolldehoff appeared throughout the film as a sleazy caricature of a German villain, complete with twirling mustache.

Because the movie was largely filmed in South Africa (and later Malta), over eighteen weeks in 1975, criticism was aimed at the filmmakers for contributing to the economy of the country's racist Apartheid regime. It did not seem to matter much to Moore, who was making several other films in the region at the time. The entire production comes off as if it really did not seem to care about the inhabitants of the region, which is not surprising, as it was directed by James Bond veteran Peter Hunt with a mostly Bond-related production crew. The film has some moments of interest, but the overall effect is one of a retread cliché that had been done better in earlier films, including Marvin's performance, which is also a retread of Ben Rumson from *Paint Your Wagon*.

Marvin had actually recorded a bawdy musical number entitled "Shagging O'Reilly's Daughter" that was cut from the film. It still appears on the film soundtrack, credited as performed by Lee Marvin and The Barflies. "There's nothing you can do about it," he said at the time. "You talk to them, and then, when you go away, they say, 'Next,' and forget it. Sure, you get upset when you're young. I'm not young."

Marvin still dutifully publicized the film, resulting in such tongue-in-cheek quotes as, "Has it ever occurred to you that some of the actors who won't talk have nothing to say, anyway. Reporters don't make actors sound stupid. Some actors can take care of that themselves. I don't care what's written about me as long as it's interesting."

TIME's staff writer Stefan Kanfer remembers a typical example of a Lee Marvin encounter with the press. The meeting took place while Marvin was in New York to promote his latest film. Kanfer and his assistant, Jay Cocks, were to meet him in his hotel room, and called from the lobby. Kanfer remembers, "I called from downstairs and he said, 'I don't have my pants on yet.' I said, 'Well, put your pants on. We're coming up.' See, I knew that if you didn't give him lip like he gave you, it would go nowhere. He'd control the interview. So, we went upstairs and he was there with his p.r. guy. When we walked in, you couldn't see him. But from the next room [we hear] 'Are the assholes in, yet?' So, I said, 'Did you get your pants on, yet?' He said, 'No,' and he came out in his underwear. He was not a heavily muscled man, but he kept trim. He had that kind of Marine build, you know?

"I wasn't gonna take any shit from him, and he knew it… Then he began to smile, and we had a terrific interview. He's a very nice guy. I said to him quite openly, 'I don't think that *Cat Ballou* is your best performance, by a long shot.' He said, 'I do agree with you. But y'know, you run this track and that's the track that the racers are on; it's the Oscar track. It really isn't based on skill as much as it's based on luck and popularity.'"

Kanfer's assistant, future Oscar-nominated screenwriter Jay Cocks, had been greatly looking forward to meeting Marvin, and was not disappointed. Asked what he thought of the meeting, he said he was "Over-awed and amused. Great, crazy fun. Talked like a bop musician and whistled for emphasis and punctuation. Hearing him talk was like listening to Dizzy Gillespie play."

After promoting the slate of AIP films, Marvin was not seen on the screen again for a full three years. The sabbatical was partly by choice, but also a matter of circumstances based on his inability to find worthy projects for which he felt any enthusiasm. He continued to battle the bottle, on and off the wagon, while pursuing his other passion, deep-sea fishing. He had long ago given up motorcycles after injuring his knee, and big game hunting had also fallen by the wayside.

Fishing for the giant marlins found along Australia's Great Barrier Reef gave him the thrill he had not known since World War II. This obsession began in 1973 when he met Australian charter boat captain Dennis "Brazaka" Wallace in Hawaii, who convinced him to visit "Down Under." When Marvin arrived in Australia, he claimed that the first fishing trip correlated to the night he was hit on Saipan thirty years earlier. Hooking the mammoth marlin prompted the actor to state, "Then you realize he has you hooked, and I must say that never since World War II have I experienced such fear. The funny thing is, that when it's over and you've made a kill, you're glad it's you who won in the end, but by the same token, here's this dead beautiful thing, and you're responsible for it. You get some sleepless nights over it, believe me…"

Lee Marvin finished the decade with the tepid Cold War spy thriller *Avalanche Express*. Based on a novel by Colin Forbes, the needlessly convoluted plot had Robert Shaw as a KGB agent defecting to the west with CIA agent Marvin using the defection as bait to catch arch-nemesis Maximillan Schell.

The cast was a strange ensemble consisting of NFL great Joe Namath,

TV detective Mike Connors, fading German film star Horst Bucholz, and future "Dynasty" star Linda Evans. To his fans, the three years Marvin had been off the screen proved quite jarring. He looked surprisingly drawn and haggard for his fifty-five years.

Marvin made the film as a chance to work with Shaw, but Shaw himself was plagued with heart trouble throughout the production, and died before his dialogue could be re-recorded. Veteran director Mark Robson had also died, suffering a heart attack near the end of the film's production, and the entire fiasco was turned over to cult director Monte Hellman who had the thankless task of trying to salvage something for release.

According to Hellman, "There were script problems as well as production problems… I never read the book, but I assumed a lot of the problems came from the original material. We actually wrote a new script. We brought in a writer to rework the script, given the material that had already been shot, and see what we could shoot in addition that would make it a better movie. So, we felt that the problems went back to the script. The reason I say thankless is because you never solve the problems, and I don't think it's a good movie now."

For Lee Marvin, who had pioneered the innovative portrayal of violence in American films, the latter years of the 1970s were spent making substandard films that were throwbacks to a previous style of filmmaking: *Spike's Gang* and *Great Scout* were embarrassing westerns; *The Klansman* was a badly rendered melodrama; *Shout at the Devil*, a poorly scripted old-fashioned adventure film; and *Avalanche Express*, an outdated and ill-fated Cold War spy thriller.

It was ironic for Marvin that the most popular film of the decade was George Lucas's 1977 opus *Star Wars*, a revamped nostalgic take on the old Flash Gordon and Buck Rogers serials, albeit on a much more stylish scale then any of the retro-like films Marvin had made at the time. The door that had begun to close by the mid-70's had slammed shut by decade's end. The wildly popular *Star Wars* series of films sealed the fate of smaller studio productions, making it that much more difficult for Marvin to ever return to such innovative films as *Monte Walsh* or *Point Blank*. He wryly commented at the time, "I know my career is going badly because I'm being quoted correctly."

His career at the end of the decade looked longingly over his shoulder. When he attempted to look forward again, the white eye was staring resolutely back at him. Just when it seemed that such a downturn would force him to slip into relative obscurity, the California State Court of Appeals prepared to hear the landmark case that would thrust Lee Marvin back into the national limelight.

CHAPTER 13

May the Best Script Win

D URING THE NOW infamous palimony suit, Lee Marvin was asked by a reporter outside the courtroom who he thought would win. "The one with the best script," he quipped. The next day in court, opposing attorney Marvin Mitchelson had the actor on the witness stand and asked him why he thought his script would win the case. The actor stated, "Because my script is real, based on fact. Yours is based on fiction." Revisiting the chronology of events of Lee Marvin and Michele Triola's relationship, via the individuals who witnessed and participated in it, sheds considerable light on Marvin's script metaphor. It then becomes quite apparent that Marvin, while no angel, was hardly the chauvinist portrayed in the media at the time, nor was his ex-girlfriend the victim she claimed to be.

From the start of their relationship, Michele Triola had exhibited behavior that those closest to Lee Marvin found questionable. "She was having one scene after another," recalled the actor's first wife. "She went in every place where I shop, had my hair done, it didn't matter. She went in and introduced herself as Mrs. Lee Marvin. Everybody got so mixed up. Everybody would say things like, 'Well, Mrs. Marvin, you made a reservation for yesterday.' It was crazy." The actor's friend Ralph O'Hara lived near Marvin's Malibu property and witnessed the way in which Triola had worked her way into Marvin's life following their first encounter during the making of *Ship of Fools*: "Then, he bought the house on La Costa Beach. Pretty soon, she's down there doing the laundry with one little ditty bag. Pretty soon the other bag, and another bag, and she was there."

From October 1964, when the actor was still married but separated from his wife, until May of 1970, Michele Triola and Lee Marvin co-habitated in Malibu. In March 1966, Marvin diplomatically told columnist Sheila Graham, "We [he and Betty] separated a year and a half ago, while I was making *Cat Ballou*… Success brings a form of acceptance, so there is a greater availability of more interesting people. Also, an individual undergoing success becomes more introspective. Therefore his demands on his wife become more picayune. He wants more, he is not satisfied with less. I'm filing for divorce as soon as our attorneys arrive at a reasonable settlement on what is community property. But I'm more than willing to have them share in my success. They suffered with me when I was struggling to make it." When Graham asked if Michele Triola would be joining him in London later in the year to film *The Dirty Dozen*, he responded, "Good grief, no!"

From the onset of their relationship, columnists had been reporting the couple were engaged, would marry soon, or any number of allusions to their deepening bond. In truth, Marvin had enjoyed the physical aspect of his relationship with Triola as long as nothing else was required. "They had a good relationship," recalled Keenan Wynn's son, Ned. "They seemed happy within the framework of partying and doing those kind[s] of things. There was a place in Malibu where we would all meet and have a good time. It was all the same thing with my dad and Lee." Marvin admittedly always had a drinking problem, but it escalated unchecked once he became a major star.

As previously mentioned, Marvin first met Ralph O'Hara at one of his favorite watering holes in Malibu called The Raft, where O'Hara was tending bar. A friendship developed in which O'Hara was able to see for himself the extent of the actor's drinking behavior while filming *Point Blank* and later *Paint Your Wagon*. "Lee was generally around people who worked with him who were unprofessional. They didn't know their lines. He was tired of doing the same scene; take twelve, take thirteen, you know. To him, that's bad news. Then he would start to get uptight and get these anxiety attacks. I call them anxiety attacks because I've had them myself. I could see it coming on him when he'd start to get nervy. He'd start to get unsettled from his normal self.

"A prime example is if he were on a set doing a take and retake and somebody couldn't remember their lines or whatever. He'd get up and say, 'I'll be back when you all get it together.' So, he would leave. What he would end up doing is, if he had a driver, he would get the driver to take him out. 'Let's go and hit the first bar.' He'd find a bar full of strangers and he'd start to talk to them. He'd pick their brains and he loved this type of conversation. This was his thing."

When Lee was married to Betty he would often drink too much, feel contrite, and then try unsuccessfully to quit. When he was with Triola he gave up all attempts at sobriety, which initiated some of his most notorious drinking escapades, such as riding on the top of John Boorman's car, several drunk driving arrests, attempting to reenlist in the Marines in the middle of the night, and more. According to his business manager Ed Silver, "I don't want to be that negative about Michele because she was good for him. He was stoned. She would take care of him; try to get him to al-anon and these things. She went through a lot of situations when he was drunk. It was not that easy to live with him. His mind was often out in the clouds…"

Unfortunately, when he would binge drink, Marvin often found even his debauchery exacerbated by Triola's presence. While filming *The Professionals* in Las Vegas, Marvin and Tony Epper played blackjack, with Epper witnessing a rather distressing side to Triola. "He had ten thousand dollars sitting right there. She's taking ten before he hit the twenty grand," recalled Epper. "She'd come and grabbed it. She'd say, 'That's none of your business.' I really didn't get involved with her. I really just backed away from all that. But it came out later in the trial. I said I saw her. I can tell you, plus what he was giving her, she must have stole twenty, thirty thousand dollars off the tables."

It was during the making of *The Professionals* that one of the most legendary nights of Marvin's heavy drinking days took place, the story of which was to reemerge during the palimony suit a decade later. "A couple of girls wanted to be stunt girls," recalled Tony Epper. "so, we tied sheets around them and hung them out the goddamn window. We did do that. They were just dancers and they were drunk and screaming and hollering. It did scare the crap out of them. It should have. They didn't want to be stunt women after that. Sixteenth floor of the Mint Hotel… But they were safe. I wouldn't let anything happen to them. We had bed sheets tied to their foot, or something, I don't know. Lee was there when we hung the young ladies out. Matter of fact, it was his idea, if the truth must be known."

Then, according to Epper's testimony, as the party crept into the wee hours, he, Marvin, and Strode continued to drink and take decisive action. Earlier in the day, Marvin had told a reporter that he wanted to shoot the famous Vegas Vic sign as well as the giant inflatable King Kong in front of the Mint Hotel. The next morning, both goals had been accomplished and the blame—or credit, depending on one's point of view—was placed squarely on the proud shoulders of Lee Marvin. "They ended up calling it in the newspaper, 'The Robin Hood Party,'" remembered Epper. "Today, they'd lock you up forever, I don't care who you are, forever."

When Marvin's success was at its zenith, publicist Paul Wasserman had the unenviable task of dealing with the couple. "My greater association with him was with Michele, who I always tried not to do interviews with in their home in Malibu, and things like that," recalled Wasserman. "Not 'At-home-with-Lee-and-Michele,' and that's what she wanted. Those few times when we did things at the house, I would always say to her, 'Can we be alone?' She wanted to be a star. Anything that interfered with her being a star, she got ugly about." Of the relationship, Wasserman observed, "I didn't see any feelings of love. I looked at it like most marriages I know: a convenience." The actor's business manager concurred, "Sometimes, Lee talked positively, but a lot of times he talked negatively. He said to me once, and this is a quote: 'When I think of Michele, it goes down.'"

Tony Epper saw a similar aspect as the relationship deteriorated, adding, "He lived in a very 'alky' world in those days… He was more afraid of her than cared for her. How can you fight with somebody like that? It's like throwing a bag of wildcats on you every time you opened your mouth to her. He'd have to kill her. Kind of psychotic? She was a nut and I witnessed it personally." Director John Boorman wrote in his autobiography of witnessing one of Triola's suicide attempts in which an emotionally non-responsive Marvin did nothing, a scene that would be eerily reenacted in *Point Blank*. Ralph O'Hara also witnessed her unstable behavior, adding, "He didn't want to have a confrontation. I've seen her pick up an entire plate of food and shove it in his face in a restaurant. That was just the nature of the beast. That's what we're talking about."

The problem in dealing with Triola financially was left to Ed Silver. "I didn't think it was going to be that long-term of a relationship, he stated candidly. "I used to talk to her every day. When Michele called, it was a half-hour to an hour, practically every day. She'd call me about something. The point is she had nothing to do with his business affairs. She didn't sign one check. I used to give her an allowance. I set up a special account for her and I used to deposit money in that account every month... I didn't give her any household money. That was the money she used to maintain herself in the household. I'll tell you something, that was so important in the Marvin vs. Marvin suit. If I would've co-mingled that money, if she would've had anything to do with the household or anything, that would have been a major, major blow in her favor."

By the time Marvin had made *Paint Your Wagon*, the relationship with Triola had become almost too much for the actor to bear. Tony Epper also took note of how badly Marvin's relationship with her had deteriorated during the difficult film. The many fights and blowups had reached critical mass as symbolized by one particular incident in which Epper was a more than willing participant: "He had rented a house and we had two or three days off. Now whether this is true or not, I don't know, but one of his pals called and said she was servicing Glenn Ford. She wasn't going to be back until Sunday afternoon and this was a Friday. Lee kept going on about the vibrators: 'I told that bitch to throw those vibrators away!' I said, 'Why don't we do something better than that?' We went to town and bought every extension cord and vibrator we could get... This is what gin does to you.

"We had a master plug and plugged it in. When she came in, that's all she got were vibrators going off everywhere! We dived under the bed and must have looked like an elephant hiding under a rock. She had a filthy mouth and was kicking us, throwing vibrators at us, shouting,

'You motherfuckers!' I remember Lee and I just took off across this big old lawn, vibrators whizzing by us and the neighbors were standing out there as if it was the damnedest thing they ever saw!"

Possibly as an act of contrition, Marvin continued to do things to help Triola realize her dream of show business success. "You know when Lee made *Paint Your Wagon*, he had that hit record, 'Wanderin' Star,'" stated Ed Silver. At Marvin's request, "I established a company called Santana Records, funded from royalties by that record. It was around fifty thousand dollars that he got for that record. What we did with that money was cut four sides for Michele. She cut four sides. She was a good singer. She was a professional singer. She played at clubs on Sunset, or whatever. Nothing ever came of it [the record] as far as breaking out."

Such noble gestures on Lee's part were typical for the actor—which also included expensive gifts as well—but did little or no good to improve their time together. "He tried to leave several times," said Epper. "He didn't want to have anything to do with her. He'd say, 'She threatened to kill me. What'll I do?' He actually told me that… *Paint Your Wagon* is where it really got into it. That's where I became cognizant of all this crap. I didn't ever enter into their private life at home, or anything. She never invited me over. I was the last person she wanted around Lee. She was afraid somebody was going to get the money and not her."

After filming *Paint Your Wagon*, Marvin was at his wit's end with Triola. Dan Moultharp, who worked for Meyer Mishkin, recalled: "I remember this one time he was passed out. He always had his money spread out all over the bar and he was out. He was out on the bar. There was some other people sitting there. Then, all of a sudden, he woke up." Miming Marvin, Moultharp shook his fist in the air and shouted, 'Damn you, Michele!' I saw that happen. It was during *Monte Walsh*."

The point of no return for Marvin was upon discovering that Triola had legally changed her name. He then sheepishly looked to O'Hara for advice. "It must have been early 1970," recalled the former bartender. " He came over to me and he had discovered that Michele had her name changed to Marvin. He said to me in these words, 'What the fuck do you do with a broad like this? How do you get rid of a broad like this? Ralph, you got broads coming out of here all the time. You get rid of them and you don't seem to have any trouble. What do you do?' I said to him, 'Lee, you got enough money to go anywhere you want and do anything you want. Why don't you just go back in the house? Don't even get dressed. Just pick up the keys to the car, your wallet, and go out. Turn it over to your lawyers. Let your lawyers handle it and just disappear until she's gone. Come back when she's gone."

Marvin decided to take his friend's advice, much to Michele Triola's immediate displeasure. She began calling every hotel in the area as well as everyone they knew in an attempt to find Marvin. While she was on the phone, Marvin had pulled into the driveway, having gone to the movies for the evening. When he saw her silhouette in the window, he slowly pulled back out, turned the car around, and drove down to Del Mar, letting his lawyers and Meyer Mishkin deal with the task of getting Triola out of the house.

The law firm of Goldman & Kagon had represented Marvin for quite some time and were very familiar with both the relationship and their client's occasional legal run-ins. When Marvin had drunkenly grabbed a banjo player's instrument in a bar and broken it over his head, Goldman & Kagon's legal assistance was elicited to make the expensive out of court settlement. Lou Goldman handled most of Marvin's previous legal responsibilities, but when it came to dealing with Michele Triola, Goldman's decades-long partner A. David Kagon stepped up to the plate.

It certainly helped that Kagon genuinely liked his client, stating, "My wife, who is an artist and professionally trained interior designer, who didn't know Lee very well other than the casual meetings we'd have at the house for dinner, would tell me, 'This man has abundant knowledge about silver, sterling silver, china, fabrics, historical knowledge!… I'm amazed!' The depth of the man never really came out, except when you saw him on the screen. You knew there had to be something inside him that could create images that he wanted to convey to you."

According to Betty Marvin, it was while her ex-husband was hiding out from Michele Triola that he had attempted yet another reconciliation. Her reaction was to tell him, "Why would I want to break back into prison?" It was tearful, according to Betty, who went on to Rome and came back to discover her ex-husband had married Pam Feeley. "He got very, very drunk and then he forgot, which he did a lot. He'd literally black out. Then the next thing, there he was with Pam in Las Vegas, married." Betty's own opinion of the union was to state, "Pam had four children from four different husbands. Like another Michele in a different way."

Much was made in the media at the time of the surprise wedding. A typical example was, "Lee had said at a press conference here in Hollywood that he didn't think he would ever marry again. Then the very next afternoon he was saying 'I do' with his press agent Jim Mahoney as his best man." When Triola was asked to comment, she cheerfully said, "Lee and I live at Malibu just four doors down from each other and he frequently drops in for breakfast and we take walks on the beach. He is very thoughtful of me. Just recently he gave me a new car, a Mercedes." She also added that, at that time, she was dating Adam West, TV's "Batman," but there was no romance.

Other media reports of the October 10, 1970 marriage included *Newsweek*'s misstatement that it was the second marriage for both Lee and Pam. The *Los Angeles Times* columnist Joyce Haber profiled the newlyweds' history, interviewing both Lee and Pam in early 1972 without either one ever mentioning his previous relationship. "I had six years on my own and I find it very lacking," claimed the actor. "As you get older, you get more serious about things… I think the bachelor dream is someone who subscribes to *Playboy*. Which isn't quite for me."

Lee Marvin's marriage to Pam Feeley ended the thousand-dollar-a-month payments he was voluntarily making to Michele Triola. According to David Kagon, the payments were made, "At a time when a thousand bucks a month was significant. This goes back to the late 1960's… According to his own statement, he agreed to pay her for a period of about five years. This was an oral agreement—and she agreed to that—provided that she didn't interfere with his life. Well, unfortunately, what happened was, he remarried. When he remarried, Ms. Triola saw fit, apparently, to speak to the new Mrs. Marvin. When the new Mrs. Marvin, Pamela, discovered that Lee was making these payments, you can imagine the reaction she had to that… I don't believe she [Pam] was aware at the time she married Lee that he was making these payments." Lee stopped making the payments in November, 1971. Less than four months later, just as he was about to step on stage in front of a live audience to tape an episode of "The Flip Wilson Show," Lee Marvin was served with papers, stating that Michele Triola was suing him for half of his wealth from the time they were together.

Michele Triola's lawyer from her short-lived first marriage was Marvin Mitchelson, a flamboyant headline-grabbing divorce attorney who came up with a plan to sue Lee Marvin. The plan included a carefully constructed strategy to win first in the court of public opinion. It began with a constant barrage of media-related interviews so the public would perceive Michele Triola not as the Glenn Close character from *Fatal Attraction* that Lee Marvin's associates witnessed, but as *Mildred Pierce*, who sacrificed unflinchingly for the person she loved, only to be emotionally and financially spurned for her efforts. Magazines ran interviews with Triola sporting such titles as *Coronet*'s "My Six Lost Years with Lee Marvin," and *Ladies Home Journal*'s "Divorce Without Marriage: The Curious Case of Lee Marvin's Common Law Wife."

Not surprisingly, the media loved the less than savory aspect of the public spectacle and did not attempt to check some of Triola's statements, such as: "Of course I knew Pam. She was Lee's best friend. They'd been to school together as kids. I used to speak to her on the phone often and Lee would write to her from time to time." She then claimed she was a dancer in Jose Greco's dance troupe in *Ship Of Fools*. In referring to her time with Marvin, she boldly stated, "There were many hard times during those early years. We were settled in as a couple a long time before he was a big name. He had his own TV show but he was not the superstar that they say he is now." When she had legally changed her name, which had so upset Lee Marvin, she said, "It was with Lee's approval. It was a joint idea. We had the name changed, not just I. We purposely kept it quiet."

The media blizzard occurred over the several years in which Mitchelson attempted to sue Lee Marvin for the newly minted phrase Mitchelson coined and defined as, "Palimony, alimony for a pal." Marvin was willing to make a large sum payment, but Mitchelson was seeking millions. Beginning in 1972, every attempt made by Mitchelson was thrown out of court. One effort found Kagon easily arguing on the grounds that his client was still married during the time the claim was being made. Superior Court Judge William Munnell dismissed the case in less than three minutes. Mitchelson plugged on, and in December 1976, the California State Supreme Court overturned the ruling of the lower court, giving the media-happy lawyer a glimmer of hope. In the interim, Mitchelson was caught off-guard by Kagon's countersuit and stated, "This move is one we didn't expect. It's very clever."

In early January of 1977, *Newsweek* reported that the number of unmarried couples in America had risen eight-fold according to census figures. It was their lead-in report to a new decision by the California State Supreme Court regarding Marvin vs. Marvin: "that the mere fact that a couple have not participated in a valid marriage ceremony cannot serve as a basis for a court's inference that the couple intend to keep their earnings and property separate and independent." Mitchelson was ecstatic and gleefully exclaimed, "This is going to open the floodgates to the courts. It's a Christmas present to all the unmarrieds." Lee Marvin was pragmatic by comparison, stating, "It could be several more years before we have a judgment of any kind." The legal wrangling did indeed continue for some time, with Mitchelson consistently coming up short for his client. In the interim, he had managed to find Triola work as a receptionist at the William Morris Agency where she met and began dating Dick Van Dyke in 1976.

The case finally was set for trial in California Supreme Court, January 1979. Lee Marvin remained steadfastly pragmatic, stating, "It doesn't disturb me. It's just that I'm sure it will embarrass my family and my friends. That's part of the position I'm in." In preparing the case, Kagon humorously noted of his client, "This was a man that probably did not own more than one or two suits. Matter of fact, at the time of the initial trial, he had to go out and buy three suits because we didn't know how long the trial would last. Obviously, he had to come into court wearing appropriate clothing."

The stage was set, the players in place and the cameras whirred. Television and print editorials were everywhere as daily accounts of the trial made front-page news. Nevermind the oil crisis, the recession, or any other daily occurrences. The water cooler discussion of 1979 was Marvin vs. Marvin. Triola basked in the spotlight as Rock Hudson famously told her at a party one night, "What a can of worms you've opened." The media circus surrounding the trial was aided by Triola's legal team and avoided by Marvin's. According to Marvin's lawyer David Kagon, "We were not going to try the case in the press. This case was going to be tried in the courtroom. As a matter of fact, we learned more about their case by reading newspaper articles. It made it that much easier."

Inside the courtroom, Mitchelson's histrionics hammered Judge Arthur K. Marshall with the point that Michele Triola gave Lee Marvin the best years of her life. The actor was even asked this when he testified. "No," he responded. "I gave her the best years of her life." Mitchelson also made an attempt to bring the couples' sex life into open court by having several letters admitted as evidence. All of Mitchelson's strategies were easily deflected by Kagon without once ever bringing up Michele Triola's past employment as a prostitute. When Triola testified on her own behalf, she broke down in tears as regularly as a "Perry Mason" defendant. The only words ever spoken by Lee Marvin to his ex-girlfriend in open court were during one of her crying jags, when he asked her to speak up.

The salacious aspect of the case involving the couple's sex life naturally gained the most media attention. Although the details were avoided in court, it was nevertheless insinuated that Triola had had an abortion. "There was an effort to show, to demonstrate, how devoted she was to him," recalled Kagon, "how he had treated her very badly in regards to her wanting to have children and he insisted on the abortion and gave her money to have an abortion. That raised a specter that really was very distasteful to Lee Marvin himself. Fact is, it wasn't true. We were prepared to demonstrate that it was physically impossible, but eventually the judge called us into chambers and told us that he didn't feel this line of testimony was really necessary and so we discontinued it."

The case dragged on for months as Triola laid claim to not only Marvin's successful film career, but that she had made Herculean efforts to salvage his reputation. She testified in court that she was the one responsible for saving the women dangling out of the window during the infamous "Robin Hood Party." Kagon elicited the aid of Ralph O'Hara to track down and find Tony Epper who had to sheepishly recount the actual events of that night, disproving Triola's account with simple physics. He also admitted to being the only culprit capable of shooting out the Vegas Vic sign and the inflatable King Kong. Business manager Ed Silver and publicist Paul Wasserman testified as well on Marvin's behalf. David Kagon stated he also received regular phone calls from show business agents without any knowledge of the case asking if their clients could testify just for the publicity.

The trial itself was not entirely without other moments of levity. Kagon recalled a moment that was a result of Mitchelson's flamboyant style: "He was a great showman. No question about that. Now one might debate what his legal skills were from the standpoint of his many times during the course of the trial... Here's an anecdote. I wasn't there, but it's a great story. Two other attorneys, assistants, were standing on either side of him, one on his left and one on his right. He was trying to impress the court with his sincerity. 'Judge, if I'm lying to this court may I be struck by a bolt of lightning right now!' and both attorneys jumped to the side." Lee Marvin's dark humor was also on display during the trial. The actor made no secret of his dislike of Mitchelson especially when the attorney suffered a major asthma attack in court and was rushed to a hospital. As the gurney wheeled Mitchelson out of court, Lee Marvin leaned over and said dryly, "Gee, I hope it's nothing trivial."

One of Mitchelson's attorneys, the one David Kagon claimed was the only one on their team with any brains, came to Kagon with an offer for a settlement. When Kagon asked him how much, the response was one hundred thousand dollars. He went to his client with the offer, who initially was willing to pay even more before the case had gone to trial. However, once the legal proceedings had begun, Kagon recalled his client's reaction to the offer: "When I mentioned it to Lee, he said two words, and they aren't the two words you think they are. He said 'No thanks.'"

When the April 1979 verdict came in, Judge Marshall's thirty-three-page verdict found Lee Marvin victorious on all counts. The fact that the trial judge ruled that Marvin should pay Triola one hundred and four thousand dollars so she might be able to get training in a new profession, has led many to believe Marvin lost the case. It lead to more speculative editorials in the media, a famous debate sketch on "Saturday Night Live," and several similar high profile cases including the likes of Nick Nolte, Peter Frampton, and Rod Stewart. For all of the media outcry vilifying Lee Marvin, he was proud to point out, "Not one feminist organization came out for Michele. All the big-time feminists were mum on it. Every woman I'd see on the street—every single one—said, 'I hope you win.' Old ladies, young ladies. So all I got was positive vibes, which is a boost to any actor's ego, right?'" It should also be noted that his wife Pam Marvin remained faithfully by his side throughout his court appearances.

Immediately following the trial, the Los Angeles District Attorney's office investigated the possibility of filing perjury charges against Marvin. The charges stemmed from an interview he gave with *Daily News* columnist Jimmy Breslin in which he claimed the only thing he learned from the trial was how to lie in court. Kagon quickly stepped in and clarified the actor's statement, saying Marvin meant he learned by watching others lie in court. The investigation was dropped, but it allowed Marvin the opportunity to expand on what he said without fear of reprisal. When asked in 1981 why he did not simply settle out of court, he said, "I never considered settling. Was it a matter of principle? Who'd spend that kind of money I've spent on anything else but principle? And yet, a smarter man might have just paid it off, just gotten rid of it, but I couldn't do it. I just cannot stand a lie and so I refused to bow out. What I'm trying to say is, I don't deal with trash."

Of the major players in the case, Michele Triola remained involved but unmarried to Dick Van Dyke, until her death from lung cancer in 2009. Van Dyke made a point in his autobiography that he gave her the $104,000 the court had first ordered. Triola often said she would pen her own version of the trial events, but like her long sought marriage contract, it never saw the light of day. Marvin Mitchelson was eventually disbarred for inappropriate behavior based on complaints filed by several of his clients and later jailed for tax evasion. He died in 2004.

The case did indeed change California family law, via the precedent-setting proceedings that allowed it to move forward. However, the flood of further palimony suits did not inundate the courts as the media and Marvin Mitchel-son had predicted. The only financial compensation Triola ever received was from Van Dyke. Marvin's lawyers appealed the ruling and received a judgment that not only won back the $104,000, but also made Triola pay the $6,000 in court costs, ironically, on the same day she was arrested for shoplifting in a Beverly Hills boutique. David Kagon, who passed away December 20, 2008, had agreed to be interviewed for this book in 1994. As if to prove that the best script did indeed win, Kagon sat back slowly in his wingback office chair and stated with a smile, "We didn't collect."

CHAPTER 14

The Last of the Wintry Heroes

IN THE 1980S, the blockbuster syndrome was in full effect, with the youth market taking over, and where even casual film fans were well aware of a film's opening weekend box office numbers. Despite the even younger audience members, a few postwar actors had experienced a renaissance, such as Burt Lancaster in *Atlantic City* (1981) and Paul Newman in *The Verdict* (1982), which were exemplary vehicles for their well-known screen personae. For Marvin, already in the winter of his years, it was not to be, at least not in his lifetime. It did not help that Marvin's years of hard drinking and a five-pack-a-day cigarette habit had aged him considerably beyond his fifty-six years. Coming off the successful palimony suit, he did luckily have a film about to be released that could capitalize on his notoriety and, more importantly, would showcase what he did better than any other actor of his generation.

Sam Fuller's *The Big Red One* had been the maverick director's "Holy Grail" for decades. Beloved in Europe for such strikingly independent films as *Shock Corridor* (1963) and *The Naked Kiss* (1964), the former newspaperman and WWII veteran had a distinct in-your-face style that matched his cigar-chomping, tough-talking personality. His dream project was based on his own nightmarish experiences in the war with a rifle company through North Africa, Sicily, the D-Day Invasion, and culminating with the liberation of the Falkenau concentration camp in Czechoslovakia. His main character was an unnamed veteran sergeant of "The Great War" who leads his four young riflemen through these pivotal battles of WWII.

"John Wayne wanted to do *The Big Red One* in the 50s, and got me a deal at Warners," recounted Fuller. "As much as I admired The Duke, it would have been a heroic picture —with Lee's persona it was a tragic picture of survivors. Closer to reality than a John Wayne picture. Lee was physically and emotionally my Sergeant."

The task of securing Marvin for the part began nearly twenty years before the film was even made. Although the two men had worked together previously on television's "The Virginian" and almost again on *The Klansman*, the film Fuller had dreamed of making with Marvin predates both projects. "I ran into Lee at the cigar store on Fairfax and he asked me about my pet project, *The Big Red One*," said Fuller. "I promised him right there and then the part of the Sergeant. Lee had one of the most sensitive souls and understood people immediately. No lengthy explanations. He knew right away what I wanted from him. There was this feeling of mutual trust and understanding. Even though he was playing a fictional character, he knew how much was based on a real history, real characters. Painful events and memories I lived through and survived." The conversation ended with a handshake in which Marvin promised, "If you ever get funding for this, I'm your Sergeant."

A circuitous path to funding followed, that included everyone from Peter Bogdanovich to Roger Corman's brother Gene, until a relatively small budget was finally secured. Once the contract had been signed, Marvin was true to his word and ready to play Fuller's Sergeant. Production began in Israel in 1978 with Marvin and Mark Hamill, Robert Carradine, Bobby Diccio, and Kelly Ward as his charges. Observing the interaction between Marvin and Fuller, Kelly Ward stated, "There was a lot that went unsaid because it was just a natural. Lee would nod, 'I know what to do.' Sam would smile, 'Atta boy. What a lad!' There was a real nice collaboration between the two because they made things happen. Kind of infused the whole cast with confidence."

Not since the likes of Robert Aldrich, John Ford, Frankenheimer, and Boorman had Marvin been so in tune with a director. The two men not only instinctively knew what was required of the other by virtue of their own war experiences; they also shared a vision of creativity that went beyond the norm of film making. There was no effort toward glorification or heroism. It was a story of survival, with both men making the challenge a greater one; putting it across viscerally to an audience.

Fuller claimed that the Sergeant he created was based partly on his commanding officer. "For me, I was inspired for the Sergeant by Terry de la Mesa Allen, who hit the covers of *Time* and *Newsweek*," Fuller stated proudly. "We loved him. He made the statement, 'Dead men made me a general.' He was an anti-Patton character, modest, taciturn, no overblown ego."

For Marvin, the inspiration came elsewhere but was just as strong. "He was a fifty-year-old first sergeant in an antiaircraft battalion that fought across Europe while I was in the South Pacific," the actor said of his inspiration. He also elaborated that, "He was a lieutenant in the First War, then when World War II came along, he enlisted as a private. My brother and I had enlisted, and all the junior executives in his firm were going in as lieutenant colonels right off the street. He didn't believe in that. Being a military man himself, he thought he could do more in the sergeant ranks. He became a high-powered sergeant… His paternal feelings for the men in his squad… hoping that someone would do the same for his two boys, wherever they were." Monte Marvin would have been proud of his son's assessment.

Fuller and Marvin put the young actors through a mini-boot camp of their own just prior to filming. "We were all shooting M-1's, the exact specs of which we were made to memorize at the time, but Lee had them down," remembers Ward. "We all put rifles to our shoulders, and shot very carefully at empty gas cans. They complimented everybody after you squeeze off eight rounds, which is the magazine of the weapon. Then, the clip pings out. They gave us little tips like, only shoot seven rounds. Don't shoot the eighth round because when the clip pops out of the rifle that can tell the enemy, if he's close enough, that you're empty, man. You're a target… It was an intense education in a very short period of time. The thing that was impressive was that, after we were all shooting properly—guns at shoulder level —he [Lee] grabs a rifle, puts in a clip and walks these steep banks. We were on a berm. Now, with the gun at hip level, he shot the gas can and hit it. It pings up in the air. At hip level, the real thing!"

The filming was tough in the blistering desert, though not entirely without moments of levity. Extras on the Israeli location consisted of residents in the area appropriately costumed for the scene. "To see those guys wearing those German coal-scuttle helmets, pull them off, and have yarmulkes on underneath—that was really something!," chuckled Fuller.

Another lighter moment occurred during one of the many hot and cramped scenes filmed in the hold of a ship as the men prepared to attack the shores of a French beachhead Marvin tells them is named "Colleville-sur-mer." "He couldn't say 'Colleville-sur-mer,' recalled Ward. "He would always flub the line on those words. I heard it in so many variations that day. Plus, it was 130 degrees in that vehicle. The cameras were seizing because the gears were expanding and they wouldn't turn the film. They had to put ice packs on the cameras. The lights made it even hotter. Lee kept going after 'Colleville-sur-mer.' Even to this day, in the film, the one take where he said it close to right, is in the film. It's a very deliberate reading: 'Nothing but combat rejects on the beach at 'COLLEVILLE-SUR-MER.' Nobody would notice but there's a kind of 'There! Fuck that line!' look all over his face. We all kidded him about it. We'd say, 'Get rid of this fucking guy. Let's get James Coburn.'"

Marvin was professional throughout the filming, and often surprised those gathered with impromptu vignettes not caught on film. A sequence shot in a Roman amphitheater earlier in the day was the perfect setting for one such moment. His training from the American Theater Wing intact, he walked up to the center of the stage just as the sun was setting. The natural lighting and his aged yet still resonant voice complemented the classical setting as Marvin recited a soliloquy from Shakespeare's "King Lear." All in attendance listened in awed silence as the drama and power of the extemporaneous performance filled the ancient arena that had stood silent for centuries.

The concentration camp sequence that climaxes the film remains one of the most moving moments Marvin would ever have on screen, accomplished without almost any dialogue. Each of the soldiers react to the horror they are witnessing in their own way, and for Marvin's

Sergeant, it is through the eyes and fading life of a malnourished child. "The kid was not supposed to drop the apple," recalled Ward. "Now again, it's an interesting and ironic touch in the film that most of the communication between the four soldiers and Lee is all hand gestures. It also enables him to communicate with this kid. He communicates with hand gestures." In a moment left in the final cut of the film that proved to be a fortuitous accident, "He gets the kid on his back and the kid is eating the apple. And the kid drops the apple and Sam only does one take. The take is in the film and you see Lee go, 'Aw shit.' But you know? It was honest. It was an honest moment."

When *The Big Red One* opened in the summer of 1980 after premiering at the Cannes Film Festival, it received mixed reviews albeit with the lion's share of praise going to Marvin. The actor went out of his way to promote the film. When he was asked why he wanted it to succeed he said it was, "My chance to make my own personal statement —with a good script, a good director and marvelous actors to work with. Sam shot all the stuff I felt about combat, the madness, the no-recall aspect. It's so fast when it's happening that everybody has a different story about the same instance."

Fearing the film would not attract an audience, Lorimar Pictures cut it down by more than an hour, rendering it almost incomprehensible and ensuring its failure at the box office. Fuller was so disgusted, he left the U.S. for France and did not return until shortly before his death in 1996.

For Lee Marvin, who gave his last great performance in the film, the film's failure raised the level of scorn he felt for contemporary audiences. When asked in an interview at the time what he thinks the current audience expects, he said, "Well besides complete idiocy, they want lack of respect. They want all the rules broken. The underdog has now become the leading man. He's the heavy, because he's kicking mother or shooting a bazooka into the sheriff's office. Next, he's got to burn down the town until there's nothing left. And the audience reaction is, 'Geez, ain't he great?' I think this all reflects on our times."

The contentment of semi-retirement in Tucson had reached its limit for him by 1981. Ralph O'Hara visited Marvin and remembers being told by the actor, "He said, 'Avoid any script that says, 'As you were riding the horse, you fell off and went down the hill, head over heels.' Avoid those scripts. Avoid the scripts that say, 'As he put on his snowshoes...' which he ended up doing with Bronson up there in Canada with Angie Dickinson."

That particular script was originally titled *Arctic Escapade*, and although Marvin's first reaction to the title was that it "sounds like a bunch of gays in Eskimo outfits," he was enticed by the prospect of working once again with director Robert Aldrich and costars Charles Bronson and Angie Dickinson. Ultimately, Peter Hunt directed this fictionalized account of the greatest manhunt in Canadian history. Retitled *Death Hunt*, it had Bronson cast as fugitive 'Albert Johnson' with Marvin as the grizzled career Mountie 'Edgar Millen' who leads a ragtag posse in pursuit of the outlaw.

Angie Dickinson, who had worked with him more than any other actress ("M Squad," *The Killers* and *Point Blank*) noticed a very different Lee Marvin on the chilly Alberta, Canada location. "He was quite bitter. Not so much sad as bitter. I'd say, 'Lee, look at the mountains!' 'Yeah, I saw 'em. I've been looking at them for two months.' He was drinking. We all just hated to see it."

She was still impressed, however, with what Marvin could do wordlessly in the film's best scene in which he goes through the aged contents of his foot locker: "It was a tough sequence because it was written a certain way, and Lee didn't want to do it. There I am with fourteen lines in the whole movie and all that. It was testy... The recall in his hands and in his eyes with every article! What is it like? It's thrilling to be part of the scene and a witness to the scene."

Marvin dutifully promoted the film on talk shows and the like, but often did so while inebriated. He slurred to one interviewer, "...with this kind of picture, if you just tell them the title, they know a lot. Charles Bronson and Lee Marvin. *Death Hunt* leaves no doubt in their minds. They know it's not a love story..."

Good scripts for actors in the winter of their years were getting harder to come by, especially for an actor who looked ten years older than he was. There were glimmers of hope in projects he felt would make excellent films, such as the deep-sea fishing adventure novel *Tournament*. There was also talk of a possible return to the stage in a worthy production. Unfortunately, none came to pass for almost three years, and funding for interesting projects such as *Tournament*, were nonexistent. As John Boorman so eloquently stated: "He picks through the midden of scripts, tossing them into the ashcan after a few pages. Only big-game fishing truly absorbs him today, but he reads on, waiting for the big one—the one that will redeem the rest, test him, draw out his powers in primal combat. He awaits the challenge, the call to heroic action. Part of him knows with a terrible clarity that such a test will not come, its time has passed. So it is with a cynical lilt of a smile that he greets the visitor... He casts the long shadow of Australopithecus, our mysterious animal ancestor that invented weapons and gave us our genetic compulsion for meting out death."

Given the strenuous challenge of his last films, *The Big Red One* and *Death Hunt*, Marvin was more than ready for a change of pace. "Those films absolutely kill me and I always get those kind of parts," he complained. "I must say, I'm looking forward to those executive parts, because the knees are gone. You know, it's true. The legs are the first to go."

True to his word, his return to the screen came with 1983's *Gorky Park*, based on the bestselling thriller by Martin Cruz Smith, and the first in a series of popular books featuring the lead character of 'Arkady Renko.' 'Renko' is a Soviet police investigator searching for a killer after three mutilated bodies are found in the titular locale, which leads to a complicated tale of political intrigue. The whodunit featured an international cast with William Hurt as 'Renko,' Marvin as American businessman 'Jack Osborne,' Polish actress Joanna Pacula, Brian Dennehy, Britain's Ian Bannen, and a host of other veteran British actors.

Noted British director Michael Apted was excited to work with Marvin in the handful of scenes in which the actor was scheduled to appear. Unfortunately, when Marvin and his wife got off the plane to the Helsinki locale, he had to be rushed to the hospital. "What I remember most vividly was that we rehearsed in hospital," recalled Apted. "Bill [Hurt] and I went into intensive care where he was in a bed. Had kind of tubes on it. We were rehearsing in hospital, which I must say, is a first and only time I've ever had to do that… Lee had such a huge commitment to doing it, and he wanted to do it well. He was prepared for the kind of indignity of having to be in hospital and rehearsing at the same time."

After Marvin was released, this commitment did not waver, and he rose to the challenge of playing the slickly dressed sable merchant who parries continually with Hurt's 'Renko.' Wearing expensive tailor-made suits, and immaculately groomed, he was almost exactly as Cruz-Smith had described him: "Into the alcove stepped a man, middle-aged, tall, lean and so dark that at first Arkady believed he might be an Arab. Straight white hair and black eyes, a long nose and an almost feminine mouth made an extraordinary combination, equine and handsome. On the hand carrying his towel he wore a gold signet ring. Arkady saw now that his skin was leathery, tanned rather than dark, tanned everywhere… He regarded Arkady without curiosity. Even his eyebrows seemed groomed. His Russian was excellent, as Arkady had known, but the tapes had missed the quality of animal assurance." Not since Vince Stone in 1952's *The Big Heat* had Marvin portrayed such a character, the major difference being that this individual, 'Osborne,' was much older and infinitely smarter. The scene, as quoted from the book, in which 'Osborne' and 'Renko' first confront each other in a public sauna, was depicted in the film, and according to Apted, "I remember him laying his towel on the bed and that great scene when he was dressing afterwards. He had an immaculate sense of timing so everything came together; the dialogue and the points. See, I remember that was one of his best days on it. He really enjoyed that."

The filmmakers had their hands full trying to recreate Soviet Russia in the Helsinki location, as well as dealing with the conflicts within the cast. Hurt grappled with the character and the cast but, surprisingly, found a comrade in Marvin. "Marvin was incredibly supportive of him," stated Apted, "much more so than the English actors around him. He [Marvin] really understood what Bill was going through, how difficult it was to do a role of this size and this responsibility. Lee was very generous with Bill and very supportive of him. For me, [he was] a real kind of good, solid rock, a good friend to have around. Although we didn't share much history together... we got along very well. He was just very supportive for me and for Bill." The other cast members recognized him for the cinematic legend he had become and treated him like royalty. As to his equally legendary drinking, "His reputation preceded him, being quite a heavy drinker," stated Apted. "I think what he did was have one night a week when he would drink on a Saturday night. Otherwise, he seemed to be totally off that sort of stuff; totally focused on what he was doing."

Released in December, 1983, the movie was not the box office hit the filmmakers had hoped for. It is unfortunate, as the film has merit despite its noticeable flaws. Apted felt the failure was cultural, stating, "I don't think Western audiences became interested in Russia until Gorbachev came around. There's a lot of interest in the film in Europe but it did very poorly here, which is disappointing. The very thing that interested me about it didn't interest an American audience. I loved that I was going into a new environment, to something I'd never been to before. Creating a new world very much as I had done in a film I had done a bit earlier, *Coal Miner's Daughter...*" One of the film's few fans was Lee Marvin, who took the time to write Apted and tell him how pleased he was with the finished film. The actor had good reason to be pleased, as he had never before appeared in so elegantly sinister a role on screen and, sadly, never would again.

The Marvin brood had a reunion of sorts when the actor's daughter Cynthia married in 1982. Marvin readily admitted over the years that he had never really been much of a father, and on occasion could be out and out cruel. When Betty had informed Lee that daughter Courtenay was dealing with issues concerning her sexuality, he managed to hurt his children's feelings with the statement, "Great, she could be the son I always wanted." He and Pam attended the California wedding and the actor was on his best behavior. When he asked Betty privately if he was expected to pay for the affair, she said, "Well, I think that's your privilege, dear."

On the heels of *Gorky Park*, he agreed to make his first foreign film, a poorly executed European film entitled *Dog Day* in which he played an aged American criminal on the lam from a botched bank robbery, hiding out in the French farmhouse of an extremely dysfunctional family. "I'd always wanted to work in France and this was a French production with a good script," rationalized Marvin. He also considered dubbing his own dialogue in French but ultimately felt he was not up to the challenge. The film had potential in the way it commented on the American folklore of gangsters and criminals which may have been what attracted Marvin to the project; but the execution bordered on the sleazy and pornographic.

The sole benefit for the actor was to be back in France for the Deauville Film Festival to which he was invited as Guest of Honor. "I enjoyed that," Marvin told the *L.A. Times.* "They're such cinema fans in France. They told me stuff about myself I'd forgotten years ago. Best of all, Henry Hathaway was there. He came up behind me as I was talking to some journalists. 'Still talking instead of listening,' he said. Then we went off and had an evening together. He's the man who put me in pictures, remember."

Dog Day did not receive much of a reception when it was released in 1984, and quickly found its way on to the dollar rental shelf of video stores. Public appearances for Marvin consisted mostly of the occasional talk show in which he joked about his career, or regular appearances on one of Bob Hope's specials. It was quick and fairly easy work for him but on one such occasion, Meyer Mishkin accompanied his client along with Pam Marvin.

Mishkin remembers the taping of the show vividly because of a telling incident: "Lucille Ball was on the show," recalled the agent in 1994. "She comes off and sees me. We hug, then kiss, she says hello to Lee and his wife and then walks away. As she's taking a few steps away, she turns around, comes back. I think she saw something on Lee's wife's face that was negative. She comes back and she said almost directly to Lee's wife about me, 'And he's the best,' and walks off... Angie [Dickinson] comes off and stops and kisses me on the cheek, so forth and so on. Lee, when I look at him, Lee's going and making a face. Something must have happened there that Lee caught from his wife's face about me. I don't know but Lucy caught it... See, over the years I've learned that when an actor is represented by you, and he gets married, within six months, he leaves you... He [Lee] wouldn't do it. I mean if it did come up, he wouldn't do it... I talk with Pam now about once a week. Very friendly now. Very friendly."

Through marriages, affairs, career highs and lows, and more than three decades of every possible scenario, with the sole exception of the brief sabbatical during "M Squad," Mishkin and Marvin had been through it all, together. Agents are not often given their due in the film industry, and often there is good reason for this. One of the rare times they were acknowledged took place at a tribute dinner held at the Beverly Hills Hilton in 1981. Many stars attended to make jokes at their agents' expense, but the most surprising of all was Lee Marvin. He took to the podium to state: "He was my friend always, and then my agent. I have never discussed any of my work with anybody —my family, the elevator operator, nobody. I discuss it with Meyer. Including my personal problems. If there's a fee involved, I'm not concerned about it. I like Meyer."

Professionally, the downward spiral continued for Marvin. His son Christopher was present when he was considering his next project. "I went to visit him, and we're sitting in his kitchen. He had this nice counter in the middle of the kitchen you could, like, lean against it, eat crackers and sardines, and just talk across the thing. I saw the script and said, 'What's this?' He said, 'Aww, some goddamned sequel to *The Dirty Dozen*. Listen to this line from this. Isn't this shit or what?' I said, 'Yeah dad, you don't have to do that shit.' I called him a month later, and he said; 'I gotta leave.' I said, 'Where you going?' He said, 'I gotta do this thing.' When he told me, I teased him with, 'You asshole!' He said, 'Yeah, shit, I know I told you I wasn't going to do it.' I said, 'Well, enjoy it, man.' I mean it was just pure hell. He said he needed the kick, man. That's how it works."

The 1985 TV-movie, *The Dirty Dozen: The Next Mission* had the original cast members Richard Jaeckel and Ernest Borgnine returning with Marvin in a sequel to the original movie with a host of young actors as a new dozen. The story in the sequel takes place only months after the first film, but Marvin looked ancient compared to his earlier rugged appearance in 1967. The ratings were strong enough however to rate several more sequels featuring Telly Savalas, and even a short-lived TV series.

Aside from a Marine Corps. training film, Lee Marvin's cinematic swan song was the 1986 Chuck Norris action opus *Delta Force*. Based loosely on real events, Marvin played 'Colonel Nick Alexander,' the leader of an antiterrorist group with Norris as the star player who wipes out an entire Arab terrorist organization single-handedly. The Israeli-produced film boasted a cast of Martin Balsam, Joey Bishop, Robert Forster, Lainie Kazan, George Kennedy, Hanna Schygulla, Susan Strasberg, Bo Svenson, Shelley Winters, and Robert Vaughn. "I got a call from the producers," Marvin explained at the time of the film's release, "they told me the story in about fifteen minutes. I said, 'Sounds good to me,' my agent met with them, and twenty minutes later, the deal was made. No sweat. Four weeks later I was off to Israel; ten weeks later it was shot and done and I was back in Tucson. No bull. Just BANG."

After a recent TV viewing of the film, Meyer Mishkin wistfully recalled, "Lee looked so bad. The booze and the smoking… I had said to him, 'Why do you want to…' He said, 'I gotta get out of the house.' I think he got fifty thousand dollars. He just wanted out of the house.... If you look at *Delta Force*, you'll see an aging, aging man. It was almost as if he was saying, again, 'I'm a Marine. I dare you to kill me.'" Robert Vaughn, who played Marvin's superior in the film, remembered, "He was very pleasant but he was fragile; getting up very slowly, getting down very slowly. He was not in good health."

Despite Marvin's frail appearance, Vaughn is quick to point out, "I just thought he was a classic case of movie star appeal. There was just nobody else like him. The X Factor, sex appeal, whatever you want to call it, Lee was Lee, and he was a tremendous force on screen." Tragically, that tremendous force was wasted in the live-action Chuck Norris cartoon. The action film that Marvin had so brilliantly pioneered in his ascent to screen prominence was now crumbling around him in a sensationalized exploitation of American jingoism shown through a display of superior firepower. In promoting the film, he fully understood the difference between real events and what the film depicted, stating, "Go see *Delta Force*. The bad guy gets it. If we can satisfy the public with the visual action of getting even and still utilize diplomacy, we've solved the problem, haven't we? In the movies you get even; in life diplomacy is best."

Back in Tucson, the aging soldier filled his days with work on his house, catching up on his reading, raising and nurturing the giant saguaro cacti indigenous to the region, and the occasional foray into oil painting. He also welcomed and entertained old friends such as Mitch Ryan. "I would often go down there and watch old movies," recalled Ryan. "He had a great collection. We would watch old Bogart movies. We would pick one or he'd find one that he'd get… I remember one time we watched Boorman's movie about King Arthur, *Excalibur*. And *Casablanca* we watched, one time."

Asked if they ever watched Marvin's old films together, Ryan responded, "No, we never did. We watched *Monte Walsh* together once and he was a little upset at the cut. But he said, 'It's all right. What the fuck. The guys gotta do what they do.' He was kind of amazing about that. He said it was kind of a shame. He didn't spend any time grinding it out, or anything."

Another factor as he got older that Marvin had to confront was the loss of his oldest and closest friends. He had attended the funeral of Robert Aldrich in 1983, and spoke briefly at Sam Peckinpah's memorial the following year. He chose his words carefully, quoting the Bible passage, "I have fought the good fight, I have finished the course, I have kept the faith."

Hardest of all to deal with, however, was the death of his old friend, Keenan Wynn. The two had not been in much contact since their wild days in Malibu, but when Marvin received word of Wynn's inoperable pancreatic cancer, he made a special trip to see his seventy-year-old comrade. "Lee went in there by himself for a while," stated Ned Wynn. "I don't know what was said because I wasn't there. My dad told me later. He said he loved Lee, and Lee told my father that he loved him. It was probably very tearful. Keep in mind, my father was really dying. There was no kidding about it from the doctors. They didn't dangle any false hope to hang on to. They gave him six months, but he hung in for eight. Anyway, Lee came out and talked a little bit about Arizona. He loved it out there…"

Lee Marvin's own health began to rapidly deteriorate. He was hospitalized in December, 1986 for intestinal surgery after complaining of abdominal pain. Doctors at Tucson Medical Center discovered that his colon was inflamed but there were no signs of a feared malignancy. He continued to smoke despite crippling coughing jags. He was supposed to be on oxygen but it did little to curtail his behavior. "Christopher used to drive over there to see him and felt very strongly that at the end he really didn't care about living," recalled his first wife, Betty Marvin. "It was interesting. He'd still take off the oxygen mask and smoke."

Other health issues ensued following his intestinal operation. According to Ralph O'Hara, "He got hepatitis from the blood. That's why he couldn't recover from the operation. They put a colostomy bag on him and he walked around with coveralls."

O'Hara kept a vigil from his home in Santa Monica and recalled, "I could tell he was losing it because he was bedridden. I kept saying, 'Hang in there, you son-of-a-bitch. Don't you dare fall down. C'mon, fight it!' He'd say, 'I'm all right. I'll be up tomorrow.' I'd say, 'Get up today! You stupid fuck, get up!' I felt he was going to die. I started crying on the phone when I talked to him. I told him I couldn't hack it, because my other friend had just died while on the phone as I was talking to him. Here I was talking to Lee now, and I had the same feeling. Lee was not going to survive this. I could tell by his voice. He didn't sound well at all."

Marvin was back in the hospital again in mid-August following another coughing attack that this time seriously hampered his breathing. His son Chris remembers visiting his father: "When I first went in and saw him, the skin was draped over him like a skeleton and he was just skin and bones. I saw a tube in his nose, in his mouth, in his ear, in his asshole, in his dick. There he was and it was like 'Am I a human being?' I looked at these young doctors and I was so mad at them…"

Pamela Marvin steadfastly and dutifully remained by her husband's bedside during the difficult hospital stay. Mitch Ryan was there visiting on August 29 and saw the condition his friend was in. "He was very uncomfortable and very… he had a look on his face like, 'What the fuck, you know? If you live like I do, this is probably the way you end up.' I read that into his face. I don't know if it was that … he did make some kind of derogatory comment about all the fucking machines that were tied up to him. It was sort of like, 'Look at this. What the fuck is this?' or 'How about this?'"

The Ryans left later that day but heard what had transpired. "I wasn't there at the time he had this breathing attack. He couldn't breathe… It's why he went to the hospital; emphysema, or something. The windpipe has closed down due to inflammation. So, he went to a hospital and they gave him huge, massive shots of steroids to relax the throat so he could start breathing. What it did was perforate his liver and his kidneys. As they found out later, you don't give alcoholics steroids because it's very dangerous. The doctors somehow didn't know that. They figured we got to get him breathing so we'll take the chance or something. Anyway, he closed up again and when they tried to put tubes down his throat he wouldn't let them. He fought it so violently he had a heart attack…"

Lee Marvin, the last of the wintry heroes, passed away at Tucson Medical Center at the premature age of sixty-three, with Pam at his bedside. As he had once inferred to Mitch Ryan, he did indeed suffer the consequences of living life on his own terms. He also spent that lifetime committed to expressing a simple truth. As his Great Uncle Ross Marvin learned tragically, and his father tried unsuccessfully to forget, man's capacity for inhumanity is boundless.

Towards the end, it was expressed with Marvin's signature dark humor, sardonically providing a mission statement to his entire cinematic career. In playing *Death Hunt*'s weathered Canadian Mountie, leading a posse through the frozen north, Marvin's character has begrudgingly been taking orders from a much younger "by-the-book" officer. In a nighttime scene around a campfire, one of the posse teases the young greenhorn incessantly, until he finally loses his temper and strikes back in primal anger. Watching the proceedings and peering over his coffee cup, the wizened Marvin smiles conspiratorially and growls, "Look who just got uncivilized."

EPILOGUE

As Depression-era hobo "A-No. 1" in 1973's Emperor of the North, *the Marvin persona was on full display: tough, unsentimental, prone to indescribable violence if provoked, and willing to mentor a young prodigy with such wisdom as, "You could be a meateater, kid. And I mean people, not their garbage."*

The Inglorious Bastard Sons of Lee

IN THE TWENTY-FIVE plus years since his untimely death, the Lee Marvin cult has been steadily on the rise. In 1992, independent film maker Jim Jarmusch wrote in *Film Comment* magazine, "One actor I'm a big fan of is Lee Marvin. Just the idea of Marvin's characters being outsiders and very violent appeals to me. Some seem to have a very strong code—even if it's a psychotic one—that he follows rigidly."

He then went even further, recounting a tale involving a secret organization known as "The Sons of Lee Marvin" whose members include Jarmusch, musicians Tom Waits and Nick Cave, and several others. The sole requirement for entry, other than being a fan, is to bear a physical resemblance to Marvin himself. No details were given other than the following anecdote: "Six months ago, Tom Waits was in a bar somewhere in Northern California, and the bartender said, 'You're Tom Waits, right? A guy over there wants to talk to you.' Tom went over to this dark corner booth and the guy sitting there said, 'Sit down, I want to talk to you.' So Tom started getting a little aggressive: 'What the fuck do you want to talk to me about? I don't know you.' And the guy said, 'What is this bullshit about the Sons of Lee Marvin?' Tom said, 'Well, it's a secret organization and I'm not supposed to talk about it.' The guy said, 'I don't like it.' Tom said, 'What's it to you?' The guy said, 'I'm Lee Marvin's son' —and he really was. He thought it was insulting, but it's not, it's completely out of respect for Lee Marvin."

Lee Marvin would have been the first one surprised by the posthumous grassroots interest in his career. In the months leading up to his death his disposition had considerably soured. In his last interviews he denigrated almost all of the films he had made. His marriage to Pam had not been the storybook romance the media had claimed. A few months before his death he even attempted to throw her out of the house. She refused and remained at his bedside.

Lee Marvin's death earned respectful obituaries, but the news of his passing was overshadowed by the death of John Huston the day before. Pam had her husband's remains cremated and interred at Arlington National Cemetary. Betty returned from Europe shocked by the news, and held a memorial by the beach attended by several friends and all of his children.

In spite of a twenty-two-page will, as his executor, Pam incurred the usual wrangling from family members over her husband's substantial estate. Although his biological children reportedly received twenty thousand dollars each, Pam's children received considerably more. The debate rages on to this day as Pam and her daughter continue to be in legal dispute over the home in Tucson.

While Lee Marvin's property may still be the object of debate, his professional legacy has grown exponentially through the years. The appreciation of his work on a more esoteric level began as early as 1968 when Marvin's career was at its apex. The next generation of filmmakers had grown up on a steady diet of his film performances in both movie theaters and television showings.

Martin Scorsese, who is of this generation, and arguably the greatest filmmaker in America currently working, had made his directorial debut with the semi-autobiographical 1968 film, *Who's That Knocking at My Door.* In one standout scene, the lead character, played by Harvey Keitel, talks about his love of bad guys in movies to his would-be girlfriend, and expounds on his personal favorite: "Lee Marvin. Now there's a real bad guy. You see, he doesn't just play a tough guy, he has to go all the way. He dresses in black, you know. He snarls. He breaks things. He kicks people. He bites. That's right. He was in this movie *Liberty Valance.* You ever see that one? Anyway, he comes into a room in the picture. He can't just walk into a room. He walks in. He snarls. He kicks over a few chairs and tables. He breaks a few things. And then he sits down. I mean, that's really a bad guy... You know, Marvin just can't do anything normal. He's gotta... You know, if he, like, if he picks up a drink with his hands, he's gotta look like he's gonna squash it. Imagine what women think. To them, he's the worst kind of bad guy. He not only kills people, he breaks furniture."

Scorsese would also go on to redefine the use of violence and its intensity in cinema even more, especially with such films as *Taxi Driver* (1976), *Raging Bull* (1980) and *Goodfellas* (1990). Hs first major critical success was 1973's *Mean Streets* and when the street savvy characters decide to go to the movies, the viewer sees the marquee poster to *Point Blank* prominently displayed in the movie house lobby.

It would be almost two decades before another young filmmaker would pay homage to Marvin's influence on screen by a director who would also redefine American film violence for an entirely new generation. Quentin Tarantino's directorial debut was the low-budget heist film *Reservoir Dogs* (1992), and a scene in which Michael Madsen and, again, Harvey Keitel almost come to blows, ends with Madsen stating, "I bet you're a big Lee Marvin fan, aren't you? Me too. I love that guy." Also, Tarantino's signature film, 1994's *Pulp Fiction,* included two professional hit men played by Samuel L. Jackson and John Travolta who appear to be clearly modeled after Marvin's and Clu Gulager's characters in *The Killers.*

In 1995 a group of Generation X'ers from Southern California heard about The Sons of Lee Marvin and took it upon themselves to create the Bastard Sons of Lee (BSOL). Founder Ron 'Liberty Valance' Walker told the *L.A. Times,* "Lee's sort of the wild man. So, maybe we live vicariously through him."

Chris Marvin read the article and got in touch with the BSOL, receiving a warm reception. As for the more secretive Sons of Lee Marvin, they do indeed exist; however Chris proved that the aforementioned confrontation with Waits was more apocryphal than fact. Marvin, a studio drummer, knew Waits professionally, and remarked, "I hadn't seen Tom in a few years. I asked him about the Jarmusch article and he said, 'Aw, Chris, it's Jim Jarmusch's crazy nightmare. It wasn't me!' That kind of threw me off… I'd be honored though, to hang out with them." The real son of Lee Marvin keeps his father's legacy alive without the aid of Jarmusch and Company. Christopher cultivates his own cacti grafted from the cuttings of his father's original plants.

Director Joe Dante, known for the popular 1984 film *Gremlins* and a true purveyor of "Baby Boomer" pop culture, directed the 1998 film *Small Soldiers*. The fantasy plot involved action figure dolls doing battle with their more peace loving counterparts. The lead action figure, named Chip Hazard, bore more than a passing resemblance to Marvin. Lending his voice to the character was Tommy Lee Jones, an actor whose resemblance to Marvin is more than coincidental. For good measure, Dante hired the likes of Ernest Borgnine, Jim Brown, Clint Walker, and George Kennedy to provide the voices of the other action figures. "They were using us for name value. They were getting everybody they could from *The Dirty Dozen*," stated Walker. "I think the toy soldiers were a great deal."

In the original 1967 classic, singer/actor Trini Lopez had made an abrupt exit from the film after demanding more money from Aldrich. Ironically, when *Small Soldiers* went into production, Clint Walker recounted, "Trini Lopez was there, but again, I guess they couldn't make the deal. He never did anything, so I don't know." It did not spoil the reunion, as he added, "I think everybody enjoyed seeing everybody. It was good. I enjoyed seeing the fellas."

Like Bogart's legacy before him, the Marvin cult continues to lives on. *The Big Red One* was reassembled to great acclaim at the 2004 Cannes Film Festival. The popular 2009 Tarantino film *Inglorious Basterds* borrowed more than a little from *The Dirty Dozen* and is the most financially successful film of Tarantino's career. MTV also offered an unexpected tribute to Lee Marvin in 2009. The network polled young filmmakers for "Our Greatest Movie Badasses," and of the top ten, only two were not part of a recent production. *The Wild Bunch*'s Pike Bishop (co-created by Marvin) was #7 while *Point Blank*'s Walker took the #5 spot. Quite an honor considering the participants were infants when Lee Marvin died.

Film historian John Farr gave the actor's lasting impact a rallying cry in the following 2010 *Huffington Post* entry: "With precious few exceptions, all I see is a lot of boys in Hollywood these days, both real and aging. Since Lee Marvin's been gone so long, there's a whole new generation of young adults out there who likely don't even know who he was. Let's change that." Let us indeed.

My Father

When Dwayne asked me if I would be interested in writing a brief piece to be included in his biography about my father, Lee Marvin, I was at first reluctant, since I had turned down many such invitations before. But, after reading the book, it brought back many loving memories of my father...

He could be very stern at times, and yet very sensitive and tender, kissing me on the lips, with "How goes the battle?" and delivering one-liners to explain himself.

When I was a boy, around the age of ten, I used to take long walks on the beach with my father, collecting beach glass. It was a serious pursuit - looking for the perfectly smooth, well-rounded pieces of Milk-of-Magnesia blue or Coca-Cola green, and, if we were lucky, an occasional piece of Japanese glass buoy. I still follow this tradition, walking the beach every day, searching for beach glass to make my mosaic artwork. I go with my Australian Shepherd, Liberty, named after my father's dog, a Puli breed.

Around that time he gave me a Swiss Army knife, which he tied to a notched leather band, so I could easily retrieve it from my back pocket. I lost it playing in the park with my pals. I was very upset and not sure how my father would react, but Dad laughed and said, "Just like a kid."

We loved listening to music together. He taught me to appreciate the likes of Leadbelly, Blind Lemon Jefferson and other blues artists of an earlier time. On the other hand he appreciated my music of the sixties—Jimi Hendrix, the Rolling Stones, Jeff Beck, and English Blues.

He loved the desert. In my twenties, when I used to visit him in Arizona, we would take long walks and he would explain how the different types of cactus cohabited with each other. I learned to appreciate his love of these plants. Now I spend time with him every day in my own garden full of many varieties of cacti.

It makes me sad he died so young at age sixty-three and I, thirty-four at the time, thought I knew it all, and did not appreciate all he had to offer. Now that I am more mature at sixty, I would like to have lengthy, in-depth conversations with him.

Toward the end, my sisters and I drove down to see him in the hospital after surgery. He said, "Come here." When I leaned over him in his hospital bed, he whispered, "Get out of here while you still can." He hated hospitals and did not want me to see him in such a frail condition. He died not long after.

Aside from being a great actor, my father was very complex. He was independent, kind, funny, generous, and could spot a phony a mile away. Hopefully, I have inherited some of these qualities.

I miss him.

Christopher L. Marvin
November, 2012

The oldest child and only son of Lee Marvin, Christopher Marvin was a professional drummer and session musician, who recorded and toured with many notable musicians. He lived in Santa Barbara where he also plied his craft as a mosaic artist, working exclusively with beach glass. Mr. Marvin died in 2013 shortly after this book's hardcover publication.

Acknowledgments

PRESIDENT OBAMA's claim that "If you were successful, somebody along the line gave you some help," is never truer than when it comes to producing a book credited to one person. I first considered writing as a career after meeting the late Tony Thomas who encouraged me to pursue my dream. Years later, a conversation with author Marshall Terrill became the genesis of *Lee Marvin: Point Blank* and he has remained one of this project's biggest cheerleaders. The research took many twists and turns but through it all there was always Larry Edmunds Bookshop, Hollywood Book & Poster, Cinephile, Eddie Brandt's Saturday Matinee, the Margaret Herrick Library, Hollywood Movie Posters, UCLA Television Archives and the Museums of Television & Radio.

If I have forgotten anyone, please be assured that is for no other reason than failing memory and not lack of gratitude. I am greatly indebted to the more than one hundred individuals who have shared their memories of Lee Marvin with me. Although I may not have quoted all of them in the text, they were each important to my research and are noted individually in the bibliography.

The ongoing research could not have been possible without the additional help of Dyann Bacci, Sandra Diaz, Wolf Forrest, Feliks Gailitis, John Gloske, Tara Gordon, Mark Haggard, Loren Janes, and Robin Roberts of the Screen Actors Guild.

As the book progressed, I was aided considerably by Harriette Ellis, still one of the best editors I have ever had the privilege to work with. She also graciously put me in contact with her nephew, Harold Meyerson. As an editor with *L.A. Weekly*, he did not hesitate for a moment when I asked him to recommend the best literary agent he could think of.

Which brings me to Mike Hamilburg. Every author claims to have the world's greatest agent but Mike truly is. When the project lay fallow for several years and I was ready to return to it full time, I was not sure that Mike would still be interested. He was indeed and with an enthusiasm that still impresses. He truly is the best of the best.

Kudos must also go out to Nicole Rakozy and her predecessor at Lucent Books Chandra Howard, for helping me hone my skills in biographical writing, and in realizing the value of a good theme. Mike Miller, Fujiko Miller and Bill Krohn helped to mold the project in its earliest stages. Ted Okuda, Mike Stein, Mai-ly Nguyen, Ted Nelson, Christine Atkinson and Phil Snyder all supported this project in their own unique way and for their efforts I humbly thank them.

Several personal friends deserve credit for their generosity during the length of this project and they know why. Michael Arold, Michael Barrow, Gregg Fry, Roy Lee Lewis, Greg Lynch, Brett Koth, Dan Silverman, and the brethren of the BSOL: I am forever in your debt.

To bring this book to print required the impressive talents of Jake Kiehle, Villette Harris, Meaghan Miller, Jonathan Kirsch, Bonnie Winings, Barry Smith, Betsy Hulsebosch, and the only publisher in America with any vision, Tim Schaffner.

My parents have both passed on since the inception of this project but they believed in it and supported it all along. The same can be said of both my sisters, Belinda Becerra and Fern Epstein, and my nieces, Natalie and Danielle, as well as the rest of my family and friends.

I have purposely saved the best for last. The amount of words required to properly thank her would take the amount of text in this book and then some. She was there from before the beginning and long after the end. She means EVERYTHING to me. I love you, Barbara.

READING GROUP GUIDE

for

LEE MARVIN: Point Blank
by Dwayne Epstein

Q&A with the Author
by Andrew Kemp, Contributing Editor, ATL RETRO.COM,
1/31/2013

A History of Violence: Dwayne Epstein Aims POINT BLANK to Uncover the Real Lee Marvin in First Definitive Biography

LEE MARVIN is an icon of 1960s cinema, a legendary screen tough-guy who punched hard and lived harder, or at least that's how the story goes. Before he became famous on the screen, Marvin worked for years in thankless villain roles and bit parts, often outshining his co-stars, and it took over a decade of hard work and a few unhappy years in series television before he finally saw a reward for his effort. During his Hollywood peak, Marvin starred in a string of classics that rewrote the rules on screen violence and forever changed the landscape of American cinema, including *The Professionals* (1966), *The Dirty Dozen* (1967), and *Point Blank* (1967).

Dwayne Epstein has spent almost two decades researching the life and legacy of Lee Marvin. Epstein had unprecedented access to the Marvin family and a mountain of records and personal letters, and the result is the first major biography of Marvin to dig into the roots behind the actor's history of violence, his unusual family legacy, and the demons that drove him to alcoholism and hell-raising....ATLRetro recently spoke with Epstein to ask him about the book and about Marvin's storied career.

ATLRetro.com: *You've written a large number of Hollywood biographies for the youth market. LEE MARVIN: POINT BLANK is the first adult biography that you've written.*

Dwayne Epstein: That would be accurate. The other biographies I've written were for a company called Lucent and they were for a series called "People in the News." A lot were what you would call Hollywood biographies, but also about political figures. I wrote about Hillary Clinton and Nancy Pelosi, as well as Adam Sandler, Will Ferrell, Denzel Washington.

Why Lee Marvin as the subject of your first major biography, then?

Lee Marvin has always fascinated me. I'm a baby boomer and I grew up watching *The Dirty Dozen* on TV, way back when they were showing it in two parts. I can watch it now and distinctly remember when the first part would end and the second part would begin. In all of his films, he was always very distinct to me, even when he was not the leading actor. Even more so after I decided to write a book on him, and the more I found out about him. He was much more than he was on screen, obviously, just like most people are. He was a fascinating man. When I researched the book, I discovered he really was the first of his kind, I mean of the post-war actors; he pretty much created the modern America cinema of violence as we know it. It came from him, not from Clint Eastwood. Lee Marvin predated Clint Eastwood by a couple of years.

You say you've been researching the book for a long time, and the research is obvious when you read it. How long did you research and work on the book?

I began it in 1994, so that went on about 18 years. Many of the people I interviewed for the book are no longer with us, and it was a real saving grace in some ways that I was able to do it when I did. Such as his brother, who had never been interviewed before.

How did that come about?

That became kind of a cool story. Like I said, he had never been interviewed, and I found that his brother had worked for the New York City school district and that he was a teacher. I have a cousin in New York who works in the teacher union, and I contacted her and asked her if she knew of a way to get into contact with Robert Marvin, and she said if he had any connection with the teacher's union at all, [she'd] find him. And she did. At the time, he still lived in the Marvin family home up by Woodstock, NY. I took a shot and gave him a call, and I wasn't on the phone with him two seconds when I knew I had Lee Marvin's brother. He sounded just like him.

Yeah, he had a distinct voice.

Yes, he did. That voice was one of his many, many great attributes as an actor.

You mention in the book that there had been studio biographies written on Lee Marvin, but that they had inaccuracies. Why did it take this long for someone to get to the definitive Lee Marvin story?

When I say studio biographies, I mean something produced by the studio to promote the film. Not an actual print biography. Press books and press releases, what have you. Some of the misinformation that's been put out there is a result of Lee Marvin himself. He created his own mythology. One or two other books had been printed previously, and if there's been misinformation there, it's because Lee Marvin loved to tell stories. He was a heck of a storyteller. He knew a good story when he made one up, and he would promote it.

Your book is getting beyond all of that and collecting the facts from everyone else, though.

Right. As often as I could, I would verify a particular story from one source with another source. I would compare one version of a story to another, such as how he got started as an actor – him often saying he was fixing the toilet at the Maverick Theater in Woodstock when his destiny called. But there are several quotes from people in that same time period who say that would be pretty hard to do since the Maverick Theater didn't have a toilet.

When reading the book, Lee Marvin's family is just as important to the book as his career. He had the great uncle who died in Robert Peary's North Pole expedition.

That's one of the most fascinating things I discovered while doing the research. I was blown away to find out the true story behind Ross Marvin.

It's kind of mind-blowing. Like, this guy had such a family history.

That was one of the early connections I made to create the theme of the book. If you believe in this thing about fate or destiny or what have you, it was there in Marvin's life before he was even born. His trail was preset, as it was. It dates back even before Ross Marvin.

In what way?

I love this story, and Lee Marvin loved to tell this story, too. The earliest Marvins in America helped settle the colony of Connecticut, and there was a puritan named Matthew Marvin who would go on fiery pub raids to get the farmers out of the pubs and into the churches. There was fire and brimstone in Lee Marvin's ancestry. He also had a varied history in terms of the colorful characters in it. He was related to George Washington and Robert E. Lee, which is why he has the name that he has. His older brother's name is Robert, and he's Lee. His mother was a very conscientious Virginia southern woman, and that kind of thing was important to her.

You talk about the theme of his family, and I noticed that there's another theme running through his story about absent fathers. His father was always traveling, and his father was raised by his uncle who passed, and Lee Marvin was always traveling.

You're right about that aspect, but to give it even more perspective, I would say that dysfunctional family was really a looming shadow in Lee Marvin's life. The violence that was perpetrated during World War II did propel his career as an actor, but it wasn't the end-all, be-all. Before that, he had travails in his family. There was alcoholism, there was abuse, all kinds of stuff. And like many families like that, there was still love. Everybody in the family loved each other, they just didn't quite know how to handle their emotions.

I want to talk for a second about this interesting chapter that you wrote. Marvin is in the Pacific Theatre in World War II, and you construct his military career almost entirely through the letters that he was sending home. You have some commentary, but almost the whole chapter is just his letters. What was it about his letters that you found so compelling that you wanted to just let him take the stage?

I'm glad you mentioned that. That was a conscious choice based on a crisis I was facing. I knew how critical that chapter was. It was the very foundation to a lot of Lee Marvin's life, and I didn't want to screw it up. I've never seen battle, and badly written battles or wartime remembrances are untrue and they can really turn the reader off to the rest of the book. If it's done well, listen, I'm not Ernest Hemingway. I can't write that kind of thing. And it was quite a dilemma for me how to approach it, and then I realized while doing the research that if I put the letters that I had that had been previously given from Lee's family in chronological order, I realized that he could write this chapter himself and he should. And that was the hardest part of doing that, deciphering what he wrote. He was dyslexic, and he had terrible handwriting. It was a lot like being an archaeologist, deciphering what he wrote. Putting them together, I realized this is Lee Marvin's voice. Let him tell the story himself.

In one of those letters he writes, towards the end of his time in the war, he's had his fill of war. But he spent a huge portion of his career recreating war and violence on film. Was he working through his experience, or was it just another job for him?

No, it was not another job for him, I can tell you that. There was something I discovered while researching the book, and I'll take the heat for this if anyone gets mad at me. It was my diagnosis, for lack of a better word, that Lee Marvin had post-traumatic stress disorder. I had never read that anywhere, I came to that conclusion myself researching and reading about PTSD and reading about the symptoms. His pretty much matched all of them, and it really went unknown and undiagnosed until about 1980. Marvin died in 1987, so most of his life was spent without any knowledge of that. Consequently, in having these symptoms, he had to channel a lot of the anger and emotions and the symptoms of PTSD, nightmares, alcoholism, survivor's guilt, a need for violence. All of these things kind of came together and he had to filter it somehow. Probably the most acceptable way to do so, aside from getting arrested on a daily basis, was becoming an actor. He prided himself on being able to do things on stage and on film that people weren't allowed to do in everyday life.

Throughout his whole life, he had struggles with marriages and struggles with alcohol. There was that infamous Robin Hood party in Vegas. What is he, dangling women out of a window with bedsheets? Do you think his alcoholism was related to his PTSD?

I think there was a vicious circle kind of thing. He drank to forget, and when he drank, he became—there's not any one thing, of course, but there was antisocial behavior, and being in Hollywood and being a big movie star in the 1960s, that kind of behavior became the talk of the town. People loved it. It's not like working as a plumber in small time America, where it's "did you see what Lee did at the party?" In Hollywood, it's like "Wow! Wasn't Lee great drunk at the party last night?" That kind of social strata encouraged it. It also ruined his marriages. A marriage, anyway.

I want to talk about Cat Ballou *for a minute, the film that gave Lee Marvin his only Oscar.*

One for one. One nomination, one Oscar.

The funny thing about that movie and it being his only Oscar is that it's not really the kind of movie you'd associate when you think of Lee Marvin. Why Cat Ballou? *Why did it resonate?*

It's interesting. A few years before he passed away, a reporter said to Marvin "I don't really think you deserve the Oscar for *Cat Ballou*, it's not really your best work." He surprised the reporter by saying "You're right. It wasn't my best performance, and I don't know if I did deserve the Oscar for that. But there is such a thing as being on the Oscar track, and I was on the Oscar track with that film." He was as surprised as anybody to see how successful it turned out. I interviewed the film's director Elliot Silverstein, who told me some fascinating stories about the making of that movie. Lee didn't play that movie for comedy. The main character, I mean, because it was a dual role. He played the main character of the drunken, burned-out gunslinger as a tragic figure. He played the character as someone who is past his prime, and what do you do with a gunslinger when nobody wants him anymore? He compared it to many things, an old soldier, a broken-down prizefighter, a retired athlete who had his day in the sun and is now making change, that kind of thing. There's a wonderful moment when Jane Fonda tells her father, "How would I know he was going to be a drunk?" And when she says that, Marvin looks over his shoulder at her, with a look of pain in his eyes. It's some of the best acting he's ever done. But it's not something that normally wins Oscars.

Well, if the movie came out today, I feel like it would be the kind of role to get you an Oscar. It's a dual role, which is difficult, and he's playing outside of his type.

He is, but what's interesting, too, is that he was cast because in a weird way he was making fun of the stuff he had done before. There's a lot of Liberty Valance in Tim Strawn, Kid Shelleen's brother. There's a little bit of that in Kid Shelleen. Silverstein said that the reason he was casting Marvin in the first place is that a couple of nights before, he had seen Marvin in *The Wild One* (1953), and he remembered the way he fell off his motorcycle. He did that in a very funny way; he knows how to move. There's a little bit of a lot of other things Marvin had done on film that come across.

I noticed that myself, that dual role is kind of spoofing on his Liberty Valance role. If it was just the old coot, if it was just Kid Shelleen, does Marvin get the part, or does Jack Palance get it like he wanted?

The funny thing is, Palance let everyone know that he wanted the role. Apparently he wasn't even considered for the part. [both laugh] And if Palance had done it, he would have been parodying the character that he played in *Shane*, which is what put him on the map. But for Marvin, there were several major actors at the time that were considered and for some reason or another—well, we know specifically that Kirk Douglas passed on it. Jose Ferrer was considered, Burt Lancaster. Several others. As years go by, there's a debate about how much of this is actual and factual and how much was urban legend. But I do know that once Lee Marvin got the part—and he had to be convinced, too, by his wife and his agent—and once he got the script, he started quoting the dialogue in the party circuit, because he thought it was the best dialogue he'd read in a long time. He had problems with the character because it was a physical character to play. You have to sell it broad, but with it being broad, you've got to be believable, or the audience is going to say a few seconds into it that this is just a cartoon. And yet, he was able to pull it off.

To me, he definitely deserved the Oscar.

That's another thing, too. Comedies don't generally win Oscars, and he pulled it off.

It was fairly late in his career when he won that Oscar, but it was also fairly late in his career when he became a household name. Why do you think it took so long for audiences to warm up to him?

There's another question outside of film in general, and that's do the times make the man or does the man make the times? With Lee, I think it was a combination of wonderful things converging at the right time. He wouldn't have made it as a star in the 30s, 40s, and 50s because it was a different thing required by both the studios and audiences. The 60s were a very interesting time cinematically, culturally, in this country in that the rules were changing, both on film and in the culture at large. There was the civil rights movement, the women's movement, the generation gap, war, assassinations, rioting in the streets. This cultural basis helped Lee Marvin become a star. He wasn't the only one, there were other stars at that time. You look at somebody like Steve McQueen. They're different actors, but Steve McQueen wouldn't have made it in the 40s and 50s. There's always exceptions of course, Humphrey Bogart was the anti-hero of his time and didn't look like a matinee leading idol, but Lee Marvin got something across to the audience that the audience wanted to see and hear, which is that man is a violent animal and I'm going to show you how violent he can be! And that was a component of the 1960s, a violent time. And movies like *The Dirty Dozen* and *Point Blank*, which really wasn't as accepted in its day as it became later on, a cult film, they were saying that guys in the middle class, with white hair and ties—they can do some pretty despicable things if they have to. And that's what Lee Marvin was about. He was perfect for the 60s at that level.

One of the stories that jumped out at me from the book is that we talk about Lee Marvin redefining screen violence through his films, but another film that's often credited with redefining screen violence The Wild Bunch *(1969). Now he didn't star in that film, but there's a bit in the book about him helping to write the screenplay!*

He did. He was the one who introduced the story to Sam Peckinpah. A friend of Lee Marvin's had been working on the script, and Lee would periodically go over and help him a bit and mold it. And that part—if ever a part had Lee Marvin written all over it, it was the role of Pike Bishop in the *The Wild Bunch*. But unfortunately, as things turn out, he made *Paint Your Wagon* (1969) instead. And I think it's one of the greatest ironies of all time, that a man who defined modern American screen violence missed out on making the most important violent film of all time. It changed everything. He missed out on that. You look at the American Film Institute [which] does that greatest 100 American Fims of All Time, and Marvin has always just kind of missed the mark for being on those lists, for having his name-above-the-title type film in that list. It would have been *The Wild Bunch*, and he missed that, which is very sad.

So here's a question, just for your opinion on his work. As he got older, a lot of aging actors go through that sad part of the career where they do a bunch of stinkers, and he did a few towards the end of his career. But he didn't seem to sink as low as some have. He wasn't Joan Crawford doing brain-dead horror movies.

Yeah, *Trog* (1970).

Yeah, yeah. So he had a knack for elevating material. Is there one film or performance in that forgotten section of his career you wish could be found again? Can you rescue something from the scrap heap?

The films themselves are of various quality—[but there are] ones that I think are worthy of being discovered. The film itself isn't that good, but I thought he was wonderful in *Death Hunt* (1981). He did some wonderful things in that movie. Also, *Gorky Park* (1983). It wasn't a very good film; it wasn't well-received. It was based on a popular novel, but he'd never played a guy like that before. He played an American businessman who was very rich and exported sable from the Soviet Union. He's just this wonderfully deadly guy who can wear a three-piece suit and do something heinous at the same time. Just a great performance on his part. Like I said, something he had never done before. And probably the best of them all was *The Big Red One* (1980), which he did about five or six years before he died, Sam Fuller's epic retelling of his own experiences in World War II. Lee Marvin is a nameless sergeant who—he does things in this movie that I've never seen him do, in that film acting. There are a lot of elements to film acting, and one of them is being able to convey without dialogue because it's a visual medium. There's a sequence at the end of the film where he's helping a concentration camp refugee. He's just liberated a concentration camp, and he helps a little boy. There's almost no dialogue in that sequence for like 9 or 10 minutes, and it's all played on Lee's face. He's very poignant, and he's not over the top. It's some of the best film acting I've ever seen. And it's kind of being rediscovered. It's important and it should be, because it's a great performance and a great film.

Actually, when I was young, probably about 9 or 10 years old, I would grab everything at the video store and try to watch it, and I saw THE BIG RED ONE then. I'm pretty sure it was my first Lee Marvin movie, and even as a kid watching it, I absolutely loved that movie. I still have a soft spot for it all the way to today.

I think in 2006, there was a restoration done.

I haven't seen the restoration yet. I loved it in the original version, so I'd imagine I'd really love it now.

My personal opinion [is] I don't think it was improved on all that much. I know it was meant to be a three-hour film and it got taken away from Sam Fuller, who by the way I got to know, he's one of the many people I interviewed for the book. He loved Lee. That's one of the tragedies, that they didn't work together more. They worked together on television a couple of times. That was Sam Fuller's opus, and he's another film director being rediscovered. They discovered him in Europe first. He's an American director, but in America he was considered a hack, and in Europe, he's God. Now American film fans are starting to rediscover his work. He was quite an individual filmmaker. Nobody else could make a movie like *The Naked Kiss* (1964) or *Shock Corridor* (1963) or *The Big Red One.* There are things that are done in that movie that had never been done before in film, no matter how long we'd been making World War II films. The four lead characters with Lee Marvin looked like young soldiers. They don't look like actors playing soldiers, they all looked to be the age 17 to 19, and they're swimming in their uniforms, you know, the way it would be in real life. Things like that.

OK, so, it's a topic that never seems to go away. Throughout his career, Lee Marvin had to field questions about cinema and violence in society. And unfortunately, your book is arriving at a moment when that conversation is back in the news.

Indeed it is. Unfortunately. The timing is badly fortuitous in terms of the book, but that conversation is out there.

Well, you quote Lee Marvin a couple of times in the book; basically his quote boils down to he wants the violence in his movies to be incredibly brutal and realistic because he thinks it acts as a deterrent. The rougher the violence, the less likely someone is to try it.

Right, that was his belief. I don't necessarily hold to that belief, but Lee Marvin professed that. He believed that the more brutal you made it, the more you would turn people off. I don't know if that's necessarily the case. He made those statements before there were warfare videogames and things we see on the news on a regular basis that were much more graphic. The kind of violence Lee Marvin was talking about is not the kind of violence that, say, a Jason Statham action film has, where it's quirky and cartoony, but it's in your face every two seconds. It's not like that MTV editing style that's quick cutting, that's not about the impact you would have on another human being. It's like a videogame or cartoon. Let's blow up as many cars as we can. Let's shoot as many things as we can. Marvin's point was, let's show the threat of violence. I'm paraphrasing here, but he said, if I'm going to shoot somebody, I'm going to knock them down, walk over, shoot them two times, and then roll them over and shoot them again. And sell it! Not just have it happen quick and go on to the next thing. That's not really what he thought violence was about. Violence is ugly, so show it to be ugly.

It's funny. You have this image—well, before I read your book, Lee Marvin seems to appeal to a certain stereotype of a conservative tough-guy, pro-war cinema. Was Lee Marvin pro-war?

Let me tell you something, that's one of my favorite things about this book. I've been reading blogs or comments about Lee Marvin. He's often been called "America's favorite badass," "he's not a wussy," and "he would go out there and kick Obama's ass!" Things like that. And people who say stuff like that don't realize that Lee Marvin was not John Wayne. Most of his life, politically, Lee Marvin was a liberal Democrat. He worked for John F. Kennedy's campaign in 1960. After Kennedy's assassination, he kept his politics to himself, but the only thing he was really a hawk on was indeed gun control. He believed very strongly in the 2nd amendment and he would tell friends that, but politically, he was a liberal. I hate to disappoint John Wayne fans out there. By the way, John Wayne and Lee Marvin were friends. They worked together, but Lee Marvin would definitely not be put in the category of a Tea Partier. Another point, too, is that you can be a liberal and be a badass. [laughs]

In the book, there are two other actors that you explore the similarities and kind of dismiss those similarities with Lee Marvin, and that's Humphrey Bogart and Clint Eastwood. If those two aren't good comparisons, who is the best comparison to Lee Marvin, in your opinion, before and after his time?

There are elements in terms of being antiheroes—and by the way, what I wrote in the book about Bogart was really comparisons to Bogart before he was famous. Comparisons can be made, because Bogart's career was very similar to Lee Marvin's. He played a lot of bad guys and secondary roles before he made it with *High Sierra* (1941) and *The Maltese Falcon* (1941) and *Casablanca* (1942) and those films, but when Lee Marvin was doing supporting and secondary roles, he really tried to sell it and do the best job he could. If you look at Bogart in those early Warner Brothers films before he was famous, he looked so uncomfortable. He didn't look like he was enjoying himself or having a good time. He looked like he was working, whereas Lee Marvin always tried to give a little more to the character, like saying to the audience, "I'm going to do something despicable here, and we're going to have fun." And that was a weird thing, too, that nobody had ever done before. There's a lot of elements of Lee Marvin in other actors, you know? There's a great quote by Errol Flynn in *The Adventures of Don Juan* (1948). He's about to chase a girl, and he'd said he would never do that again. His friend says "I thought you weren't ever going to do this again," and Errol Flynn as Don Juan says "You know, there's a little Don Juan in every man, and if I am Don Juan, there must be more of him in me!" The same goes for Lee Marvin. There's a little Lee Marvin in a lot of actors, but there's only one Lee Marvin, and there's more of Lee Marvin in him than anyone.

One last question. Besides the obvious connection to one of his most well-known films, why choose the title POINT BLANK for your book?

I had a devil of a time coming up with a title. I had several things I was thinking of, but once I wrote the introduction, I realized that what Lee Marvin did that nobody else had done before him was that he presented violence on film like nobody had done before and consistently. That's the other thing. There were moments of violence in American cinema that were pretty bad, like when Richard Widmark pushed a lady in a wheelchair down a staircase [in *Kiss of Death* (1947)], but after Richard Widmark did that, he never played that kind of character again which is, you know, a tragedy. But Lee Marvin, once he established himself, never walked away from how violent mankind can be. He was in your face with the way it was presented. I thought if I could come up with a name for that style, and that was point blank. Just that's how he was. He was point blank, in your face, no excuses.

Andrew Kemp is a screenwriter and game writer who started talking about movies in 1984 and got stuck that way.

He writes at www.thehollywoodprojects.com and hosts a bimonthly screening series of classic films at theaters around Atlanta.

Topics and Questions for Discussion

1) Having read *Lee Marvin Point Blank*, how has your opinion of Lee Marvin changed?

2) The author asserts that Lee Marvin's ancestry helped set the stage for the actor's predetermination towards violence. Do you agree or disagree with this assertion?

3) It's been said that an individual's parents are the first and most pervasive social role model in a person's life. In what way did Lee Marvin's parents influence his life? How did Marvin's mother effect his opinion of women?

4) When Lee Marvin was going to school he was considered well liked but troublesome. What do you think teachers and/or administrators would do differently if Lee Marvin were a student today?

5) Lee's older brother Robert is on record as stating he was jealous of his younger brother's success. What do you think Lee thought of his brother?

6) Lee Marvin often said he learned how to act in the Marines. What do you think he learned in the USMC that he channeled into his acting?

7) At the start of his acting career, Lee Marvin chose to forsake the Broadway stage for Hollywood. If he had stayed in New York, do you think he would have succeeded? Why or why not?

8) From small parts, to secondary roles, to lead villain to leading man, Lee Marvin's film career had several stages. What do you think was his best and worst performance in each of these stages?

9) Paradoxically, Lee Marvin hated the medium of television and yet he proved to be more versatile in it than on film. Why do you think that was?

10) In interviews Lee Marvin consistently stated that the violence portrayed in films should be more graphic as a deterrent to real-life violence. Do you agree or disagree with his point of view?

11) As a leading man, Lee Marvin wanted to play the romantic lead more often but very rarely did. Which actresses do you think he would have had good screen chemistry with had he made a love story?

12) Each of the characters he has played represents a certain aspect of Lee Marvin's real life persona. Which of his characters do you think is the most and least like the real Lee Marvin?

13) The political opinion of some stars are very well known, such as Jane Fonda and John Wayne, yet some readers have been surprised to discover that Lee Marvin was fairly liberal in his politics. Why do you think that is?

14) The 1960s were a period of immense change in American filmmaking, with movies like *Bonnie & Clyde* and *Easy Rider* becoming unlikely surprise hits with both audiences and critics. However, audiences and critics disliked *Point Blank* but became a cult hit years later. Why do you think that was the case?

15) Frequent costars Angie Dickinson, as well as French actress Jeanne Moreau have both said they found Lee Marvin to be incredibly sexy. What do you think his appeal was to female audience members?

16) There are several films Lee Marvin almost made but ultimately didn't throughout this career, most notably, *The Wild Bunch*. How do you think his performance would have differed from that of William Holden's?

17) In the late 1970s, the infamous palimony suit brought Lee Marvin back into the media spotlight. Although most people incorrectly remember the trial's outcome, do you think the actual verdict was fair?

18) Had Lee Marvin lived, and his age was not a factor, what other films do you think he could have starred in?

19) Some film stars have become more popular in death than they ever were life, such as Marilyn Monroe, Humphrey Bogart and James Dean. Do you think that will happen with Lee Marvin? Why or why not?

20) If the story of Lee Marvin was made into a film, who would you like to see portray him and why?

Important Dates in the Life of Lee Marvin

SEPTEMBER 2, 1896: Mother Courtenay Washington Davidge born in Virginia.

DECEMBER 19, 1896: Father Lamont 'Monte' Waltham Marvin born in Elmira, NY.

SEPTEMBER 3, 1921: Parents marry.

JULY 18, 1922: Brother Robert Davidge Marvin born in Washington, D.C.

FEBRUARY 19, 1924: Lee Marvin born in New York City.

SEPTEMBER 25, 1926: *New York Times* article announces murder of Ross Marvin.

1929-1940: Is enrolled and expelled from several public and private schools along the eastern seaboard.

SEPTEMBER, 1940-JUNE, 1942: Enrolled in Lakeland Florida's St. Leo Academy. Drops out before senior year to join the Marines.

AUGUST 12, 1942: Joins the U.S. Marine Corp.

JUNE 18, 1944: Wounded in action during the battle of Saipan.

JULY 24, 1945: Officially discharged from the USMC.

JUNE, 1947: Makes professional acting debut in Woodstock's Maverick Theater production of "Roadside."

1947-1951: Appears in summer stock, Off-Broadway, military training films, short subjects and live TV while also taking classes at the American Theater Wing under the G.I. Bill as of April, 1948.

FEBRUARY 10, 1951: "Billy Budd" opens, marking Lee Marvin's sole appearance on Broadway.
1951: Leaves New York for California, having met agent Meyer Mishkin while filming bit part in *You're in the Navy Now* (February, 23); Seen as extra in *Teresa* (April 5).

1952: Appears in *Diplomatic Courier* (June 13), *We're Not Married* (July 11), *Duel at Silver Creek* (August 1), *Hangman's Knot* (November 15), and is third billed in *Eight Iron Men* (December, 30).
FEBRUARY 2, 1952: Marries Betty Ebeling in Las Vegas.
NOVEMBER 22, 1952: First child and only son Christopher Lamont born.

1953: Appears in *Down Among the Sheltering Palms* (March 1), *Seminole* (March 15), *The Glory Brigade* (May 20), *The Stranger Wore a Gun* (July 30), *The Big Heat* (October 14), *Gun Fury* (November 11), and *The Wild One* (December 30).

1954: Appears in *Gorilla at Large* (May), *The Caine Mutiny* (June 24) and *The Raid* (August 4).
MAY 7, 1954: Daughter Courtenay Lee born.

1955: Appears in *Bad Day at Black Rock* (January 7), *Violent Saturday* (April), *Not*

as a Stranger (June 28), *A Life in the Balance* (July 1),
Pete Kelly's Blues (July 31), *I Died a Thousand Times* (November 9)
and *Shack Out on 101*(December 4); Befriends costar Keenan Wynn.

1956: Appears in *Seven Men From Now* (August 4), *Pillars of the Sky* (October 12),
Attack! (October 17), and *The Rack* (November 2).
JUNE 8, 1956: Daughter Cynthia Louise born; Makes final stage appearance in La
Jolla Playhouse production of "Bus Stop" (June 26-July 8).

1957: Appears in *Raintree County* (December 20).
September, 1957: "M Squad" premieres on NBC.

1958: Appears in *Missouri Traveler* (January 21).
March 8, 1958: Daughter Claudia Leslie born.

JUNE, 1960: Last episode of "M Squad" airs.
1960: Endorses Kennedy for president and appears on star-studded TV special (July
10).

1961: Stars in TV's "People Need People " (October 10) and receives Emmy-nom-
ination; Appears in *The Comancheros* (October 30).

1962: Helps to stage amateur production of "People Need People" at San Quentin
(March); Appears in *The Man Who Shot Liberty Valance* (April 22).

1963: Hosts and narrates short-lived syndicated TV series "Lawbreakers"; Appears
in *Donovan's Reef* (June 12).
MARCH 23, 1963: Mother Courtenay dies suddenly of a cerebral hemorrhage.

1964: Appears in first made-for-TV movie *The Killers,* but network considers
it too violent in the wake of the Kennedy assassination. Universal successfully
releases it in theaters (July 7).

OCTOBER, 1964: Begins relationship with Michele Triola.

1965: Appears in *Cat Ballou* (June 24) and *Ship of Fools* (July 29).

1966, APRIL 18TH: Wins Best Actor Oscar for *Cat Ballou.*
1966: Appears in *The Professionals* (November 2).

JANUARY, 1967: Divorced from Betty Marvin.
MARCH 21, 1967: Hosts and narrates WWII-era documentary "Our Time In Hell"
for ABC and defers salary to Marine charity.
1967: Appears in *The Dirty Dozen* (June 15) and *Point Blank* (August 30); Appears
briefly in documentary *Tonight, Let All Make in London* (September 26) from set
of *The Dirty Dozen*; Is named number one male box-office star in U.S. by Motion
Picture Herald magazine (December).

1968: Television drama *Sgt. Ryker* released in theaters (February 1); Appears in
Hell in the Pacific (December 18).

1969: Earns first million dollar paycheck and Golden Globe nomination for *Paint
Your Wagon* (October 15); Single "Wanderin Star" reaches number one spot in
U.K. music charts, outselling The Beatles.

APRIL, 1969: Receives honorary doctorate of fine arts from St. Leo.
1970: Has liaison with Jeanne Moreau; Appears in *Monte Walsh*
(October 7) Ends relationship with girlfriend when she legally changes name to Michele Triola Marvin.
OCTOBER 10, 1970: Marries former Woodstock girlfriend Pamela Feeley in Las Vegas.

APRIL 6, 1971: Father dies in Florida after slipping into a coma.

1972: Appears in *Pocket Money* (February 1) and *Prime Cut* (June 28).

MARCH 11, 1973: Frequent costar Robert Ryan dies of cancer at age 63 in New York City.
1973: Appears in *Emperor of the North* (May 23) and *The Iceman Cometh* (November 10).

1974: Appears in *Spikes' Gang* (May 1) and *The Klansman* (November 13).

1975: Moves to Tucson, Arizona.

1976: Appears in *The Great Scout and Cathouse Thursday* (June 23) and *Shout at the Devil* (November 24); Two separate episodes of "The Virginian" spliced together, one with Marvin and another with Charles Bronson released to theaters as *The Meanest Men in the West* (March).

1978: August 9, costar Robert Shaw dies from a heart attack before *Avalanche Express* is complete.

JANUARY-APRIL 1979: Unsuccessfully sued by Michele Triola for palimony.
1979: Appears in *Avalanche Express* (October 19); Appears in Dutch documentary *Samuel Fuller and The Big Red One*.

1980: Appears in *The Big Red One* (July 18).

1981: Appears in *Death Hunt* (May 22).

1982: Daughter Cynthia marries Edward Michaels

1983: Matthew Michaels, Lee Marvin's grandson is born.
Is honored at France's Deauville Film Festival (August)
Director Robert Aldrich dies in L.A. at age 65 of kidney failure,Dec.5th.
Appears in *Gorky Park* (December 15).

1984: Appears in *Dog Day* (released on video in US on October 7, 1985).
1984: Director Sam Peckinpah dies in Inglewood, California at age 59 of heart failure, December 28th.

1985: Appears in TV-movie, "The Dirty Dozen: Next Mission," aired on NBC February 4.

1986: Appears in *The Delta Force* (February 14).
Admitted to hospital for colon surgery. November 18th.

1987: Appears in TV special "The Spencer Tracy Legacy: A Tribute by Katherine Hepburn" (March); Appears in short military training film *Combat Leadership:*

The Ultimate Challenge for the USMC in what would be his last film appearance (May 12).

Dies in Tucson Medical Center at age 63 of a heart attack August 29, 1987; cremated remains buried at Arlington National Cemetery (October 7, 1987).

Posthumous Events Related to Lee Marvin

1989: Director Jim Jarmusch makes first public mention of "The Sons of Lee Marvin."

1990: Daughters Courtenay and Cynthia earn screen credit as a sound editor and TV costumer, respectively.

1997: *Lee, A Romance* by Pamela Marvin published by Faber & Faber.

1998: Cable television airs "Lee Marvin: A Personal Portrait by John Boorman."
1998: *Dirty Dozen* cast members reunite to voice characters in Joe Dante's *Small Soldiers.*

AUGUST 8, 1999: Brother Robert dies in Benedictine Hospital in Kingston, New York at age 77.
OCTOBER 9, 1999: Career long agent Meyer Mishkin dies at age 87 in L.A.

AUGUST, 2003: Frequent costar Charles Bronson dies in L.A. from complications of Alzheimer's disease at the age of 81.

AUGUST 2004: *The Big Red One: The Reconstruction* is rereleased with deleted footage restored by film historian/critic Richard Schickel.

NOVEMBER 19, 2006: Frequent costar Jack Palance dies in Monteceito, California at age 87.

MAY-JUNE, 2007: Film Society of Lincoln Center pays tribute to Marvin with a retrospective of his films.

FEBRUARY, 2009: MTV votes Walker in *Point Blank* number 5 of the top ten badasses in movie history.

OCTOBER 29, 2009: Michele Triola dies of lung cancer at age 76 in Malibu home where she lived with Dick Van Dyke.
2009: Quentin Tarantino's *Dirty Dozen*-like *Inglorious Basterds* released.

JULY 2011: Original play "Lee Marvin Be They Name" by Nick Zagone opens for limited run in Modesto, Calif. with actor Jack Souza as Marvin.

SEPTEMBER, 2011, "Tales of A Hollywood Housewife" by Betty Marvin published by iUniverse.

JULY 8, 2012: Frequent costar Ernest Borgnine dies in L.A. at age 95.

2012: Youngest daughter Claudia succumbs to liver disease.

FEBRUARY, 2013: Hollywood's American Cinematheque show four Marvin films for a screening entitled "Call in the Marine: A Tribute to Lee Marvin."
OCTOBER, 2013: Son Christopher succumbs to cancer.

The Unmade Films of Lee Marvin

Oklahoma! (1955): Auditioned for the role of Jud that was played in the film by Rod Steiger.

How the West Was Won (1962): It is unknown which role Marvin turned down.
Billy Budd (1962): Having been in the play, Marvin wanted to play Claggart but director Peter Ustinov decided on Robert Ryan who was more well-known at the time.

The Longest Day (1962): MCA turned down the John Wayne role for Lee Marvin
Andersonville (1965): Marvin was to play a sadistic sergeant but the film was never made.

Synanon (1965): Turned down the film that eventually flopped at the box office.

The Petrified Forest (1965): Financing fell through on the planned remake.

The Hallelujah Trail (1965): Marvin passed on the role of the stern calvary officer played by Burt Lancaster in John Sturges' over-the-top and unsuccessful comedy.

Bette Davis/Lee Marvin Comedy (1965): Made instead as *Bunny O'Hare* with Ernest Borgnine.

In Cold Blood (1966): Marvin liked the script but the detective was played by John Forsythe.

Reflections in a Golden Eye (1966): Turned down by Marvin, the role went to Marlon Brando.

Roman Polanski Project (1967): Erotic thriller Marvin immediately turned down after reading it.

April Morning (1967): The Revolutionary War saga to be directed by Howard Hawks was made for TV with Tommy Lee Jones in 1988.

The Diamond Story (1967): A caper film to be made in conjunction with *The Wild Bunch.*

Petulia (1968): Based on a popular novel made instead with George C. Scott and Julie Christie.

The Wild Bunch (1969): The film Marvin helped create was nixed instead for *Paint Your Wagon.*

Patton (1970): Marvin was one of the actors who turned down the role played by George C. Scott.

Two Mules for Sister Sarah (1970): Clint Eastwood's role had been written for Marvin.

Tender Loving Care (1971): Marvin as a cop protecting a young girl but backing fell through.

Cat Ballou sequel (1971): Made as an unsuccessful TV-movie with Jack Elam as Kid Shelleen.

Deliverance (1972): Marvin and Brando in the roles that went to Jon Voight and Burt Reynolds.

Carriman, They Called Him (1972): A Sam Peckinpah western/comedy that never panned out.

John Cassavetes Project (1972): To costar Anthony Quinn, it never came to fruition.

Custer's Last Stand (1973?): Director Robert Totten wanted Marvin to play legendary outlaw D. B. Cooper as a descendant of General Custer but claims Pam Marvin talked him out of it.

The Yakuza (1974): Made instead with Robert Mitchum.

Earthquake (1974): Charlton Heston eventually played the lead role Marvin was offered.

Jaws (1975): The role that went to Robert Shaw.

Moontrap (1977): A western Jack Nicholson would direct starring Marvin that went unfinanced.

Apocalypse, Now! (1978): A recently discovered handwritten letter shows Coppola imploring Marvin to play the Marlon Brando role of Kurtz but the actor never responded.

Canadian Film Project (1979): Marvin claimed the script was awful and turned it down.

Wolf Lake (1980): A thriller by Burt Kennedy eventually released with Rod Steiger.

Henderson the Rain King (1980): Saul Bellow novel Marvin coveted but could not get the rights.

Paradise Road (1981): Peter Bogdanovich's project of degenerate gamblers Frank Sinatra, James Stewart, Lee Marvin, Charles Aznavour, Dean Martin and Jerry Lewis that never materialized.

Tournament (1981): Marvin's dream project on deep-sea fishing, he never found any backers.

Glory Bars (1981): Based on a novel by William Smith concerning a 30-year Marine Sgt. training recruits in the 70s it was to be directed by Robert Aldrich.

That Championship Season (1982): The role of the basketball coach went to Robert Mitchum.

Runaway Train (1983): Kurosawa wanted Marvin in the role played by Jon Voight in 1985.

Iwo Jima Documentary (193): Announced as its narrator, the film was never made.

Godard's King Lear (1987): The director's updated Shakespeare settled on Burgess Meredith.

Track 29 (1987-88): Having befriended writer Dennis Potter on *Gorky Park*, Marvin was considered for the role later played by Christopher Lloyd.

Untitled Jim Jarmusch Project: Jarmusch was formulating a story in which Marvin would play a drunken father to three grown sons who hated each other. Unfortunately, Marvin passed on.

Films Lee Marvin Could Have Made

Although he died in 1987 at the age of 63, it is worth considering what roles Lee Marvin might have played had he lived a few more years. It is of course, a purely speculative list:

The Untouchables (1987): Jim Malone, Sean Connery's Oscar-winning role.

City Slickers (1991): Curly, Jack Palance's role.

A Few Good Men (1992): Col. Nathan R. Jessup, Jack Nicholson's role.

Scent of a Woman (1992): Lt. Col. Frank Slade, Al Pacino's role.

Unforgiven (1992): Will Munny, Clint Eastwood's role.

The Fugitive (1993): Sam Gerard, Tommy Lee Jones' role.

The Shawshank Redemption (194): Brooks Hatlen, James Whitmore's role.

Lone Star (1996): Charlie Wade, Kris Kristofferson's role.

Affliction (1997): Glen Whitehouse, James Coburn's role.

Three Kings (1999): Maj. Archie Gates, George Clooney's role.

Magnolia (1999) Earl Partridge, Jason Robards' role.

Man on Fire (2004): John Creasy, Denzel Washington's role.

Million Dollar Baby (2004): Frankie Dunn, Clint Eastwood's role.

Sin City (2005): Det. John Hartigan, Bruce Willis' role.

End Notes

AI=Author interview

"I concluded it's every man for himself,": "A Cool Head Hits it Hot,"
Martin Cohen, *True*, Oct. 1965.

PART I: BOOT CAMP

Chapter 1: The Guilty Puritan
"I remember fighting with my brother": "A *Redbook* Dialogue: Lee Marvin & Johnny Carson," *Redbook*, Nov. 1967.
"You've just been deposited there": Ibid.
"Maybe blood is thicker than water": Letter from Courtenay to Lee, Feb. 2, 1944.
"I think he was a guilty puritan,": AI, March 13, 1996.
"During the Civil War...": "A Cool Head Hits it Hot," Martin Cohen, *True*, Oct. 1965.
"the charcoal gray sheep...": "'Killer' Lee Marvin is Back In Action," Louella Parsons, *Herald Examiner*, March 16, 1965.
"In 1863, while Sheriff McCann was in charge": "Marvin Lost Life with Peary," *Elmira Star Gazette*, Sept. 9, 1909.
"Marvin fought his way into everything": Ibid.
"I may say that your application": Letter from Peary to Ross Marvin, June 30, 1905.
"Went out to Denver to see his father": "Drinks with Liberty Valance," Robert Ward, *Rolling Stone*, Sept. 3, 1981.
"Quiet in manner, wiry in build": *North Pole*, Robert E. Peary, NY: Stokes Co, 1910. p. 319.
"He who had shrunk from loneliness": Ibid., p.318.
"Uncle was a big bookie...": AI, July, 21, 1994.
"As a matter of fact, he said he was out in Leavenworth,": Ibid.
"My father was the classic puritan,": "Drinks with Liberty Valance," Robert Ward, *Rolling Stone*, Sept. 3, 1981.
"He said it was in a building in New York City,": AI, July, 21, 1994.
"William Jr. ['Willie'] died in a car accident": AI, July, 21, 1994.
"I didn't make my fortune,": "Woodstock: Thumb Box Sketch" *Catskill Mountain Star*, March 6, 1958.
"I see you again, just as you were...": Letter from Courtenay to Monte, Sept. 3, 1941.
"Since I can't send you a gift...": Undated letter from Courtenay to Monte.
"A very hot Saturday afternoon,": Ibid.
"Their gestures were different,:" AI July 21, 1994.
"I once tried to figure out the first time I felt guilt,": "A *Redbook* Dialogue: Lee Marvin & Johnny Carson," *Redbook*, Nov. 1967.
"He lost his temper,": "Eskimo Killed Prof. Marvin" *New York Times*, Sept. 25, 1926.
"If I didn't know about it,": AI July 21, 1994.
"I wasn't having any too much discipline,": Martin Cohen, "A Cool Head Hits it Hot" *True*, October 1965.
"I left kindergarten,:" "A Redbook Dialogue: Lee Marvin & Johnny Carson," *Redbook*, Nov. 1967.

Chapter 2: Dogface Vs. St. Leo
"I am a good boy": Lee's letter to Santa dictated to Courtenay, Dec. 1929.
"She had a job in the Depression": AI, July 21, 1994
"He started off in the Bank of Montreal": Ibid.

"Well, there was money but there was no wealth": AI, Feb. 12, 1995.

"Here's a little insight": Ibid.

"Lee had the most difficult time with his mother,": Ibid.

"I always envied the street kids": "How Getting Shot Saved Lee Marvin's Life," Tom Seligman, *Parade*, April 27, 1986.

"My parents just didn't know...": "Marvin as in Marlin," Roger Vaughan, *Motorboat & Sailing*, May, 1977.

"I didn't like school": "Lee Marvin: Tough, Gentle Heart," *Family Weekly*, Peer J. Oppenheimer, April 1, 1966.

"Please see that Lee gets to school on time," Report card from P.S. 166, Feb. 1936.

"Yes, and so is his son" AI, Feb. 12, 1995.

"Oh yes and he would recite Robert Service": Ibid.

"It was a pattern,": Ibid.

"I've never been able to accept any kind of discipline": "A Rebel's Creed," *This Week*, [no author credited] Aug. 14, 1966 .

"I once kicked Uncle Don in the shins": "Lee Marvin: O'Neill's the Tough Guy," Anthony Mancini, *NY Post*, Oct. 13, 1973.

"My father rarely punched my brother": AI, July 21, 1994

"My brother owed some kid some money": Ibid.

"Very liberal boarding school": Ibid.

"It was an outgrowth of the little Red schoolhouse-type": "The Klansman," Judy Stone, *Playgirl*, July, 1974.

"I am writing this letter at the point of a gun": Lee's letter to parents, undated.

"Lee is an exceedingly restless...": Manumit Fall/Winter term, William Mann Fincke, Group Teacher, March 18, 1937.

"We were smoking, that's all": "The Star You Love To Hate," Arnold Hano, *Pageant*, May 1966.

"Today we took four guys": Letter to Robert, Feb. 11, 938

"He took the sweepings and dumped them out the window": "The Star You Love To Hate," Arnold Hano, *Pageant*, May 1966.

"The asked me to go home and commune with god": "Drinks with Liberty Valance," Robert Ward, *Rolling Stone*, Sept. 3, 1981.

"My uniform cost eight hundred dollars": "The Star You Love To Hate," Arnold Hano, *Pageant*, May 1966.

"...Wild harmless, innocent but crazy kid": "Lee Marvin: O'Neill's the Tough Guy," Anthony Mancini, *NY Post*, Oct. 13, 1973.

"I'm not knocking what my parents were trying to do" "Oh! Those Movie Meanies," Cynthia Lindsay, *Cosmopolitan*, Sept. 1966.

"The past few weeks seemed unbearable": Undated.

"For god's sake don't let anything that can happen..." From Courtenay to Monte, Jan 28, 1941.

"As to money, Oh hell": Ibid.

"My father had him in public high school": AI, July 21, 1994.

"Here on the afternoon of June 21, 1940": Letter to Monte.

"I live in fear of you today": Ibid.

"Lee just appeared": "Lakelanders Recall Former Resident, Actor Lee Marvin," *Lakeland Ledger*, Travis Ingham, April 20, 1966.

"When I was fourteen": AI w/ Betty Ballantine, June 14, 1996.

"Lee just though his father hung out the sun,": "Ex-Lakelander Lee Marvin's Name Is Really Lee Marvin," Larry Vickers, *Tampa Tribune*, April 21, 1966.

"If you don't see a father as often": AI, July 21, 1994.

"He had very keen eyes": "Ex-Lakelander Lee Marvin's Name Is Really Lee Marvin," Larry Vickers, *Tampa Tribune*, April 21, 1966.

"He didn't care much for the academic part": AI May 8, 1996.

"We called him 'Dogface'": *Pioneer College: The Centennial History of Saint Leo College, Saint Leo Abbey, and Holy Name Priory*, James J. Horgan, St. Leo College Press, 1989, page 461.

"I bopped him one time": Ibid.

"This evening I was 'told' to go out for track": Letter to Courtenay, Nov. 4, 1940

"Making a little wine out of the citrus fruit'": AI, June 15, 1998.

"Well, Lee won and I came in second": Ibid.

"The auditorium was filled to capacity": "Brother Orchid's Monks and Gangsters Wow Local Audiences," *St. Leo Chronicle*, March 27, 1942.

"This is the last you will ever see an address...": Monte to Courtenay, Aug. 1941.

"I and four other boys": Letter to parents, Dec. 4, 1941.

"I think that I have finally come to a decision": Letter to Courtenay, May, 1942.

CHAPTER 3: "I HAVE HAD MY FILL OF WAR"

"It could not be taken by a million men": *World War II: The War in the Pacific*, DVD. Writer/

Director Don Horan, New Video Distribution, 1993.

"He gave me his .45": "Drinks with Liberty Valance," Robert Ward, *Rolling Stone*, Sept. 3, 1981.

"[It was] also then that Monte proceeded to seduce Lee's girlfriend": AI Feb. 12, 1995.

"The war had an effect on me": "The Star You Love To Hate," Arnold Hano, *Pageant*, May 1966.

"On Kwajalein there were six guys": "Old Foes with a New View of War," P.F. Kluge, *Life*, Sept. 27, 1968.

"He was assigned to go knock out a foxhole": AI August 17, 1995.

"He popped out of the hole like a little animal": "Hollywood's Tough Loner" *Hollywood Confidential*, Tedd Thomey, NY: Pyramid Books, 1967 p.27

CHAPTER 4: "THESE HORRIBLE, ANIMAL MEN"

"I won't repeat exactly what I said...": "Lee Marvin" Leatherneck, Robert Johnson Jr., July, 1985.

"Your brother is quite a man": Letter from Courtenay to Robert, April 11, 1945.

"It ruined him": "Drinks with Liberty Valance," Robert Ward, *Rolling Stone*, Sept. 3, 1981.

"Outstandingly meritorious service": Copy of citation provided by Robert Marvin.

"I just got home from school,": Letter to Robert postmarked Oct. 27, 1945.

"It made no sense": "The Star You Love To Hate,": Arnold Hano, *Pageant*, May, 1966.

"Natural hazards effecting apple crop": 1946 resume provided by Robert Marvin.

"What I am trying to put over here": Undated story provided by Robert Marvin.

"The greatest dive I've ever seen in my life": AI Bill Heckeroth, June 12, 1996.

"When Lee would come home": AI Robert Marvin, July 21, 1994.

"You Marines are alot of bullshit": Ibid.

"I was wearing a good pair of pants": Ibid.

"A guy digging ditches": "Assorted Blasts From An Angry Man," Bob Johnson *TV Guide*, Oct. 3, 1959.

"It wasn't long after, the state police arrived": AI Bill Heckeroth, June 12, 1996.

"My next film is going to be your life story" Ibid.

"We fished": AI David Ballantine, June 14, 1996.

"I fought WWII in the Zone of the Interior,": Ibid.

"I knew Monte and Courtenay,": Ibid.

"The gargle": Ibid.

"Lee's performance was the most hilarious,": "From Maverick to Filmland Marvin Left Them in Aisles," Tobie Geertsma, *Kingston Daily Freeman*, April 19, 1966.

"The director needed a tall loudmouth": Marvin, Donald Zec, NY: St. Martin's Press, 1980. p. 47

"Nothing could be further from the truth": "From Maverick to Filmland Marvin Left Them in Aisles," Tobie Geertsma, *Kingston Daily Freeman*, April 19, 1966.

"I got swocked,": "The Star You Love To Hate,": Arnold Hano, *Pageant*, May, 1966.

"He was a very impressive character": AI Betty Ballantine, June 14, 1996.

"It grabbed me just like that!": "How Getting Shot Saved Lee Marvin's Life," Tom Seligman, *Parade*, April 27, 1986.

"Lee Marvin as 6'3" 'Texas': "At the Maverick," *Ulster County News*, June 29, 1947

"He had such presence on stage": AI Betty Ballantine, June 14, 1996.

"It was the closest thing to the Marvin Corp.":

"Acting is a search for communication":

"Hard work and no crap, no doubt about it": AI James Doohan, Oct. 5, 1996.

"When I put on the rags": "How Getting Shot Saved Lee Marvin's Life," Tom Seligman, *Parade*, April 27, 1986.

"We slept in cabins": AI James Doohan, Oct. 5, 1996.

"Lee was a killer": AI Betty Ballantine, June 14, 1996.

"He also of course had an affair with the company's leading lady": Ibid.

"Let me tell you, pal, touring was fuckin' tough": "Lee Marvin's Great, Goddamned Moments of the Big Kavoom,": Grover Lewis, *Rolling Stone* Dec. 21, 1972.

"Lee told my father he wanted to be an actor": AI Robert Marvin, July 21, 1994.

"It was marvelous, like a halfway house": "Marvin is still at it and holding up well," Chris Chase, *LA Herald-Examiner*, May 21, 1981.

"Lee walked in and they showed him the saber": AI David Ballantine, June 14, 1996.

"I could turn that part inside out": *Datebook*, Dec. 22, 1948.

"There used to be an agent in New York": AI Bert Remsen, Nov. 23, 1994.

"I think he might have very well ended up...": AI Betty Ballantine, June 14, 1996.

"New York is a totally different scene": AI Leo Gordon, Jan. 26, 1999.

"Look, I'm a trained killer" AI Betty Ballantine, June 14, 1996.

"PTSD went undiagnosed until 1980": "Troubled Homecoming," Thomas Childers, *VFW*, April, 2009.

"If veterans of WWII were mentioned at all": Ibid.

"I hung around for three days": "Marvin is still at it and holding up well," Chris Chase, *LA Herald-Examiner*, May 21, 1981.

"Dear Lee, good luck tonight": Feb. 10, 1951, photocopy provided by Robert Marvin.

"There I was in a theater,": "Lee Marvin, Hollywood's Most Dedicated Hell-Raiser," Jim Sirmans, *Saga*, June, 1974.

"He stood at attention through three acts": AI David Ballantine, June 14, 1996.

"I said, 'Give Hollywood a try'": AI James Doohan, Oct. 5, 1996.

"It was a damned bore": "A Cool Head Hits it Hot," Martin Cohen, *True*, Oct. 1965.

PART II: IN THE TRENCHES

CHAPTER 5: THE MERCHANT OF MENACE

"Can't I take crap on my own time?" AI, July 23, 1994.

"Let me see him work": Ibid.

"Before you showed up": Ibid.

"In my first picture I played seven sailors": "Drunkest Gun in the West," *Life*, June 11, 1965.

"I said to him, 'Before you go, I want you to do something'": AI, July 23, 1994.

"Hollywood is the funniest place": Undated letter to Monte on Screenland stationery.

"No, I didn't have that kind of deal": AI, July 23, 1994.

"Things are still going very well for me out here": Letter to Robert, Dec. 1, 1951.

"The episode Lee was on was a three-man piece": "Portrait of a Star: Lee Marvin," Rick Spalla Productions, 1968.

"Everything he did in the early days": AI, July 23, 1994.

"My offices used to be on Sunset Blvd.": Ibid.

"I remember his telling me about a scene": AI, June 14, 1996.

"I was very attracted to his one Brooks Brothers jacket" AI, Feb. 12, 1995.

"Here's one of the dearest memories I have of Lee": Ibid.

"Lee was very shy as a man with women": Ibid.

"Lee from the beginning, knew every method used in acting": Ibid.

"I know that Webb made sure a lot of influential people..." : AI June 23, 1996.

"For instance, when he put on his clothes": AI Sept. 7, 1996.

"Oh, he was a wonder": Ibid.

"I can't re-sign with you": AI, July 23, 1994.

"He went around and about": AI, Feb. 12, 1995.

"We had no witnesses,": "The Star You Love To Hate," Arnold Hano, *Pageant*, May 1966.

"On our honeymoon": AI, Feb. 12, 1995.

"He cried when I had a baby": Ibid.

"Did you see the pictures of Christopher?": Letter to Robert, Dec. 28, 1952.

"You don't make friends with the guys who are above you": "Drinks with Liberty Valance," Robert Ward, *Rolling Stone*, Sept. 3, 1981.

"He would have been with Raoul Walsh and Barrymore": AI July 13, 1995.

"That quality of violence in Lee showed up on screen": AI, June 14, 1996.

"Meyer had a whole bunch of people who were really busy": AI July 13, 1995.

"We met when he was coming up heading toward the bus": AI April 8, 1997.

"Fort Lost in the Woods of Misery" Ibid.

"I think the biggest thing about Lee that stands out": Ibid.

"I did ask [Lang] if there was anything that he wanted to tell me": "Marvin," Roy Pickard, *Photoplay Monthly*, July, 1976.

"We're sitting around a coffee table between scenes" AI Jan. 15, 1995.

"Lee's girlfriend, Gloria Grahame, had a scene": Ibid.

"In those days, the [3-D] cameras, weren't quite as effective": AI Jan. 26, 1999.

"He was a pretty muscular gun nut:" Ibid.

"When he was a young actor and we were just married": AI, Feb. 12, 1995.

"There are big things in the wind": Letter to Robert, Dec. 28, 1952.

"Lee passed me coming in over at the Columbia Ranch": AI April 8, 1997

"When the director [Laslo Benedek] walked down the street": Ibid.

"He [Marvin] and Marlon Brando...": AI Nov. 4, 1994

"They got along but it was a tolerance" Ibid.

"Lee was always in the tense scenes" AI, Feb. 12, 1995.

"When they did The Wild One, he was our son's baby-sitter": Ibid.

"Just don't make eye contact" Ibid.

CHAPTER 6: YOU LOOK LIKE YOU NEED A HAND"

"I was a troubleshooter": "Maverick Marvin," Kirk Honeycutt, *NY Daily News*, Feb. 11, 1986.

"I caught Lee's first screen triumph": AI June 14, 1996.

"He was a goofball but he was a fun goofball": AI Sept. 7, 1996.

"There they were, Admiral this and General that": AI July 21, 1994.

"Lee Marvin plays his role more than effectively": "Films Arrive," A.O. Scott, *New York Times*,

Aug. 21, 1954.

"I was mainly hired as the dummy": Some Enchanted Egos, Donald Zec, NY: St. Martin's Press, 1973, p. 256.

"We had babies one right after another": AI, Feb. 12, 1995.

"The first house we bought was up in Hollywood Knolls": Ibid.

"Lee had never sung": Ibid.

"Like Lee, he was another guy who did things...": AI Oct. 4, 1999.

"I also knew the first time I met him that he was unusually bright": Ibid.

"I didn't have anything in the script about that": Ibid.

"See, Lee was the kind of guy that hated gimmicks": AI April 8, 1997.

"You look like you need a hand": Bad Day at Black Rock, Warner Home Video DVD, 2005.

"I'll grant you one basically fine actor is Spencer Tracy": "Lee Marvin: Tuesday's Story": Ralph Story, KNXT-TV.

"One night there was this poker game in his home": AI April 8, 1997.

"Like on my birthday he would give me a bicycle...": AI, Feb. 12, 1995.

"What's the matter, don't you serve servicemen here?": *Forgive Us Our Digressions: An Autobiography*, Jim & Henny Backus, NY: St. Martin's Press, 1988.

"All you had to do was meet Lee": AI May 5, 1999.

"If you just ignore Victor Mature,": "Don't Just Twinkle, Rise and Shine," Judith Crist, *NY Herald Tribune*, Dec. 5, 1965.

"Sincerity and giving the role a character beyond what was written": AI Nov. 4, 1994.

Page 120) "I got to do things on film...": How Getting Shot Saved Lee Marvin's Life," Tom Seligman, *Parade*, April 27, 1986.

"I think everybody was certainly in awe of Ella": AI June 23, 1996.

"Lee was an amazing actor:" AI Oct. 17, 1994.

"They even gave me advice on how to treat men": Ibid.

"They were the best of friends and always got along": AI Oct. 11, 1995.

"Yeah, I guess there were a time or two they'd be in the shop": AI Aug. 8, 1995.

"This kid's good,": AI Budd Boetticher Oct. 30, 1994.

"Lee comes out and he's got this coat on": AI May 31, 1995.

"Lee was great": AI Oct. 30, 1994.

"He was one of the few actors who really knew how to handle a gun": Ibid.

"If I lose another man on account of you," "Attack" Pressbook, UA, 1956.

"Well, we made that local...": AI Oct. 25, 1994.

"He was totally in charge": AI Dec. 12, 1997.

"Lee, in those days, was very much...": AI June 23, 1996.

"Ward, what war did you fight in?": AI Peter Levinson Feb. 2, 1996.

"After the play": AI April 22, 1997.

"I feel very strongly that the longer you stay away from the stage...": Feb. 12, 1995.

"There's a scene in the bar in which he goes kind of wild": AI Oct. 4, 1999.

"I think he felt like I did and felt sorry for him": AI July 26, 1995.

"Lee was on location so I called our business manager Ed Silver...": AI, Feb. 12, 1995.

"If you ever talk to my wife again...": Ibid.

CHAPTER 7: MAN IN A STRAITJACKET

"No matter how fast they are...": "The Man for Vicaries," Richard Schickel, *TIME*, June 4, 1965.

"Lee is a mythomaniac" "Black Eye," Rip Torn, *TIME*, May 6, 1966.

"The fight was supposed to last about four minutes": AI Dec. 11, 1997.
"We would walk down the hall to go to the cafeteria" AI Sept. 25, 1994.
"In the early days, he was doing a show with Reagan": AI July 23, 1994.
"I did 'Bailout at 43,000' on 'Climax!' in 1956" AI July 13, 1995.
"He was a terrific personality": AI Nov. 21, 1994.
"You must understand that anthology TV is a very difficult form" AI Feb. 19, 1998.
"The truth is it was Lee Marvin's show": Ibid.
"I've sunk in one of these before!" CBS Television [viewed at The Paley Center, 1995]
"In those days I did a lot of 'Studio One": AI Nov. 10, 1995.
"Everybody knew me....": "Marvin Says Keep Cool If Goal Is A Real Whopper," Bob Thomas, Associated Press, May 27, 1965.
"That kid really smokes": "'Angry' Lee Marvin is Happy With New Dramatic Opportunities,": Bob Brooks, *L.A. Mirror*, Oct. 4, 1961.
"No broads, no mother, no sleep, no eat...": "The Man for Vicaries," Richard Schickel, *TIME*, June 4, 1965.
"Making movies rather than television": "Marvin's 'Pitching' in the Majors," Harold Hildebrand, *L.A. Examiner*, Oct. 29, 1961.
"Cops and robbers series sell": "Lee Marvin Candid Character," Joe Hyams, *Herald Tribune TV Guide*, Oct. 27, 1957.
"They arrested our cameraman twice": Ibid.
"I'm never ashamed of anything I do": Ibid.
"You never quite knew what he was going to do": AI Sept. 25, 1994.
"That is one of my good early jobs": AI Aug. 2, 2001.
"We had themes and what not": AI, Feb. 12, 1995.
"We got on the subject of the Brooklyn Dodgers" AI July 21, 1994.
"When Lee became somewhat successful.": AI Feb. 12, 1995.
"Lee told me a story during the time of 'M Squad'": AI Aug. 26, 1995.
"I would get out of the series....": "Man in A Strait Jacket" *TV Guide*, Feb. 7, 1959.
"We were really tight it seems to me until 'M Squad'" AI Feb. 12, 1995.
"Well, Lee was wined and dined by MCA,": AI June 26, 1995.
"He said, 'I don't want to do M Squad any more'": AI Feb. 12, 1995.
"Creatively, an actor is limited in TV": "Marvin's 'Pitching' in the Majors," Harold Hildebrand, *L.A. Examiner*, Oct. 29, 1961.
"Ida Lupino was directing that one": AI Jan. 18, 1998.
"He called me..." "Re-creating A Footnote To History, *TV Guide*, Mar. 26, 1960.
"I regard the series as a public service...": "He'll Play It Straight On New TV series, actor Lee Marvin won't act," Jack Leahy, *Sunday News*, Aug. 25, 1963.
"Violence on the screen is totally different," "There's not ENOUGH VIOLENCE on TV!" Lee Marvin as told to Peter J. Levinson, *TV-Radio Mirror*, Dec. 1963.
"What I remember most was his eyes" AI Nov. 23, 1994.
"By the time we got back from the hospital all stitched up,": AI June 23, 1996.

CHAPTER 8: "LADY, I JUST DON'T HAVE THE TIME"
"He's been around this town ten years": AI Feb. 2, 1996.
"It will be the site of a huge new housing development": "The Comancheros," Pressbook, 20th Century Fox, 1961.
"Ford gave Lee a piece of direction...": AI July 13, 1995.
"I think he's one of the most intelligent directors...": "Lee Marvin: Tuesday's Story": Ralph Story, KNXT-TV.
"It was a kick in the head workin' with Ford...": "Drinks with Liberty Valance," Robert Ward, *Rolling Stone*, Sept. 3, 1981.

"Here's how we meet...": AI Sept. 3, 1994.

"We were just sitting there bored with the whole thing": AI April 8, 1997.

"I move faster on screen,": "Drinks with Liberty Valance," Robert Ward, *Rolling Stone*, Sept. 3, 1981.

"I can work with tough directors," "Lee Marvin Shoots Off His Mouth!" Julie Paul, *Motion Picture*, Nov. 1968:

"We had a dog named Liberty, too": AI March 5, 1995.

"I remember once, when I was about twenty-two or twenty-three": AI Oct. 11, 1995.

"Absolutely fantastic": AI August 17, 1995.

"I remember one time, he and Neville Brand were in his car": AI April 8, 1997.

"A couple of times he used to wake me up": AI March 5, 1995.

"I remember when he didn't drink": AI Feb. 12, 1995.

"There might have been a hundred people there": AI July 8, 1995.

"I also knew when he wasn't drinking": AI Feb. 12, 1995.

"His drinking was getting pretty bad": Ibid.

"The guy never said anything": "Hanging Tough with Lee Marvin," Jane Wilson, *LA Times West*, Aug. 27, 1967.

"There's a thing that happens with actors" AI Oct. 9, 1999.

"He's quite kid, isn't he?" AI Feb. 12, 1995.

"Don't you want you and your family to get brown as berries?": *Print The Legend: The Life and Times of John Ford*, Scott Eyman, NY: Simon & Schuster, 1999, p.493.

"Have I ever had a part where I didn't get killed?": "Lee Marvin Alive and Tired of Dying It Up," Don Alpert, *LA Times,* Feb. 10, 1962.

"Duke would talk slow": AI Feb. 12, 1995.

"I won't jump out a third story window": "He'll Play It Straight On New TV series, actor Lee Marvin won't act," Jack Leahy, *Sunday News*, Aug. 25, 1963.

"This is like six in the morning": AI August 17, 1995.

"I was talking to what's-his-name, Eddie G. Robinson": "The Ultimate Drinking Buddy," Lewis Grossberger, *New York Magazine*, Aug. 25, 1980.

"On the plane is where he said to me": AI Feb. 12, 1995.

"Yet they still suffer from recurring nightmares": "Troubled Homecoming," Thomas Childers, *VFW*, April, 2009.

"As you progress from bit to feature player,": "Maverick Marvin," Kirk Honeycutt, *NY Daily News*, Feb. 11, 1986.

"When he was really lucid": AI August 17, 1995.

"I called the parents of the kids I invited": AI Feb. 12, 1995.

"Movies went to TV from the the the theaters until The Killers": AI Aug. 2, 2001.

"Are you going to play the older killer?": *A Siegel Film*, Don Siegel, London: Faber & Faber, 1993,

"He was, in my view, one of the foremost actors of his time": AI Jan. 20, 1997.

"He started putting down and condemning every other actor on the set,": Ibid.

"I used to look at his body language": AI Oct. 6, 1996.

"He was a gifted actor who could rehearse and perform": AI Aug. 2, 2001.

"This guy couldn't act worth a shit": AI Jan. 20, 1997.

"That's the greatest death scene I believe I've ever seen": Ibid.

"Schools like NYU, UCLA and USC...": Ibid.

"Lady, I just don't have the time": *The Killers* DVD, Criterion Collection, 2003.

PART III: TAKING THE POINT

CHAPTER 9: "TENSION, BABY, JUST TENSION"

"Lee, don't be schmuck!" AI Oct. 9, 1999.

"Lee is in kind of a special category in Hollywood,": "'Killer' Lee Marvin is Back In Action," Louella Parsons, *Herald Examiner*, March 16, 1965.

"It was at that moment that I realized my career...": "Remembering Lee Marvin" Michael Burkett, *Orange County Register*, Sept., 1, 1987 [reprint].

"Whatever picture I do next, had better be the right one": "'Killer' Lee Marvin is Back In Action," Louella Parsons, *Herald Examiner*, March 16, 1965.

"John Wayne was the toughest of them all": AI Oct. 11, 1995.

"Hell no. A book by a seventy-two-year-old broad? Not me": "Marvin Plays His Father," Jerry Parker, *Newsday*, Aug. 3, 1980.

"In essence it's the 'Ugly American,' ": Ibid.

"I think he drank sometimes to stop the pain,": AI Feb. 12, 1995.

"Yes, he could be irrationally enraged,": Ibid.

"Yeah, he got the guns out after a certain point": AI Oct. 11, 1995.

"If he just showed his head just an inch," AI Feb. 12, 1995.

"We were at the intersection of Wilshire and Westwood Blvd.": Ibid.

"He would look at you from under his eyebrows," AI Nov. 15, 1995.

"He literally would black out,": AI Feb. 12, 1995.

"I was in Robinson's Dept. Store,": AI Nov. 15, 1995.

"Lee got drunk and he [Cabeen] put him in the [motel] room," AI Dec. 10, 1995.

"I didn't even know they were coming to my house,": AI Nov. 15, 1995.

"The first thing was his personality,": AI July 4, 1994.

"Among those that stand out in the best sense,": "Reviewing Stand," Archer Winsten, *NY Post*, July 29, 1965.

"I think he was a hell of an actor,": AI July 4, 1994.

"He was the seventh guy after six of them turned it down,": AI August 17, 1995.

"We had lunch in Bel-Air at Harold's house,": AI May 31, 1995.

"The first script was rather a female adventure story," AI Feb. 23, 1998.

"I was concerned that Kirk Douglas, as a major star,": Ibid.

"I told him, 'It'll get you out of playing heavies,' ": AI Feb. 12, 1995.

"I started laughing when I read the first line,": "Lee Marvin: A New VIP in the Pecking Order," Joseph N. Bell, *National Observer*, Feb. 28, 1966.

"There's too much chaos here,": AI Feb. 23, 1998.

"He was a wild man,": AI Oct. 12, 1995.

"As filming went on, we socialized in California at my house...": AI Oct. 9, 1995.

"What bothered Lee about Jane...": AI Oct. 12, 1995.

"I remember early on, Lee had the driver stop...": Ibid.

"He had seen Harold call me over each time,": AI Feb. 23, 1998.

"Well, I remember one day," AI Oct. 9, 1995.

"Another funny incident was on the last day,": Ibid.

"If you watch that scene closely," AI Feb. 23, 1998.

"I was in a changing room in I. Magnin's trying on something,": AI Feb. 12, 1995.

"This woman called and I answer...": Ibid.

"I wish you well but it's so hard for me to understand...": Ibid.

"When I first came to town...": AI Feb. 23, 1998.

"The horse crossed his legs...": Ibid.

"The film was a lucky strike,": Ibid.

"I've been doing good things for years...": "Lee Marvin: A New VIP in the Pecking Order," Joseph N. Bell, *National Observer*, Feb. 28, 1966.

"The slow growth for me was actually planned ahead,": "Ballou Goes Up" *Briefing*, Sept. 1965.

"I went to a [prerelease] screening of Cat Ballou," AI March 13, 1996.

CHAPTER 10: EVERYBODY GETS THEIR "VI-CARIES"

"Let's just you and me face it, buddy,": "Lee The Marvel," *Stage & Cinema*, Sept. 8, 1967.

"If someone's going for my life...": "Lee Marvin," Pat McCabe, *Tiger* Magazine, Summer, 1968.

"Most people only wise up...": "Hanging Tough with Lee Marvin," Jane Wilson, *LA Times West*, Aug. 27, 1967.

"The only thing in life that's really interesting....": Ibid.

"The whole thing of success is just a big accident,": Ibid.

"I like a martini. I like rum,": "The Star You Love To Hate," Arnold Hano, *Pageant*, May 1966.

"When I do a scene I make it as rough as I can,": "A Cool Head Hits it Hot," Martin Cohen, *True*, Oct. 1965.

"People get a vicarious thrill out of what I do," "'Bad Guy' Marvin Enjoys Role," Roderick Mann, *Miami Herald*, April, 30, 1966.

"He had a body language that was altogether different..." AI April 8, 1997.

"They were some group," AI May 7, 1995.

"Shooting was postponed one day because of rain": "Lee Marvin" *Leatherneck*, Robert Johnson Jr., July, 1985.

"From then on [after Valance], we were cool,": AI Sept. 3, 1994.

"See how I was cut out in that vest?": Ibid.

"He had no fear,": AI May 7, 1995.

"Lee Marvin told me one thing that set in my mind...": AI Oct. 29, 1994.

"Yeah, he'd do a lot of fight scenes,": Ibid.

"He's crazy. He pulled a thing once, geez!": Ibid.

"I saw it when we'd drive to the set,": AI Sept. 3, 1994.

"The sober people on that film gave me more trouble....": AI May 7, 1995.

"Cabeen was an asshole,": Ibid.

"Oh if it weren't for Lee Marvin, I wouldn't get billing,": AI Sept. 3, 1994.

"Oh -- I didn't think it was all THAT funny,": "Candid Hollywood," *New Bedford Standard Times*, June 5, 1966.

"Two will get you twenty...": "A Frank Fellow,": Florabell Muir, *Daily News*, March 11, 1966.

"I want to be in competition with the best,": "Lee Marvin Talks Marriage," Sheila Graham, *New York World-Telegram*, March 15, 1966.

"The men with whom I'm competing....": "Lee Marvin Academy Award Nominee, Talks of Many Things on Visit Home," *Kingston Daily News*, April 12, 1966.

"I just said, 'Oh Lee, I think you should reconsider it,' ": AI Feb. 12, 1995.

"Lee was on the aisle. I was next to him,": AI Oct. 9, 1999.

"Thank you, thank you all, very much,": "Lee Marvin: Hollywood's Straight Shooter," *A&E Biography* DVD, 2001.

"He certainly didn't act like that tough, hard-drinking character..." "Julie New Darling of Oscar Set" Sheila Graham, *NY World Telegram & Sun*, April 21, 1966.

"Yes and no. Yes because everybody likes...": AI Feb. 23, 1998.

"I was willing to try it and Lee mumbled something....": Ibid.

"Well, the English government wouldn't allow American...": AI Oct. 25, 1994.

"The Yank stabbed me mate,": AI August 26, 1995.

"Bob Aldrich used to always say...": Ibid.

"He wants to intimidate you but...": "Lee Marvin Finds his Spot in Gorky Park": Roger Ebert, *Gazette Telegraph*, Jan. 8, 1984.

"What a character,": AI Dec. 16, 2011.

"Lee's a pro,": AI April 6, 1999.

"I had cut my finger..." Ibid.

"As a patriotic American...": "Rep. Corman Lauds 3M Co., Mascott, Marvin for Hell": *Hollywood Reporter*, Jan. 25, 1967.

"Marvin asked: 'I have script approval?' ": "Lee Marvin: A Dying Breed, John Boorman, Close-Ups, NY: Workman Publishing, p. 406.

"*The Killers* had a different situation already,": AI Aug. 2, 2001.

"He was endlessly inventive...": "Lee Marvin: A Dying Breed, John Boorman, Close-Ups, NY: Workman Publishing, p. 406.

"Lee was having one of these anxiety attacks....": AI Dec. 10, 1995.

"He really liked her," Ibid.

"Well, I'm really flattered by that," AI Aug. 2, 2001.

"So, Carroll said to Lee during the film," AI Feb. 12, 1995.

"I saw *Point Blank* at a film festival...": "My Style," Richard Stayton, *LA Herald-Examiner*, Feb. 4, 1985.

"We sit down in the master bedroom," AI Feb. 12, 1995.

CHAPTER 11: "I AIN'T SPITTIN' ON MY WHOLE LIFE"

"A female reporter from New York came to the London set,": AI Aug. 26, 1995.

"He didn't have a place to live...": AI Jan. 16, 2011.

"I don't know if I remember it correctly...": AI March 13, 1996.

"He was one of the few stars that would bring...": AI Aug. 17, 1995.

"Lee and I, from the beginning, would see Japanese films,": AI Feb. 12, 1995.

"This guy hypnotizes you with his genius,": "Marvin Plays His Father," Jerry Parker, *Newsday*, Aug. 3, 1980.

"It all paralleled beautifully,": "'Hell In the Pacific' Was Just That for Film Crew," Wayne Warga, *LA Times*, May 31, 1968.

"Mifune is beyond professionalism,": Ibid.

"Those who died, if they were still alive,": "Old Foes with a New View of War," P.F. Kluge *Life*, Sept. 27, 1968.

"We had limo that we had come in from the hotel,": AI Oct. 9, 1999.

"They released it during the Christmas weekend in Westwood," AI July 13, 1995.

"Screw'em. Let'em do their own killing,": AI w/ L.Q. Jones, July 13, 1995.

"A friend of Lee Marvin's called Roy Sickner...": Special collections file, Margaret Herrick Library of Academy of Motion Pictures Arts & Sciences.

"I don't think there were six pages of mine left....": "Mad As Hell: The Life and Work of Paddy Chayefsky, NY: Random House, 1994, page 249.

"I saw what happened there,": AI Oct. 29, 1994.

"He and I were standing there by the microphone,": AI May 5, 1998.

"They had a screening at Warners and Marvin was invited,": AI Nov. 20, 1994.

"[Sam] approached me about doing The Wild Bunch,": "Lee Marvin's Great, Goddamned Moments of the Big Kavoom," Grover Lewis, *Rolling Stone* Dec. 21, 1972.

"Lee Marvin is a superb...": David Denby, *New York Magazine*, Oct. 1969.

"Nobody gets to be a cowboy forever, Monte": "Monte Walsh," Paramount/CBS DVD.

"I would love to do love scenes,": "Lee Marvin Alive and Tired of Dying It Up," Don Alpert, *LA Times*, Feb. 10, 1962.

"It was really very strange,": AI Jan. 14, 2012.

"One of the other things he did was when we first got there," Ibid.

"Lee Marvin was not a tough guy acting like a tough guy,": AI Oct. 9, 1994.

"I remember one time we were in some restaurant...": AI Sept. 1997.

"One thing that Lee and some of the other stuntmen said was..." AI Jan. 14, 2012.

"Then came Jeanne Moreau,": Ibid.

"He says more in less words,": "Lee Marvin, Hollywood's Most Dedicated Hell-Raiser,"

Jim Sirmans, *Saga*, June, 1974.

"The decision to cut the film is unfortunate,": "Bill Fraker Directing Bow," Larry Cohen, *The Hollywood Reporter*, Oct. 7, 1970.

"I ain't spittin' on my whole life,": "Monte Walsh," Paramount/CBS DVD.

"It's Pam Feeley, from Woodstock,": AI March 13, 1996.

"It's kind of a comedy of a couple of con men...":

"They didn't get it,": AI March 3, 2012.

"When the Chief died...": "Drinks with Liberty Valance," Robert Ward, *Rolling Stone*, Sept. 3, 1981.

"Lee invited Gene and me to drive out with him...": AI Dec. 9, 1995.

"Actually, I thought Lee was protective of her in that thing,": Ibid.

"I have made some mistakes I wish I hadn't.": "Lee Marvin's Great, Goddamned Moments of the Big Kavoom,": Grover Lewis, *Rolling Stone* Dec. 21, 1972.

"I met Lee Marvin in Bob [Aldrich's] office,": Will the Real Me Please Stand Up, Christopher Knopf, GA: Bear Manor Media, p.123.

"Bob has a knack for gettin' a kind of cast together...": "Lee Marvin's Great, Goddamned Moments of the Big Kavoom,": Grover Lewis, *Rolling Stone* Dec. 21, 1972.

"We were on that damned thing for a week,": AI Oct. 25, 1994.

"I get a special kick playing rebels...": "Lee Marvin the railroad hobo in *Emperor Of The North*..." Bert Reisfeld, *Photoplay*[UK], October, 1973.

"He has that wonderful face," AI July 13, 1995.

"I saw him someplace and he gave me the shooting script...": AI March 13, 1996.

"Yeah, it was at a stage in my career where I wasn't sure...": AI March 26, 2012.

"In acting there are certain unspoken rules,": Ibid.

"Marvin came in literally carrying an entire case of beer ..." AI Jan. 19, 2012.

"Lee just couldn't handle it,": AI July 13, 1995.

"Lee Marvin was sometimes not called for a week and a half,": "Frankenheimer's 'Iceman': Another Chance for U.S." Gregg Kilday, *LA Times*, Sept. 13, 1973

"We went over the points we wanted to make, the beats,": July 13, 1995.

PART IV: THE REAR ECHELON,
"He was born to be my sergeant," AI June 1, 1995.

CHAPTER 12: THE WHITE EYE

"It's getting very difficult to be an actor ...": "Lee Marvin Sitting in bahnhof watching the trains go by," Colin Dangaard, *LA Herald-Examiner*, May 27, 1978.

"I could see his eyes widen a bit...": AI May 5, 1999.

"Spikes is not only a bank robber...": "Lee Marvin the railroad hobo in Emperor Of The North..." Bert Reisfeld, *Photoplay*[UK], October, 1973.

"As they say, it never opened...": AI May 5, 1999.

"It's dangerous for the same reason antiwar films are dangerous,": "The Klansman," Judy Stone, *Playgirl*, July, 1974.

"I'll either drink the town dry or I won't touch a drop,": "Women Like to be Scared of a Guy," Phillip Judge, *Girl Talk*, Oct. 1975.

"I said to Lee, 'I have to go back...": AI Oct. 4, 1999.

"There wa a film that Lee Marvin and Cameron Mitchell did...": AI Jan. 18, 1998.

"I was gong to direct it," AI June 1, 1995.

"Yeah, Lee was very good,": AI Oct. 4, 1999.

"It's a load of bull,": "Women Like to be Scared of a Guy," Phillip Judge, *Girl Talk*, Oct. 1975.

"Can you tell I did that one for the money?": AI w/ Paul Wasserman, March 13, 1996.

"The thing I look for now is how I really feel,": "Lee Marvin, Hollywood's Most Dedicated

Hell-Raiser," Jim Sirmans, *Saga*, June, 1974.

"I was always proud of what I did with Lee,": AI Jan. 16, 2012.

"Well, to tell you the truth, Lee changed,": AI Sept. 23, 1995.

"It's a thing you continually do,": AI Dec. 10, 1995.

"We were at the Holiday Inn, or something like that,": AI Sept. 23, 1995.

"I'm going to be very candid about this...": AI Feb. 12, 1995.

"You couldn't have gotten seven people who were more different," AI Jan. 21, 2012.

"He's not a man of many words," Ibid.

"Any time you do something like that,": "Marvin's 'Great Scout' a Replay,": Ann Guarino, *NY News*, June 23, 1976.

"A fun picture, a summer romp": "Lee Marvin. Sees 'Great Scout' As Fun Picture...Nothing More," *Chicago Tribune*, Donald Kirk 7/25/76.

"There's nothing you can do about it,": Ibid.

"Has it ever occurred to you that some of the actors...":

"I called from downstairs," AI Dec. 14, 2012.

"Over-awed and amused," AI June 21, 2012.

"Then you realize he has you hooked,": "Marvin," Roy Pickard, *Photoplay Monthly,* July, 1976.

"There were script problems as well as production problems," AI Nov. 7, 1996.

"I know my career is going badly...": AI w/ Myer Mishkin, July 23, 1994.

CHAPTER 13: MAY THE BEST SCRIPT WIN

"The one with the best script": AI w/ David Kagon, July 20, 1994.

"Because my script is real,": Ibid.

"She was having one scene after another,": AI Feb. 12, 1995.

"Then he bought the house on La Costa Beach,": AI Dec. 10 1995.

"We [he & Betty] separated a year and a half ago,": "Lee Marvin Talks Marriage," Sheila Graham, New York World-Telegram, March 15, 1966.

"They had a good relationship,": AI Oct. 11, 1995.

"Lee was generally around people who...": AI Dec. 10, 1995.

"I don't want to be that negative about Michele,": AI Jan. 16 2012.

"He had ten thousand dollars sitting right there," AI Oct. 29, 1994.

"A couple of girls wanted to be stunt girls,": Ibid.

"They ended up calling it in the newspaper, 'The Robin Hood Party',": Ibid.

"My greater association with him was with Michele," AI March 13, 1996.

"He lived in a very 'alky' world in those days,": AI Oct. 29, 1994.

"I didn't think it was going to be that long-term a relationship,": AI Jan. 16 2012.

"He had rented a house and we had two or three days off,": AI Oct. 29, 1994.

"You know when Lee made Paint Your Wagon...": AI Jan. 16 2012.

"He tried to leave several times,": AI Oct. 29, 1994.

"I remember this one time he was passed out,": AI Aug. 14, 1995.

"It must have been early 1970,": AI Dec. 10 1995.

"My wife, who is an artist and professionally trained...": AI July 20, 1994.

"Why would I want to break back into prison?": AI Feb. 12, 1995.

"Lee had said at a press conference...": "A Surprise Wedding," *Modern Screen*, Nov. 1970

"Lee and I live at Malibu just four doors down...": "Marvin, Girl Friend Still Friends," Dorothy Manners, *LA Herald Examiner*, Aug. 12, 1970.

"I had six years on my own and I find it very lacking,": "Lee Marvin Philosophical" Joyce Haber, *LA Times*, March 25, 1972.

"At a time when a thousand bucks a month was significant,": AI July 20, 1994.

"Of course I knew Pam,": "My Six Lost Years with Lee Marvin," Bernard Barry, *Coronet*, June, 1972.

"There were many hard time during those early years,": Ibid.

"It was with Lee's approval'": "The Girl Lee Marvin Never Married Sues Him for Divorce," *Movie Star Life*, Brenda Shaw, Feb. 1972.

"Palimony, alimony for a pal,": AI w/ David Kagon, July 20, 1994.

"This move is one we did not expect,": "Lee Marvin's $1-M Battle of The Sexes" Leon Freilich, *Midnight/Globe,* Nov. 1977.

"That the mere fact that a couple have not participated...": "Lee Marvin's Other 'Wife'" *Newsweek*, Jan. 10, 1977.

"This is going to open the floodgates to the courts,": Ibid.

"It could be several more years before we have a judgment...": "Lee Marvin's $1-M Battle of The Sexes" Leon Freilich, *Midnight/Globe*, Nov. 1977.

"It doesn't disturb me,": "It's Round Two of the Marvin Affair," Victor Junger, *People* Jan 22, 1979. 1/22/79

"This was a man who probably did not own...": AI July 20, 1994.

"What a can of worms you've opened,": "Lee Marvin May Have to Cough Up Big Bucks," *People*, Jan. 17, 1077.

"We were not going to try the case in the press,": AI July 20, 1994.

"I gave her the best years of her life,": Ibid.

"There was an effort to show...": Ibid.

"He was a great showman,": Ibid.

"When I mentioned it to Lee, he said two words,": Ibid.

"Not one feminist organization came out for Michele,": "The Penthouse Interview: Lee Marvin," Fred Robbins, *Penthouse*, Feb. 1980.

"I never considered settling,": "Marvin Plays His Father," Jerry Parker, *Newsday,* Aug. 3, 1980.

"We didn't collect," AI July 20, 1994.

CHAPTER 14: THE LAST OF THE WINTRY HEROES

"John Wayne wanted to do The Big Red One in the 50s,": AI June 1, 1995.

"I ran into Lee at the cigar store on Fairfax,": Ibid.

"There was a lot that went unsaid...": AI April 30, 1996.

"For me, I was inspired by for the Sergeant by ...": AI June 1, 1995.

"He was a fifty-year-old first sergeant in an antiaircraft battalion,": "Marvin Plays His Father," Jerry Parker, NEWSDAY, Aug. 3, 1980.

"We were all shooting M-1's,": AI April 30, 1996.

"To see those guys wearing those German coal-scuttle helmets...": "Sam Fuller Lands with The Big Red One," Bruce Cook, *American Film*, June, 1979.

"He could say Colleville-sur-mer,": AI April 30, 1996.

"The kid was not supposed to drop the apple,": Ibid.

"My chance to make my own personal statement,": "Marvin Plays His Father," Jerry Parker, *Newsday*, Aug. 3, 1980.

"Well besides complete idiocy, they want lack of respect,": "The Penthouse Interview: Lee Marvin," Fred Robbins, *Penthouse*, Feb. 1980.

"He said, 'Avoid any script that says...' ": AI Dec. 10, 1995.

"Sounds like a bunch of gays in Eskimo outfits,": "Marvin Plays His Father," Jerry Parker, *Newsday*, Aug. 3, 1980.

"He was quite bitter,": AI Aug. 2, 2001.

"It was a tough sequence because it was written a certain,": Ibid.

"...With this kind of picture, if you just tell then the title,": "Marvin is still at it and holding up well," Chris Chase, *LA Herald-Examiner,* May 23, 1981.

"He picks through the midden of scripts,": "Lee Marvin: A Dying Breed, John Boorman, Close-Ups, NY: Workman Publishing, p. 407.

"Those films absolutely kill me...": "The Ultimate Drinking Buddy," Lewis Grossberger, *New York Magazine*, Aug. 25, 1980.
"What I remember most vividly was that we rehearsed in hospital,": AI Mar. 9, 2012.
"Into the alcove stepped a man,": Martin Cruz, Smith, *Gorky Park*, London: William Collins & Sons, 1981, p.89.
"I remember him laying his towel on the bed...": AI Mar. 9, 2012.
"Marvin was incredibly supportive of him,": Ibid.
"His reputation preceded him, being quite a heavy drinker,": Ibid.
"I don't think Western audiences became interested in Russia until...": Ibid.
"Great, she could be the son I always wanted,": AI Feb. 12, 1995.
"Well, I think that's your privilege, dear,": Ibid.
Page 301) "I'd always wanted to work in France...": "A Mellower Lee Marvin: To Helsinki and Back," Roderick Mann, *LA Times,* Dec. 25, 1983.
"I enjoyed that,": Ibid.
"Lucille Ball was on the show,": AI Oct. 9, 1999.
"He was my friend always, and then my agent,": "Unsung Agents Get Their Rewards," Sondra Lowell, *LA Times*, Feb. 21, 1981.
"I went to visit him and we're sitting in his kitchen,": AI Mar. 5, 1995.
"I got a call from the producers": "Remembering Lee Marvin" Michael Burkett, *Orange County Register,* Sept., 1, 1987 [reprint].
"Lee looked so bad,": AI Oct. 9, 1999.
"He was very pleasant but he was fragile,": AI Jan. 18, 1998.
"I just thought he was a classic case of movie star appeal,": Ibid.
"Go see Delta Force,": "Maverick Marvin," Kirk Honeycutt, *NY Daily News*, Feb. 11, 1986.
"I would often go down there and watch old movies,": AI Jan. 14, 2012.
"No, we never did,": Ibid.
"I have fought the good fight,": "My Style," Richard Stayton, *LA Herald-Examiner,* Feb. 4, 1985.
"Lee went in there by himself for a while," AI Oct. 11, 1995.
"Christopher used to drive out there to see him...": AI Feb. 12, 1995.
"He got hepatitis from the blood,": AI Dec. 10, 1995.
"I could tell he was losing it because he was bedridden,": Ibid.
"When I first went in and saw him,": AI Mar. 5, 1995.
"He was very uncomfortable," AI Jan. 14, 2012.
"I wasn't there at the time he had his breathing attack,": Ibid.
"Look who just got uncivilized,": "Death Hunt," Anchor Bay DVD, 2005.

Epilogue: The Inglorious Bastard Sons Of Lee
"You could be a meat eater, kid,": "Emperor of The North," 20th Century Fox DVD, 2006.
"One actor I'm a big fan of is Lee Marvin": "Jim Jarmusch's Guilty Pleasures," *Film Comment*, May, 1992.
"Six months ago, Tom Waits was in a bar somewhere in Northern California,": Ibid.
"Lee Marvin. Now there's a real bad guy,": "Who's That Knocking At My Door," Warner Brothers DVD, 2004.
"I bet you're a big Lee Marvin fan, aren't you?": "Reservoir Dogs," Lion's Gate DVD, 2003.
"Lee's sort of the wild man,": "Keepers of The Flame" Jim Washburn, *LA Times*, Feb. 29. 1995.
"I hadn't seen Tom in a few years," AI Mar. 5, 1005.
"They were using us for name value,": AI April 6, 1999.
"Trini Lopez was there,": Ibid.
"With precious few exceptions, all I see is a lot of boys...": "Where is Lee Marvin When We Really Need Him?" John Farr, *Huffington Post*, Feb. 20, 2010.

Bibliography

Books

Abrams, Joanne, Unterburger, Amy L. (ed), *International Dictionary of Films & Filmmaking*, UK: St. James Press, 1997.

Alloway, Lawrence, *Violent America: The Movies 1946-1964*. NY: The Museum of Modern Art, 1971.

Anderson, F.W. et al. *The Death of Albert Johnson, Mad Trapper of Rat River*. Surrey, B.C: Heritage House, 1986.

Ann-Margret, My Story. NY: Putnam, 1994.

Ashley, Elizabeth, Actress: *Postcards From the Road*. NY: M. Evans & Co. 1979.

Baxter, John, *Sixty Years of Hollywood*. NY: A.S. Barnes, 1973.

Biskind, Peter, *Easy Riders, Raging Bulls: How the Sex-Drugs-and-Rock 'n' Roll Generation Saved Hollywood*. NY: Touchstone Books, 1998.

Blum, Richard A., *American Film Acting, The Stanislavski Heritage*. Ann Arbor, MI: UMI Research Press, 1984.

Bogdanovich, Peter, *Who the Devil Made It*. NY: Ballantine Books, 1997.

_____, *Who the Hell's In It*. NY: Ballantine Books, 2004.

Boller, Paul F, Davis, Ronald, L. *Hollywood Anecdotes*, NY: Ballantine, 1988.

Boorman, John, *Adventures of a Suburban Boy*. London, England: Faber & Faber, 2003.

Borgnine, Ernest, *Ernie: The Autobiography*. New York, NY: Citadel, 2008.

Brando, Marlon, & Lindsey, Robert, *Songs My Mother Taught Me*. NY: Random House, 1994.

Brode, Douglas, *The Films of the Fifties*. Secaucus, NJ: Citadel Press, 1976.

_____, *The Films of the Sixties*. Secaucus, NJ: Citadel Press, 1980.

Bronson, Harriett, *Charlie & Me*. Woodland Hills, CA: Timberlake Press, 2011.

Buford, Kate, *Burt Lancaster, An American Life*. Cambridge, MA: Da Capo Press, 2000.

California Civil Code, *Marvin v. Marvin*. LA., December 27, 1976.

Chanslor, Roy, *The Ballad of Cat Ballou*. NY: Little Brown, 1956.

Chapman, John, ed. *The Best Plays: 1950-1951*. NY: Dodd, Mead, 1951.

Charity, Tom, *John Cassavetes: Lifeworks*. London: Omnibus Press, 2001.

Clarkson, Wensley, *Quentin Tarantino: The Man, The Myth and His Movies*. London: John Blake, 2007.

Clinch, Minty, *Burt Lancaster*. NY: Stein & Day, 1986.

Considine, Shaun, *Mad As Hell: The Life and Work of Paddy Chayefsky*. NY: Random House, 1994.

Coxe, Louis O, & Chapman, Robert, *Billy Budd*. NY: Hill & Wang, 1962.

Crist, Judith, *The Private Eye, The Cowboy and The Very Naked Lady*. NY: Holt/Rinehart, 1968.

_____ *Take 22: Moviemakers on Moviemaking*. NY: Viking, 1984.

Daniel, Douglass K., *Tough As Nails: The Life and Films of Richard Brooks*. University of Wisconsin Press, 2011.

Deschner, Donald, *The Films of Spencer Tracy*. Secaucus, NJ: Citadel Press, 1968.

Dickens, Homer, *The Films of Gary Cooper*. Secaucus, NJ: Citadel Press, 1970.

Dmytryk, Edward, *It's a Hell of a Life But Not a Bad Living*. NY: Times Books, 1978.

Douglas, Kirk, *The Ragman's Son*. NY: Simon & Schuster, 1988.

Druxman, Michael B., *Make it Again, Sam: A Survey of Movie Remakes*. NY: Barnes, 1975.

Eames, John Douglas, *The MGM Story*. NY: Crown, 1985.

Evers, Alf, *Woodstock: History of an American Town*. NY: Overlook Press, 1989.

Eyman, Scott, *Print the Legend: The Life and Times of John Ford*. NY: Simon & Schuster,

1999.

Fine, Marshall, *Accidental Genius: How John Cassavetes Invented the American Independent Film*. NY: Miramax Books, 2005.

Finler, John W. *The Movie Directors Story*. NY: Crescent Books, 1985.

Fishgall, Gary, *Against Type: The Biography of Burt Lancaster*. NY: Scribner, 1995.

Forbes, Colin, *Avalanche Express*. NY: Fawcett Crest Books, 1977.

Froug, William, *The Screenwriter Looks at the Screenwriter*. NY: MacMillan, 1972.

Fleischer, Richard, *Just Tell Me When to Cry*. NY: Carroll & Graf, 1993.

Fonda, Jane, *My Life So Far*. NY: Random House, 2006.

Fuller, Sam, *The Big Red One*. NY: Bantam Books, 1980.

_____ *A Third Face: My Tale of Writing, Fighting, and Filmmaking*. NY: Knopf, 2002.

Galbraith, Stuart IV, *The Emperor and the Wolf: The Lives and Films of Akira Kurosawa and Toshiro Mifune*. London: Faber & Faber, 2002.

Garner, James & Winokur, Jon, *The Garner Files*. NY: Simon & Schuster, 2011.

Goldstein, Toby, *William Hurt: The Man, the Actor*. NY: St. Martin's Press, 1987.

Heath, W.L., *Violent Saturday*. NY: Harper & Row, 1955.

Hamblett, Charles, *Paul Newman*. Chicago: Regnery, 1975.

Hemingway, Ernest, *The Complete Short Stories of Ernest Hemingway*. NY: Simon & Schuster, 1987.

Hickman, Dwayne & Hickman, Joan Roberts, *Forever Dobie: The Many Lives of Dwayne Hickman*. NY: Birch Lane Press, 1994.

Hirsch, Phil, ed. *Hollywood Confidential*. NY: Pyramid Books, 1967.

Horgan, James J, *Pioneer College: The Centennial History of St. Leo College, St. Leo Abbey and Holy Name Academy*. FL: St. Leo College Press, 1989.

Jacobs, Diane, *Hollywood Renaissance*. NY: Delta Books, 1980.

Kaminsky, Stuart, *Don Siegel: Director*. NY: Curtis Books, 1974.

Kass, Judith M., *The Films of Montgomery Clift*. Secaucus, NJ: Citadel Press, 1979.

Kennedy, Burt, *Seven Men From Now*. NY: Berkley Press, 1956.

Kingman, Russ, *A Pictorial Life of Jack London*. NY: Crown, 1979.

Knopf, Christopher, *Will the Real Me Please Stand Up*. Albany, GA: Bear Manor Media, 2010.

Lentz, Robert, *Lee Marvin: His Films and Career*. Jefferson, NC: McFarland Press, 2000.

Levy, Shawn, *Paul Newman: A Life*. NY: Harmony Books, 2009.

Livingston, Leon Ray (a.k.a. 'A- No 1'), *From Coast to Coast with Jack London*. Sullivan, IL; The Depot, 1987.

Lockridge, Ross, Jr, *Raintree County*. Boston: Houghton Mifflin, 1948.

Logan, Josh, *Movie Stars, Real People & Me*. NY: Dell, 1978.

London, Jack, *Novels and Social Writings (The Road)*. NY: Viking Press, 1982.

Lovell, Glenn, *Escape Artist: The Life & Films of John Sturges*. University of Wisconsin Press, 2008.

McDougal, Dennis, *Five Easy Decades: How Jack Nicholson Became the Biggest Movie Star in Modern Times*. Hoboken, NJ: Wiley & Sons, 2008.

McGivern, William P, *The Big Heat*. NY: Pocket Books, 1952.

Maltin, Leonard, *TV Movies & Video Guide*. NY: New American Library, 1989.

Marvin, Betty, *Tales of a Hollywood Housewife*. Bloomington, IN: iUniverse, 2009.

Marvin, Pam, *Lee: A Romance*. London, England: Faber & Faber, 1997.

Medved, Harry & Michael, *The Hollywood Hall of Shame The Most Expensive Flops in Movie History*. NY: Perigree, 1984.

Michener, James A., *Centennial*. NY: Random House, 1974.

Mitchelson, Marvin, *Made in Heaven, Settled in Court*. NY: Warner Books, 1979.

Mitchum, John, *Them Ornery Mitchum Boys*. Pacifica, CA: Creatures At Large Press, 1989.

Mordden, Ethan, *Medium Cool, The Movies of the 1960s*. NY: Knopf, 1990.

Nathanson, E.M., *The Dirty Dozen*. NY: Dell Pub. 1965.

Norst, Joel, *The Delta Force*. NY: St. Martin's Press, 1986.

O'Neill, Terry, *Legends*. NY: Viking, 1985

O'Rourke, Frank, *The Professionals (aka A Mule for the Marquesa)*. NY: William Morrow & Co., 1964.

Osborne, Robert, *The Academy Awards Illustrated*. CA: ESE, 1975.

Palmer, R. Barton, ed., *Larger Than Life: Movie Stars of the 1950s*. New Brunswick, NJ: Rutgers University Press, 2010.

Peary, Danny, *Alternate Oscars*. NY: Delta, 1993.

_____ *Close-Ups: The Movie Star Book*. NY: Workman, 1978.

Place, J.A., *The Non-Western Films of John Ford*. Secaucus, NJ: Citadel Press, 1979.

Porter, Katherine Anne, *Ship of Fools*. NY: Little, Brown, 1945.

Quirk, Lawrence, *The Films of Paul Newman*. Secaucus, NJ: Citadel Press, 1981.

Reed, Oliver, *Reed All About Me*. UK: Coronet Books, 1979.

Reynolds, Burt, *My Life*. NY: Hyperion, 1994.

Roote, Mike, *Prime Cut*. NY: Award Books, 1973.

Rose, Thomas, ed, *Violence In America*. NY: Random House, 1969.

Scorsese, Martin & Wilson, Michael Henry, *A Personal Journey with Martin Scorsese Through American Movies*. NY: Miramax Books/Hyperion, 1997.

Server, Lee, *Robert Mitchum: "Baby, I Don't Care."* NY: St. Martin's Griffin, 2001.

Seydor, Paul, *Peckinpah The Western Films*. Ill: University of Illinois, 1980.

Shapiro, Richard, *The Great Scout & Cathouse Thursday*. Terre Haute, IN: Popular Library,1976.

Shipman, Donald et. al. *Duke: The Life and Times of John Wayne*. NY: Doubleday, 1985.

Shipman, David, *The Great Movie Stars: The International Years*. NY: St. Martin's Press, 1972.

_____, *Movie Talk*. NY: St. Martin's Press, 1988.

Siegel, Don, *A Siegel Film*. London, England: Faber & Faber, 1993.

Signoret, Simone, *Nostalgia Isn't What It Used to Be*. NY: Pengin, 1979.

Silver, Alain & Ursini, James, *What Ever Happened to Robert Aldrich?* NY: Limelight, 1995.

Sinclair, Andrew, *John Ford*. NY: Dial Press, 1979.

Smith, Martin Cruz, *Gorky Park*. NY: Random House, 1981.

Smith, Wilbur, *Shout at the Devil*. London: Wm. Heinemann Ltd, 1968.

Stallings, Penny, *Forbidden Channels*. NY: HarperCollins, 1991.

Stark, Richard (Westlake, Donald E.), *Point Blank (aka The Hunter)*. NY: Pocket Books, 1962

Stowell, James Vinton, *Ross G. Marvin A Tragedy in The Artic*. Elmira, NY: Chemung County Historical Society, 1954.

Strode, Woody & Young, Sam, *Goal Dust*. Lanham, MD: Madison Books, 1990.

Thomas, Bob, *Marlon: Portrait of the Rebel as an Artist*. NY: Ballantine, 1973.

_____ *Golden Boy, The Untold Story of William Holden*. NY: Berkely Books, 1983.

Thomas, Tony, *The Great Adventure Films*. Secaucus, NJ: Citadel Press, 1980.

Thomey, Tedd, *The Glorious Decade*. NY: Ace Books, 1971.

Thompson, Morton, *Not As a Stranger*. NY: Scribner's, 1954.

Thomson, David, *The New Biographical Dictionary of Film*. NY: Knopf, 2010.

Tippette, Giles, *The Spikes Gang (aka The Outlaw)*. NY: MacMillan, 1970.

Tomkies, Mike, *The Robert Mitchum Story*. NY: Ballantine Books, 1973.

Travers, Peter, ed. *The Rolling Stone Film Reader*. New York, NY: Pocket Books, 1996.

Van Dyke, Dick, *My Lucky Life in and Out of Show Business*. NY: Crown, 2011.
Verimyle, Jerry, *The Films of Charles Bronson*. Secaucus, NJ: Citadel Press, 1981.
Vineberg, Steve, *Method Actors: Three Generations of an American Acting Style*. NY: Schirmer Books, 1991.
Weddle, David, *If They Move… Kill'em!: The Life and Times Of Sam Peckinpah*. NY: Grove Press, 1994.
Wellman, Paul I, *The Comancheros*. NY: Doubleday, 1952.
Williams, Tony, *Body & Soul: The Cinematic Vision of Robert Aldrich*. Lanham, MD: Scarecrow Press, 2004.
Willoughby, Bob & Schickel, Richard, *The Platinum Years*. NY: Random House, 1974.
Windeler, Robert, *Burt Lancaster*. NY: St. Martin's Press, 1984.
Wise, James E. & Rehill, Anne Collier, *Stars in The Corps: Movie Actors in the United States Marines*. Annapolis, MD: Naval Instiute Press, 1999.
Woodruff, Paul & Willner, Harry A, ed. *Facing Evil: Light at the Core of Darkness*. Lasalle, IL: Open Court, 1988.
Whittemore, Henry, *Geneological Guide to the Early Settlers of America*, Baltimore: General Publishing Co. 1967.
Winters, Shelley, *Shelly II: The Middle of My Century*. NY: Simon & Schuster, 1989.
Wynn, Ned, *We Will Always Live in Hollywood*. NY: William Morrow & Co. 1990.
Yule, Andrew, *Life on the Wire: The Life and Art of Al Pacino*. NY: Donald I. Fine Inc, 1991.
Zec, Donald, *Some Enchanted Ego*. NY: St. Martin's Press, 1973.
_____*Marvin: The Story of Lee Marvin*. New York, NY: St. Martin's Press, 1980.
Zicree, Mark Scott, *The Twilight Zone Companion*. NY: Bantam Books, 1982.
Zinneman, Fred, *A Life in the Movies*. NY: Scribner's, 1992.

Periodicals

Alpert, Don, "Lee Marvin Alive and Tired of Dying It Up," *LA Times*, February 10, 1962.
Alpert, Hollis, "The New Repertory Cinema: Eight Enchanted Evenings of Ely Landau," *World*, August 28, 1973.
Anon, "Man in a Strait Jacket," *TV Guide*, February 7, 1959
Anon, "Assorted Blasts From An Angry Man," *TV Guide*, October 3, 1959.
Anon, "Drunkest Gun in the West," *Life*, June 11, 1965.
Anon, "Lee Marvin Charged in Collision," *LA Times*, September 24, 1965.
Anon, "Lee Marvin, Academy Award Nominee, Talks of Many Things on Visit Home," *Woodstock News*, April 12, 1966.
Anon "Lee Marvin -- A Year Later On Eve of Oscar," *LA Herald-Examiner*, April 9, 1967.
Anon "A Rebel's Creed," *This Week*, August 14, 1966.
Anon "Lee The Marvel," *Stage & Cinema*, September 8, 1967.
Anon "Long "Live the Debonair, Magnificent Lover," *LA Herald-Examiner*, Decmber 1, 1968.
Anon "Why Lee Marvin is Being Sued for 'Divorce' by the Woman He Never Married," *Motion Picture*, 1972.
Anon, "Lee Marvin's Other Wife," *Newsweek*, January 10, 1977.
Anon, "Lee Marvin May Have to Cough Up Big Bucks to His Ex-Lover," *People*, January 17, 1977.
Anon, "The Paladin of Paramours," *Time*, January 15, 1979.
Anon, "Lee Marvin Hangs Up His Guns," *The Globe*, August 13, 1985.
Archerd, Army, "Just For Variety," *Daily Variety*, April 28, 1983.
Baker, Bob & Morrison, Patt, "Lee Marvin, Menacing Gunman of Film, Dies," *LA Times*, August 30, 1987.

Barry, Bernard, "My Six Lost Years with Lee Marvin," *Coronet*, June, 1972.

Barthel, Joan "He's Way Up On Top, Baby!" *TV Guide*, September 28, 1968.

Bell, Joseph N, "Lee Marvin: A New VIP in the Pecking Order, *National Observer*, February 28, 1966.

Benson, Walter, "Success Came Too Late Says Lee Marvin," *National Enquirer*, May 15, 1966.

Bond, Jeff, Bettencourt, Scott & Kendall, Lukas, "Criminal Existence," *Point Blank CD Soundtrack Liner Notes*, 2000.

Borgnine, Ernest, "Unpublished Interview," *Filmfax*, 2006.

Breslin, Jimmy "Lee Marvin Says He Learned 'How To Lie,'" *NY Daily News*, May 20, 1979.

Brill, Steven, "Revenge For the Jilted?" *Esquire*, May 9, 1978.

Brooks, Bob "Angry' Lee Marvin Is Happy With New Dramatic Opportunities," *LA Mirror*, October 4, 1961.

Buckley, Tom, "How Marvin Went to War for The Big Red One," *NY Times*, August 1, 1980.

Burkett, Michael, "Remembering Lee Marvin, *Orange County Register*, September 1, 1987.

Casselman, Ben, "Lee Marvin's Widow Lists His Tucson Home, *Tucson Citizen*, April 20, 2007.

Chase, Chris, "Marvin is Still at it and Holding Up Well," *LA Herald-Examiner*, May 23, 1981.

Childers, Thomas, "Readjusting to Postwar Society: Troubled Homecoming," *VFW*, April 2009.

Cohen, Larry "Natgen's 'Monte Walsh' Top BO, Critical Film Success," *The Hollywood Reporter*, October 7, 1970.

Cohen, Martin "True's Who: Lee Marvin," *True*, October, 1965.

Connolly, Mike, "Lee Marvin: Some Tough Guy," *Screen Stories*, October, 1966.

Cook, Bruce, "Sam Fuller Lands with the Big Red One," *American Film*, June, 1979.

Cowan, Ronnie, "Divorce Without Marriage: The Curious Case of Lee Marvin's Common-Law Wife," *Ladies Home Journal*, October, 1973.

Crist, Judith, "Don't Just Twinkle, Rise and Shine, *NY Herald-Tribune*, December 5, 1965.

Crowther, Bosley "The Marvel of Lee Marvin," *NY Times,* September 24, 1967

Dent, Alan "Cinema," *Illustrated London News*, August 26, 1967.

Dangaard, Colin, "Lee Marvin: Sitting in the Bahnhof Watching the Trains Go By," *LA Herald-Examiner*, May 27, 1978.

Darrach, Brad, "And the Best Bad Guy Leaves a Few Words to Live By," *People*, September 14, 1987.

Dolgoff, Stanley, "Screen Gems: The Dirty Dozen," *Cable Guide,* November, 1990.

Dorsey, Helen, "That Salty Old 'Puritan,' Lee Marvin," *Family Weekly,* April 4, 1976.

Downing, Henderson, "Fishing with Lee," *Outside Left*, April 1, 2004.

Drew, Bernard, "Marvin Always a Commanding Presence," *NY Times*, August 20, 1980.

Ebert, Roger, "Lee Marvin Finds His Spot in Gorky Park," *Chicago Sun-Times*, January 8, 1984.

Epstein, Dwayne, "Lee Marvin: The Mind Behind the Muscle," *Outré*, 1996.

Evans, Max, "Max Evans Remembers 'The Wild Bunch,'" *New Mexico*, June, 1994.

Farr, Bill "No Perjury Prosecutions in Marvin Case, D.A. Says," *LA Times*, August 5, 1980.

Footlick, Gerald K., Kasindorf, Martin, "An Unmarried Woman," *Newsweek*, April 30, 1979.

Galante, Giselle, "Lee Marvin: My Principle Sport Consists of Avoiding My Wife," *Paris Match*, January 20, 1984.

Gallet, George, "Theresa High Wins Catholic Crown," *Miami Daily News*, May 4, 1941.

Garland, Robert, "Woe Floods a Play That Isn't Very Good," *NY Journal-American*, March 28, 1949.

Geertsema, Tobie "From Maverick to Filmland Marvin left Them in Aisles," *Kingston Daily Freeman*, April 19, 1966.

Giles, Sue, "The Stars Shine for Consortium Party," *Tucson Lifestyle*, March 9, 1981.

Givens, Bill & Carpozi, George Jr., "The Woman Who Filled Lee," *Star*, September 15, 1987.

Graham, Sheila, "Lee Marvin Talks Marriage," *NY World Telegram & Sun*, March 15, 1966.

_____ "Lee Marvin Gets Kick From Oscar," *Tribune*, April 6, 1967.

Greenberg, Abe, "Meet Lee Marvin -- An Outspoken Star," *Hollywood Citizen News*, October, 18, 1969.

Gross, Milton, "Jimmy Brown—On Camera," *NY Post*, May 31, 1966.

Grossberger, Lewis, "The Ultimate Drinkig Buddy," *New York*, August 25, 1980.

Guarino, Ann, "Marvin's 'Great Scout' a Replay," *NY News*, June 23, 1976.

Haber, Joyce "Honor For Lee Marvin," *LA Times*, April 24, 1969.

_____ "Lee Marvin: Best-Loved Bad Guy in Hollywood," *LA Times*, February 20, 1972.

_____ "Lee Marvin Philosophical," *LA Times*, March 25, 1972.

Hall, William, "Soul on Ice," Uncut, July 1998.

Hall, Sterling "Bus Stop At The Playhouse," *La Jolla Journal*, June 28, 1956.

Hampton, Howard, "Return of the Body Snatchers," *Film Comment*, Nov-Dec. 1996.

Hano, Arnold, "The Star You Love To Hate," *Pageant*, May 1966.

Harold, Clive, "The Real Lee Marvin—By the Woman He Married After Dumping Michelle," *London Sun*, 1979.

Herman, Ellen "The Story That Had to Be Told," *Inside Movies*, January, 1966.

Hevesi, Dennis, "Lee Marvin, Movie Tough Guy, Dies," *NY Times*, August 31, 1987.

Hildebrand, Harold, "Mavin's Pitching in the Majors," *LA Examiner*, October 29, 1961.

Honeycutt, Kirk, "Maverick Marvin," *Daily News*, February 11, 1986.

Hudson, Donald, "Woman Sues Lee Marvin for Half Million 'Alimony'" *National Enquirer*, 1972.

Hughes, David, "Lee Marvin: Fans Never Mob Me," *National Enquirer*, 1978.

Hull, Bob, "Our Time In Hell," *Herald Examiner TV Weekly*, March 19, 1967.

Hyams, Joe, "Lee Marvin: Candid Character," *Herald Tribune*, October 27, 1957.

Ingham, Travis, "Lakelanders Recall Former Resident, Actor Lee Marvin," *Lakeland Ledger*, April 20, 1966.

Jackovich, Karen G. "At 56, Lee Marvin is Cooling Out in Tucson Between Wars," *People*, October 13, 1980.

Jacobs, Alexandra, "How Palimony Began," *Entertainment Weekly*, February 16, 1996.

James Nick, "The Marines Taught Him the Subtlety of Violence," *London Observer*, September 7, 1997.

Jarmusch, Jim, "Guilty Pleasures," *Film Comment*, May, 1992.

Johnson, Robert Jr (2nd Lt.) "Lee Marvin," *Leatherneck*, July 1986.

Judge, Phillip, "'Women Liked to Be Scared of a Guy,'" *Girl Talk*, November, 1975.

Junger, Victor, "It's Round Two of the Marvin Affair and the Stakes are 1.5 Million for Michelle," *People*, January 22, 1979

Kaiser, Joan, "A Painter for the 'Wagon'" *LA Herald-Examiner*, 1969.

Kilday, Gregg," Frankenheimer's 'Iceman'; Another Chance for US," *LA Times*, October 21, 1973.

Kirk, Christopher, "Lee Marvin: From Bad Guy To Glad Guy?" *NY Daily News*, April 17, 1966.

Kirk, Donald, "Lee Marvin Sees 'Great Scout' As Fun Picture… Nothing More," *Chicago Tribune*, July 25, 1976.

Klinger, Rafe, "Lee Marvin's Family still Feuding over His Estate," *Examiner*, January 12, 2009

Kluge, P.F. "Old Foes with a New View of War," *Life*, September 27, 1968.

Latta, John "What Stars Did Before They made It," *National Enquirer*, May 7, 1985.

Leahy, Jack "He'll Play It Straight," *Sunday News,* August 25, 1963.

Levin, Gerry, "Lee Marvin: Why I Have Turned Down $10 Million in Commercials," *National Enquirer*, March 27, 1979.

Lewis, Grover "Lee Marvin's Great Goddamned Moments of the Big Kavoom," *Rolling Stone*, December 21, 1972.

Lewis, Richard Warren, "Playboy Interview: Lee Marvin," *Playboy*, January 1969.

Liebenson, Donald, "These World War II Heroes Were Dirtier by the 'Dozen,'" *LA Times*, May 19, 2000.

Lindsay, Cynthia, "Oh! Those Movie Meanies," *Cosmopolitan*, September, 1966.

Lindsey, Robert, "Lee Marvin Told to Pay $104,000 But Judge Prohibits Property Split," *NY Times*, April 19, 1979.

Lowell, Sondra "'Unsung Agents Get Their Rewards," *LA Times*, February 21, 1981.

Luther, Claudia, "Judge Orders Probe of Marvin Testimony," *LA Times*, June 27, 1979.

Lyons Donald, "We Don't Murder, We Kill," *Film Comment*, July 1992.

McCabe Pat, "Lee Marvin," *Tiger*, Summer, 1968.

McCombie, Brian, "Warriors of the Silver Screen," *VFW*, February, 1998.

McGilligan, Patrick, "William Fraker's Magic Camera," *American Film*, April 1979.

Mancini, Anthony, "Lee Marvin: O'Neill's The Tough Guy," *NY Post*, October 13, 1973.

Mann, Roderick, "'Bad Guy' Marvin Enjoys Role," *Miami Herald*, April 30, 1966.

_____ "Not All's Golden for Marvin," *Chicago Sun-Times*, January 14, 1979.

_____ "Sam Plays it Again with The Big Red One," *LA Times*, June 1, 1980.

_____ "A Mellower Lee Marvin: To Helsinki and Back," *LA Times*, December 25, 1983.

Manners, Dorothy, "Has it ever occurred to you that some of the actors...": "Marvin Has Something to Say," *LA Herald-Examiner,* Nov. 28, 1976.

Manners, Dorothy "Lee Marvin's Romance a Question Mark," *LA Herald-Examiner*, August 20, 1966.

_____ "Secret Flight for Lee Marvin," *LA Herald-Examiner*, June 27, 1969.

_____ "Marvin, Girlfriend Still Friends," *LA Herald-Examiner*, August 12, 1970.

_____ "Executive of the Day Lee Marvin," *LA Herald-Examiner*, 1972.

_____ "Marvin Has Something to Say," *LA Herald-Examiner*, November 28, 1976.

Margulies, Edward "The Klansman Ought to Have Been Called Crakerz n The Hood," *Movieline*, October, 1996.

Marleaux, Mimi, "The 'Truth' About Lee and Michelle," *The Globe*, May 15, 1979.

Martin, Tom, "Lee Marvin Tells About the Woman Who Has Finally Tamed Him," *The Star*, May 8, 1979.

Marvin, Lee, & Levinson, Peter, "There's Not Enough Violence on TV," *TV-Radio Mirror*, December, 1963.

_____ "The Huge Elk Was King of the Mountain, And I Didn't Want to Shoot him," *Gun World*, May, 1964.

_____& Johnny Carson, "A Redbook Dialogue," *Redbook*, November, 1967.

_____ "The Dubious Dynamics of Dove Downing," *Gun World*, December, 1967.

Meyer, Rod, "The Mellow Lee Marvin," *Arizona Republic*, June 20, 1971.

Michaelson, Judith, "Marvin Rule: Revolution in Getting 'Split,'" *LA Times,* May 17, 1979.

Montgomery, Charles, Rubin, Sam & Taylor, Richard, "Hell-Rasing Drove Lee Marvin to an Early Grave at 63," *National Enquirer*, Septmber 15, 1987.

Mori, Steve, "Lee Marvin: The Klansman and the Horse He Rode In On," *Cinema Retro*, Autumn, 2009.

Muir, Florabel "A Frank Fellow," *Daily News*, March 11, 1966.

Oliver, Myrna, "Palimony Proves to be an Elusive Pot of Gold," *LA Times*, January 30, 1986.

Olsen, Dale "Lee Marvin At Liberty," Variety, April 26, 1962.

Oppenheimer Peer J. "Lee Marvin: Tough Guy, Gentle Heart," Family Weekly, April 17, 1966.

Padgett, Nina, "Lee Marvin: Hollywood's Iron Horse Cowboy, " Cycle World, July, 1994.

Page, Don, "Marvin, Ex-Marine With Good Cause," LA Times, March 15, 1967.

Parker, Jerry, "Marvin Plays His Father," Newsday, August 3, 1980.

Parsons Louella, "'Killer' Lee Marvin is Back in Action," Herald Examiner, May 16, 1965.

Paul, Julie, "Lee Marvin Shoots Off His Mouth!" Motion Picture, November, 1968.

Payne Don, "The Professionals Invade Las Vegas," Nevada Highways and Parks, Fall, 1966.

Peretz, Jack, Wasserman, Joanne, "Lee: What I Agreed to Pay Years Ago," NY Post, April 19, 1979.

Pickard, Roy "Booze, Fishing, Acting, Violence and Me!" Photoplay Film Monthly, July, 1976.

Politzer, Milt, "Did Lee Mavin Really Mean What He Said?" LA Herald-Examiner, June 27, 1979.

Putnam, George Palmer, "Eskimo Killed Pro. Marvin..." NY Times, September 25, 1926.

Pye, Michael, "Sam Fuller's Last Testament," London Telegraph, October 7, 2004

Redman, Nick, "A Man and His Train," Emperor of the North Soundtrack CD Liner Notes, 2008.

Reisfeld, Bert, "Lee Marvin the Railroad Hobo in Emperor..." Photoplay, October, 1973.

Robbins, Fred, "Penthouse Interview: Lee Marvin," Penthouse, February, 1980.

Robinson, Robert, "Screen Tough Guy Marvin, 63, Dies of Heart Attack," Variety, August 31, 1987.

Robles, "The Courtroom Eye," Los Angeles, September, 1982.

Roditte, L.N. "Experience and the Best Teachers," Theater Arts, January, 1950.

Rogers, Kathleen, "Hollywood Tough Guy Marvin Dead at 63," Hollywood Reporter, August 31, 1987.

Salisbury, Ann, "Ex-Mate Claims Marvin Urged Abortions," LA Herald-Examiner, January 17, 1979.

Saragossi, Steve, "A Forgotten Slice of 70s Mayhem," Cinema Retro, Autumn, 2009.

Schickel, Richard, "The Man For Vicaries," Time, June 4, 1965.

_____, "Reconstructing Sam Fuller's The Big Red One," Film Comment, May/June, 2004.

Schreiberg, Stu, "Lee Marvin: Master of the Uphill Battle," USA Today, February 4, 1985.

Schriener, Harry, "Lee Marvin's Most Closely Guarded Secret," Movie Life, September, 1969.

Seligson, Tom "How Getting Shot Saved Lee Marvin's Life," Parade, April 27, 1986.

Selznick, Daniel, "An Old Pro on the Go Again," NY Times Sunday Magazine, ???, 1980.

Sirmans, Jim, "Lee Marvin Hollywood's Most Dedicated Hell-Raiser," Saga, June, 1974.

Silverman, Jeff, "Nullimony," LA Herald-Examiner, August 12, 1981.

Skolsky, Sidney "Tintypes...Lee Marvin," NY Post, October 17, 1965.

Smith, Tom, "Tough Guy Lee Marvin: Real-Life Violence Makes Me Ill," National Enquirer, March 3, 1981.

Stayton, Richard, "My Style," LA Herald-Examiner, February 4, 1985.

Stone, Judy, "Tha Klansman," Playgirl, July, 1974.

Sufrin, Mark, "Lee Marvin, Brawler, Beachhead Hero, Hollywood's Toughest Hombre," True Man, March, 1968.

_____ "Lee Marvin Cries: 'I Can't Stand Myself!'" Movie World, November, 1969.

Sweet, Matthew, "How We Met: John Boorman & Pam Marvin," London Independent, June 28, 1996.

Taylor, Charles, "Tough Minded," AMC Magazine, November, 1998.

Taylor, Norman "The Dirty Dozen," ABC Film Review, November 1967.

Thomas, Bob "Acting Like Fishing," AP Wire, May 1965.

_____ "A Little Respect For Lee Marvin," AP Wire, May 17, 1966.

_____ "Marvin Sounds Off on Co-star Hurt," *AP Wire*, December 30, 1983.

Thompson, Howard, "How to Succeed By Trying to Be Bad," *NY Times*, May 23, 1965.

Thomson, David, "As I Lay Dying," *Sight and Sound*, June, 1998.

Townsend, Dorothy, "Marvin Appeals Award to Ex-Lover," *LA Times*, September 20, 1979.

Umley, Marian "Woodstocker Wins Oscar," *Ulster County Townsman*, April 21, 1966.

Vaughan, Roger, "Marvin as in Marlin," *Motorboat and Sailing*, May, 1977.

Vickers, Larry "Ex-Lakelander Lee Marvin's Name Is Really Lee Marvin, *Tampa Tribune*, April 21, 1966.

Warbeck, Jack "Lee Marvin Combats Terrorist Fury with the Delta Force," *Prevue*, April, 1986.

Ward, Robert, "Drinks with Liberty Valance," *Rolling Stone*, September 3, 1981.

Warga, Wayne "'Hell in the Pacific' Was Just That for Film Crew," LA Times, May 31, 1968.

Warren, Elaine, "Triola vs. Marvin," *LA Herald-Examiner*, November 30, 1978.

Washburn, Jim, "Keepers of the Flame," *LA Times*, February 21, 1995.

West Richard, "$104,000 Marvin Case Award Upset," *LA Times*, August 13, 1981.

White, Brynn, "Ballad of a Soldier," *Film Comment*, May/June 2007.

Wilson, Earl, "A Bit of Bogart..." NY Post, April 25, 1966.

_____ "Lee Marvin: My Ship Has Come In..." *NY Post*, February 12, 1972.

Wilson, Jane "Hanging Tough with Lee Marvin," *LA Times West Magazine*, August 27, 1967.

Marv Wolf, "Making War Movies," *Soldier of Fortune*, August, 1981.

Wukovits, John F, "'Hell Is On Us,'" *Pacific War: Special Edition*, 2003.

Yount, Dave, "The ABCs of Crime," *Video Eyeball*, Vol. II No. 6.

Pressbooks, presskits & souvenir programs from all of Lee Marvin's films.

Author Interviews

Eddie Albert: April 24, 1997-Phone & December 11, 1997 & in person @ his home. [deceased]

Norman Alden: January 18, 1998-In Person @ Beverly Garland Hotel. [deceased]

Chris Alcaide: January 15, 1995-In Person @ Beverly Garland Hotel.[deceased]

Steve Allen: September 22. 1997-In Person @ his Burbank office [deceased].

Michael Apted: March 9, 2012-Phone.

Betty Ballantine: June 14, 1995-In Person @ her Woodstock house

David Ballantine: June 14, 1995-In Person @ Robert Marvin's house.

Henry Beckman: January 18, 1998-In Person @ Beverly Garland Hotel [deceased]

Joseph Biroc: October 25, 1994-Phone. [deceased]

Budd Boetticher: October 30, 1994-Phone. [deceased]

Jeff Bridges: Mach 26, 2012-Phone interview.

J.P.S. Brown, March 3, 2012-Phone.

David Busey, February 25. 2012-phone

Frank Cady: April 22, 1997-Phone. [deceased]

Michael Callan: October 9, 1995-Phone

Charles Champlin: October 8, 1994-In Person @ Lone Pine Film Festival

Jay Cocks: June 21, 2012, e-mail.

John Dennis: September 25, 1994-In Person @ Beverly Garland Hotel. [deceased]

Paul DeGuenther: June 15, 1998-Phone.

Angie Dickinson: August 2, 2001: In Person @ her home.

James Doohan: October 5, 1996-In Person @ Wyndham Hotel [deceased]

Edward Dymtryk (& wife Jean): September 7, 1996-In Person @ Musso & Franks. [deceased]

Bud Ekins: August 8, 1995-Phone. [deceased]

John Ericson: October 8, 1994-In Person @ Lone Pine Film Festival.

Tony Epper: October 29, 1994- In Person @ his Agua Dulce home. (deceased)

Norman Fell: October 6, 1996-In Person @ Beverly Garland Hotel. [deceased]

Richard Fleischer:In Person @ Cinematheque April 2, 1999 May 5, 1999-Phone. [deceased]

Vito Franco: October 8, 1994- In Person @ In Person @ Lone Pine Festival.

John Frankenheimer: July 13, 1995-His office. [deceased]

Sam Fuller: Mail 1st, June 1995. [deceased]

Christa Fuller: Mail 1st, June 1995.

Beverly Garland: September 25, 1994-In Person @ Her Hotel. [deceased]

John Gloske: January 18, 1998-In Person @ Beverly Garland Hotel.

Don Gordon: November 6, 1994-phone

Leo Gordon: April 3, 1999-Phone. [deceased]

Clu Gulager: January 20, 1997-In Person @ The Farmer's Market.

Don Gurler: August 17,1995- his office.

Bill Heckeroth: June 12, 1996-In Person @ his shop.

Monte Hellman: November 7, 1996-His home.

Dwayne Hickman: October 12, 1995-Phone

Fr. James Hoge, OSB: May 5, 1998-Phone.

Robert Horton: July 8, 1995-In Person @His home.

L.Q. Jones: July 13, 1995-In Person @ his Hollywood home.

David Kagon: July 20, 1994- In Person @His office. [deceased]

Stefan Kanfer: December 14, 2012-phone.

Millard Kaufman: October 4, 1999-Phone. [deceased]

Burt Kennedy: May 31, 1995-In Person @ His home. [deceased]

Dr. Hans Kohler: July 11, 1995-In Person @ His home.

Stanley Kramer: July 4, 1994-In Person @ Sportsman Lodge. [deceased]

Buzz Kulik: November 21, 1994-Phone [deceased]

Peter Levinson: February 2, 1996-In Person @His office. [deceased]

Kay Lenz: January 21, 2012-Phone interview.

Barbara Luna: November 15, 1995-In Person @Her home.

Grover Lewis: Sept, 1994-Phone [deceased]

Leslie H. Martinson: February 19, 1998-Phone.

Betty Marvin: February 12-13, 1995-In Person @ her home in Cambria.

Christopher Marvin: March 5, 1995-In Person @ Ventura friend's house.

Joan Marvin: October, 31, 1995-In Person @ her home. [deceased]

Robert Marvin: July, 21, 1994 (phone), October 31, 1995+ & June 8, 1996-his home. [deceased]

Martin Milner: July 23, 1996-In Person @ his Carlsbad home.

Meyer Mishkin: July 23, 1994-In Person @ his home. [deceased]

John Mitchum: October 8, 1994-In Person @ Lone Pine. [deceased]

Alvy Moore: April 8, 1997-In Person @ his Palm Springs home. [deceased]

Carolyn Moore: April 8, 1997-In Person @ her Palm Springs home. [deceased]

Terry Moore: October 17, 1994-Phone.

Dan Moultharp: August 14, 1995-phone & August 17,1995-his office

Ralph O'Hara: December 10, 1995-In Person @ The Sand Castle in Malibu.

Jack Palance: September, 1997-In Person @ Queen Mary [deceased]

Phil Parslow: May 7, 1995-Phone. [deceased]

Bob Phillips: August 26, 1995-In Person @ Lunch in the Valley.

Paul Picerni: January 18, 1998-In Person @ Beverly Garland Hotel. [deceased]

Jean Porter: September 7, 1996-In Person @ Musso & Franks.

George Rappaport: August 17, 1995-In Person @ His home.
Bert Remsen: November 23, 1994-In Person @ Lone Pine. [deceased]
Fr. Paul Romf, OSB (archivist): May 1, 1998-In Person @ St. Leo College.
Cheyney Ryan: January 19, 2012-Phone.
Lisa Ryan: December 16, 2011-Phone.
Mitch Ryan: January 14, 2012-Phone
Charles Saunders: May 13, 1998-Phone.
Christiana Schmidtmer: October 24, 1994-phone. [deceased]
Ed Silver: January 16, 2012-Phone.
Elliot Silverstein: February 23, 1998-In Person @ Mirabelle restaurant.
Rick Spalla: January 20, 1998-In Person @ his studio. [deceased]
Woody Strode: September 3, 1994-In Person @ Glendora his home. [deceased]
Neil Summers: October 9, 1994-In Person @ Lone Pine
Terry Swindoll: August 15, 2010-e-mail.
Rod Taylor: July 26, 1995-Phone
Robert Totten: January 15, 1995-In Person @ Beverly Garland Hotel. [deceased]
Fr. Gregory Traeger, OSB: May 1, 1998-In Person @ St. Leo College.
Robert Vaughn: January 18, 1998-In Person @ Beverly Garland Hotel.
Gregory Walcott: December 9, 1995-In Person @ Beverly Garland coffee shop.
Bob Walker: June 6, 1995-In Person @ his Office. [deceased]
Clint Walker: April 6, 1999-Phone.
Ron Walker: In person@ his Garden Grove home
Kelly Ward: April 30, 1996-In Person @ The Encino Radisson.
Paul Wasserman: March 13, 1996-In Person @ The Daily Grill [deceased]
David Weddle: November 20, 1994-In Person @ forgotten restaurant.
James Whitmore: April 3, 1996 (Mail) [deceased]
Ned Wynn: October 11, 1995-Phone.
Tracy Wynn: September 23, 1995-Phone.

Index

.45 automatic pistol, father's, 42, 44, 47
"19th Hole of Europe, The" (play), 63

A
Abbott, Bud, 103
abortion, Pamela Feeley's, 60
Academy Awards, Oscar for *Cat Ballou*,
147-148, 156-158
acting, education in
    American Theater Wing (ATW), 60,61
    Manumit school, 21
    St. Leo's School for Boys, 27
acting, Lee Marvin's view of, 59
action heroes, modern, 156
ADD (Attention Deficit Disorder), 19,26
Admiral Faragut Naval Academy, 23
Africa, 196
agents. See Mishkin, Meyer
aging, 125, 225-227
Akins, Claude, 85,127
Albert, Eddie, 70,94,100
alcoholism
    aging due to, 215
    Ann Davidge's, 10
    anxiety attacks, relation to, 202,203
    automobile accidents from, 136, 142
    bars, behavior in, 56,64,160
    Betty's reaction to, 118-120
    Cat Ballou, 141, 1444-145
    Donovan's Reef incident, 122-123
    drinking after filming, 76
    drinking quote, 157
    family fights related to, 53
    Fern Lea incident, 173
    harassment of women and, 120
    Iceman Cometh, The 184-187
    interviews, drunk for, 223
    Ira Hayes, portrayal of, 110-111
    The Klansman, while filming, 191
    Lamont Marvin's, 51
    Michele Triola contribution to, 203-
        204
    not drinking, difficulty with, 120-121
    The Professionals, 203-204
    PTSD and, 125
    "Route 66" incident, 112-113
    on set drinking, 116, 143
    Ship of Fools portrayal of, 135
    therapy for, 121

Alcaide, Chris, 80
Aldrich, Robert (director), 94, 158-161,
    181-182
All Quiet On the Western Front, 18, 70
Allen, Elizabeth, 123
"American, The, (TV)" 110-111
American International Pictures (AIP), 195
American National Theater and Academy
(ANTA), 64
American Theater Wing (ATW), 60-61
ancestors of Lee Marvin, 4-10
anger, childhood, 3
anthology TV shows, 100-101
anti-heroes, 133, 155
anxiety attacks, 202-203
Apted, Michael (director), 221-223
Arctic Escapade, 220
Arctic exploration by Ross Marvin, 5-9,
    13-14
Arlington National Cemetery, 110, 234
art imitating life, 163
Ashley, Elizabeth, 134
Astor Drug Store, 63
athletics, high school participation in, 27
Attack!, 94-95
Attention Deficit Disorder (ADD), 19, 26
ATW (American Theater Wing), 60-61
audiences, changing over time, 62, 223
auditions
    early New York, 62-64
    Oklahoma!, 87
    You're In the Navy Now, 69
automobiles owned by Lee Marvin
    accidents in, 136, 142
    Bristol Ace, 118
    Ford convertible, 73
Avalanche Express, 198-199
awards
    Best Actor in a Comedy, Golden
Globes, 146
    Best Foreign Film Actor, British
Academy Award, 129
    Emmy nomination for "People Need
People," 110
    Oscar for *Cat Ballou*, 147, 156-158

B
Bad Day at Black Rock, 88, 191
bad guys, ability to play, 234, 235
"Bailout At 43,000," 101-102
Baker, Oregon, 172

Ball, Lucille, 224
Ballantine, Betty, 58-61,62,63
Ballantine, David55-56, 57, 59
Ballantine, E. J., 21, 57
Ballantine, Ian, 57,63
Ballantine, Stella, 21, 57
Ballinger, Lt. Frank, character, 104-110
Balsam, Martin,226
Bancroft, Anne, 84,86, 91
banjo incident, 207
bank robbery films
    Dog Day, 223-224
    Spike's Gang, 189
    Violent Saturday, 89-90
Bannen, Ian, 221
Barger, Sonny, 83
baseball, "How Charlie Faust Won a
    Pennant for the Giants," 102
Basie, Count, 105
Bastard Sons of Lee (BSOL), 235
Beatty, Warren, 165
Beetles, The, 83
Bellamy, Ralph, 151
Benedek, Laslo (director), 82-83
Benny Goodman, 43
Best Actor in a Comedy, Golden Globes,
    156
Best Foreign Film Actor, British Academy
    Award, 129
Best, James, 86
Betty Marvin. See Marvin, Betty Ebeling
Big Heat, The, 79-80, 222
Big Red One, The, 50, 215-220, 236
"Big Story, The" (TV), 100
"Billy Budd" (play), 64, 70, 71
Biltmore Theater, 64
Biroc, Joe, 94, 159, 182
birth of Lee Marvin, 12
Bishop, Joey, 226
blues music, 77, 118-119
Bob Hope specials, 224
Boetticher, Budd (director), 93
Bogart, Humphrey, 84-86, 91, 165
"Bonanza," (TV), 110
Bond, Ward, 95
Bonnie & Clyde, 165
books, favorite, 18, 150
Boone, Richard, 150
Boorman, John (director), 161-163, 169-
    171, 204
Borgnine, Ernest

Bad Day at Black Rock, 88
Dirty Dozen, The, 158-161
"The Dirty Dozen: The Next Mission,"
    226
Emperor of the North, 181-182
Small Soldiers, 235
stardom, achieved before Lee's, 99
Stranger Wore A Gun, The, 78
Violent Saturday, 89
Brand, Neville, 88, 118, 127–128
Brando, Jocelyn, 105, 110
Brando, Marlon, 81-83
Brennan, Walter, 89
Bridges, Jeff, 183-184
Bristol Ace automobile, 118
British Academy Award, Best Foreign Film
    Actor, 129
Broadway productions, 64-65, 70
Bronson, Charles, 64,70,76,105, 159-162,
    220-221
Brooklyn, New York18, 53, 106
Brooks, Richard (director), 151-156
"Brother Orchid," (play) 28
Brown, Jim, 159-162, 235
Brown, JPS, 178
BSOL (Bastard Sons of Lee), 235
Bucholz, Horst199
burial site of Lee Marvin, 234
Burr, Raymond, 84
Burton, Richard, 156, 190-192
"Bus Stop (play)," 95
Bush, Billy Green, 175

C
Cabeen, Ty, 138, 155
Cady, Frank, 95-96
Caine Mutiny, The,84-86
Callan, Michael, 141-143
Camp Pendleton, 39
Canada, filming in, 220-221
Cannes Film Festival, 219, 236
Canyon City, Colorado, 143-144
Cardinale, Claudia, 151
Carradine, Keith, 181-182
Carradine, Robert, 216
Cassavetes, John, 127, 158-161,165
Cat Ballou, 140-148, 156-158
Catholic school (St. Leo), 26-29
Chandler, Jeff, 94-95
Chanslor, Roy, 139
Chapman, Bob, 64

character acting, 83, 99
Chayefsky, Paddy, 172-174
Chicago, 50-51
childhood of Lee Marvin
    kindergarten violence, 3
    movies, favorites, 18-19
    in New York City, 16-18
    running away from home, 15
    schools attended. See education
    Walker family, with, 25
children of Lee Marvin
    antagonism with Pam Marvin, 195
    Christopher Lamont. See Marvin,
Christopher Lamont
    Claudia Leslie, 87
    Courtenay Lee, 87, 223
    Cynthia Louise, 87, 223
    estate, disposition of, 234
    stepchildren, with Pamela Feeley, 208
    "The Sons of Lee Marvin," 249–251
Chino, character, 68, 83
Christine, Virginia, 127
Christmas 1929, 16
cigarette habit, 104, 215, 229
Civil War
    ancestors fighting in, 4
    Raid, The, 86-87
    Raintree County, 96-97
    reading about, 19
Clark, Matt, 175
Clift, Montgomery, 96
"Climax!" (TV), 101
Cobb, Lee J., 84
Coburn, James, 105, 218
cockiness on set, 95
Cocks, Jay, 197
Cohen, Larry (critic), 177
Cole, Nat 'King', 141-142
Colleano, Bonar, 76
Comancheros, The, 116
combat. See war, real; war, theatrical
"Combat!" (TV), 110
comedies
    Cat Ballou, 140-148, 156-158
    Donovan's Reef, 122-123
    Great Scout and Cathouse Thursday,
    The, 195,-196
    "How Charlie Faust Won a Pennant for
    the Giants," 102
    Pocket Money, 178
    "Joke's On Me, The," 103

concentration camp scene in *The Big Red*
    One, 220
Connors, Mike, 198-199
contract player system, 72
Cook, Dr. Frederick, 7-9
Cooper, Gary, 70
Cornell University, 5-7, 9
costumes, originality with, 93
Crowther, Bosley, 165
Culp, Robert, 195-196
cult of Lee Marvin, 231-236
Curtiz, Michael (director), 116

D
3-D work, 78,81,84
Dade County, Florida, 24-26
Davidge, Courtenay Washington. See
Marvin, Courtenay Washington Davidge
Davis, Jim, 175
D-Day, 45, 158-161
Dean, James, 62
death. See also violence
    acting, ability with, 129
    feelings about playing characters who
    die, 122
    Lee Marvin's, 228-229
    writings about, 51-52
Death Hunt, 220-221, 229
Deauville Film Festival, 224
DeGuenther, Paul (classmate), 27
DeHavilland, Olivia, 91
Delta Force, 226
demolition training, 41
Dennehy, Brian, 221-223
Dennis, John, 105-106
Denny, Reginald, 143
Denver, Colorado, 6
DeWilde, Brandon, 97
Diccio, Bobby, 216-220
Dickinson, Angie
    Death Hunt, 220-221
    Killers, The, 126-129
    "M Squad" episode, 224
    Meyer Mishkin endorsement, 224
    Point Blank, 163-167
Dillman, Bradford, 183-184
Diplomatic Courier, 71
directors. See individual directors/films
Dirty Dozen, The, 76-77, 156, 158-161, 165
"Dirty Dozen: The Next Mission, The,"
(TV), 224-225

disability payments for war wound, 50
divorce. See also palimony suit of Michele Triola
    from Betty Ebeling, 167
    of parents, threatened, 25-26
Dmytryk, Edward (director), 76-77, 85
Doctor of Fine Arts Degree, 173
Dog Day, 223-224
'Dogface,' nickname, 26
Donovan's Reef, 121-123
Doohan, James, 59-60, 65, 71
Douglas, Kirk, 141
Douglas, Melvyn, 179
Down Among the Sheltering Palms, 78
"Dr. Kildare" (TV), 110
"Dragnet," 72-73, 75
drugs
    alcohol. See alcoholism
    "smoke," 54
drunk driving arrests, 203
drunkenness. See alcoholism
Duel At Silver Creek, 72
Dullea, Keir, 111
Dunn, Michael, 134,139
dying, realistic, 76. See also death; violence
dyslexia, 19

E
Eastwood, Clint, 130,173-176
Ebeling, Betty. See Marvin, Betty Ebeling
Ebsen, Buddy, 95
education
    Admiral Faragut Naval Academy, 23
    American Theater Wing (ATW), 60-61
    attitude towards, 18-19
    Chicago night school, 50
    dyslexia, effects of, 19
    expulsions from schools, 21-22
    fights during childhood, 18
    Florida public schools, at, 23-24
    Kingston High School, 51
    Manumit school, 21-22
    Oakwood Academy, 22-23
    St. Leo's School for Boys, 25-28
    truancy, 20
Egan, Eddie, 181-182
Egan, Richard, 89
Eight Iron Men, 75-76
Ekins, Bud, 93
Elmira, New York, 4-5
Emmy nomination, 110

Emperor of the North, 181-182
emphysema, 228
England, filming in, 158-161
Eniwetok, battle of, 44-45
Epper, Tony, 153-154, 172, 203-206, 211-212
Erlene (childhood nanny), 16
Erickson, John, 89
"Escape" (TV) 100
Eskimos, 7-8
estate, disposition of, 234
Evans, Linda, 190-192, 198-199

F
Falana, Lola, 190-192
family members
    ancestors, 4-9, 11
    brother. See Marvin, Robert Davidge
    children. See children of Lee Marvin
    father. See Marvin, Lamont Waltham (Monte)
    mother. See Marvin, Courtenay Washington Davidge
    Robert Marvin. See Marvin, Robert Davidge
    wives. See Marvin, Betty Ebeling; Marvin, Pamela Feeley
Farr, John, 236
fatherhood. See children of Lee Marvin
Feeley, Pamela. See Marvin, Pamela Feeley
Feldman, Phil, 171-172
Fell, Norman, 126-127
fencing class, 61
Ferrer, Jose, 85,136,143
fighting. See also violence; war, real
    banjo incident, 207
    bar room fights, description of
    picking, 63
    childhood, 3
    class issues resulting in, 17
    Dade City High School, with, 28
    in English pub, 160
    freight train, on a, 182
    high school, at, 25
    between Lee's parents, 25-26
    love for fight scenes, 80
    postwar, with father and brother, 53
    quotes on, 149-150
    "Route 66" (TV) incident, 112-113
    teenage, 26
    ten-year old, incident as a, 20-21
    TV gaffe involving, 100-101

"Fighting Fourth" Marine Division, 38-39,42-47

Fincke, William Mann (Manumit), 21-22

firearms

.45 automatic pistol, father's, 42, 44, 47

care of on sets, 153

Garand M-1, 81

gunpowder incident, 56

misuse of, 136, 144

M-1's, 217-218

practicing draws of, 93

TV gaffe involving, 100

fishing, love of, 18, 74, 76-77, 199

"Fist of Five," (TV), 110

Fitzgerald, Ella, 91

Fix, Beverly and Paul, 136

Fleischer, Richard (director), 89-90, 190

Flippen, J.C., 141

"Flip Wilson Show, The" (TV), 209

Florida State Citrus Commission, 24-26, 29

Flynn, Errol, 18

Fonda, Jane, 141-148

football, high school, 29

Ford convertible, ownership of, 73

Ford, Glenn, 79-80, 205

Ford, John, 114-118, 121-124

Forster, Robert, 226

Fort Leonard Wood, Missouri, 80

"Fragile Fox" (play), 94

Fraker, William (director), 175

France, filming Dog Day, 223-224

Francis, Anne, 89

Frankenheimer, John (director), 102, 110-111, 182-185

Frankovich, Mike (producer), 137

Franz, Arthur, 76-77

French Haute Couture salon, 109

Fuller, Sam (director), 110, 188, 191-192, 215-220

G

gaffes on early live TV, 100-101

gambling, 203

Garand M-1 rifles, 81

gardening, 227

Garland, Beverly, 101

Garner, James, 89

"General Electric Theater," 101-102

Gibbs, Wolcott (critic), 65

girlfriends

1943, unnamed, 42, 44

affairs leading to separation with Betty, 137

Betty Ebeling. See Marvin, Betty Ebeling

Maverick Theater actresses, 60-61

Michele Triola. See Triola, Michele

New York reporter, with, 167-168

Pamela Feeley. See Marvin, Pamela Feeley

Glory Brigade, The, 79-80

Gloske, John, 192

Golden Globes

Best Actor in a Comedy award, 156

nomination for Paint Your Wagon, 174

Goldman & Kagon (law firm), 207-214

Gordon, Don, 103-104

Gordon, Leo, 63-64, 81-82

Gorilla At Large, 84, 192

Gorky Park, 221-224

Grahame, Gloria, 81, 92

Grant, Cary, 73

Graves, Peter, 86

Great Depression, 16-17

Great Scout and Cathouse Thursday, The, 189-190

Greco, Jose, 134

Green, Walon, 174

Greenwich Village drinking bouts, 53-54

Gregory, James, 112

Grimes, Gary, 190

Guadalcanal, 36, 48

Gulager, Clu, 127-130

Gun Fury, 81-82

Gunn, Moses, 184-185

gunpowder incident, 56

guns. See firearms

Gurler, Don, 140, 168-169

Guth, Ray, 175

H

Hackman, Gene, 180-181

Hadnot Point, North Carolina, 32-35

Hamill, Mark, 216-220

hand-to-hand combat, 46-47

Hangman's Knot, 73

harassment of women, 120

Harrigan (Inukitsoq), 8-9. 13-14

Hart, Colonel Franklin, 85

Harte, Bret, 19

"Hasty Heart, The" (play), 63

Hathaway, Henry (director), 65,69-71,224

Hawaii, 122-124

Hayes, Ira, 110-111

Hecht, Harold (producer), 140-148

Heckeroth, Adolph, 54-55, 59

Heckeroth, Bill, 54-55

Heflin, Van, 86-87

Hell in the Pacific, 169-171

Hellman, Monte (director), 199-200

Hell's Angels, 83

Hemingway, Ernest, 126

Henson, Matthew, 7-8

Hepatitis,228

heritage of Lee Marvin, 4-9, 11

Heston, Charlton, 108

Hickman, Dwayne, 141-143

history, Lee's interest in, 19-22

hobos, 182-183

Hoge, Fr. James, 27, 173

Hollywood

    Courtenay Marvin's characterization of, 71-72

    decision to prioritize over Broadway, 66

    first visit to, 41

    moves to, 71-72

"Home of the Brave (play)," 63

homecoming, postwar, 48

homosexuality, 107-108

honesty, 146

honeymoon with Betty Ebeling, 76

Hopkins, Bo, 175-176

Horton, Robert, 119-120

Hosford, Mary, 98

hospitalization

    in 1986, leading to death, 228-230

    during *Gorky Park*, 222

    war wound, recuperation from, 49

houses owned by Lee Marvin

    Hollywood Knolls, 87

    Malibu beach house, 146, 152, 168

    Tucson home, 193-195, 227

    Uplifter's Ranch, Santa Monica, 98

"How Charlie Faust Won a Pennant for the Giants," 102-103

Howard, Ron, 190

Hudkins, John, 175

Hudson, Rock, 81, 211

Huie, William Bradford, 190

humor, sense of, 74

Hunt, Peter, 197

Hunter, The (novel), 163

Hurt, William, 221-224

Hyman, Ken, 171-172

hypocrisy, disdain for, 27

I

I Died a Thousand Times, 92

I Never Sang for My Father, 180-181

Iceman Cometh, The, 103, 183-186

illnesses. See hospitalization

Indio, California, 155

instincts, acting, 102

interviews with press, 149-151

Inukitsoq (Harrigan), 8-9, 13-14

investments, 193-194

Israel, filming in, 216, 218, 226-227

Iwo Jima, 109-110

J

Jacksonville, Florida, 29

Jaeckel, Richard, 95, 159-162, 225-226

Japanese soldiers, 36, 45-48, 166-168

Jarmusch, Jim, 234, 237

Jaws, effect on film industry, 189

jazz, 91-92

Jefferson, Blind Lemon, 76

Jim Kane (novel), 179-180

"Joan of Arc at the Stake" (play), 87

"Joke's On Me, The" (TV) 103

Jones, L.Q., 78-79, 89, 115-116

Jones, Tommy Lee, 237

K

Kagon, A. David, 138, 108-115

Kanfer, Stefan, 197-198

Kaufman, Millard, 88, 97, 191-192

Kaye, Stubby, 141-142

Kazan, Lainie, 226

Keitel, Harvey, 235-236

Kelly's Army of 1894, 182

Kennedy, Arthur, 110

Kennedy, Burt, 93-94, 141

Kennedy, George, 159-162, 226, 237

Kid Shelleen character, 140-148

Kiley, Richard, 103

Killers, The, 126-130, 236

kindergarten, 3, 15

King Kong incident (Las Vegas), 204

Klansman, The, 190-193

Knopf, Christopher, 179-180

Kolldehoff, Reinhard, 197-198

Korean War movies

Glory Brigade, The, 79-80
Rack, The, 94-95
Korvin, Charles, 134
Kramer, Stanley (producer/director), 69-70, 82-84,, 85-86, 84, 134-139
Kudluktoo, 8-9, 13-14
Kulik, Buzz (director), 99
Kwajalein incident, 43

L
La Jolla Playhouse, 96
Lakeland, Florida, 26-27, 29
Lamour, Dorothy, 123
Lancaster, Burt, 151-156
Landers, Hal (producer), 175
Lang, Fritz (director), 80-81
Las Vegas, 77, 153-154, 203-204
Latimer Productions, 103-104
Laughlin, Tom, 106
"Lawbreakers, (TV)" 111-112
Lee, Peggy, 92
Lee, Robert E., 4, 12-13
Leigh, Vivien, 134-139
Lemmon, Jack, 149
Lenz, Kay, 195-196
Lerner, Alan Jay, 172-173
lesbianism, 224
Levinson, Peter, 114
Life in the Balance, A, 92
Linderman, Mitch, 140
live theater vs. film acting, 96-97
Livingston, Leon R. (A#1), 182-183
Logan, Josh (director), 172-173
London, Jack, 19,74, 182
Lone Pine, California, 89
Lopez, Trini, 159-162,237
love scenes, 175
Luna, Barbara, 134, 137-138
Lupino, Ida (director), 111

M
"M Squad" (TV), 105-110
Mahoney, Jim, 208
Malibu, California
    beach house, 146, 152,168
    The Raft bar, 164
Malick, Terence, 179
Man Who Shot Liberty Valance, The, 115-118, 121-122, 241
Mann, Abby, 134
Manumit school, 21-22

March, Fredric, 184-186
Marine Corps, U.S.
    acting, applying lessons from, 60
    boot camp and training, 31-34
    Camp Elliott, 38-42
    Corporal, promotion to, 38
    demolition training, 42
    drunken reenlistment attempts, 203
    Eniwetok, battle of, 46-47
    enlistment in, 30-31
    "Fighting Fourth" Marine Division, 40-41, 44-49
    hospital ship, recuperation on, 49
    Iwo Jima, 110-111
    Marshall Islands campaign, 45
    Military Occupational Specialties training (MOS), 38-40
    negative attitude towards, 39
    "Our Time in Hell, (TV)" 161-162
    Purple Heart, receiving while serving in, 48-49
    Quartermaster School., 34-38
    rejection for reenlistment, 50-51
    Saipan, battle of, 46-48
    scout/sniper activity, 45
    training film for, 226
    visits with his father while in, 42-44
    war crimes witnessed while in, 44-45
Marley, John, 141
marriages
    Betty Ebeling, to, 77 See also Marvin, Betty Ebeling
    of daughter Cynthia Louise, 224
    Pamela Feeley, to, 178-182. See also Marvin, Pamela Feeley
    parents, Lee Marvin's, 11
Marshall Islands campaign, 45
Martin, Strother, 195-196
Martinson, Leslie (director), 103-104
Marvin, Betty Ebeling
    Academy Awards, missing from, 157-158
    bossing around Lee, 119
    Cat Ballou, reading of script, 141
    children's relationship with Pam Marvin, 195
    dating, 73-75
    defense of by Lee, 98-99
    divorce from Lee, 167
    drunkenness, reaction to Lee's, 118-120

French Haute Couture salon, 108
gifts given to, 89-90
girls, birth of, 87
"M Squad," toll on marriage, 105-107
Marlon Brando and, 82-83
Michele Triola, encounter with, 145
O'Connor, Carroll, friendship with, 164
proposal to, 76
rebuffing Lee before Feeley marriage, 175-176
reconciliation attempts, 140, 166, 207
separation from Lee, 135-136
Uplifter's Ranch home, discovery of, 98
wedding ceremony, 77
Marvin, Christopher Lamont (son)
birth, 70,78
BSOL and, 251–252
Dirty Dozen sequel, discussion of, 225-226
illness of Lee, 229
relationship with Lee, 118-119, 126
Marvin, Claudia Leslie (daughter), 87
Marvin, Courtenay Lee (daughter), 87 , 224
Marvin, Courtenay Washington Davidge
ancestry of, 10-11
career of, 11-12, 16
death of, 125
divorce from Lamont threatened, 25-26
Hollywood, characterization of, 71-72
Lee's relationship with, 17-18, 27
marriage to Lamont Marvin, 11
separation from Lamont, 24
"Thanksgiving in Strange Places" radio show, 54
Woodstock, life in, 51
Marvin, Cynthia Louise (daughter), 87, 224
Marvin, Edward, 5
Marvin, Elizabeth (paternal grandmother), 6
Marvin, Henry (paternal grandfather), 6
Marvin, Joan (sister-in-law), 10
Marvin, Lamont Waltham (Monte)
Academy Award, reaction to, 157
admiration of Lee for, 39
adoption by Ross Marvin, 6-7
The Big Red One, as Lee's model for Sergeant, 215-220
childhood and education of, 6-7, 9-10
death of, 180-181
death of uncle Ross Marvin, 9, 14-15
divorce threat from Courtenay, 25-26

early career of, 10-11
Eastman Kodak, working for, 17
Florida State Citrus Commission, work for, 24-26. 29
Frank Seaman Agency work of, 13
marriage of, 11-12
New York and New England Apple Institute work, 51
postwar alcohol and family fights, 53
punishment of Lee, 20-21
retirement, 51
return from World War II, 48-50
reunion with Lee in Woodstock, 175-176
second marriage of, 177
suicide attempt of, 49
World War I service, 10-11
World War II visits with Lee, 42-44
Marvin, Mary (paternal great-grand-mother), 5
Marvin, Matthew (ancestor), 4
Marvin, Michele. See Triola, Michele
Marvin, Pamela Feeley
abortion of, after dating Lee, 61
children from previous marriages, 194
estate, struggle over, 235
Lee's attempt to throw out, 235
marrying Lee Marvin, 178-179
McLeod, Duncan, prior marriage to, 106
Meyer Mishkin's friendship with, 225
move to Tucson, 194
at palimony trial, 214
rivalry with Michele, 209
sickness and death of Lee, 229-230
wedding to Lee, 208-209
Marvin, Robert Davidge (brother)
Academy Award, reaction to, 157
birth of, 12
childhood fights with Lee, 2
enlistment in Army Air Corps, 30
envy of Lee's success, 107
Lee's love for, 37
Oakwood Academy, attendance at, 24
postwar alcohol and family fights, 53-54
teaching career, 107
Marvin, Ross Gillmore (great uncle), 5-9, 13-16, , 229
Marvin, Seth (ancestor), 4
Marvin vs. Marvin. See palimony suit of Michele Triola

Matthau, Walter, 103
Mature, Victor, 90-91
Maverick Theater, 57-61
MCA (Music Corporation of America), 109
McCann, William (ancestor), 4-5
McLeod, Duncan, 106
McNally, Stephen, 90
McQueen, Steve, 93, 149
Mean Streets, 236
"Medic, (TV)" 101
Meeker, Ralph, 159
Melville, Herman, 19
memorial services for Lee Marvin, 235
memorization ability, 19
"Merchant of Menace," 81
method actors, 128-129
Mexico, 76, 179-180
Mifune, Toshiro, 169-171
Military Occupational Specialties (MOS)
    training, 38-40
military service
    of ancestors, 4-6
    Lamont's, 10-11, 42-44
    Lee's. See Marine Corps, U.S.
    Robert's, 30
military training films, 62, 226
Milner, Martin, 95, 113-114
Mint Hotel incident, 204
Mishell, Dr. Dan, 78
Mishkin, Meyer
    ability to get work for clients, 79
    Academy Awards, at, 156-157
    cleaning up by, 136
    Hell in the Pacific, 169-171
    Lee's tribute to, 225
    loyalty of Lee Marvin to, 76, 225
    Lucille Ball with, 225
    "M Squad," problems from, 108-109
    signing of Lee Marvin by, 69-73
    TV, pushing Lee to, 99-100
    Wild Bunch, The 171-172
    Missouri Traveler, The, 98-99
"Mister Roberts" (play), 42-43
Mitchell, Cameron, 84, 191-193
Mitchelson, Marvin, 209-214
Mitchum, Robert, 91
mobsters, playing
    The Big Heat, 80-81
    The Killers, 126-130
    Prime Cut, 180-181
    Violent Saturday, 90-91

money, as a motivation, 105
Montalban, Ricardo, 91
Monte Marvin. See Marvin, Lamont
    Waltham (Monte)
Monte Walsh, 175-178, 227
Moore, Alvy, 79-80, 83, 89, 117
Moore, Roger, 197-198
Moore, Terry, 92-93
Moreau, Jeanne, 175-178
Morey, William, 180-181
MOS (Military Occupational Specialties)
    training, 38-40
mother of Lee Marvin. See Marvin,
    Courtenay Washington Davidge
motorcycle gangs, portrayal of, 83
motorcycles, love of, 93
Moultharp, Dan, 207
Mountie role in *Death Hunt*, 220-221, 230
M-1's, 81, 217-218
MTV badasses list, 237
"Murder in the Cathedral" (play), 63
murder of a civilian in war, 44-45
murder of Ross Gillmore Marvin, 13-15
Music Corporation of America (MCA), 109
music recordings, "Shagging O'Reilly's
    Daughter," 197

N
Naish, J. Carroll, 90
Namath, Joe, 198
Nardini, Tom, 141
NBC, 129
New River, North Carolina, 32-34
New York and New England Apple
    Institute, 51
New York City
    childhood in, 16-18
    drinking bouts in, 53-54
    Lamont Marvin in, 10-11
    postwar return to, 48-49
New York State, 4-5
New York Times, The
    Courtenay Marvin's work at, 11-12
    Firing of Bosley Crowther, 165
    Ross Marvin murder story, 13-15
New York University (NYU), 10
Newlan, Paul, 104
Newman, Paul, 95, 149, 178-179
nightmares, post-military, 53
Nimoy, Leonard, 105
Noonan, Tommy, 90

Norris, Chuck, 226-227
Not As A Stranger, 90
nudity in *The Professionals,* 151

O
Oakwood Academy, 22-23
obituaries, 235
O'Connor, Carroll, 164
O'Hara, Ralph, 194, 202-203, 206-207, 211, 219, 228
Oklahoma! audition, 87-88
Olivier, Laurence, 156
O'Neill, Eugene, 183-186
O'Rourke, Frank, 150
Oroville, California, 191-193
Oscars
 for *Cat Ballou,* 147, 156-158
 nominations for *The Dirty Dozen,* 165
"Our Time in Hell" (TV), 162
"Outlaw's Reckoning" (TV), 100-101

P
Pacula, Joanna, 221-224
Paint Your Wagon, 63, 172-175
painting, 227
Palance, Jack, 92, 93-94, 99 150, 153, 175
palimony suit of Michele Triola
 California Supreme Court trial, 210-215
 inception of, 200-202
 initiation of, 209-215
Paramount, 172-173
Parkins, Barbara,197-198
Parris Island, South Carolina, 31-33
Parslow, Phil, 153-154
Parsons, Louella, 133
parties, 1950's industry, 73-74
Patrick, Nigel, 97-98
Patton, turning down, 168
Payback, 165-166
Pearl Harbor, 29-31, 36, 85
Peary, Robert, 5-9
Peckinpah, Fern Lea, 174
Peckinpah, Sam (director), 113-114, 168, 171-174, 182, 228
Peleliu, 170
"People Need People" (TV), 111
Pete Kelly's Blues, 91-92
pets, 2
Phillips, Bob, 127, 159-161
phoniness, disdain for, 27
Photoplay, Courtenay Marvin writing for,

27
Picerni, Paul, 110
Pierson, Frank, 140, 158
Pillars of the Sky, 95
plays, amateur, 57
plays, professional
 "Billy Budd," 65-66, 71
 "Bus Stop," 95
 first, 57-58
 "Joan of Arc at the Stake," 88
 Maverick Theater other plays, 60
 off-Broadway, 63
 road company (1946-1947), 61
 "Roadside," 58-59
 "The Rainmaker," 96
plumbing apprenticeship, 54-55, 59
Pocket Money, 178-179
Point Blank, 161-163, 169-171, 204
poker playing, 89
police roles
 "Lawbreakers," 112-113
 "M Squad," 106-110
political support for John F. Kennedy, 126
Porter, Katherine Anne, 134
post-traumatic stress disorder
 alcoholism and, 125
 nightmares, 53
 "People Need People," 111
 survivor guilt, 47-48, 64
 symptoms of, 64
press relations, 149-150
Prime Cut, 180-181
producer role of Lee Marvin, 104-105, 175
producers. See individual films
production code demise, 149
Professionals, The, 150-155, 203-204
prostitutes, 39
PTSD. See post-traumatic stress disorder
publicist, use of, 148
Pulp Fiction, 236
puritanism, 4, 10
Purple Heart, receiving, 48-49
Putnam, George Palmer, 13

Q
Quartermaster School, U.S.M.C., 34-38
quotations from Lee Marvin
 meateater, 233
 press, interviews by, 148-150
 "spittin' on my whole life," 178

R

racism, 191-193, 197-198
Rack, The, 95-96
radio, part work for, 62
Raid, The, 86-87
Railroads,179-180
"Rainmaker, The" (play), 96
Raintree County, 97-98
Rappaport, George (neighbor), 45-46, 124, 126
rating systems, 149
reading abilities, 19
Reagan, Ronald, 102-103, 126-130
Real Steel, 110
realism
    Attack!, 95
    audience demand for, 63
    brought by Lee to early TV roles, 73
    Eight Iron Men, contribution to, 85-86
    police in "Lawbreakers," 111
    "There's Not Enough Violence on TV!" article, 112-113
Reed, Donna, 73, 81
Reed, Oliver, 195-197
Reisman, Major John, character of, 158-161, 164-165
religious upbringing, 26-27
Remsen, Bert, 62-63, 111, 113-115
Reservoir Dogs, 236
retirement, 227-228
revenge theme, 165-166
Revolutionary War, 4
Reynolds, Burt, 106
Richards, Max, 42-43
Ritchie, Michael, 178
Ritt, Martin, 189
"Roadside" (play), 58-59
Roberts, Bobby (producer), 175
Robin Hood Party, The, 204, 212
Robinson, Edward G., 124
Robson, Mark (director), 199
Roosevelt, the, (Ship), 7-8
Ross, Marion, 111
"Route 66" (TV), 112-113
running away from home, 15, 19
Russia, 221-224
Ryan, Cheyney, 195-196
Ryan, Lisa, 160
Ryan, Mitch, 176-178, 227, 229-230
Ryan, Robert, 87, 150-151, 158-161, 184-186

S

Saint, Eva Marie, 97
Saipan, battle of, 46-48, 85
salesmen, playing, 183-186
San Diego, 38-41
San Quentin, 111
Santana Records, 206
Santelli, Giorgio, 62
"Saturday Night Live," (TV), 213
Savalas, Telly, 158-161
Scaife, Edward, 158-161
Schaefer, Jack, 175
Schaffner, Franklin (director), 103
Schell, Maximillan, 199-200
Schiffrin, Bill (producer), 192
schooling. See education
Schygulla, Hanna, 226
Scorsese, Martin, 235-236
Scott, Randolph, 79, 93-94
Scourby, Alexander, 81
scout/sniper activity, 45
scripts, evaluation of, 168-169, 189
Seberg, Jean, 172-173
Segal, George, 134
Seminole, 78
Service, Robert, 19
Seven Men From Now, 94-94
sex
    advice to Terry Moore, 92
    reporter, with, 167-168
    palimony trial, role in, 212
    prostitutes, with, 39
Shack Out on 101, 92-93
"Shakedown Cruise" (TV), 103-104
Shaw, Robert, 199-200
Shearer, Leroy Channing, 5
Ship of Fools, 134-139, 201-202
Shout at the Devil, 197-198
Sickner, Roy, 179, 171-172, 174
Siegel, Don, 127-130
Signoret, Simone, 134
Silver, Ed
    investments through, 193-194
    Michele Triola, dealing with, 205
    purchase of Malibu beach house for Lee, 168
    Santa Monica house purchase, 98
    testimony in palimony suit, 212
Silverstein, Elliot (director), 140-148, 157-158
Simpson, O.J., 191-193
Sinatra, Frank, 91, 126

singing, 86-87

Small Soldiers, 237

Smith, Charlie Martin, 190

Smith, Cruz Martin, 221

Smithers, William, 195

"smoke," 54

"Sons of Lee Marvin, The," 234-236

"Sound of Hunting, A" (play) 63, 75

South Africa, 196

Spacek, Sissy, 180-181

Spike's Gang, 190

Spradlin, G.D., 175

spy thriller, *Avalanche Express*, 199-200

S.S. Seahorse (Woodstock bar), 52-53

St. Leo Doctor of Fine Arts Degree, 173

St. Leo's School for Boys, 26-29

"Star Trek" (TV), 60

Star Wars, effect on film industry, 200

stardom, pursuit of, 99

"Steel" (TV), 109

Steiger, Rod, 70, 99, 156-157

Stewart, Jimmy, 116-117

Stranger Wore A Gun, The, 78

Strasberg, Susan, 226

Strauss, Robert, 95

"Streetcar Named Desire, A" (play), 63

Strode, Woody, 116-117, 150-155, 204

"Studio One" (TV), 102-104

studio system demise, 149

stuntmen, 162-163, 173, 203-206, 212

stunts, ability to do own, 97, 124, 129, 153

Sturges, John (director), 87

success, quotation on, 149-150

suicide

    Lamont Marvin's attempt, 49

    Michele Triola's attempts, 163, 205

Summers, Neil, 176-177

"Suspense" (TV), 100

Sutherland, Donald, 158-161

Svenson, Bo, 226

swimming ability, 27-28, 97-98

Sydney, Silvia, 90

T

Tarantino, Quentin, 236

Tashman, Lilyan, 72

Taylor, Don (director), 196

Taylor, Elizabeth, 104, 191

Taylor, Rod, 97-98

Teddy Valentine, 58

teenage years in Florida, 24-29

"Ten Nights In a Barroom" (play), 57

terrorism, 226-227

Texas, first professional acting role as, 58-59

20th-Century Fox, 65, 70, 115

"Thanksgiving in Strange Places" (radio show), 54

The Raft (Bar), 163

therapy, 121

Theresa, 65, 71

"T-Men In Action" (TV), 100

tobacco, sponsoring of shows by, 104

Tokyo, 170

Tombstone Street, 115

Tompkins, Angel, 180-181

Toms River, New Jersey, 23

Torn, Rip, 100

track, high school participation in, 27-28

Tracy, Spencer, 87-88

tributes to Lee Marvin, 235-238

Triola, Michele

    Academy Awards, at, 156-157

    alcoholism of Lee, contribution to, 203-204

    Betty Marvin, harassment of, 145-146, 201-202

    breakup with Lee, 207

    death of, 214

    Dick Van Dyke, dating, 211-214

    fight with Ty Cabeen, 154

    financial relationship with Lee, 205

    first encounters with Lee Marvin, 137-138

    Marvin, legal name change to, 207

    nature of relationship with Lee, 168, 202

    payments to, end of, 209

    Santana Records recordings of, 206

    shoplifting arrest, 215

    suicide attempts of, 163, 205

    thefts from Lee, accusations of, 203

    vibrator incident, 205-206

    troubleshooting role, 84

Tucson, Arizona, residence in, 194-195

Tully Crowe character, 115

TV career

    anthology shows, 102-103

    attitude towards acting in TV, 99-100, 110

    "Dragnet," (TV) 72-73, 75

    early part work for, 62

    "M Squad," (TV) 104-110

made-for-TV movies, inception of, 127
post "M Squad," 110
summary of early career in, 100
"There's Not Enough Violence on TV!"
    article, 112-113
"Twilight Zone," (TV) 110

U
union membership, plumber's union, 54
U.S.S. Teakettle, 70
"Untouchables, The" (TV), 110

V
Valley of Fire desert, Nevada, 152
Van Dyke, Dick, 201-204
Vaughn, Robert, 226-227
Vegas Vic sign shooting incident, 204
Vernon, John, 163
vibrator incident, 205-206
"vicaries," 150, 155, 165
Vietnam veterans, PTSD of, 64-65
Vince Stone, role as, 80-81
violence. See also fighting; war, theatrical
    acting, quality showing up in, 79
    banjo incident, 207
    beatings by his father, 26
    childhood, 3, 26
    confessed need for, 64
    kicking Uncle Don, 20
    between Lee's parents, 25-26
    murder of Ross Gillmore Marvin, 13-15
    Oakwood Academy, at, 22-23
    quotes on, 149-150, 171
    "Route 66," (TV) incident, 112-113
    sources of interest in, 14-15
    "There's Not Enough Violence on TV!"
        article, 112-113
    Wild Bunch, The, 173-174
Violent Saturday, 90-91
"Virginian, The" (TV), 110, 216
vocabulary, creativity with, 150

W
"Wagon Train," (TV), 110, 119-120
Waits, Tom, 234-235
Walcott, Gregory, 180-181
Walker, Bob, 109
Walker, Clint, 158-161, 237
Walker family (childhood neighbors), 26
Walker, Ron (BSOL founder), 226
"Wanderin' Star," (Song) 174, 206

war, real. See also Marine Corps, U.S.
    compared to theatrical, 149-150
    hand-to-hand combat, 46-47
    horror of, statement, 112
    Marshall Islands campaign, 45
    mortar fire, nearly wounded by, 47
    murder, equating it with, 50
    negative reaction to, 44-46
    scout/sniper activity during, 45
    wounded at Saipan, 48
war, theatrical
    Attack!, 94-95
    Big Red One, The, 184, 215-218, 237
    The Dirty Dozen, 75-76, 156-161, 164-
        165, 225-226
    Eight Iron Men, 74-75
    Glory Brigade, The, 79-80
    Hell in the Pacific, 169-171
    Shout at the Devil, 197-198
    "The American" (TV), 110-111
Ward, Kelly, 216-220
Warden, Jack, 70, 122
Washington, D.C., 11-12, 29
Washington, George, 4
Wasserman, Lew, 120, 127
Wasserman, Paul (publicist), 148, 168, 178-
    179, 184, 204-205, 212
Wayne, John, 93-94, 115-117, 122-123, 149,
    165, 216
Webb, Jack, 70 72-73, 75, 91-92
Webber, Robert, 158-161
Werner, Oskar, 134, 156
westerns
    Bad Day at Black Rock, 88, 191
    Cat Ballou, 140-148, 156-158
    Comancheros, The 116
    Gun Fury, 81-82
    Man Who Shot Liberty Valance, The,
        115-118, 121-122, 241
    Monte Walsh, 175-178, 227
    "Outlaw's Reckoning" (TV) 110-111
    Paint Your Wagon, 172-175
    Pillars of the Sky, 95
    Professionals, The, 150-155
    Rip Torn shoot out gaffe, 100
    Seven Men From Now, 93-94
    Spike's Gang, 190
    Stranger Wore a Gun, The, 77
    Wild Bunch, The,168, 171-174
Weddle, David, 173-174
Westlake, Donald E., 162

Whiskey (family dog), 2
"white eye, the", 189
Whitney, Cornelius Vanderbilt, 98-99
Who's That Knocking at My Door, 235-236
Wild Bunch, The, 179, 171-174
Wild One, The, 70, 82-83
Williams, Adam, 81
Willner, Dr. Harry, 111
Willoughby, Bob, 97
Winters, Shelley, 92, 226
wives of Lee Marvin
    Betty. See Marvin, Betty Ebeling
    Michele (alleged). See Triola, Michele
    Pam. See Marvin, Pamela Feeley
Woodstock, New York, 18, 51-54, 178-179
work as a plumbing apprenticeship, 54-55,
    59
World War I, Lamont Waltham in, 10
World War II. See also war, real
    Attack!, 94-95
    Big Red One, The, 50, 191, 215-220,
      236
    Dirty Dozen, The, 76-77, 156, 158-161,
      165
    Eight Iron Men, 75-76
    Hell in the Pacific, 169-171
    Shout at the Devil, 197-198
    "The American" (TV), 110-111
Wouk, Herman, 84-85
wound suffered in World War II, 48-49
Wynn, Elizabeth and Thomas7, 9-10
Wynn, Keenan, 92-93, 157, 162-166, 194,
    228
Wynn, Ned, 93,118 135, 202, 228
Wynn, Tracy Keenan, 194

Y
"Year of Lee Marvin, The," 133
Young, Terence (director), 192
You're In the Navy Now, 69

Z
Zinnemann, Fred (director), 70

Photographic Credits

Cover Photo: "M Squad": NBC/Universal

PHOTOGRAPHS FOR SECTION BREAKS:

Front of Book. Lee Marvin in *The Dirty Dozen*: Photofest, Inc

I. Lee Marvin, Robert Marvin, and dog: Used with Permission of the Authorized Representative of the Robert Marvin Archive

II. Lee Marvin as 'Chino' in *The Wild One* holding son Christopher: Permission granted courtesy of Betty Marvin

III. Lee Marvin in *The Professionals*: © 1966, renewed 1994 Pax Enterprises, Inc. All Rights Reserved. Courtesy of Columbia Pictures

IV. Lee Marvin in *Delta Force*: Photofest, Inc.

V. Lee Marvin in *Emperor of the North*: Photofest, Inc.

Afterword. Lee Marvin and Christopher Marvin in sandbox: Permission granted courtesy of Christopher Marvin

INSERT

• Ross Marvin: Courtesy of the Chemung County Historical Society, Elmira, N.Y.
• Monte Marvin in WWI uniform: Used with Permission of the Authorized Representative of the Robert Marvin Archive
• Lee Marvin as a baby: Used with Permission of the Authorized Representative of the Robert Marvin Archive
• Courtenay Marvin with Lee and Robert in park: Used with Permission of the Authorized Representative of the Robert Marvin Archive
• Lee Marvin at Manumit School: Used with Permission of the Authorized Representative of the Robert Marvin Archive
• Lee Marvin and friends in Florida: Used with Permission of the Authorized Representative of the Robert Marvin Archive
• Lee Marvin at St. Leo's School for Boys: Used with Permission of the Authorized Representative of the Robert Marvin Archive

- Lee Marvin, Courtenay and Monte: Used with Permission of the Authorized Representative of the Robert Marvin Archive
- Lee Marvin's USMC ID Card: Used with Permission of the Authorized Representative of the Robert Marvin Archive
- Lee Marvin and platoon members: Used with Permission of the Authorized Representative of the Robert Marvin Archive
- 4th Marine Division patch: Used with Permission of the Authorized Representative of the Robert Marvin Archive
- Lee Marvin and Wade Rayborn with captured weaponry: Used with Permission of the Authorized Representative of the Robert Marvin Archive
- Memorial Day parade: Courtesy of "The Daily Freeman" Kingston, N.Y. and Christopher Marvin
- Lee Marvin in "Roadside": Used with Permission of the Authorized Representative of the Robert Marvin Archive
- Lee Marvin in "Billy Budd": Used with Permission of the Authorized Representative of the Robert Marvin Archive
- Lee Marvin ATW Shakespeare production: Used with Permission of the Authorized Representative of the Robert Marvin Archive
- Sea Horse card: Used with Permission of the Authorized Representative of the Robert Marvin Archive
- "Dragnet": Photofest, Inc.
- *The Glory Brigade*: Photofest, Inc.
- *Bad Day at Back Rock*: Photofest, Inc.
- *The Man Who Shot Liberty Valance*: Photofest, Inc.
- "M Squad": Photofest, Inc.
- *Ship of Fools*: Photofest, Inc.
- On set of *Donovan's Reef* in Hawaii with family: Permission granted courtesy of Betty Marvin
- Monte, Lee and Christopher Marvin: Used with Permission of the Authorized Representative of the Robert Marvin Archive
- Lee Marvin and Keenan Wynn with Oscar: UPI Photo
- *Cat Ballou*: Photofest, Inc.
- *The Professionals*: Photofest, Inc.
- *Point Blank*: Photofest, Inc.
- *The Dirty Dozen* cast reading: Licensed by: Warner Bros. Entertainment, Inc. All Rights Reserved
- Phillips, Mishkin, and Marvin: Licensed by: Warner Bros. Entertainment, Inc. All Rights Reserved, and courtesy of Bob Phillips collection
- *Hell in the Pacific*: Photofest, Inc.
- Monte on set of *Paint Your Wagon*: Used with Permission of the Authorized Representative of the Robert Marvin Archive
- Lee Marvin on set of *Paint Your Wagon*: Permission granted courtesy of Christopher Marvin
- *Monte Walsh*: Photofest, Inc.
- *The Iceman Cometh*: Photofest, Inc.
- Lee and Pam Marvin after "Palimony" decision: AP Images
- *Gorky Park*: Photofest, Inc.
- Lee Marvin, Sam Fuller, and John Boorman on location for *The Big Red One*: Permission granted courtesy of Christa Fuller
- *The Big Red One*: Photofest, Inc.
- Lee Marvin and daughter Cynthia at wedding: Permission granted courtesy of Betty Marvin
- Lee Marvin relaxing in Tucson: Permission granted courtesy of Christopher Marvin
- Lee Marvin with son Christopher in Tucson: Permission granted courtesy of Christopher Marvin
- *Shack out on 101*: Photofest, Inc.
- *Raintree County*: Photofest, Inc.
- *The Comancheros:* Photofest, Inc.
- *Point Blank*: Photofest, Inc.
- *The Killers*: Photofest, Inc.
- *Pocket Money*: Photofest, Inc.

About the Author

DWAYNE EPSTEIN, a native of New York's Coney Island, was born in 1960, then at age eight, moved with his family to Cerritos, Ca. As a young man he moved back east where he attended Mercer Community College in New Jersey. His first professional writing credit was as a film reviewer for Hearst Community Newspapers, and from there he took a job as assistant editor for the five area newspapers put out by Cranbury Publications,

He later went on to freelance for film publications, and his articles on such figures as Bobby Darin, Steve Allen, Sam Fuller, and John Belushi, appeared regularly in *FilmFax* Magazine. He has contributed to the international publication, *Cahiers du Cinema*'s "Serious Pleasures" and to Bill Krohn's bestselling books, "Hitchcock at Work" and "Joe Dante and the Gremlins of Hollywood."

Epstein has also authored several young adult biographies for Lucent Publications' "People in the News" series, and he has appeared on both A&E and Entertainment networks to discuss the life and careers of, respectively, Lee Marvin and Hillary Swank. *LEE MARVIN: Point Blank* is his first adult biography and was the Bronze Medal winner of the 2013 Independent Publishers Book Award (IPPY) in that category.

Having resettled in California in the early 90s, Dwayne makes his home in Long Beach with his fiancée Barbara Troeller, a writer and millinery historian. When not writing, he enjoys reading about and watching movies, and collecting rare soundtracks.

For further information about the author and this book, visit www.pointblankbook.com.

PHOTOGRAPH BY BARBARA TROELLER